GOETHE'S PLAYS

GOETHE'S PLAYS

JOHANN WOLFGANG VON GOETHE

Translated
with Introductions by
Charles E. Passage

Frederick Ungar Publishing Co.
New York

Copyright © 1980 by Frederick Ungar Publishing Co., Inc.

Printed in the United States of America

Designed by Peter McKenzie

Three of these plays have been previously published:
  Götz von Berlichingen. Copyright © 1965 by Frederick Ungar Publishing Co., Inc.;
  Iphigenia in Tauris. Copyright © 1963 by Frederick Ungar Publishing Co., Inc.;
  Torquato Tasso. Copyright © 1966 by Frederick Ungar Publishing Co., Inc.

Library of Congress Cataloging in Publication Data

Goethe, Johann Wolfgang von, 1749–1832.
   Goethe's plays.

   Bibliography: p.
   Includes index.
   1. Passage, Charles E.
PT2026.A5   1980   832'.6   79-4834
ISBN 0-8044-2258-3

TABLE OF CONTENTS

PREFACE

The present volume is intended to serve a dual purpose: first, to collect seven dramatic works of Goethe in English translation within convenient compass, and second, to survey some forty other dramas, parts of dramas, and ideas for dramas that belong to his lifelong career as a playwright.

In the two chapters devoted to this second purpose all items are listed, but discussions are cursory or more detailed according to their uneven merits. Texts were read in the volumes numbered 7, 11, and 12 of Goethe's collected works as published by the Deutscher Taschenbuch Verlag (DTV) of Munich. Number 7 contains most of the small works before 1775 and an afterword by Peter Boerner (1962). Number 11, with an afterword by Walther Migge (1962), and Number 12, with an afterword by Benno Reifenberg (1963), contain the less familiar works after 1775. Occasional details of information have been borrowed from the respective afterwords, but the judgments expressed are those of the present writer. The material of these two surveying chapters is not easily found in English, and the overview presented is even harder to discern amid the sea of Goethe's total literary production or amid the ocean of books about Goethe and his works.

The seven translations are all by the present writer. Three of them have been separately in print for some time: *Götz von Berlichingen* (1965), *Iphigenia in Tauris* (1963), and *Torquato Tasso* (1966); separate publication of *Egmont* is pending. The separately published introductions have here been rewritten, shortened, and coordinated with each other and with the rest of the present material. Relevant information about each play is given immediately preceding the translation, but all our prose sections have been fitted into a biographical frame, from the opening page to the final page.

To these four major and independent dramas two fine, early pieces have been prefixed: *The Lover's Whim* and *Fellow Culprits,* which restore the Rococo segment of Goethe's production usually ignored by nineteenth-century critics. Thus our volume has three panels, of two plays each: the Rococo, as mentioned; the "Storm and Stress" or "pre-Romantic" panel, with *Götz* and *Egmont*; and the classical, with *Iphigenia* and *Tasso*.

To the middle panel has been added our English version of the original sketches for *Faust,* the *"Urfaust,"* with lines keyed to the complete *Faust, Part I* so as to indicate discrepancies of omission, subtraction, and addition between the first and final texts. Lines common to both texts are repeated from the present writer's translation of the total *Faust,* Parts I and II, as published by the Bobbs-Merrill Publishing Company in 1965. For the permission to repeat those lines we wish to thank the Bobbs-Merrill Company most kindly, and, in particular, Ms. Lois Stewart, who dealt with our request for the permission. In our concluding pages we try to state succinctly why "Goethe's *Faust* is not a "play" and why it *is* one of the greatest dramatic achievements in the world.

Nearly fifty dramatic pieces by Goethe are mentioned in this book. A few are trivial; some are lost in their own era; many are "interesting"; and a few are masterworks. Under the circumstances, the disparities were probably inevitable. But, as Aristotle might say, from all the facts assembled there arises a certain grandeur.

C. E. P.

Dansville, New York
September 1, 1979

PART I

DRAMATIC WORKS TO 1775

THE DRAMATIST'S PREPARATION

Unusual experiences crowded in upon Johann Wolfgang Goethe even in his boyhood. Before age six he was watching with wonder as his family's house was rebuilt around him in a form more befitting his lawyer-father's prosperity. At age ten he saw that house requisitioned by the French army for an officer's billet. His father might sulk, his mother and younger sister might be discommoded daily in their own home, but he himself enjoyed conversing in French with the unwelcome guest, and from him he learned something about why his juvenile paintings were imperfectly conceived. He was fourteen when he first heard the seven-year-old Mozart play in concert. He was fifteen when he witnessed the ancient coronation rituals for Joseph II of Hapsburg as King of Germany. At the same age he was already exploring his native city of Frankfurt-on-the-Main, sometimes, according to his autobiography, in the company of dubious associates, both male and female.

His education was all by tutors under the parental roof. Besides such old-fashioned subjects as penmanship, geography, and pencil-and-paper mathematics, there was the usual in-depth study of Latin and Greek. He also acquired French, which was indispensable for polite conversation; Italian, which was indispensable for the arts; enough English to compose a letter in that language; and, in his adolescent ramblings about town, even a smattering of Yiddish. He had some musical training and sang with an amateur's pleasure. At age sixteen he tended to think that his future lay with painting and the graphic arts, with literature probably as a sideline.

His earliest preserved poem is a set of verses presented to his maternal grandparents by way of a New Year's greeting. He was then seven and a half. Over the years he composed a good many poems, but at the approach of maturity he took pains to destroy all of those that he could find.

For his fifth Christmas he received from his paternal grandmother the momentous gift of a puppet theater. At first he watched and listened avidly while his elders manipulated the puppets and read the lines, but in time he was to adapt the little pieces to other playlets composed by himself. In a later chapter we shall have occasion to mention the small fragments of three serious attempts at drama in his teenage years. While the French troops were occupying Frankfurt he was able to attend performances of the French classics and other dramas by acting troupes from France. Before age twenty he and his sister and their friends were themselves giving amateur performances of those French classics, so that he had Racine's cadences in his ear from a very early date.

Save for those amateur performances, all this took place between his birth, on August 28, 1749, and his departure for the University of Leipzig, then a distant city in eastern Germany, in September of 1765. Besides "hearing" various subjects in the usual lecture halls he studied painting and copper engraving with prominent teachers of those disciplines. Intellectual pursuits posed no difficulties for him, but fashionable Leipzig found his manners and his wardrobe provincial, with the result that numerous teachers volunteered to initiate him into the social graces. He learned willingly and rapidly.

After three years at the university Goethe left Leipzig on his nineteenth birthday and returned to his father's house. Professional study was yet to be decided upon and arranged for. In his returning luggage he brought the completed manuscript of a one-Act verse play entitled *The Lover's Whim (Die Laune des Verliebten)*.

THE LOVER'S WHIM

Again and again in Goethe's works there recurs the odd theme of cheerful versus noncheerful spirits. The latter include not only petulance and ill-temper, but also fretful worry—"the borrowing of trouble,"—and, in particular, a certain irrational contrariness that destroys one's own pleasure and that of others. Cheerful spirits betoken happy acceptance of an infinite variety of things and a joy in all that life has to offer, short of physical misery. Goethe's own vacillation between the sunny and the dark troubled him, and he sometimes wrestled, as with a demon, to rid himself of "Care." The English word "care" includes less than half of the spectrum covered by German *Sorge*. In his drama of *Egmont* the title-hero precipitates tragedy because his supremely sunny temperament rejects all claims of Care, and the eighty-year-old author will show Faust at age one hundred still fending off the attacks of a ghostly Dame Care.

During his Leipzig days Goethe once so indulged his bent for irrational contrariness that, by way of atonement—so he says in Book VII of his autobiography—he composed "the little piece, *The Lover's Whim,* amid the innocent quality of which may also be discerned the compulsion of a seething passion." The offended girl was a lively, pretty lass, worthy of being set up like a little saint in the shrine of his heart. In recalling her, he names her Annie, though it is known from other sources that she was really Anna Katharina Schönkopf, usually called Käthchen (Katie). He saw her daily. She helped prepare the food he ate, she served him his evening wine, and, with a small company, the two of them shared in harmless parlor games. In time, he tells us, he began tormenting her by way of venting his frustrations in literary endeavor. With unfounded jealousies he spoiled the pleasantest days for himself and for her, until he perceived at last that she had ceased to care for him. Whereupon he fell really in love with her:

5

> Finally I entered into the girl's former role. I tried everything possible to be agreeable . . . because I would not give up hope of winning her back. Only, it was too late. I had really lost her.

In the play "Annie" became Amina and the moody Eridon a part of Goethe himself. A significant point is the author's imaginative transfer of himself into the girl's place and his seeing of the whole matter from the feminine point of view.

This little play of 1767–68 followed an established pattern. Since mid-century such German writers as Gellert and Gleim had popularized the one-Act pastoral, even to the regular casting of two pairs of lovers—one pair in harmony, the other pair in disharmony—the dramatic action arising out of the disharmony. The hexameter couplets imitated the Alexandrine couplets of French tradition. The stylized shepherds and shepherdesses had haunted the literature and the pictorial arts of western Europe for three centuries, stemming from classical models in Vergil's ten *Eclogues,* published in 37 B.C., which in turn imitated the *Idylls* composed by Theocritus in the third century B.C. Such figures are most familiar to us in the paintings of Fragonard and other Rococo artists, as well as from the descendants of these in the lacy valentines of the nineteenth century, but let us note that Marie Antoinette's real-life "shepherds" and "shepherdesses" had not yet, as of 1767–68, herded their beribboned flocks about the picturesque glades at the outer limits of the Versailles gardens.

In German literature of the 1750s and 1760s the pastoral play (*Schäferspiel*) was almost the only genre in which an author could be worldly, gracious, witty, and "pagan," without obligation to display either maudlin piety or bluenose morality. It was the antidote to Klopstock's excess of angel-feathers. Specimens of German pastoral antecedent to *The Lover's Whim* might well be insipidly sweet, but they afforded an avenue of escape from the literary dullness of the mid-eighteenth century.

The sequence of German pastorals ended with this present play; it seemed to have carried the slender tradition as far as it would reach and left no more to be done with it. Of all the German plays of this kind, *The Lover's Whim* is the only readable—and playable—

example. It has elegance of meter and rhyme and diction. It has (intentionally) quotable lines. It is stageworthy. It is also humanly and poetically valid, and it steadily holds the focus of young adulthood upon the life of young adults.

*

All translations in this volume number the scenes within Acts according to the English system whereby only a shift of setting warrants a new scene, and not according to the continental system whereby the entrance or departure of a major character requires the indication of a new scene.

THE LOVER'S WHIM

A One-Act Pastoral Play in Verse

(Die Laune des Verliebten
Ein Schäferspiel in Versen und einem Akt)
1767–1768

CHARACTERS

EGLE	⎫	
AMINA	⎭ shepherdesses
ERIDON	⎫	
LAMON	⎭ shepherds

The scene represents an unidentified spot
with grass and trees.
The time is both of 1767–68 and timeless.

Amina and Egle are sitting at one side of the stage twining garlands.
To them comes Lamon bringing a little basket of flowers.

LAMON (*setting the little basket down*):
    More flowers for you.
EGLE: Good.
LAMON: Just see how fine they show!
    For you, child, this carnation here.
EGLE: The rose!
LAMON: No, no,
    Today Amina gets the season's prize to wear:
    A rose is what I like to see in raven hair.
EGLE: Am I supposed to take that as a courtesy?
LAMON: You've loved me, how long now, without quite knowing
                                           me?
    I'm perfectly aware you love me, me alone,
    And my heart also is eternally your own,
    You know that. Yet you'd have me deeper in your spell?
    Is it so wicked finding others fair as well?
    I don't forbid your saying: "There's a handsome lad;
    Oh, that one's jolly, this one's nice!" I don't get mad,
    I let you.
EGLE: Don't get mad; I'll keep my temper too.
    We both have lapses. I'll admit I often do
    Encourage suitors; and some shepherdesses hear
    Sweet things you say to them at times when I'm not near.
    The heart may bow to orders, playful jest will not;
    Light conduct must preserve us from a fickle thought.
    With even less good grace than you would I be jealous.
                        (*to Amina*)
    You smile at us: what are you thinking, darling? Tell us!
AMINA: Not much.
EGLE: Enough to feel my joy and your distress.
AMINA: How so?

EGLE: How so? Why, just when Amor's drowsiness
    Should be dispelled by laughter, put to headlong flight,
    Your grief begins when your beloved comes in sight.
    There's no man more inclinded to self-indulgent whim.
    You think he loves you: I see deeper into him.
    He sees that you obey him, so his whole affection
    Is for a person who will follow his direction.

AMINA: Oh, he obeys me too.

EGLE: So he can have next chance.
    Aren't you obliged to steal his every look and glance?
    The power which was placed by Nature in our gaze,
    Which charms a man, or which dismisses and dismays,
    You have surrendered to him, till you are well pleased
    If he looks kindly at you. With his forehead creased,
    His brows knit in a frown, his eyes all gloom, intense,
    His lips compressed—a charming picture he presents
    Day after day, till pleading, kisses, mournful sighs
    Dispel the wintry harshness from his somber eyes.

AMINA: You have not loved him, do not know him well enough.
    It is not selfish whim that makes his brow so rough;
    His heart is troubled with a fitful moodiness
    That turns our fairest summer days into distress.
    And yet I'm gratified when, at the sight of me,
    His moods will vanish under my cajolery.

EGLE: A signal happiness that one could do without.
    But name me one enjoyment he has yet allowed.
    The prospect of the dance thrilled your heart through and through;
    Your lover fled the dance and kept you from it too.
    He can't bear your attending any festival
    Because he grudges meadow grass your footprint's fall;
    In your pet bird he sees a rival for his place.
    He can't bear watching partners clasp you in embrace
    Who will, while he is circling through the dancing rings,
    Be pressing close and whispering all the sweetest things.

AMINA: Don't be unfair just when today, at my request,
    He's letting me attend with you two as your guest.

EGLE: You'll pay for that.

AMINA: How so?

EGLE: Why does he stay behind?

AMINA: He doesn't care for dancing.

EGLE: It's some trick, you'll find.
When you come back delighted he'll ask mockingly:
"You had a good time, did you?"—"Very good."—"I see.
Game playing?"—"Forfeits."—"Oh. Damoetas surely came?
You danced?"—"Around the tree."—"To think I missed that
                                                    game!
He dances well? What keepsake did you give the boy?"
                        (*Amina smiles.*)
You smile?

AMINA: You've struck the very note he does employ.
—More flowers!

LAMON: Here. These are the best ones.

AMINA: But it's fine
He grudges everybody every glance of mine.
My lover's envy shows how fondly I'm esteemed,
And all the pangs of my small pride are then redeemed.

EGLE: I pity you, my dear. Since you dote on your pains
You are beyond all rescue. You now clank your chains
And tell yourself it's music.

AMINA: One bow more, right here,
But all the ribbon's gone.

EGLE (*to Lamon*):   There's one you took this year,
The one that tied the May-crown they awarded me.

LAMON: I'll fetch it.

EGLE: But you must come back immediately.

AMINA: He doesn't set much store by presents, as he ought.

EGLE: I don't myself just like my lover's ways of thought.
He isn't much impressed by dalliances of love
And trifles that a tender heart thinks so much of.
There is a lesser pain in being loved the less,
However, than in being loved to great excess.
Devotion I admire, but to our lives it must
Give full repose in full tranquillity of trust.

AMINA: Oh, such a tender heart is precious, I believe.

He often hurts me, but he grieves to see me grieve.
If he finds fault, if his displeasure is incurred,
I have to do no more than say one kindly word
And right away he changes, temper disappears;
He even weeps with me when he sees me in tears,
Kneels down before me and entreats me for forgiving.

EGLE: And you forgive him?

AMINA: Always.

EGLE: What a way of living!
    Forever ready pardons and forever slighted,
    Such effort in Love's cause, and ever unrequited!

AMINA: What can't be altered—

EGLE: Can't be altered? It's quite plain
    That changing him is easy.

AMINA: How?

EGLE: Let me explain.
    Both your distress and Eridon's own discontent
    Result from—

AMINA: What?

EGLE: Your over-tender sentiment.

AMINA: That, I should think, would bring him to a sweet surrender.

EGLE: You're wrong. Be hard and strict, and you will find
                                          him tender.

    Just try it once, arrange to cause him some slight pain:
    Men crave to win by conquest, safety is no gain.
    When Eridon comes for an hour's company
    He's well aware how effortless success will be.
    The number of his rivals causes him no fear,
    He knows you love him more than he has held you dear,
    His luck is far too good, he's an absurdity:
    For want of misery, he makes up misery.
    He sees that you love nothing more than him on earth
    And only doubts because you give him no doubts worth
    The doubting. Treat him as though he's expendable;
    He'll rage, of course, but take it as dependable:
    He'll soon prize one glance more than any present kiss.
    Let him have cause to fear, and he will find it bliss.

AMINA: Yes, that's all well and good, but carrying out the part
   Is quite beyond me.

EGLE: Why lose courage at the start?
   You're too soft-hearted. But look there!

AMINA: My Eridon!

EGLE: I thought so. Trembling at the sight you look upon.
   Oh, this won't do. If change in him is what you seek,
   See him approach with calm and calmly hear him speak.
   What flutterings of the heart, what blushes you display,
   And—

AMINA: Let me go! Amina cannot love that way!
       (Enter Eridon slowly, with arms folded.
       Amina gets up and runs to meet him. Egle
       remains seated at her task.)

AMINA: *(seizing him by the hand)*:
   Beloved Eridon!

ERIDON *(kissing her hand)*:   My girl!

EGLE *(to herself)*:   Oh, happy day!

AMINA: What lovely flowers! Who gave you that nice bouquet?

ERIDON: My loved one.

AMINA: Oh?—Those are the ones that came from me?
   Still fresh from yesterday?

ERIDON: A gift from you, you see,
   Is prized. But where are mine?

AMINA: I used them here to twine
   Those garlands for the dance.

ERIDON: For that! How you will shine!
   You'll rouse lads' hearts to love and be the envy of
   The girls.

EGLE: Be glad you have the sweet devoted love
   Of such a girl for whom so many lads contest.

ERIDON: When I am envied all around I cannot rest.

EGLE: You could, though. Who has more security than you?

ERIDON *(to Amina)*:
   Tell me about the dance. Damoetas will come too?

EGLE *(interrupting)*:
   He told me he would never miss such an affair.

ERIDON (*to Amina*):

    My dear, whom will you choose to have as partner there?
        (*Amina is silent; he turns to Egle.*)
    See that she gets the one who's dearest to her heart.

AMINA: Impossible, my friend, since you will not take part.

EGLE: No, listen, Eridon. Enough's enough, you know.

    Do you enjoy tormenting poor Amina so?
    If you think she's unfaithful, leave her, set her free;
    If you believe she loves you , stop this cruelty.

ERIDON: I'm not tormenting her.

EGLE: Would you call it delight?

    To cast vexation on her pleasure out of spite?
    Forever doubting, when she gives no cause to feel
    A doubt—

ERIDON: You'll pledge me that her love for me is real?

AMINA: My love for you not real!

ERIDON: When will you prove it? When?

    Who let herself steal saucy Damon's nosegay, then?
    Who let young Thyrsis give her that nice ribbon too?

AMINA: My Eridon!

ERIDON: You will admit that it was you?

    You're good at kissing: doubtless they both got their share.

AMINA: My darling, don't you know?

EGLE: Oh, little does he care.

    What you can tell him, you have told him long ago;
    He heard it all, and still accuses even so.
    And if you tell him everything again today,
    He will accuse anew tomorrow anyway.

ERIDON: Perhaps quite rightly too.

AMINA: When has Amina ever

    Shown evidence of being faithless to you?

ERIDON: Never.

    I can't and don't claim that.

AMINA: In all my life, has any

    Occasion made you think so?

ERIDON: Occasions have been many.

AMINA: When have I been untrue?
ERIDON: Why, never from intent;
    From indiscretion, often. That's what I resent.
    Things I set store by, you deem trivialities;
    Things that annoy me, you can overlook with ease.
EGLE: Well, if Amina doesn't mind, why should you care?
ERIDON: She's often asked me that. The point is: I do care.
EGLE: Amina grants your rivals little hope, I'm sure.
ERIDON: Too little for distrust, too much to feel secure.
EGLE: She loves you as no woman's heart loved you before.
ERIDON: By dancing, pleasure, jesting, she sets equal store.
EGLE: None but a mother could love someone not thus blessed.
AMINA: Stop, Egle! Eridon, stop making me depressed!
    Go ask our friends how to you my thoughts always rallied,
    Yes, even in your absence when we laughed and dallied.
    How often, with chagrin that spoiled the time for me
    Because you weren't along, I asked: Where can he be?
    Oh, if you don't believe me, come along today
    And then claim I'm not true to you in every way.
    I'll dance with none but you, no arm but mine shall grasp
    Your arm, no hand but mine will hold yours in its clasp.
    If my behavior gives you any hint of taint—
ERIDON: Yes, but no love was ever proved by self-constraint.
EGLE: Just see the tears now flowing to implore your grace.
    I never would have thought your heart could be so base.
    On one hand, insatiety that knows no bounds,
    That ever craves for more, the more supply abounds,
    And on the other hand your pride that won't endure
    To share her heart with youthful joys however pure,
    With alternating grip upon your heart take hold.
    Her love leaves you unmoved, her grief too leaves you cold.
    I'm fond of her, and from you I shall henceforth guard her;
    Avoiding you is hard, but loving you is harder.
AMINA (*to herself*):
    Why must my heart with so much love be torn and riven?

(Eridon is motionless for a moment, then he
timidly goes over to Amina and takes her by
the hand.)

ERIDON: Amina, dearest child, can I still be forgiven?

AMINA: Have I not proven that these many times before?

ERIDON: O noble heart, here at your feet let me implore!

AMINA: Stand up, my Eridon!

EGLE: Too much thanks may be wrong.

What's too intensely felt is not felt very long.

ERIDON: But my intense devotion to her is supreme—

EGLE: It would be better far if it were less extreme.

Your lives would be more calm, and both her pain and yours—

ERIDON: Forgive me yet this once, I'll learn a wiser course.

AMINA: Go, dearest Eridon, and pick me a bouquet;

If it's from you, no other could me so array.

ERIDON: You've got the rose already.

AMINA: Lamon's gift. I do

Think it becomes me.

ERIDON (*touchily*):   Yes . . .

AMINA: But I'll give it to you,

So you won't be annoyed.

(Eridon takes it and kisses her hand.)

ERIDON: I'll pick you that bouquet.

(Exit.)

EGLE: You poor, good-hearted child, you won't succeed that way.

The more you give, his hungry pride will ask for more;

See that he doesn't rob your love of all its store.

AMINA: So long as I don't lose him, that's what I would hate.

EGLE: That's sweet. But one can see your love's of recent date.

Beginnings are like that; once loving, you'll discover

One has no thoughts except as one thinks of the lover.

And if we read a sighful novel then, about

How gently this one loved, how that one's faith held out,

How grand that tender hero stood in danger's hour

And how his prowess in the fray came from love's power,

Our heads then fairly swim; ourselves we see portrayed,

We crave to suffer and to conquer unafraid.

A young heart quickly takes a novel's influence,
A heart that loves may take it with intemperance.
We go on living so, until one day we see
Our faithfulness was just the heart's absurdity.

AMINA: But that is not my case.

EGLE: As fever patients say:
"But, Doctor, I'm not feverish at all today."
Do we believe them? No. Despite their protestations,
As in this case of yours, we give them medications.

AMINA: That's how we speak of children, but you won't imply
That I'm a child?

EGLE: You love.

AMINA: You too!

EGLE: Then love as I!
Abate the storm that has been whirling you around.
One can be very calm when love is most profound.

                    (Enter Lamon.)

LAMON: Here is the ribbon.

AMINA: Very nice.

EGLE: How long you took!

LAMON: Well, Chloris called me over to her by the brook:
Some flowers on her hat brim had to be attached.

EGLE: What did she give you?

LAMON: Nothing but the kiss I snatched.
A kiss is, I maintain, when all is said and done,
The best reward a girl can give to anyone.

AMINA *(showing Egle the garland with the bow now on it)*:
How's this?

EGLE: Fine.—Here!
          (She drapes the garland around Amina so
          the bow rests on her right shoulder. While
          doing so she addresses Lamon.)
          The order now is: Romp and laugh!

LAMON: In frolic unrestrained! A pleasure's cut in half
When it is well-behaved and we must worry whether
Our doings, lovers, and digestion go together.

EGLE: You're right.

LAMON: Of course!

EGLE: Amina, sit so I can see.

(*Amina sits down. Egle arranges flowers in her hair and goes on talking.*)

That kiss your Chloris gave you, give it back to me!

LAMON (*kissing her*):

With all my heart!

AMINA: A curious pair you make, you two!

EGLE: If Eridon did so, it would be best for you.

AMINA: I wouldn't want his kiss bestowed on any comer.

LAMON: Where is your rose?

EGLE: She had to let him take it from her

To soothe his feelings.

AMINA: It's my duty, giving in.

LAMON: You're right. Forgive each other: that's the way to win.

I've noticed you outdo each other causing spite.

EGLE (*as a sign that she is through adorning Amina's hair*):

There!

LAMON: Lovely!

AMINA: But without the others its's not right,

The flowers Eridon is bringing.

EGLE: Wait and see.

Stay here while I get ready. Lamon, come with me.

We'll leave you by yourself but soon be back with you.

(*Lamon and Egle go out.*)

AMINA: Ah, how I envy the devotion of those two.

How I would like—but does it lie within my powers?

—to see contentment come into this love of ours.

Had I not given him so great control of me,

I would be better satisfied and so would he.

But now to try undoing that control in turn—

My coldness would feel his indignant fury burn!

I know his anger and I tremble. O my heart,

How unconvincingly you will enact the part!

Yet if you once did get these matters so in hand

That where he once commanded, you will then command—

Today's my chance, and not to miss it, I will start
At once—Oh, here he comes! Control yourself, my heart!
> (*Enter Eridon.*)

ERIDON (*giving her the flowers*):
　　They're not too nice, my child. I'm sorry. Will they do?
　　I picked in haste.

AMINA:　　　　　　　　　It is enough, they come from you.

ERIDON:　　They're not so fresh-blown as the roses Damon took
　　Away from you.

AMINA (*fastening them over her heart*):
　　　　　　　　　But I'll be glad to keep them. Look:
　　Where you are, that is where these flowers too shall go.

ERIDON:　　Will they be safe there—

AMINA:　　　　　　　　　Safe? Do you imagine—?

ERIDON:　　　　　　　　　　　　　　　　No!
　　I don't imagine anything. I only fear.
　　The best heart can forget, when sporting far and near
　　Amid the merry din and pleasures of the dance,
　　Forget what wisdom bids and duty's governance.
　　You may remember often even in your pleasure,
　　But you forget to hold your freedom within measure,
　　And young men quickly feel entitled to the best
　　When liberties are granted even as a jest.
　　They're vain enough that trifling pleasures are believed
　　Real tenderness.

AMINA:　　　　　　　Suffice it that they are deceived.
　　It's true that troops of sighing swains around me bask,
　　But my whole heart is yours, so what more can you ask?
　　Allow the poor things' rights to stand and look at me;
　　They think it's even—

ERIDON:　　　　　　　No! Their thoughts just shouldn't be!
　　That's what annoys me so. I realize you're mine,
　　But one of them may think he shares my lucky sign
　　And in your eyes sees kisses as a certainty,
　　Or even gloats at getting you away from me.

AMINA: Then spoil his triumph. Come along and let me show
   How you stand first in my affection—
ERIDON: Thank you, no.
   It would be cruel to accept that sacrifice.
   My wretched dancing would be much too high a price.
   At dances I know whom you think most highly of:
   The one who dances well and not the one you love.
AMINA: That's true.
ERIDON (*with suppressed mockery*):
                    Oh, what a shame I do not have the gift
   Of Damaran, the so-much-praised, the fleet, the swift!
   How he can dance!
AMINA: So all his rivals' claims collapse.
ERIDON: And every girl—
AMINA: Admires—
ERIDON: No, loves him for it.
AMINA: Perhaps.
ERIDON: Perhaps? Of course they do!
AMINA: Why do you look so wild?
ERIDON: Aren't you tormenting me? You drive me crazy, child!
AMINA: No, you bear all the blame for all our differences!
   Oh, cruel Eridon, how can you be like this?
ERIDON: I must; I love you. Love bids me cry my dismay;
   If I loved less, I wouldn't bother you this way.
   I feel my tender heart swept up into the skies
   At pressure from your hand or laughter from your eyes.
   I thank the gods for giving me this happiness,
   But no one else must share the thing that I possess.
AMINA: But no one else does share it, no one ever will.
ERIDON: And you put up with them. Your every look should kill.
AMINA: Why kill?
ERIDON: Because they love you and because they flirt.
AMINA: A likely reason!
ERIDON: You don't want to see them hurt.
   You must indulge them, else your joy is lessened there.
   Unless you—

AMINA: Eridon, you're being most unfair.
Does love entail withdrawal from the human race?
A heart in love with one, finds hating others, base.
The tender feeling won't permit that ugly notion,
At least with me.
ERIDON: You do defend with great emotion
The tender sex's way of being gratified:
Of twenty fools that kneel, all twenty are belied.
Today your haughtiness will feed on adoration
And, goddess-like, you will lend ear to supplication;
For you, still more young hearts will kindle into flame,
You won't have smiles enough to answer every claim.
Remember me amid that swarm of fools, then say
That I come first.
AMINA (*to herself*):   Oh, my frail heart, he wins the day.
Is spoiling my good times his reason for existence?
Do I see misery stretching to the furthest distance?
                    (*to Eridon*)
You make a heavy yoke of love's most fragile bond,
You torture like a tyrant, yet I still am fond.
With tenderness I answer even as you chide:
I yield on every count; still you're not satisfied.
What have I not renounced? You ask more than your share.
You want today's good time. All right, I yield it. There!
                    (*She takes the garlands from her hair and
                    from her shoulder, throws them aside, and
                    goes on speaking in a tone of forced calm.*)
You like me better this way, don't you, Eridon,
Than dressed up for the dance? Now is your temper gone?
You stand and stare. Have I done something to be blamed?
ERIDON (*falling to his knees*):   Amina, dearest, I am sorry
                                        and ashamed.
Go to the dance.
AMINA: No, here with you is where I'll stay,
And tender melody shall while the hours away.
ERIDON: My darling, go!

AMINA: Go fetch your flute and play for me.
ERIDON: All right!

(He goes out.)

AMINA: He looks sad but rejoices secretly.
On him, your tender sympathy will go for naught.
This sacrifice has touched him? Hardly as it ought.
He takes it as his due. Oh, why do you complain,
My heart, and choke my breast? Did I deserve this pain?
You did, indeed! You see he won't renounce his grim,
Tormenting ways, yet you still go on loving him.
I cannot bear it any longer. Hark! The dance
Is starting, and my heart and feet begin to prance.
I shall! Why does my bosom choke with pangs so dire?
How terrified I feel! My heart is all on fire.
I shall go to the dance!—He holds me back.—Poor lass,
The happiness of love has brought you to this pass.

> *(She throws herself down on a plot of lawn
> and weeps. As the others appear, she dries
> her eyes and gets up.)*

Oh, here they come. Now I must face their taunts and jeers.

(Egle and Lamon come in.)

EGLE: The crowd is forming. Quick! Amina! What? In tears?
LAMON (*picking up the garlands*):   The garlands?
EGLE: Who took those from where I had them fitted?
AMINA: I.
EGLE: You don't want to come?
AMINA: Yes—if I were permitted.
EGLE: Who's to permit you? Come, don't be ridiculous.
No need to speak in riddles, don't be shy with us:
Did Eridon—
AMINA: Yes.
EGLE: As I thought! You're all the more
A goose to grieve yet be no wiser than before.
You promised him to stay here with him, I surmise,
And while away this lovely day in soulful sighs?
I have no doubt he'd rather see you dressed this way.

(After a pause, she gives Lamon a sign.)
But, child, you do look better in your fine array.
Come, put this on; now this around your shoulder; so.
Now you look beautiful.

> *(Amina stands with downcast eyes and
> allows Egle to do as she will. Egle gives
> Lamon a sign.)*
> Oh my, it's time to go.

LAMON: Your humble servant, lovely child. The dance won't wait.
AMINA (*in distress*):   Farewell.
EGLE (*starting to leave*):   Amina! Aren't you coming? We'll be late!

> *(Amina gazes at her sadly and does not
> answer. Lamon takes Egle by the hand to
> escort her away.)*

LAMON: Oh, let her be! I'm tired to death of all this folly:
She has to spoil the dance that might have been so jolly.
There's no one else can do the dance with Lefts and Rights,
I counted on her for it; now she sets her sights
On staying home. Come on, I have no more to say.
EGLE: So you're not going. Child, you're in a sorry way.
It will be fun. Farewell.

> *(Egle starts to kiss Amina. Amina falls into
> her arms, weeping.)*

AMINA: Oh, I can't bear it! Stay!
EGLE: In tears?
AMINA: My heart's in tears, it chokes my breathing so.
I'd like to—Eridon, I think I hate you! Oh!
EGLE: He does deserve it. Still, a lover can't be hated.
But you must love him without being dominated.
I said so long ago. Come on.
LAMON: On to the dance!
AMINA: And Eridon?
EGLE: Go on ahead. I'll take the chance
Of getting him to join us for the afternoon.
You'd like that?
AMINA: Oh, so much!

LAMON: Come on, then! Hear that tune
　　The shawms and flutes are playing!
　　　　　(*He takes Amina by the hand and sings and dances.*)
EGLE (*singing*):   If you have a lover that's jealous and odd,
　　　　　　　　　Begrudges a smile and begrudges a nod,
　　　　　　　　　Complains you are fickle, complains you are false,
　　　　　　　　　You can't hear him scold while you sing and you waltz.
　　　　　　　　　(*Lamon dances Amina out of sight.*)
AMINA (*as she goes*):   Do bring him along!
EGLE: Now we shall see! I've waited for this chance a long,
　　Long while to change this shepherd. First, I had to reach him.
　　Today my wish is granted, now I'm going to teach him.
　　Torment her, will you? Well, I'm taking you to task.
　　He's coming.
　　　　　　　　　(*Enter Eridon.*)
　　　　　　Eridon—
ERIDON: Where is she?
EGLE: How you ask!
　　She's over with my Lamon where the shawms are playing.
　　　　　　　(*Eridon throws his flute on the ground and
　　　　　　　tears up his songs.*)
ERIDON: The faithless creature!
EGLE: Temper?
ERIDON: She said she was staying.
　　The hypocrite removed the garlands from her head
　　And with a smile upon her face stood there and said:
　　"I won't go dancing." Did I ask her not to?—Wouldn't—
　　　　　　　(*He stamps his foot and kicks away the torn
　　　　　　　songsheets.*)   ·
EGLE   (*in an even tone*):   May I inquire what right you have to say
　　　　　　　　　　　　　　　　　　　　　she couldn't?
　　Do you demand a heart that loves with all its might
　　Shall have no happiness except within your sight?
　　Do you think every joyous impulse has been stilled
　　As soon as a girl's heart with tenderness is filled?
　　She gives you her best hours, which is your proper due,

And when you are away her thoughts remain with you.
So it is folly keeping her in such commotion;
She can love dance and play with no loss of devotion.
                    (*Eridon folds his arms and gazes aloft.*)
Eridon: Ah!
Egle: Tell me, do you think that this is love, maybe,
    This keeping her with you? No, it is slavery.
    You come: to everyone else there she must be blind;
    You go: she must not fail to follow right behind;
    And if she hesitates, you give her looks that wither;
    But if she follows you, her heart does not go with her.
Eridon: So?
Egle: Still, one listens when embitterment lifts cries.
    Where freedom is denied, there every pleasure dies.
    That's how we are. A child may be inclined to song,
    But tell him: Sing!, and not a sound will come along.
    Allow her freedom and she will not be untrue,
    But if you are too hard, she'll wind up hating you.
Eridon: Hate me?
Egle: Deservedly. So use this time of stress
    To realize good fortune with real tenderness.
    None but a tender heart aglow with inner fire
    Can show true constancy or to real love aspire.
    The bird you keep shut in a cage, can you rely
    On its devotion?
Eridon: No.
Egle: But if it's free to fly
    Through fields and gardens and yet always comes back later?
Eridon: Yes, true. I know that.
Egle: Is your joy not all the greater
    To see the little creature that you love so dearly,
    And yet has freedom, giving you his preference clearly?
    And if your darling comes back from a festival
    Still quivering from the dance, and seeks you out, and all
    Her looks reveal that perfect joy can be nowhere
    So long as you, her one beloved, were not there,

And if she vows a thousand dances give less pleasure
Than just your kiss, are you not lucky beyond measure?
ERIDON (*touched*):   Oh, Egle!
EGLE: Righteous anger of the gods may shatter
   A happy man who deems his luck a trifling matter.
   Oh, be content, my friend, or they'll avenge the tears
   Of her you love.
ERIDON: If I could just dismiss my fears
   When all too many clasp her hands amid those dances
   And this one looks at her and that one gets her glances.
   Just thinking of it wrenches my heart's every string.
EGLE: Well, never mind all that. It doesn't mean a thing.
   Nor even does a kiss.
ERIDON: What's that you say? A kiss?
EGLE: One's heart must brim with feeling to be saying this,
   I think—and yet your better judgment *will* release her?
   If you show anger, nothing else can ever please her.
ERIDON: Dear friend!
EGLE (*cajolingly*):   Don't do it. You're too kind for that, I
                                           know.

   Farewell. (*She takes his hand.*)
                    You're wrought up now.
ERIDON: My pulse is throbbing so—
EGLE: Still angry? But she *is* forgiven. I must hurry
   And bring her your decision. She'll be sick with worry.
   I'll tell her: All is well. Then her anxiety
   Will ease and she'll come back the more affectionately.
                    (*She looks at him with feeling.*)
   When once the dance is over she will seek you out,
   The fonder of you for the search, beyond a doubt.
                    (*Egle moves tenderly closer, leaning on his
                    shoulder. He takes her hand and kisses it.*)
   And when at last she spies you in her sweet distress,
   Then clasp her to you in your total happiness!
   A girl grows prettier from dancing—cheeks aglow,
   Lips breathing smiles, a tress come loose and dangling low,

A bosom panting—and what gentle charms enhance
A body that has just been speeding through the dance—
The pulses throb, and from the body's rush and flight
Each nerve and muscle seems to thrill before your sight—

> (*She affects a tender rapture and falls against his bosom. He puts an arm around her.*)

What can outweigh the rapture of beholding this?
By never dancing you don't know what all you miss.

ERIDON: Against your heart, dear friend, I do know what it is!

> (*He takes Egle in his arms and kisses her. She permits him. Then she steps back and inquires in a frivolous tone.*)

EGLE: You love Amina?

ERIDON: As myself.

EGLE: And yet you can kiss me?
Just wait! I'll make you pay for this duplicity,
Disloyal creature!

ERIDON: You don't think that just because—

EGLE: I think as I may think. A tender kiss it was,
My friend, and I was satisfied completely by it.
.And so were you. Your ardent lips would like to try it
Again, I fancy. Poor Amina should be here.

ERIDON: Oh, if she were!

EGLE: It would go ill with you, I fear.

ERIDON: She'd scold me. But she mustn't know it did occur.
I kissed you, it is true, but where's the harm to her?
And if she kissed me just as warmly, where's the harm
In feeling that your kiss is also full of charm?

> (*Enter Amina.*)

EGLE: Ask her that.

ERIDON: Ah!

AMINA: I have to see him even so!
Oh, Eridon beloved, Egle made me go.
I broke my word, I'm sorry. Right here's where I'll stay.

ERIDON (*to himself*):   I'm false!

AMINA: Still angry with me? Please don't turn away!

ERIDON (*To himself*):   What can I do?

AMINA: One tiny little act of treason,
Does it deserve such vengeance? You have every reason
To blame me—

EGLE: Let him be! He just gave me a kiss;
He's relishing.

AMINA: A kiss!

EGLE: So tenderly.

AMINA: Ah, this
Is too much for my heart! Is love so soon converted
To hatred? Have I been abandoned and deserted?
To kiss another means he is prepared to jilt.
Since I have loved you, when have I incurred such guilt?
To my lips no young man dared so much as aspire;
I hardly gave the kiss that Forfeit games require.
As much as yours, my heart is gnawed by jealousy,
But I'll forgive you if you'll only look at me.
Yet all in vain, poor heart, are you so well defended:
Since you occasioned him this pain his love is ended.
In vain our interceding friend will plead your claim.

ERIDON: What tenderness! Oh, how she does put me to shame!

AMINA: Oh, dearest Egle, how could you seduce my friend?

EGLE: Be comforted, Amina, this is not the end.
I know your Eridon, I know how true he is.

AMINA: But he—

EGLE: Yes, that is true. He did give me a kiss.
But I know how it happened, and you can forgive.
See his remorse!

ERIDON (*falling at Amina's feet*):   Amina, love for whom I live!
Be angry with her: she contrived it, to be kissed.
I was so near her lips that I could not resist.
You can excuse it, knowing my heart as you do:
A little slip like that won't spoil my heart for you.

EGLE: Amina, kiss him, since he speaks so rationally.
                    (*to Eridon*)
Your heart will not be spoiled by joy, nor will hers be,

Friend, you have judged yourself, compelled by circumstance.
Admit now: it's no crime if she enjoys a dance.
                    (*imitating him*)
And if so many clasp her hands amid those dances,
And this one looks at her, and that one gets her glances,
That doesn't mean a great deal either, as you know.
No more, I hope, will you torment Amina so.
You'll come with us now?
AMINA: Please!
ERIDON: I have to, it is clear.
That kiss has been instructive.
EGLE (*to Amina*):   We're both sorry, dear.
But if such jealousy afflicts his heart again,
Recall this kiss: you'll find it is good medicine.
—You jealous men that tease your girls with might and main,
Remember capers *you* have cut—and then complain.

FELLOW CULPRITS

Among the papers that Goethe brought home with him in September of 1768 was the sketch of a second play, entitled *Fellow Culprits (Die Mitschuldigen)*. Like its predecessor, it was intended as a one-act comedy in hexameter couplets, but in the end it worked out to three Acts. The setting is an inn, Acts I and III in the reception room, Act II in one of the chambers upstairs. The unnamed city is, of course, Leipzig.

At age sixty-three (in 1812) Goethe recalls some of the circumstances in Book VII of his autobiography. Around Easter of 1766, he reports, he went to pay a visit to an acquaintance from home who was staying at

> a small inn or tavern . . . run by an innkeeper named Schönkopf. This latter was married to a Frankfurt woman, and though he entertained few persons during the rest of the year and could not take guests in his small house, he did entertain numerous Frankfurt people at [Leipzig] Fair time, serving them meals and, in case of need, putting them up.

Soon after that visit Goethe began to take his meals regularly at Mr. Schönkopf's establishment. The person who served him his food was the innkeeper's daughter, that same Anna Katharina Schönkopf whose story was told under the name of Annie in earlier pages of the autobiography and who figured, in a somewhat different aspect, as Amina in *The Lover's Whim*. In 1766, we may add, Mr. Schönkopf was aged fifty and his daughter twenty, i.e., three years older than the student diner. She was unmarried, and her boarder's quick-kindling affections came to a declaration of love as early as April 27th. How matters went from there has already been told, but the young people's parting was amicable and Goethe sent the girl a congratulatory poem for her wedding day, May 7, 1770.

In the play the unnamed innkeeper is doubtless a fair portrait of Mr. Schönkopf. The heroine, who is decidedly less sweet-and-suffer-

33

ing than Amina, is now called Sophie, while traits of Goethe may be discerned in the elegant young lover who, under the French-classical name Alcest, is a lodger at the inn. But Sophie now is twenty-four and has a husband named Söller. He is a shabby wastrel, even a thief, and the author, with a brilliant stroke of malice, has him appear in clown costume, either ready to leave for a masquerade party or returning from one. The inn itself is arbitrarily "at the sign of the Shaggy Bear."

In its completed form *Fellow Culprits* is a comedy of manners, akin to the French Molière, the Italian Goldoni, and their German imitators, Weisse, Krüger, and Schiebeler, works by all of these being in contemporary theater repertories in Germany. The hexameter couplets show a little more tendency to run-on lines than those of *The Lover's Whim*. As a play, it is artfully contrived, full of witty lines and amusing situations, and eminently stageworthy.

The problem is that it is *too* artfully contrived in its equal distribution of guilt among the four "fellow culprits." The action takes place at only one possible point in time, leaving unanswered all questions about what went before the opening curtain and about what will happen after the final one. Each character is implausibly ignorant of precisely those factors which make this action possible, though all four of them have lived under one roof for a considerable time. For a farce, this sort of procedure is acceptable, but farce is not the ruling quality of this play. There are passages of tenderness and, still more, of bitterness. From moment to moment the whole work threatens to turn deadly serious, and at the end each of the four characters is placed in an intolerable position. Continue the story for as much as one more day and anything could happen, even to extermination of the cast by murder and suicide.

Looking back upon the work in 1812 Goethe saw all this. There is a disparity, he points out, between the lively manner of the work and its somber background,

> so that in performance the totality inspires dread even while its separate parts are amusing. Its harshly pronounced illicit actions offend esthetic and moral feelings, and for that reason the play could

not win access to the German stage, although imitations of it, by steering clear of those rocks, met with success.

The problem here runs parallel to that in Congreve's *The Way of the World* (1700), where comedy, disclosing human follies, comes upon matters too evil to be funny any more. But whereas Congreve, in writing that bitter and fine play, was a deeply experienced man of thirty, Goethe was twenty and rash and ebullient. *Fellow Culprits* is delightful to read or to see in performance, but reflective thought will burn holes right through it.

FELLOW CULPRITS

A Comedy in Three Acts

(Die Mitschuldigen
Ein Lustspiel in drey Aufzügen)
1768–1769

CHARACTERS

THE INNKEEPER
SOPHIE, his daughter
SÖLLER, her husband
ALCEST
A SERVANT

The action takes place at an inn
"at the sign of the Shaggy Bear"
The time is contemporary with the
composition of the play.

ACT I

Söller, in a domino, is sitting at a small table, on which stand a candle, a bottle of wine, and a glass. Opposite him sits Sophie, sewing a plume and a bow onto a hat. At stage-rear stands a larger table with a candle on it. Books and inkwell; an armchair.
Enter the innkeeper.

INNKEEPER (*to Söller*):   Oh, so my son-in-law's off to the ball again!
  With all this nightlife, you might skip one now and then.
  When I gave you my daughter that was not to say
  That you should spend my money turning night to day.
  I'm getting on in years, I wanted peace and quiet;
  With you to help me out I *had* hoped to come by it.
  My savings squandered: that's the help I get from you.
              (*Söller hums a tune.*)
  Yes, sing your little song! But I can sing one too.
  You're just an emptyheaded, good-for-nothing lout,
  And drink and smoking-pipes are all you care about.
  With gadding all night long and mornings sleeping late,
  No duke in all this empire boasts a cozier state.
  There sits the scamp in clown's garb la-de-da,
  His Majesty the fool!
SÖLLER (*raising his glass*):   Here's to your health, Papa!
INNKEEPER: A fine toast *that* is. It's enough to make me ill.
SOPHIE: You should be nice to father.
SÖLLER (*raising his glass to her*):   Sophie, as you will.
SOPHIE: My will is chiefly saving you from death by him.
INNKEEPER: Unless he mends his ways his chances there are slim.
  His everlasting wrangles simply have to cease;
  The way he keeps it up, the Devil might make peace.
  He's thankless, feelingless, in everything he does.
  He won't see what he is or think of what he was.
  The pauper state I saved him from, and all his debts,

39

Those are the things this cad conveniently forgets.
Not time, not bitter end, will ever cure the brash:
A piece of trash to all eternity stays trash.
SOPHIE: Oh, he will change in time.
INNKEEPER: Then shouldn't he get started?
SOPHIE: His trouble is his youth.
SÖLLER: From Sophie never parted!
                    (*He drinks to that.*)
INNKEEPER (*outraged*):   With him it goes in one, and out the other,
                                                            ear.

He doesn't listen. Do I count for nothing here?
These twenty years I've spent in honesty and thrift.
Do you expect my hard-earned status as a gift
To manage any way you choose? Oh, no! say I;
That's not the way of it, to that plan say goodbye.
My reputation stands and will stand high and fair.
The whole world knows the owner of The Shaggy Bear,
And he sees to it that his pelt keeps looking well.
Once finished painting here, up goes the sign "Hotel."
Then high-class patrons will come here to spend and spend.
But hard work is the watchword, drinking has to end.
It will be late to bed and early up again.
That's how it stands.
SÖLLER: You've got a way to go till then.
If things stay as they are and don't slack off still more.
Who all is here? The rooms are on the second floor.
INNKEEPER: There's no one leaving, is there? No one in retreat?
There *is* Monsieur Alcest up in the ballroom suite?
SÖLLER: That's something, I admit. And he is steady pay.
But minutes come at sixty to the hour, I say.
What's more, Alcest has reason to be here.
INNKEEPER (*stung*):   Does he?
SÖLLER (*reaching for his glass*):
Oh, *à propos*, Papa: long life to Paoli.[1]
INNKEEPER (*amicably*):   Long life to him, my son; his tribute should
                                                            be paid.

[1] Pasquale Paoli, the Corsican patriot before 1768.

It was no easy feat, the valor he displayed.
Disaster could not daunt his total gallantry.
I'm going to call my inn "Hôtel de Paoli."

SÖLLER: The signboard will be something journalists will prize.
I'll die of grief if it does not materialize.
How is it that you haven't read your paper yet
Today?

INNKEEPER: It's for the errand boy to go and get.
If they should make him king you'd all be glad, I vow.
My heart thumps as if I could hear the shooting now.

(*Exit.*)

SÖLLER: Nothing so bad but what the paper makes it good.

SOPHIE: Oh, humor him a bit.

SÖLLER: I don't have fiery blood.
That's his good fortune. But why ding at me like this,
As if I were—

SOPHIE: Now, dear!

SÖLLER: I do know how it is!
I'm well aware of what condition I was in
A year ago: footloose, in debt up to my chin.

SOPHIE: Don't fret so, dear!

SÖLLER: But when the worst has been conceded,
I still was just the man my little Sophie needed.

SOPHIE: I have no cheerful hour but what you always flout it.

SÖLLER: I don't blame *you*, it's just the way I feel about it.
A woman is a constant joy by just her beauty;
Love her or not, our gratitude is bounden duty.
You're beautiful, my love, and I'm not made of stone,

(*He kisses her.*)

And I'm a lucky man to have you for my own.
I love you.

SOPHIE: Yet you can torment me constantly.

SÖLLER: What if I do?—I do, though; there I must agree.
Then too, Alcest loved you, and you showed him affection
And maybe even—but, that was an old connection.

SOPHIE: Oh!

SÖLLER: No, there's nothing there but what was quite all
                                                                right.

A seedling planted grows up to its normal height,
And if fruit forms with time and no one's there to pick it,
It will bear fruit another year. There's nothing wicked
In that, and nothing that would make me start a fuss.
It's merely funny.

SOPHIE: What is so ridiculous?

Alcest may well have loved me and shown me affection,
And I loved him as well; ours *was* an old connection.
What else, then?

SÖLLER: Nothing. Nothing else was on my mind
When I made that remark. But young girls sometimes find
It's fun to toy with love, to give the thing a try;
They have an itch around their hearts, they don't know why.
The trickster Amor stalks in tender friendship's shape,
And one not knowing tigers wishes no escape.
Of mothers' scoldings girls can not make any sense;
In purity they love, and fall in innocence;
And if they also gain experience at life,
A husband's better off to get a clever wife.

SOPHIE: You do not know me.

SÖLLER: Let us drop the subject, then.

For girls a kiss is like a glass of wine to men:
First one, and then another, and so on till we sink;
If we don't want to stagger, then we shouldn't drink.
You're mine, and that's what counts—You're into your
                                                fourth year

Of Alcest's friendship and his renting quarters here:
How long was he away? Two years, I think.

SOPHIE: No. More.

SÖLLER: And now he's two weeks back, and all is as before.

SOPHIE: Dear, what use is this talk?

SÖLLER: Why, talk is good for us.

Most wives and husbands have so little to discuss.
But why has he come back?

SOPHIE: Because he likes it here.

SÖLLER: I have a notion that he holds you very dear.
Suppose he loved you: would you listen to his plea?

SOPHIE: Love has its claims, but so does my fidelity.
You think . . . ?

SÖLLER: I don't think anything. But I'm aware
A man does something more than whistle to the air.
The sweetest note that ever shepherd piped in glades
Is only one note, and in course of time it fades.

SOPHIE (*impatiently*):   I realize. But what about the note you play?
Your discontent increases with each passing day.
You pick at me till I don't have a minute's peace.
In order to be loved you first must learn to please.
Are you a man to give a girl much happiness?
Have you acquired the right to make these challenges?
And nothing to them all. You stand the house on end;
You don't earn anything and yet you spend and spend.
You live from hand to mouth, borrow from all and any,
And if your wife's in want she doesn't have a penny:
You just let her find money any way she can.
If you so want a loyal wife, then be a man.
There's no temptation worse than want in all life's book,
And hunger drives the shrewdest fish to take the hook.
My father rightly gives me nothing all along.
We need things, and yet everything is going wrong.
Today I had to ask for something anyway:
"No money? *You*?" he said, "yet Söller drives a sleigh."
And then he lectured me so both my ears still burn.
Now maybe you will tell me which way I'm to turn,
Since you're no husband to provide a wife with things.

SÖLLER: Let's wait and see, my darling, what tomorrow brings.
Some loyal friend may—

SOPHIE: He would be a foolish friend.
And friends are more inclined to borrow than to lend;
The ones that give and do not take I've yet to see.
No, things can not go on this way with you and me.

SÖLLER: But you have what you need!

SOPHIE: But I had that before.
One who was not deprived may still want something more.
Good luck may have from childhood furnished all we need
And yet the things we have seem very slight indeed.
The things to which all women and all girls aspire
I do not crave, but I am not without desire:
Fine clothes, a dance—I am a woman, after all.

SÖLLER: Then, as I've said before, come with me to the ball.

SOPHIE: Oh, why must business here with us come all in flurries:
A few days' rush, and then off everybody hurries.
I'd rather be alone here years on years unending.
If you will not economize, I must stop spending.
My father is annoyed enough with me already,
So I must calm him down and keep his temper steady.
No, Sir, I will not waste my money constantly;
Save some yourself, so you can spend it then on me.

SÖLLER: For just this one more time, my child, let me have fun,
Then when the Fair time comes, we'll see what can be done.

                    (*Enter a servant.*)

SERVANT: For Monsieur Söller.

SÖLLER: Yes?

SERVANT: The man from Tirinette.

SOPHIE: The gamester!

SÖLLER: Send him packing! Devil take him yet!

SERVANT: He says it's urgent.

SOPHIE: I can only wonder why.

SÖLLER (*embarrassed, to Sophie*):
He's leaving.
    (*to the servant*)   Right away.
    (*to Sophie*)   He's come to say goodbye.

                    (*Exit.*)

SOPHIE: He's here to dun him for some gambling I O U.
He'll go through everything, and nothing I can do.
So ends my happiness and all my dreams so sweet:
The wife of such a cad, and there is no retreat.
What has become of all those youths that bowed before you,

Those swarms of sweet young men who knelt down to adore you?
When each one searched your glances to decry his fate
There I in plenty stood, as though in goddess' state,
And saw my whims obeyed by servers far and wide.
It was no simple task to fill my heart with pride.
And, oh!, the things that can bring girls to sheer distress!
Give one a little beauty, and right away they press
Us with their compliments until our heads are dazed.
What girl can go through that ordeal-by-fire unfazed?
And all so honor-bright in everything you say,
You men, and then the Devil takes you all away.
We're all invited when there's hope of tidbit-fare,
But let a girl get serious: doors close everywhere.
With gentlemen these days that's just the way it goes.
From twenty candidates one half-man may propose.
Too many times I was abandoned and betrayed;
At twenty-four one can't leave any chance unplayed.
Then Söller came along, and I said I'd be pleased.
He's no great bargain, but he is a man at least.
Now here I sit, as good as dead and in the ground.
I could, of course, have suitors flocking all around,
But if a married woman has some scruples in her,
Young fellows can't be bothered taking time to win her.
From girls they're satisfied with flirting and with teasing,
They chatter their sweet nothings hours and hours unceasing,
But if a married woman is a little chaste,
They marvel at her and call for their hats in haste.
   Alcest is here again, and that's cause for dismay:
When he was here before, it was a different day.
I loved him—and still do—I can't make up my mind.
I do avoid him. He is of the brooding kind,
I am afraid of him, and have good cause to be.
If he but knew the heart that yearns inside of me!
Here he comes now. My full heart trembles at the fact;
I don't know how I want, or how I ought, to act.
              (*Enter Alcest.*)
ALCEST: Are you alone? And may a friend dare say a word?

SOPHIE: Sir!

ALCEST: "Sir!" That's not the greeting that you once
                                          preferred.

SOPHIE: Yes, time goes by, and things change with each passing
                                          year.

ALCEST: Can time have power even over you, my dear?
    Are these my own words or some actor's in a part?
    Are you Sophie?

SOPHIE (*pleadingly*): Alcest!

ALCEST: Well, are you?

SOPHIE: My poor heart
    Bleeds at your words. Alcest! My friend! I must implore you,
    Excuse me, I must go.

ALCEST: I stand here crushed before you.
    Then leave me if you must. I fancied I had struck
    A moment when you were alone, and blessed my luck.
    Now she (I hoped) will speak a tender word or two.
    Go on, now! Go ahead! Here in this room with you
    My Sophie once the fairest flames of love confessed,
    Here in this room our hearts were first together pressed,
    Here on this very spot, if you recall, you swore
    Eternal faith to me.

SOPHIE: Oh, spare me! Say no more!

ALCEST: I never will forget that lovely evening hour.
    Your eyes spoke, and I felt emboldened by their power.
    All trembling then you proffered ardent lips to me,
    And my heart still relives that thrill of ecstasy.
    With thoughts of me you then were wholly occupied,
    While now you cannot spend a moment at my side.
    You see I seek you out, you see me all forlorn.
    Go, faithless heart, and leave me victim of your scorn.

SOPHIE: I am distressed enough: is worse distress your aim?
    I never loved you? Oh, how can you make that claim!
    You were my utmost wish, you were my highest good,
    For you my heartbeat pulsed, and for you flowed my blood.
    This heart which once submitted to your total rule

Can not forget you ever, nor can it be cruel.
To time, that sweeps so much away, love will not bend,
And no one ever loved who thought his love could end.
But—Someone's coming!

ALCEST: No!

SOPHIE: It's dangerous, talking here.

ALCEST: Without a single word! Oh, put aside your fear.
It's this way all the time. The troubles one goes through!
Two weeks I've been here now, and not once talked to you.
I know you love me still, but I will die of that,
Since we can never be alone to have a chat.
Here in this room it's never quiet for a minute,
With first your father, then your husband sitting in it.
I won't be staying long; it's more than I can bear.—
But are not all things possible to those who dare?
You used to cope with obstacles of any size
To make a dragon sleep, or blind a hundred eyes.
Oh, if you only would!

SOPHIE: Would what?

ALCEST: Would only care
About not driving your Alcest to his despair.
My darling, do find opportunity somehow
For us to talk the way this room will not allow.
Why not tonight? Your husband will not be about,
It's Mardi Gras, and I too am invited out.
From rear gate to my stairs there's no cause for concern,
And no one in the house will notice my return.
I have the key right here. Just say that you're agreed.

SOPHIE: Alcest, I am amazed.

ALCEST: Then I will have no need
To think of you as false, or that your heart is hard.
It is our only way, it must not be disbarred.
We know each other; there's no shame, unless you make it.
If there were any other way I would not take it.
All right then: I'll come to your room tonight at nine,
Or if you feel it's safer, you can come to mine.

SOPHIE: Alcest, you ask too much!

ALCEST: How daintily she speaks!
"Too much! Too much!" she says, while here I wait whole weeks
For nothing. Damn! What keeps me here day after day,
If not Sophie! Tomorrow I'll be on my way!

SOPHIE: No, darling, no!

ALCEST: You see me wretched, yet you never
Show mercy. I can't stay away from you forever.
   (*Alcest paces up and down the room. Sophie stands undecided.*
   Enter the innkeeper with a letter.)

INNKEEPER: A letter. Someone high-up must be writing you,
The seal is extra-big, on vellum paper, too.

(*Alcest takes the letter and rips it open.*)
He tears the envelope to pieces in his haste.

ALCEST (*after no more than a glance through the letter*):
I leave tomorrow morning. There's no time to waste.
My bill!

INNKEEPER: In this bad time you leave so suddenly?
Your letter must convey uncommon urgency.
May I presume to ask Your Grace if such is true?

ALCEST: No.

INNKEEPER (*aside to Sophie*):   *You* ask him, I'm certain he will
                                    answer *you*.
            (*He goes to the table at the rear, consults*
            his books, and writes up the bill.)

SOPHIE (*tenderly*):   Alcest, is such the case?

ALCEST (*looking away*):   See tenderness awaken!

SOPHIE: Alcest, I beg you, do not leave Sophie forsaken!

ALCEST: All right: make up your mind and say you will receive me.

SOPHIE (*aside*):   What shall I do? What can I do? He must not leave
                                                         me,
   He's all I've got, so I must do the best I can.

ALCEST: Well, darling?

SOPHIE: But my husband . . .

ALCEST: Devil take the man!
   You will, then?

SOPHIE: Will I . . . ?

ALCEST: Well?
SOPHIE: I'll come to you.
ALCEST: I'll stay,
   Innkeeper! Hold your bill.
INNKEEPER: Ah, so?
                                 (to Sophie) What did he say?
SOPHIE: Not much.
INNKEEPER: He didn't?
                        (Enter Söller.)
SÖLLER: Where's my hat?
SOPHIE: I'll get it. Here!
ALCEST: I must be off now to my banquet.
SÖLLER: Bon plaisir!
ALCEST (taking Sophie's hand):
   Farewell, dear lady.
SÖLLER (aside):   Insolence grows on the cur.
ALCEST (to the Innkeeper):
   A light to go upstairs!
SOPHIE: Farewell, Alcest.
INNKEEPER (accompanying him):   Yes, Sir.
ALCEST: No, you stay here.
INNKEEPER: But, Sir . . .
ALCEST: Not one step of the way!
SOPHIE: Well, Söller . . . ? If I came along what would you say?
SÖLLER: It's now a little late.
SOPHIE: I said that as a joke.
SÖLLER: No, I can tell there's heart-fire burning, by the smoke.
   When someone's party-bound and someone else stays put
   It stands to reason other matters are afoot.
   Another time.
SOPHIE: Yes. It will keep. And—if you're able—
   I would suggest avoidance of the gambling table.
   Good night, Papa, I'm off to bed. It's late, you know.
INNKEEPER: Sleep tight.
SÖLLER (gazing after her):   By golly, but she is a beauty, though!
           (He hurries to overtake her and kisses her.)
   Sleep well, my lamb!

(*Exit Sophie.*)

(*to the Innkeeper*)   Well, are you also off to bed?

INNKEEPER (*aside*):   There is that devilish letter: I wonder what it
said?

(*aloud*)   Yes. Happy Mardi Gras!

SÖLLER: Thanks, and good night to you.

INNKEEPER: Oh, Söller, when you leave, make sure the gate is to.

SÖLLER: I'll see to it.

(*Exit the Innkeeper.*)

Now what am I to do? This danged
Attraction of the cards! I'd like to see him hanged,
The Jack of Diamonds!—I must use my thinking-cap.
All loans are at an end, I'm caught fast in a trap.
Let's see . . . Alcest has money; here's a key for broaching
More locks than one. Besides, I think he's done some poaching
On land of mine; he finds my wife of interest.
Supposing I drop in on him, say, like a guest?
If it gets out, though, there will be a fine ado.
But I am in dire straits and what else can I do?
I'll lose my hide unless my gamester gets his pay,
So, buck up, Söller! They're asleep: be on your way!
Why, even if they catch me, I won't come to grief:
A pretty wife can work salvation for a thief.

ACT II

The stage is divided, the main portion representing Alcest's room, the smaller portion representing an alcove.
Enter Söller in his domino, wearing a hat and holding his mask up in front of his face.
Unabashed, he comes softly in by the side door and cautiously shines a dark lantern around. Finding everything quiet, he tiptoes up to the footlights, takes off his hat and mask, and mops his brow.

SÖLLER: In life it's not so much our bravery that's demanded:
　　　One *can* get through this world by being underhanded.
　　　One fellow may set off with pistols at his sides
　　　To get a bag of money—maybe death besides—
　　　And cry: "Your purse! Be quick about it!"—as refined
　　　As if he had no more than "To your health!" in mind.
　　　Another slips up by you and by sleight-of-hand
　　　Removes your watch with lightning-swiftness as you stand.
　　　Ask him to say: "I'm stealing now, here's how I do it:
　　　Watch carefully!"—he's done it and you never knew it.
　　　Now, Nature formed me for a less distinguished part:
　　　I lack sufficient nerve, my fingers lack the art.
　　　But not to be a rogue is difficult today,
　　　With money scarce and wants increasing every way.
　　　And semi-rascals are poor creatures and forlorn,
　　　For thieves, like poets, come with geniuses inborn;
　　　The minute either botches up or shows a flaw
　　　He feels the critics' scourges or the whips of law.
　　　　All right: you're in the trap; now get yourself safe out.
　　　They think I'm at the ball and nowhere here about;
　　　My wife is sound asleep; Alcest is merry-making:
　　　A perfect constellation for my undertaking.
　　　　　　　(*He takes the strongbox from the table.*)

51

Come, sacred thing, container of my god and hero!
Without you any king is nothing but a zero.

> (*He draws a picklock from his pocket and
> goes on speaking while he is breaking into
> the strongbox.*)

Ah, jimmies open paths to lands of milk and honey;
With little jimmy's help I get Big Jimmy—money.
I once was secretary in a City Hall,
Which was no kind of job for little minds at all;
It is a noble craft and needs a skilled technician.
I had some good ideas while in that position
And lived much like a prince. They caught a thief one time,
They found his set of keys and hanged him for his crime.
Now, law-courts, as you know, keep back such properties.
I was a mere subaltern, but I got those keys.
A thing may seem so worthless that you may refuse it,
But if you wait, the time may come when you can use it.
And now . . .   (*The lock yields.*)

> Oh, lovely coins! A sheer joy to behold!

My heart expands the way that purse there bulges gold . . .
Unless it's fear—
(*He listens.*)   You coward knees, stop shaking, then!

> (*He shrinks with fear.*)

Hark!—Nothing.   (*He closes the strongbox.*)
All is well.

> (*As he goes to leave, he startles and stands rigid.*)

> No, there it is again!

There's something in the hall. It doesn't move away.
The Devil at his tricks? But what a time to play!
A cat—No, cats take care to tread with velvet paw.
The key turns in the lock!

> (*He darts into the alcove and peeps through the curtains.*)

> Ye gods! My father-in-law.

> (*Enter by the side door the innkeeper in
> nightshirt, nightcap, and slippers,
> anxiously holding a candle.*)

INNKEEPER: A skittish heart-beat is a very silly matter:
　　Do just a wee bit wrong, it starts to pitter-patter.
　　There must be in that letter things I need to see
　　For me to be here. It had Polish registry,
　　I think. Today's newspaper was inanely cold;
　　Its latest items are invariably months old;
　　The editor himself is in a wretched way:
　　The little that he knows, he's not allowed to say.
　　I'd be Prime Minister if I had rank and station:
　　Then I would see each courier's communication.
　　　　　　　　　(*He searches about.*)
　　He went upstairs, fetched hat and sword, as I recall . . .
　　I hope he didn't take the letter to the ball.
　　　　　　　　　(*He searches some more.*)
SÖLLER (*in the alcove*):   You poor old fool! The god of news and
　　　　　　　　　　　　　　　　　　　　　　thievery
　　Has plainly favored you with less esteem than me.
INNKEEPER: I just don't find it.
　　(*He startles.*)　　　　　　　　Oh!—What was that noise I heard?
　　From that room there? (*He listens.*)
SÖLLER (*frightened*):　　　Can he have smelled me?
INNKEEPER:　　　　　　　　　　　　　Something stirred.
　　It rustled like a woman's shoe.
SÖLLER:　　　　　　　　　I'm not a shoe!
INNKEEPER (*blowing out his candle*):   Pfft! Let's get out of here!
　　　　　　　(*In his haste he cannot get the lock open,
　　　　　　　and in trying, he drops the candle. Finally
　　　　　　　he wrenches the door open and rushes
　　　　　　　away.
　　　　　　　Enter Sophie by the main door.*)
SÖLLER (*astonished*):　　　　A woman's coming through!
　　I hope it's not my wife!
SOPHIE (*setting her candle on the table and coming forward*):
　　　　　　　　　　　This step is rash indeed.
　　I'm so afraid.
SÖLLER (*in caricature*):　　　It is! Oh, this is all I need!

Goodbye, poor head of mine!—But now supposing *I*
Stepped forth?—No. Then I'd bid my neck goodbye.

SOPHIE: Sophie, you've come to him. Ah, What temerity!
But what else could I do? he cannot come to me.
My bedroom and my father's room are much too near.
But here there's no one!

SÖLLER: No one! With your husband here?

SOPHIE: Yes, follow Love. With friendly looks and gestures glad
He leads you on at first.

SÖLLER: I think I'm going mad!
I mustn't, though.

SOPHIE: But when you once have lost your way,
There's no will-o'-the-wisp that leads you worse astray.

SÖLLER: A swamp would be more healthy for you than this room.

SOPHIE: However bad things were, I'm now approaching doom.
My husband goes too far, as I've tried to advise him,
But at his present rate I'm coming to despise him.

SÖLLER: You little witch!

SOPHIE: He has my hand; Alcest meanwhile
Is owner of my heart.

SÖLLER: A poison-brewer's guile
Was never worse than this.

SOPHIE: All love till his was sham;
From him I first discovered what love *could* be.

SÖLLER: Damn!

SOPHIE: How cold my heart was till it yielded to Alcest!

SÖLLER: Oh, if all husbands could once hear things thus confessed!

SOPHIE: How happy I was once.

SÖLLER: It's not worth thinking of.

SOPHIE: How kind Alcest could be.

SÖLLER: Bah! That was puppy-love.

SOPHIE: Fate soon will part us now, and by a paradox
I have to be—why have to?!—married to this ox.

SÖLLER: Who? Me, an ox! Yes, with horns sprouting from my
brow.

SOPHIE: What do I see?

SÖLLER: What, madam?

SOPHIE: Father's candle! How
  Did that get here? Perhaps—he's here and listening
  From some place hidden.

SÖLLER: Conscience, goad her with your sting!

SOPHIE: I can't imagine how he could have lost it here.

SÖLLER: She'd brave her father, but the Devil she might fear.

SOPHIE: Oh, no! The entire household has been long abed.

SÖLLER: Her pleasure counts for more than any sense of dread.

SOPHIE: My father would not—Who knows where it may be from?
  But never mind.

SÖLLER: Alas!

SOPHIE: Why doesn't Alcest come!

SÖLLER: I'd like to shake her!

SOPHIE: Longing and a fear unknown
  Take me by turns.

SÖLLER: I fear him like the Devil's own!
  If now the Prince of Darkness came into my view,
  I'd say: "Go on and take her!—Take the money, too!

SOPHIE: My over-tender heart, wherein lies your transgression?
  In pledging vows, by what right did you make concession?
  Vows to a man without a grain of decency,
  Uncomprehending, faithless, rude, and crude!

SÖLLER: Who? Me?!

SOPHIE: If such a monster does not justify my hate,
  I'll take my chances living in the Devil's state.
  He *is* a devil!

SÖLLER (*angry*):   Devil! Monster! I will burst
  If I don't have it out with her.
          (*He starts to come forward, sees Alcest, and retreats.*)

ALCEST: Why, you're here first!

SOPHIE (*smiling*):   I came to meet you.

ALCEST: But you're trembling?

SOPHIE (*pointing first to Alcest, then to the door*):   Dangers lurk
  Both here, and there.

SÖLLER: This is the prelude to the work.

SOPHIE: You know the things my heart has suffered for your sake,
And knowing my whole heart, forgive this step I take.

ALCEST (*meaningfully*): Sophie.

SOPHIE: Then I will not feel guilty if you do.

SÖLLER: Why not ask *me* if *I* may yet forgive you too?

SOPHIE: Why have I come here? I myself don't rightly know.

SÖLLER: Oh, I know all too well.

SOPHIE: I may be dreaming, though.

SÖLLER: If only *I* were dreaming!

SOPHIE: I am full of grief,
Alcest.

ALCEST: Confession of a sorrow brings relief.

SOPHIE: Be sympathetic, as you always used to be!

SÖLLER: Oh, yawn together, and you call it sympathy.
Just great!

SOPHIE: In you I found out what perfection is,
Only to go and marry your antithesis.
I have a heart from which all virtue has not died.

ALCEST: I know it.

SÖLLER: So do I.

SOPHIE: But, kindliness aside,
Alcest, I would not overstep my proper bounds
If Söller as a husband did not give me grounds.

SÖLLER: She lies! She makes me out a dummy.—Look, good Sirs:
I show a better calf than that poor stick of hers.[1]

SOPHIE: I felt obliged to give you up, though I decried him,
And be his wife.

SÖLLER: Oh, fine!

SOPHIE: And now I can't abide him.

SÖLLER: Oh, great!

ALCEST: You don't deserve a marriage of this kind.

SOPHIE: He's dumb without a heart and mean without a mind;

---

[1] Eighteenth-century gentlemen's breeches left the lower leg cased in skintight silk stockings. Males with good calves displayed them proudly; those with poor calves wore pads. See *Faust* 2501–2.

Too cowardly to be a rascal and too dull
For noble thinking; he has nothing in his skull
But quarrels, slanders, lies, and cheats.
SÖLLER: I see she's firm on
The points that should be listed in my funeral sermon.
SOPHIE: To go on living with him is past thinking of
Unless—
SÖLLER: I must escape!
SOPHIE: —I still can have your love.
ALCEST: I love and grieve, like you.
SOPHIE: That is my consolation,
That you, at least, will spare me the humiliation
Of pity.   (*She seizes his hand.*)
                  By this hand, Alcest, this hand so dear,
I beg you: let your heart keep faith with me!
SÖLLER: Just hear
The poetry!
SOPHIE: This heart that burned for you alone
Knows of no comfort-giving hand except your own.
ALCEST: But for your heart I know no remedy.
SÖLLER: Too bad!
With nothing for the heart, a woman will be glad
To find a different cure.
SOPHIE (*leaning on Alcest's arm*):   My friend!
SÖLLER (*with apprehension*):   No further, now.
        (*to audience*)   It's lucky *you*'re down there before us
                                            anyhow:
Your presence may restrain them.
                  (*Alcest puts his arms around Sophie.*)
                              He's gone overboard.
I'd grab him by the throat, except he has his sword.
SOPHIE (*distressed*):   Oh, cruel! Let me go!
SÖLLER (*beside himself*):   Of all the airs! Damnation!
"Oh, cruel! Let me go!" That's sheer capitulation.
Have they no shame at all! To sing that trite old song
When she is coasting downslope all the way along!

Who'd give a penny for her virtue?

SOPHIE: One last kiss,
   And then farewell.

ALCEST: You're leaving?

SOPHIE: I am leaving, yes.

ALCEST: You love me, and you go?

SOPHIE: I love you, as I say,
   But I would lose a friend by any further stay.
   The flow of sorrows pours its fullest in the night
   When fear subsides in some place hidden out of sight.
   The quieter we talk, the more we may expose,
   And therewith, for my sex, the greater danger grows.
   Love's first name is sweet confidentiality;
   A sorrow-softened heart amid such intimacy
   Will not deny a friend a kiss, but after that . . .
   A friend is only human.

SÖLLER: She has things quite pat.

SOPHIE: Farewell!

ALCEST: I'm still your friend until the day I die.

SÖLLER (*relieved*):   The lightningbolt has missed my head and
                                          whizzed on by.

> (*Sophie leaves; Alcest escorts her out by the
> main door.*)

(*in the alcove*)   Oh, death! He's going with her! Now at any cost
I must get out of here!

> (*He ventures half way out of the alcove and listens.*)
                                 It may be I have lost
My hearing in both ears—Can she be still around?
And yet there's not a stir . . . I do not hear a sound.
How would it be if I got closer to the stair

> (*He edges over to the main door.*)

They're whispering together!—Damn it!

> (*He thinks he hears someone coming and
> dashes back into the alcove.*)
                                          Easy there!
Why, no one's coming. (*He starts forward again.*)

Try once more!

(*He cannot bring himself to do so.*)

No, I don't dare.

(*as a travesty of distress*)

What shall I do? I am a cuckold!

(*He knocks his head against the wall.*)

There's a pair

Of horns here on my forehead, sprouting, burgeoning,
In sign of my condition.

(*He claps the purse.*) Come, you precious thing,
We'll both escape. Then lead me where wine can be had.
As long as there is drink I cannot feel too bad.
A decorated brow is not the worst of things,
And cuckolds can find comfort that no gallows brings.

(*He hurries out by the side door.*
Reenter Alcest.)

ALCEST: Declare, great spirits, that there is no purity,
That love is lust and friendship mere hypocrisy,
That not a single heart is girt with solid walls,
That, given opportunity, the strongest falls,
And that if someone's found unstained by any vice
It's just that boys are shy and girls are over-nice.
"They tremble" is your jest to inexperienced youth,
But may that not be Virtue's sign in very truth?
May not this sympathy that from our senses wells
So irresistibly be more than fever-spells?
How sweet the dreams that I in former times once dreamed
In Sophie's arms. I had no feelings, so it seemed,
Until her glance, her kiss, her hand-clasp had revealed
The ecstasy that to a novice is unsealed.
We did not meet by choice, we made no plan or claim,
We gazed at one another and stood rapt in flame.
Few questions needed asking either way; instead,
Our intuitions flashed and everything was said.
A good long time we spent sweet moments in that state,
But then at last it came to naught. I railed at Fate,

And swore that friendship, faith, and love and tenderness
Were simply vice in masquerading costume dress,
While in the whirl of sensual delights I sought
To set the worth of virtuousness and love at naught.
With lust and pride and time I got myself well steeled,
Believing tender feelings could not make me yield.
Thus I came back. How beautiful Sophie had grown!
"Her husband's probably a knight of some well-known
High Order," so I told myself, "but, then, what of it?
When you present your proposition she will love it.
Resistance would produce a sneer and nothing more.
So let it be the Faun-and-Nymph-game as before."
So *I* thought. But, on seeing her, I felt emotion:
What was it? Can you rake-hells give me any notion?
It tells me I am wrong, it warmly pleads her cause,
It undercuts my ploys and gives my boldness pause.
She terms me friend and shows her heart all clear and plain.
I had abjured all friendship, yet I feel her pain.
She says that no one is so dear to her as I;
Now, love is nonsense, but I thrill at her reply.
She loves me, yet from virtue will not be deflected;
I laughed at virtue, but in this case I respect it.
I hoped for much today, yet not one thing was claimed;
A coward's naughtiness! I ought to be ashamed.
Call me a woman: treacherous but lacking will;
Or else at vice say I'm a mere apprentice still.
What is it drives me on to find my pleasure in her?
Love? or self-interest? Do you expect to win her
By paying for it? No! I know her money's short—
Which she will not admit—and I admire her for 't.
A secret gift might be acceptable, however.
I still have money. Yes, I think that would be clever.
Let's count it.   (*He opens the strongbox.*)
                What the Devil! I've been skinned alive!
My hundred ducats now are barely twenty-five!
Just since this afternoon. I always think to lock it,

And here's the key as usual safely in my pocket.
Now, who's been in here? Ha! Sophie! She'd never do it!
Could my valet—? He's in his room, and I'll go through it.
If he's asleep, I'll rouse him with a "Did you steal it?!"
And give him such a scare that he can not conceal it.

(Exit.)

ACT III

The main room of the inn.
The Innkeeper, in his nightgown, is sitting in the large chair at the table, on which are a nearly burned-down candle, coffee things, pipes, and the newspapers. After speaking his first few lines he gets up and, in the course of the ensuing lines, gets dressed.

INNKEEPER: It seems that Poland isn't making out too well,
But I first want to hear what tale the Russians tell.
If they just go about it right they cannot fail,
And they're the fellows that can make the Turks turn tail,[1]
For there's no stopping them once they get in the race.
Here's what I'd do if I were in the Russians' place:
In front of the Seraglio I'd move up my forces
Without the Sultan's leave, and then not spare the horses.
    If I don't get that letter I will lose my mind.
It was some business of a very fishy kind.
The riddle seems to be a rugged nut to crack.
One misstep, then you dread the misstep may step back.
It wasn't in my line, and I was scared last night,
Yet for the keeper of an inn it wasn't right
To panic at the rustling of a shoe. No host
Should do so. Yet a thief is close kin to a ghost.
Why, no one was around, not Söller, not Alcest,
The waiter had gone out, the maids were all at rest—
Hold on!—This morning early, between three and four,
I heard a sound much like the squeak of Sophie's door.
She could have been the very ghost from which I fled;
It was a woman's shoe and maybe Sophie's tread.
But what would take her there?—Girls do have hankerings
To snoop around a bit and look at strangers' things,
Their linen and the like. Had I as much misdoubted,

---

[1] In 1768 Russia went to war against Turkey and Polish fugitives in Turkey.

I would have scared her and then made a joke about it;
She would have helped me search, and we'd have found it, too.
Now that I've missed my lucky chance, what shall I do?
We never think of things while there is time to act
And good ideas always trail behind the fact.

(Enter Sophie.)

SOPHIE: Imagine, Father!

INNKEEPER: No "Good Morning?" What's your
                                                      hurry?

SOPHIE: Forgive me, but my mind is frantic with new worry.

INNKEEPER: How so?

SOPHIE: Alcest just recently received a purse
    Of money, and it's lost.

INNKEEPER: I tell you, it's a curse,
    This playing faro.

SOPHIE: That was not my meaning, Father.
    It has been stolen!

INNKEEPER: What!

SOPHIE: Out of his rooms.

INNKEEPER: Now, bother
    Upon the thief! Who took it?

SOPHIE: We don't know.

INNKEEPER: From where?

SOPHIE: Right out of Alcest's strongbox on the table there.

INNKEEPER: But when?

SOPHIE: Last night.

INNKEEPER (aside):   Oh, sin of curiosity!
    They'll find my candle and then lay the blame on me.

SOPHIE (aside):   He looks so guilty, standing there the way he does.
    He had been in that room, the candle proves he was.

INNKEEPER (aside):   Was it Sophie herself? Now, that would be a
                                                      fright!
    She had run short, I know, and she was there last night.
    (aloud) He wants to cause us trouble with his stupid game.
    It's safety and low rates that give this house its fame.

SOPHIE: The injury to him is injury to us,
    And the proprietor will be notorious.

INNKEEPER: But it's a matter I can't do a thing about.
  If there's a thief here, has Alcest then found him out?
  A nasty business!
SOPHIE: I feel crushed by this disgrace.
INNKEEPER (*aside*):   Aha! She's worried.
    (*aloud, with some annoyance*)   Still, it may turn up some place.
  I wish it would.
SOPHIE (*aside*):   His conscience bothers him, I see.
    (*aloud*)   But if he gets it back, the thief, he says, may be
  Whoever it may be; he wants no one to suffer—
  And we don't either.
INNKEEPER (*aside*):   She's the thief, or I'm a duffer.
    (*aloud*)   You are an honest girl, and I have trust in you—
  One second—
            (*He goes to see that no one is near the door.*)
SOPHIE (*aside*):   Now he's going to tell me it is true.
INNKEEPER: I know you well, Sophie; I know you've never lied.
SOPHIE: From you I've had no secrets that I wished to hide.
  So I hope in this present case I merit—
INNKEEPER: Good!
  You're still my girl. What happened, happened. Understood?
SOPHIE: Papa, I surely won't be more severe than you.
INNKEEPER: It's only human, no cause for a great ado.
  That you were in that room no one but me can prove.
SOPHIE (*startled*):   You know that!
INNKEEPER (*smiling*):   I was there myself. I heard you move.
  Not knowing who it was, I quickly scooted out.
SOPHIE (*aside*):   He did, then, steal the money, now there is no
                                                 doubt.
INNKEEPER: I heard you coming back this morning early, too.
SOPHIE: And—neatly—no one would suspect it might be you.
  I found your candle.
INNKEEPER: *You* did.
SOPHIE: Yes.
INNKEEPER: The life of me!
  How shall we manage giving back his property?

SOPHIE: You simply say: "Monsieur Alcest, the thief is found,
Be merciful, and here's your money safe and sound.
An opportunity can, as you know, mislead;
No sooner had he done it than he rued the deed,
Confessed, and placed it in my hands. Forgive him, Sir!"
And then I'm sure Alcest will graciously concur.

INNKEEPER: At fixing things like this you seem to be well versed.

SOPHIE: Then give the money back.

INNKEEPER: I'd have to have it first.

SOPHIE: Why, don't you have it?

INNKEEPER: No! How should I?

SOPHIE: You ask *how*?

INNKEEPER: Unless you give it to me.

SOPHIE: But—who has it now?

INNKEEPER: Ah, who!

SOPHIE: Who else but you?

INNKEEPER: Of all the fiddle-faddle!

SOPHIE: What did you do with it?

INNKEEPER: Your wits begin to addle.
You have it, don't you?

SOPHIE: I?

INNKEEPER: Yes!

SOPHIE: How would I come by it?

(The innkeeper goes through the gestures of stealing.)

INNKEEPER: Eh?

SOPHIE: I don't understand.

INNKEEPER: How shameless to deny it.
Now you must give it back, you hem and haw about.
You just confessed the deed.

(to the audience) You, Sirs, will bear me out.

SOPHIE: Well, that's the limit! I'm the one to be repaying,
When you're the thief yourself, as you just got through saying.

INNKEEPER: You toad! Where's your respect, your filial devotion!
You make me out a thief and raise all this commotion,
When you're the thief yourself!

SOPHIE: Oh, father!

INNKEEPER: Anyway:
  Were you up there last night?
SOPHIE: I was.
INNKEEPER: And now you say
  You didn't take that money?
SOPHIE: Do you call that fair?
INNKEEPER: I do!
SOPHIE: But weren't you up there too?
INNKEEPER: I'll pull your hair
  If you don't stop this! March now, little wretch! A crime
  Is not a joke!   (*Exit Sophie in tears.*)
                    I'll tell you what! . . . She's gone! . . . High time!
  She may think she can lie her way out of this fuss . . .
  The money's gone, she stole it, that is obvious.
                (*Enter Alcest, deep in thought.*)
  (*embarrassed and pleadingly*)
  I'm much distressed to learn about this situation,
  And I am not surprised, Sir, at your irritation.
  But I entreat your patience for a little space
  Till ways are found to get your money back in place.
  In this town there are persons who, from jealousy,
  Would air this news and blame me quite maliciously.
  There was no prowler, this was done by some housemate,
  And you will get your money back if you but wait.
  May I ask what amount?
ALCEST: Some eighty ducats.
INNKEEPER: My!
ALCEST: But eighty ducats—
INNKEEPER: Damn! but that is mighty high!
ALCEST: And yet I would be quite prepared to overlook it
  If I could find out how and why the party took it.
INNKEEPER: When once the money's back, you won't much care to
                                                            know
  How, when, or where, or if by such-and-such or so-and-so.
ALCEST (*aside*):   My valet hasn't got it, and he's not a thief.
  But in my room there—No! No! That's beyond belief.

INNKEEPER: You rack your brains and ponder, all to no avail.
    I'll surely get it back.
ALCEST: You will?
INNKEEPER: Yes, without fail!
    If I don't get those eighty ducats back, and soon,
    Call me the Ace of Spades, or Monkey-in-the-Moon.
ALCEST: You know, then—
INNKEEPER: Hmm! I'll get it. Just you wait and see.
ALCEST: But tell me who it was!
INNKEEPER: Not for the life of me!
ALCEST: Who stole it? Tell me, please!
INNKEEPER: I said I couldn't say.
ALCEST: But someone *inside*—
INNKEEPER: No use going on this way.
ALCEST: Perhaps the chambermaid.
INNKEEPER: Poor little Hanna? No.
ALCEST: Well, how about the waiter?
INNKEEPER: Not so far's I know.
ALCEST: The cook's too stupid—
INNKEEPER: Chances there are pretty slim.
ALCEST: There's Hans, the kitchen boy.
INNKEEPER: We might consider him.
ALCEST: Oh might the gardener—?
INNKEEPER: Getting warmer with each guess.
ALCEST: The gardener's son.
INNKEEPER: No.

ALCEST: Could it be—?
INNKEEPER (*half whisper*):   The watchdog? Yes.
ALCEST (*aside*):   Just wait, you stupid oaf, I know your ticklish spot.
    (*aloud*)   Oh, I don't really care if I find out or not,
    So long's I get it back.
               (*He pretends to be leaving*)
INNKEEPER: True.
ALCEST (*as if struck with a sudden idea*):   Oh! . . . My inkwell's dry
    And here's this urgent letter I must answer—

INNKEEPER: My!
   So quick to answer, when it just came yesterday.
   It *must* be urgent.
ALCEST: There should not be much delay.
INNKEEPER: Ah, correspondence is a source of endless pleasure.
ALCEST: Not always. It consumes one's time in such a measure
   As cannot be made up for.
INNKEEPER: But it's time well spent.
   One letter we receive makes up for many sent.
   It must contain things of uncommon urgency,
   Your letter: might I ask?
ALCEST: Not for the life of me.
INNKEEPER: News from the north, perhaps?
ALCEST: I said I couldn't say.
INNKEEPER: It came from Poland?
ALCEST: No use going on this way.
INNKEEPER: Perhaps about the king?
ALCEST: His helpless Highness? No.
INNKEEPER: Could there be Turkish columns—?
ALCEST: Not so far's I know.
INNKEEPER: The Forty-fifth might—
ALCEST: Chances there are pretty slim.
INNKEEPER: Or maybe Paoli—
ALCEST: We might consider him.
INNKEEPER: About the comet—
ALCEST: Getting warmer with each guess.
INNKEEPER: About the Saxon ghost?
ALCEST The Jesuit specter? Yes.
INNKEEPER: You set no great store by your Humble Servant's sense.
ALCEST: Distrustful people hardly merit confidence.
INNKEEPER: About what sort of confidence do you inquire?
ALCEST: Who is the thief? Here is the letter you desire:
   It would make quite a fair exchange, I think you'd find.
   Well, do you want the letter?
INNKEEPER (*abashed but greedy*): Ah! You're much too kind.
   (*aside*) If only it were something else he'd ask of me.

ALCEST: Accept a favor, do a favor equally.

I guarantee no word of this will be repeated.

INNKEEPER: The letter is so tempting I could fairly eat it.

But what about Sophie?—Oh, she would understand.

This lure is more than any mortal could withstand.

My mouth is watering, as for some pickled hare.

ALCEST (*aside*):   He's like a greyhound sniffing ham-scent in the air.

INNKEEPER (*ashamed, yielding, but still hesitant*):

It's your suggestion, Sir, and your beneficence—

ALCEST (*aside*):   He's rising to the bait.

INNKEEPER: —compels my confidence.

     (*in doubt and half-pleading*):

You promise I may see the letter right away?

ALCEST (*holding the letter out*):

Right here it is.

               innkeeper slowly approaches Alcest.)

INNKEEPER: The thief—

ALCEST: The thief?

INNKEEPER: I have to say?

ALCEST: Well, out with it!

INNKEEPER: It's—

ALCEST: Well?

INNKEEPER (*choking up*):   My daughter!

          (*He grabs the letter out of Alcest's hand.*)

ALCEST (*astonished*):   That's not true!

INNKEEPER (*ripping open the envelope in haste and beginning to
     read*):   "Esteemed and noble Sir—"

ALCEST (*seizing him by the shoulder*):   I want the truth from you!
The truth!

INNKEEPER (*impatiently*):   Yes, she's the one. It's very hard on me.

     (*reading*)   "—and more particularly—"

ALCEST (*as before*):   It could not be Sophie.

INNKEEPER (*wrenching himself loose and continuing to read the letter
     without answering Alcest*):   "—my benefactor—"

ALCEST (*as before*):   I am at a loss for words.

INNKEEPER (*as before*):   I only wish you were.—"Sir—"

ALCEST (*as before*):   Listen!
INNKEEPER (*as before*):   Afterwards!
ALCEST: You are a stupid oaf.
INNKEEPER: Agreed.
ALCEST: Your brains are loose
    Inside your head.
INNKEEPER: Yes, Sir.
ALCEST (*to himself as he walks away*):   I'll put this to good use.
                              (*Exit.*)
INNKEEPER (*alternately reading and commenting*):
    Where was I? Has he gone? "—You've often been so kind
    In bearing with my faults that I shall hope to find
    Forgiveness now as well." Forgive him what? Let's see.
    "—I know, Sir, that you surely will rejoice with me—"
    That's good! "—for Heaven has today sent me a present.
    That rich men envy but which must delight a peasant:
    My wife has borne another child—" Oh, God in heaven!
    "—a boy, just like the others; he makes Number Seven."
    The brat! Oh, drown him now before he gets too old!
    "—Aware of all your kindness, may I make so bold—"
    Oh, I shall choke on this! "—as to beseech Your Grace—"
    Oh, hang him, with the hangman in godfather's place!
    Now, what's his name, this fellow with that brood of his?
    "Franz," Now comes Latin: "*Candidatus* . . . ?" Oh, that is
    The same as "Candidate." ". . . *theologiae*." Wait:
    There's more. "—and Tenant Cottager on your estate."
    Just wait! You will not get away with this scot-free!
    Alcest! I want you! Leave my inn immediately!
    To fool a poor old man like me is downright horrid.
    I'll bring you up on charges! I could choke you for it!
        But oh!, my erring daughter, why did I beget her!
    And I betray you for a tenant-farmer's letter!
                    (*clutching his wig with both hands*)
    A pig-eyed, donkey-eared, old ox, that's what I am!
    Between this letter and the theft I'm in a jam.
    So stupid! I must beat someone to vent my spite.

(*He grabs up a cane and goes running
around the stage with it.*)

Is there no back where I can gorge my appetite?
If I could be a breeze with several hundred wings
I'd pound the world, the sun and moon, and other things.
I'll die if I don't do it!—Someone break a dish
So I can have a reason to indulge my wish!

(*He bumps into a chair and beats it.*)

You dusty thing! Come here, I'll beat you black and blue.
Alcest! If only I could do the same to you!

(*As the innkeeper is pounding away, Söller
comes in at the rear and stands in fright.
He is still wearing his domino, with his
mask tied to his arm, and he is half-tipsy.*)

SÖLLER: What's going on here! Be alert now, be astute!
There's no use winding up that armchair's substitute.
What imp has set the old man off on this rampage?

(*to the audience*)

If one of you dares ask him, step right up on the stage.

INNKEEPER (*without noticing Söller*):
I'm all worn out. My back is aching. Oh, my arm!

(*He throws himself down in the pounded chair.*)

I'm all a-sweat.

SÖLLER (*aside*):   Well, exercise does make one warm.

(*He moves into the innkeeper's view.*)

Uh—father . . .

INNKEEPER: Ah, Monsieur, back from the night's carouse.
I suffer mortal torment, and you leave the house.
Our Shrovetide clown is off to dancing, gaming, sporting,
While here at home the Devil does his own cavorting.

SÖLLER: Why so wrought up?

INNKEEPER: I can't relive these hours of pain.

SÖLLER: What happened?

INNKEEPER: Oh! Alcest! Sophie! Need I explain?

SÖLLER: No, no.

INNKEEPER: I'd gladly see the two of them in hell.

And Devil take that wretched Candidate as well!
>   (*Exit.*)
SÖLLER (*in a travesty of anguish*):
>   What happened? Who knows what I soon may have to hear!—
>   Face boldly toward the tempest, but protect your rear!
>   My secret may be out. What terrors are aroused
>   To draw my sweat at every pore! Oh, Doctor Faust
>   Was never half this scared, nor Richard III, the Mean.
>   Hell there, the gallows there, the cuckold in between.
>>   (*He races crazily about, then finally stops
>>   to reflect.*)
>   By stolen goods no happiness was ever made.
>   Come, coward, rascal, why should you be so afraid?
>   Things may not be that bad. I'll find out soon enough.
>>   (*He catches sight of Alcest and rushes away.*)
>   Oops! There he comes. He might be bent on playing rough.
>>   (*Exit.*)
>>   (*Enter Alcest.*)
ALCEST: Such rival thoughts have never torn my heart before.
>   This sweet girl who in my imagination bore
>   The features of all virtue and propriety,
>   Who showed me what love at its loftiest could be,
>   Whom I had cherished as a goddess, girl, and friend,
>   At seeing her debased I shudder. If I end
>   By ranking her below ideals I defined,
>   She is a woman with the rest of womankind.
>   But I grow frantic thinking she could stoop so low.
>   My heart demands that I stand by her even so.
>   How small! Why can't you bring yourself to seize this chance
>   That now is offered you by Fortune's fair advance?
>   A woman past compare, for whose true love you live,
>   Needs money. Quick, Alcest! the penny that you give
>   Will bear whole dollars. But she stole it willfully.
>   All right: she still may come to live quite virtuously.
>   Go like a débauché and tell her in cold blood:
>   "Madame, I know you stole my money. Well and good,

That's quite all right with me. Feel free in spending it.
What wealth I have is yours to use as you see fit."
Then strike the semi-man-and-wifely attitude,
And Virtue's self will then decline to play the prude,
If you are deft about it. Yield herself she will.
 But here she comes, and you are flustered. That bodes ill.
Alcest, you do not have the knack for doing wrong.
Your heart is wicked, but it isn't very strong.
(Enter Sophie)

SOPHIE: All by yourself, Alcest? Are you avoiding me?
 What draws you so to solitude and privacy?

ALCEST (lightheartedly): I cannot give a reason proper to this case,
 But for no reason many monologues take place.

SOPHIE: Your loss was sizeable and you must be distressed.

ALCEST: A trifle, really. And I do not feel depressed.
 We have it, after all, and what's that paltry sum?
 If it has come into good hands, why, let it come.

SOPHIE: Excessive generosity soon turns to waste.

ALCEST: A wastrel's money often may be shrewdly placed.

SOPHIE: How do you mean that?

ALCEST (with a smile):   That?

SOPHIE: It seems to make no sense.

ALCEST: Sophie, why don't you favor me with confidence?
 The money's gone, and where it lies, there let it lie.
 If I had realized, I would have raised no cry.
 Since matters stand this way, however—

SOPHIE (in amazement):   Then, you know?

ALCEST (tenderly, as he takes her hand and kisses it):
 Your father— Yes. I know.—I love you even so.

SOPHIE (astonished and embarrassed): And you forgive—?

ALCEST: Forgive? What crime has been committed?

SOPHIE: But—

ALCEST: Let us both speak frankly, if you will permit it.
 You know I'm fond of you, as I was always fond.
 Fate may have parted us but did not break our bond.
 Your heart is ever mine, and mine is your heart still,

And all my wealth is yours, as if by deeded will.
You have an equal share in all my property.
Take anything you like, but give me love, Sophie.
   (*He takes her in his arms, but she remains silent.*)
Command me, and your every wish will be respected.
SOPHIE (*proudly, as she withdraws from his embrace*):
   But I don't need your money—and would not accept it.
   What kind of talk is this? Can I be misconstruing?
   You quite misjudge me.
ALCEST: No, I know what I am doing.
   Your humble servant knows you, knows your taking ways,
   And wonders why your anger flares to such a blaze.
   In overstepping—
SOPHIE (*astonished*):   Overstepping what?
ALCEST: Madame!
SOPHIE (*indignant*):   What do you mean, Sir?
ALCEST: Oh, forgive me—Do be calm!—
   I love you far too much to speak in franker terms.
SOPHIE: Alcest!
ALCEST: Just ask your father whether he confirms
   What he told me.
SOPHIE (*in violent outburst*):   What did my father have to tell?
   Will you be good enough to give me answer!
ALCEST: Well—
SOPHIE (*as before*):   Well, what!
ALCEST: That you absconded with my money.
SOPHIE (*turning away in fury and in tears*):   Oh!
   He is a—How much further will his malice go!
ALCEST (*pleadingly*):   Sophie!
SOPHIE (*still turning away*):   You are a cad!
ALCEST: Sophie!
SOPHIE (*as before*):   I just abhor you!
ALCEST: Forgive me!
SOPHIE: Get away! I have no pardon for you!
   My father does not shrink from speaking slanderously,
   But how could you, Alcest, believe such things of me?

I would not have admitted it to save my soul,
But now I must: my father is the thief who stole.
(She rushes away.)
ALCEST *(throwing himself into the armchair)*:
 Where do we stand, Alcest? It's yours now to decide:
 The father or Sophie: which one of them has lied?
 Yet both of them have always acted with propriety . . .
 Ha, Söller! Wait a minute! But how could that be?
 He wasn't home last night—off somewhere to a ball—
 Or else he would have been my suspect first of all.
 The penchant for sly, underhanded things is his,
 But I don't see how he could be involved in this.
(Enter Söller in everyday costume and with a hangover.)
SÖLLER: Ugh! There he sits. I hate him worse than ordinary.
 His face is like a signboard: Cuckold Veterinary.
ALCEST *(aside)*: Here he comes now.
  (aloud)   How are you, Mr. Söller?
SÖLLER: Bad.
 I've still got music spinning in my head like mad.
     (He rubs his forehead.)
 It hurts right here.
ALCEST: Were lots of ladies at the ball?
SÖLLER: The usual. Mice will come to mousetraps, after all,
 When bacon's in 'em.
ALCEST: Lots of fun?
SÖLLER: Lots.
ALCEST: All danced out?
SÖLLER: I only watched.
      (to the audience) I had some things to think about.
ALCEST: You only watched! That's dull. I'd sooner just not go.
SÖLLER: I needed cheering up.
ALCEST: Were you successful?
SÖLLER: No.
 Here in my forehead I had such a throbbing pain
 And pressure that the dancing proved too great a strain.
ALCEST: Indeed!

SÖLLER: And worst of all, the more I saw and heard,
The more I found my sense of sight and hearing blurred.
ALCEST: Too bad! The trouble came on suddenly, you say?
SÖLLER: No, ever since you've been here I have felt this way—
Or even longer.
ALCEST: Strange!
SÖLLER: I just can't seem to shake it.
ALCEST: I recommend warm compress treatments: they would
                                                    make it
Wear off, perhaps.
SÖLLER (*aside*):   I think he's laughing up his sleeve.
      (*aloud*)   That's easy said.
ALCEST: But in the long run it will leave.
Things will improve. Meanwhile it rather serves you right:
You didn't even take your wife along last night
When you went to the ball. It really wasn't nice
To leave your sweet young wife a bed as cold as ice.
SÖLLER: Oh, she likes staying home, and leaves my check-rein slack.
And getting warm without me is her special knack.
ALCEST: A trifle odd.
SÖLLER: Oh yes, a sweet-tooth is uncanny
About detecting tidbits in each nook and cranny.
ALCEST (*nettled*):   Why all these metaphors?
SÖLLER: All plain enough, I think.
For instance, there's her father's wines I like to drink;
However, he's not one to stray about or roam;
He guards what's his; and so I drink away from home.
ALCEST (*with a glimmering*):   What are these hints, Sir?
SÖLLER: Sir, all womankind's best friend.
She is, of course, my wife. But how much, in the end,
Does she care what her husband thinks about her life?
ALCEST (*with suppressed anger*):
Her husband you may be, but I'll defend your wife.
And if you venture to continue at this rate—
SÖLLER (*daunted, to himself*):
I'll wind up yet by asking him to estimate

How virtuous she is.

   (*aloud*)   My hearth is still my hearth

No matter who's the cook.

ALCEST: I much doubt you are worth

   The wife you have—so blameless, beautiful, refined,

   And generous; she has no fault of any kind.

SÖLLER: I grant the many charms with which she is endowed;

   Among her gifts I count my being antler-browed.

   To have a wife like her was my predestined doom

   For I was crowned a cuckold in my mother's womb.

ALCEST (*flaring up*):   Söller!

SÖLLER (*impudently*):   Söller what?

ALCEST (*restraining himself*):   Stop now! Right where you're at!

SÖLLER: And who's the man to force my mouth shut? Tell me that!

ALCEST: If I had you outside I'd soon teach you his name.

SÖLLER (*drily*):   I'm glad to know the champion of my wife's good

                                          fame.

ALCEST: Right!

SÖLLER: Who knows more than you if she has gone too far?

ALCEST: Damn!

SÖLLER: Oh, Monsieur Alcest, we both know how things are.

   Be patient! We will come to terms, if not just now,

   Then later. Gentlemen the likes of you somehow

   Will mow themselves a harvest field and sweep it clean

   While leaving husbands only fallen ears to glean.

ALCEST: I cannot help but marvel, Sir, at your persistence.

SÖLLER: Oh, I have had my share of tears in this existence

   And every day I seem to feel my antlers sprout.

ALCEST (*exasperated*):   This is too much. What is it that you want?

                                    Speak out!

   What damage do you think her honor has incurred?

SÖLLER (*forthrightly*):   It goes beyond belief, Sir, what was seen and

                                    heard.

ALCEST (*as before*):   What do you mean by "seen" and "heard?"

SÖLLER: Precisely that.

   The sense of sight and hearing.

ALCEST: Ha!
SÖLLER: Now hold your hat!
ALCEST (*with the resolution of extreme anger*):
   What was it that you heard, what was it that you saw?
SÖLLER (*frightened and starting to go*):   Excuse me, Sir.
ALCEST (*stopping him*):   Where are you going?
SÖLLER: I withdraw.
ALCEST: You will not leave this room!
SÖLLER (*aside*):   This devil wants me dead.
ALCEST: What did you hear?
SÖLLER: I only know what someone said.
ALCEST (*angrily insisting*):   What someone?
SÖLLER: Just a man I know.
ALCEST (*grabbing him harder*):   Speak up, you whelp!
SÖLLER (*in terror*):   A man that saw it for himself.
                    (*more boldly*)   I'll shout for help . . .
ALCEST (*taking him by the collar*):   Who was it?
SÖLLER (*trying to wriggle loose*):   Damn you!
ALCEST (*holding him fast*):   Who?! You goad me past
                                  endurance.
               (*He draws his sword.*)
   What lying rascal was it gave you that assurance?
            (*Söller falls in terror to his knees.*)
SÖLLER: Myself.
ALCEST (*threateningly*): What did you see?
SÖLLER (*in terror*):   Why, what you always see:
   The man's a man, Sophie's a woman, obviously.
ALCEST (*as before*):   What else?
SÖLLER: Well, then things went the way you'd think they might
   When he likes her and she likes him and all is right.
ALCEST: How's that?
SÖLLER: I wouldn't think you'd need to ask me that.
ALCEST: Well, Sir?
SÖLLER: Would anyone turn such a thing down flat?
ALCEST: A thing like what, Sir?
SÖLLER: Oh, enough! Be damned to you!

ALCEST: A thing like what, Sir?

SÖLLER: It is called a rendezvous.

ALCEST (*taken aback*): You lie!

SÖLLER (*aside*): Oh, here it comes!

ALCEST (*aside*): I think we've been betrayed.

(*He puts his sword back in its sheath.*)

SÖLLER (*aside*): The worst is over. He looks daunted and dismayed.

ALCEST (*recovering*): What do you mean by that?

SÖLLER (*defiantly*): You know as well as I.
That comedy last night—I saw it from close by.

ALCEST (*astonished*): From where?

SÖLLER: The alcove.

ALCEST: *So* much for your costume ball.

SÖLLER: Was it much different from your banquet, after all?
No matter how a secret may be hedged about,
You gentlemen get wind of it and still find out.

ALCEST: It may prove too that you're the thief I'm looking for.
I'd sooner daws and ravens entered through my door
Than you.—You sorry wretch.

SÖLLER: I'm anything you say.
But must you high-and-mighties always have your way?
You help yourselves to our possessions in your pride,
You flout the law, by which we others must abide.
It's always flesh or gold. Deserve the gallows less
Yourselves before you hang us for our shiftlessness.

ALCEST: You still presume, I see.

SÖLLER: I see no reason *not* to.
It's no fun wearing horns around the way I've got to.
In short, why should this issue be a cause for strife?
I stole your money, Sir, and you, Sir, stole my wife.

ALCEST (*threateningly*): What did I steal?

SÖLLER: Oh, nothing, Sir, but what was yours
Before it passed to me.

ALCEST: Shall—?

SÖLLER: I'll keep still, of course.

ALCEST: This thief shall have his noose!

SÖLLER: May I point out to you
  That there's a certain law for other people too?
ALCEST: You—
SÖLLER (*miming a decapitation*):   Tidbit-chasers also get
                                              their wind cut short.[2]
ALCEST: Habitual offenders sometimes steal for sport:
  You'll get the gallows, or at least the whipping post.
SÖLLER (*pointing to his forehead*):   I'm branded, as it is.
SOPHIE (*from offstage*):   My father still is most
  Abusive in his tone.
INNKEEPER (*from offstage*):   This girl will not retract!
              (*Enter Sophie, followed by the Innkeeper.*)
SOPHIE: There is Alcest.
INNKEEPER (*catching sight of Alcest*):   Aha!
SOPHIE: Now we'll get truth and fact.
INNKEEPER (*to Alcest*):   Sir, she's the thief.
SOPHIE (*on Alcest's other side*):   Sir, he's the thief.
ALCEST (*with a smile to each of them, then matching
     their tone of voice and pointing to Söller*):   You both are wrong:
  The thief is here.
SOPHIE: He!
INNKEEPER: He?
SÖLLER (*aside*):   Now, hide of me, be strong!
ALCEST: Yes, he's the one that's got that money.
INNKEEPER: Drive a nail
  Right through his head!
SOPHIE: You!
SÖLLER (*aside*):   Cloudburst hurtling down as hail.
INNKEEPER: I'd like to take you—
ALCEST: Sir, to anger call a halt.
  We did suspect Sophie, but she was not at fault.
  She dared to visit me upstairs, but even so,
  Her virtue justified her action—
    (*to Söller*)   as you know.

---

[2] Commoners were hanged, nobles were decapitated.

(*Sophie is astonished.*)

The night observed such silence we were unaware,
But virtue—

SÖLLER: Did she ever have me sweating there!

ALCEST (*to the Innkeeper*):   But you—?

INNKEEPER: I too came up, from curiosity.
That wretched letter . . . I was all agog to see . . .
It might be from some prince, or from a Polish magnate.
The prince turned out to be a tenant—Candidate.

ALCEST: Forgive my little joke.—I trust you will forgive
Me too, Sophie?

SOPHIE: Alcest!

ALCEST: As long as I may live
I'll never doubt your virtue. Pardon too my base
Misconduct toward you.

SÖLLER: I almost believe the grace
Includes me too.

ALCEST: You'll pardon Söller here as well?

SOPHIE (*giving Söller her hand*):
Yes, Here!

ALCEST (*to the Innkeeper*):   Allons!

INNKEEPER (*giving Söller his hand*):   But—steal no more.

SÖLLER: Ah, time will tell.

ALCEST: Now what about my money?

SÖLLER: Sheer necessity,
Sir, drove me on, the way that gambler hounded me.
It was my I O U's that forced me to the theft.
How much is gone I can't quite say, but here's what's left.

ALCEST: What's lost I'll call a gift.

SÖLLER (*to the audience*):   For this time, then:
                                        "home free."

ALCEST: I hope you'll settle down to thrift and honesty,
But any new tricks tried, or any other such—
                    (*He mimes a hanging.*)

SÖLLER: A cuckold *and* be hanged? No, that would be too much.

GÖTZ VON BERLICHINGEN

Sudden and nationwide fame came to our author in the summer of 1773 with his historical drama *Götz von Berlichingen.* Goethe had been one of the first people to sense the picturesqueness of sixteenth-century Germany, the era of Martin Luther, of the man who called himself Doctor Faustus, of Count Egmont, and of "the last of the German knights," Gottfried (commonly called Götz) of Berlichingen. In naming these four historical personages we have automatically listed the subjects of three of his best-known dramatic works, *Faust, Egmont,* and the present play. To Goethe and his contemporaries the era from about 1480 to about 1550 passed for medieval. To persons taking their orientation from English history or French history those years belong to the Renaissance, but the viewpoint from central Europe is different. Interest in the high Middle Ages—the twelfth and thirteenth centuries—would not come until around 1800, with the generation called Romantic. By English standards *Götz* is a "pre-Romantic" work; by German terminology it is not pre-Romantic, but "Storm and Stress," a catchy term that was originally the title of a stage success of 1776 by Maximilian Klinger. Under either label the new style is seen to be wholly alien to the Rococo quality of *The Lover's Whim* and *Fellow Culprits.*

After eighteen months at home in Frankfurt, Goethe set out once again in March of 1770 to study law at the University of Strassburg. The legal studies went well enough, and in August of 1771 he came away with the degree of *Doctor juris* but only half-heartedly committed to the law as a profession.

Not without relevance to the play, at least on the psychological level, was the poignant love affair of this period in Goethe's life. The girl's name was Friederike Brion, daughter of a clergyman in the Alsatian hamlet of Sesenheim. The poet had chanced upon her and her family in the course of a ride about the countryside in the autumn

83

of 1770. Before his very eyes, he fancied, the persons and the settings represented Oliver Goldsmith's *The Vicar of Wakefield* sprung into life. A strong and mutual affection developed between the pair of young people, yet in the end the aspiring poet bade farewell to the simple country girl, who had no aspirations to "the great world." In the play Goethe "confesses" his regrets and even magnifies them in portraying Weislingen's remorse over his shabby desertion of Götz's sister Maria. When a copy of the published drama was forwarded to Friederike through a friend, Goethe wrote that "poor Friederike will be somewhat consoled when the faithless one—Weislingen—is poisoned."

Of the many new friends made in Strassburg, one was Goethe's exact contemporary, Franz Lerse, "who might have been set up as a model of German youth." In the play he is given a role under his own name and bidden, as it were, to play himself.

A more important acquaintance was Johann Gottfried Herder, only five years older than Goethe but already versed in lore that struck the mind of the impressionable younger man as new and strange and wonderful. Herder's talk was of Gothic architecture and folk poetry and Shakespeare, of the philosophy of history, of the ethnic composition of Europe as a whole and the potentialities latent in the various ethnic groups, of the need to create a specifically German literature. For models Herder steered his intent listener to the Bible, to Homer, and to Ossian, and he also urged him to study the national past. Above all, he preached the wisdom of the human heart over mere reason.

The first product of this teaching was the drama *Götz*. Six years later, in 1776, one of Goethe's first recommendations to the Duke of Weimar was to bring Herder to his court. Herder was invited, came, and lived in Weimar until his death in 1803. There he published work after work of valuable scholarship, but his was the bitter experience of seeing his protégé far outdistance him in fame, so that envy and a certain cantankerousness tarnished Herder's own success.

On August 27, 1771, the eve of his twenty-second birthday, Goethe was again at his father's house in Frankfurt. Three months later, on November 28th, he wrote a Strassburg friend, a middle-aged actuary named Salzmann, that he was utterly engrossed in "dramatizing the history of one of the noblest Germans, to rescue the memory of a worthy man." By that statement he meant that he was writing a play called *The History of Gottfried of Berlichingen with the Iron Hand, Dramatized*. Late in December Salzmann lavished high praise on the work and informed Goethe that he was forwarding the manuscript to Herder. Some months elapsed before Herder replied in terms that were "unfriendly and harsh," saying that Shakespeare had "thoroughly spoiled" the young dramatist. That version of 1771 was left unpublished until after Goethe's death in 1832, but the revision entitled *Götz von Berlichingen* went to the publisher in 1773.

The work proclaimed literary revolution. Readers and audiences, especially the young ones, were thrilled by its combination of exaltation and down-to-earthness; this, they understood, was the Shakespearean method. Still more, there was delight at the glorification of the national past and of the national character—and, let us observe, there was nothing political about that glorification. One reviewer of 1773 termed the work "the most beautiful, the most captivating monstrosity," the latter word referring, of course, to the way the play shattered every rule of French-classical dramaturgy. Conservatives were less pleased. As late as 1780 Frederick the Great of Prussia, who had spent a lifetime bringing French culture to his German country, called it "une imitation détestable de ces mauvaises pièces anglaises." The première at Berlin on April 12, 1774 was a triumph. Imitations followed thick and fast, some forty having been counted in German alone. Sir Walter Scott's historical romances in prose started with his translation of *Götz* in 1799. Schiller's historical plays took their cue from it, and in France it provided inspiration for Victor Hugo, Dumas *père,* and the young Alfred de Musset.

Outside of Germany the hero and his milieu are unfamiliar, but Germans remembered Götz somewhat as Americans remember Daniel Boone or General Custer. It was the era of decayed feudalism. The uses of gunpowder had bypassed a centuries-old class of warrior knights in armor. The courses of justice were everywhere obstructed. The emperor in Vienna was remote, and access to him was more often than not by way of the very lords whose conduct was being challenged.

Economics, weaponry, and the legal system were all forcing desperate choices upon the old "free" knights of the lesser aristocracy: they might hire out as mercenaries at much the same fee as a commoner, or they might keep to their castles and live on the tolls forced out of every traveler, or they might turn their castles into robbers' strongholds. Here and there a knight might try to live gallantly by the old chivalric rules, and such were Gottfried of Berlichingen and his friend Franz of Sickingen.

As teenagers, both attended the Diet convoked at Worms in 1495 by Emperor Maximilian to bring all his subjects under the jurisdiction of imperial courts, where Roman law would provide justice. Götz, a sports-loving youth, averse to books, was then in service as a page. He was knighted soon after, and in battle soon after that he lost his right hand, which was replaced by a "sort of glove into which the arm-stump was fitted and made fast." Henceforth he was "Götz with the Iron Hand."

As a career soldier he was almost continually in battle, now in "honorable feuds" in his own interest, now in the service of others. His "operations" against the Bishop of Bamberg in 1512–13, and against merchant convoys of the city of Nürnberg, caused him to be declared an outlaw of the Empire, but he bought himself free. During larger-scale "operations" in 1519 he had to surrender at Möckmühl Castle on the River Jaxt because his supplies and ammunition had run out. The surrender terms stipulated that he and his men were to go free, but they were all arrested the minute they left the castle. Until October of 1522 he was held prisoner at Heilbronn, until Franz of Sickingen ransomed him and he swore an oath to fight no more. In 1525, however, he led a contingent in the peasant revolt, under duress, he declared, and for only four weeks. For this "service" he was arrested in 1526, released, arrested again in 1528, and imprisoned until 1530. This time his oath obliged him never to spend a night outside his home castle and never to mount a horse. The oath was abrogated by the Emperor in 1542 because there was need for skilled fighters against the Turks. In 1544 Götz was needed against the invading French, but after that he retired in peace—and composed an autobiography, the *Life History of Sir Götz of Berlichingen*. Two successive wives, both named Dorothea, bore him seven sons and three daughters.

The autobiography was, of course, Goethe's principal source, yet when he came to write his play he retained only generalities. Apart from the hero and Franz of Sickingen, the characters are purely fictional and the scenario is his own invention. The Bishop of Bamberg has only the title of the historical bishop. In I, 2, "Brother Martin" resembles Martin Luther but is not he. The delightful scene (I, 3) with Götz's small son reflects not only Goethe's own feelings, but also the new, post-Rousseauistic interest in children. As we have said, Lerse is a real person and Maria owes something to Friederike Brion. More importantly, Götz and Weislingen are aspects of the author, as are Faust and Mephisto and other pairs of males to be encountered in subsequent dramas. Significantly enough, the real dramatic power lies with Weislingen and the gorgeous Adelheid, woman of evil.

For many years Goethe was annoyed by inquiries of why he did not write more plays in the manner of *Götz*. His impatient dismissal of those questions was based on the characteristic idea that he had disburdened his heart of the emotions expressed in that work and hence had no need for further expression of them. He had also pioneered a new dramatic formula, and his desire was now not to repeat it but to adapt it to still other experiments.

To Anglo-Saxon notions, he might do well to be less fluidly "Shakespearean" than to require fifty-six changes of scene in a single drama, and he might do well to abate somewhat the breathless haste that was so conspicuous in *Götz*, but on the whole he had been wise in abandoning those rather precious continental forms and the rules for composing in "the proper way." To Goethe's notion, there *was* no proper way, nor did he wish to commit himself to any one way. Intensely as he admired Shakespeare, his aim was not to become Shakespeare's satellite. In the *Faust* scenes he was already engaged in writing in 1773–74, he was using Shakespeare's method in a rather different combination; in the subsequent *Egmont* he would try still another adaptation; and then, by a step that dismays Anglo-Saxons, he was to abandon Shakespearean models altogether. Thus *Götz* stands unique among his dramas, and a splendid work it is!

GÖTZ
VON BERLICHINGEN

with the Iron Hand

A Play
(*Ein Schauspiel*)
1773

CHARACTERS

Emperor Maximilian
Götz von Berlichingen
Elizabeth, his wife
Maria, his sister
Karl, his little son
Georg, his page
The Bishop of Bamberg
Weislingen
Adelheid von Walldorf } at the Bishop's court
Liebetraut
The Abbot of Fulda
Olearius, Doctor of both kinds of law
Brother Martin
Hans von Selbitz
Franz von Sickingen
Lerse
Franz, Weislingen's page
Ladies-in-waiting to Adelheid
Metzler
Sievers
Link } leaders of the rebellious peasants
Kohl
Wild
Lords and ladies of the Bamberg court
Imperial Councilors
Aldermen of Heilbronn
Judges of the secret tribunal

Two Nürnberg merchants
MAX STUMPF, a server of the Count Palatine
A stranger ⎫
The bride's father ⎬ peasants
The bridegroom ⎭
Horsemen of the Berlichingen, Weislingen, and Bamberg forces
A Captain, officers, and soldiers of the Imperial army
An innkeeper
The Court Summoner
Citizens of Heilbronn
The city watchman
The jailer
Peasants
A gypsy leader
Gypsies and gypsywomen

Time: An indeterminate period of years around 1520.
Place: Various localities in southwestern Germany.

ACT I

[Scene 1]

Schwarzenberg in Franconia. An inn.
Metzler and Sievers at table. Two mounted soldiers by the fire.
The innkeeper.

SIEVERS: Hänsel, another glass of brandy, and be Christian about
the measure.

INNKEEPER: You never get enough.

METZLER *(in a low voice to Sievers)*: Tell that again about Berlichingen. Those Bambergers there are so mad they're just about
purple.

SIEVERS: Bambergers? What are *they* doing here?

METZLER: Weislingen has been up at the castle for two days now
with the Count; they were his escort. I don't know where he
came from. They're waiting for him. He's going back to Bamberg.

SIEVERS: Who is this Weislingen?

METZLER: The Bishop's right-hand man, a powerful nobleman
who is laying for Götz.

SIEVERS: He'd better watch out.

METZLER *(softly)*: Keep it up! *(Aloud)* Since when has Götz been
having trouble again with the Bishop of Bamberg? Rumor
had it that everything was settled and smoothed over.

SIEVERS: Yes, *you* settle something with priests! When the Bishop
saw he wasn't getting anywhere and kept getting the short end,
he came crawling for mercy and was anxious to get a settlement
arranged. And loyal-hearted Berlichingen gave in, unbeliev-
ably, the way he always does when he has the upper hand.

METZLER: God shield him! An upright gentleman.

93

SIEVERS: Just think, isn't it a shame? There they pick off a page of his when it's the last thing he's expecting. But he'll fix them again for that!

METZLER: It's a dirty shame, though, that his last trick didn't come off. He must have been fit to be tied.

SIEVERS: I don't think that a thing like that got him down for long. Remember too that everything was reconnoitered down to the last detail—when the Bishop would be leaving the watering place, how many horsemen he had with him, which road he was traveling. And if things hadn't been betrayed by treacherous people he would have blessed that bath for him and rubbed him down besides.

FIRST SOLDIER: Why are you discussing our Bishop? I think you're looking for trouble.

SIEVER: Mind your own affairs! You've got no business at our table.

SECOND SOLDIER: Who told you to talk disrespectfully about our Bishop?

SIEVERS: Do I have to answer to you? Look at the monkey!

FIRST SOLDIER *(boxes his ears.)*

METZLER: Kill the bastard!

(They start a fight.)

SECOND SOLDIER: Come on over here if you've got the guts!

INNKEEPER *(parting them by force)*: Quiet down! Damnation! Go on outside if you've got something to settle between you! In my barroom I want things decent and orderly. *(He shoves the soldiers out the door.)* And you two donkeys, what are you trying to start?

METZLER: Don't let your tongue run away with you, Hänsel, or we'll be after your bald head. Come on, friend, we'll beat 'em up outside.

(Enter two outriders of Berlichingen's.)

FIRST OUTRIDER: What's going on?

SIEVERS: Hey! Good day to you, Peter! Good day, Veit! Where do you come from?

SECOND OUTRIDER: Don't you dare let on who it is we serve.

SIEVERS *(softly)*: Then your master Götz can't be too far off?

FIRST OUTRIDER: Shut up!—Got trouble?

SIEVERS: You ran into those fellows outside. They're Bambergers.

FIRST OUTRIDER: What are *they* doing here?

METZLER: Weislingen is up at the castle with His Grace; they were his escort.

FIRST OUTRIDER: Weislingen?

SECOND OUTRIDER *(softly)*: Peter! This is a windfall! *(Aloud)* How long has he been there?

METZLER: Two days now. But he means to leave today, I heard one of those fellows say.

FIRST OUTRIDER *(softly)*: Didn't I tell you he came this way? We could have watched a good long while over there. Come on, Veit.

SIEVERS: Help us beat up those Bambergers first.

SECOND OUTRIDER: There are two of *you*. We've got to get going. See you later!

(The outriders leave.)

SIEVERS: Stinkers! Those outriders! If you don't pay them they won't lift a finger.

METZLER: I'd swear they're on a mission. Whose employ are they in?

SIEVERS: I ain't supposed to say.—They're in service with Götz.

METZLER: Is that so!—Now let's get after those two outside. Come on! As long as I've got a club I'm not afraid of their oven-spits.

SIEVERS: If we could just once go after those princes this way, that are peeling the hides right off of us!

*

[SCENE 2]

A lodge in the forest.

GÖTZ *(beneath the linden tree in front of the door)*: What's keeping my outriders? I have to keep walking back and forth or sleep will overtake me. Five days and nights now on the lookout. It sours the little life and freedom a man has. All the same, when I get you, Weislingen, I'll call it a good job done. *(He starts to pour from the bottle.)* Empty again! Georg!—As long as there's no lack of this and of good courage I can laugh at princes' schemes and greed for power.—Georg!—Send your toady Weislingen around to your kith and kin, have him blacken my name. Go to it. I've got my eyes open. You got away from me, Bishop! So your precious Weislingen can pay the score. —Georg! Can't the lad hear? Georg! Georg!

THE PAGE *(in grown man's armor)*: Sir?

GÖTZ: Where have you been? Sleeping? What the devil kind of mummery is this? Come here! You look all right! Don't be bashful, lad. You're fine! If you could just fill it out! Is that Hans's armor?

GEORG: He wanted to take a bit of a nap and he unbuckled it.

GÖTZ: It's more comfortable than its master.

GEORG: Don't be angry. I took it away quietly and put it on, and took my father's old sword down off the wall, ran out into the yard, and drew it.

GÖTZ: And hacked about with it? That must have helped the bushes and thorns. Is Hans asleep?

GEORG: At your call he jumped up and bellowed to me that you were calling. I was trying to unbuckle the armor when I heard you the second and third times.

GÖTZ: Go and give him back his armor and tell him to be ready and to look after the horses.

GEORG: Oh, I fed them all right and put the bridles back on. You can ride whenever you're ready.

GÖTZ: Bring me a jug of wine. Give Hans a glass too. Tell him to be alert; he'll need to be. I hope any minute now my scouts will be coming back.

GEORG: Oh, Sir!

GÖTZ: What's the matter?

GEORG: Can't I go along?

GÖTZ: Some other time, Georg, when we capture some merchants and get their carts.

GEORG: Some other time! You have said that so often. O, this time, this time! I only want to run along behind, hide off to one side. I'll gather up your spent arrows for you.

GÖTZ: The next time, Georg. First you'll have to have a doublet, a helmet, and a spear.

GEORG: Take me along. If I had been along the last time you wouldn't have lost your cross-bow.

GÖTZ: You know about that?

GEORG: You threw it at the enemy's head and one of the foot soldiers picked it up, and there it was, gone. I know, don't I?

GÖTZ: Did my men tell you about this?

GEORG: Of course. And in return I whistle all kinds of tunes for them while we curry the horses, and teach them all sorts of jolly songs.

GÖTZ: You're a brave lad.

GEORG: Take me along so I can prove it.

GÖTZ: The next time, on my word. Unarmed as you are, you mustn't go into battle. The times to come will need men too. I tell you, boy, it will be a sweet time: princes will offer their treasures for a man that they now hate. So, Georg, give Hans back his armor and bring me some wine.

(Exit Georg.)

What is keeping my men? I can't understand it.—A monk! Now where is he coming from?

(Enter Brother Martin.)

Reverend Father, good evening! Where are you coming from so late? Man of holy peace, you put many a knight to shame.

MARTIN: I thank you, noble Sir. And for the time being I'm only a humble Brother when it comes to titles. Augustin is my name in religion, but I like best to hear Martin, my baptismal name.[1]

GÖTZ: You are tired, Brother Martin, and doubtless thirsty.

(Enter the page.)

Here comes some wine just at the right time.

MARTIN: A drink of water for me. I am not permitted to drink wine.

GÖTZ: Is that a vow?

MARTIN: No, gracious Sir, it is not against my vow to drink wine; but because wine is against my vow, I drink no wine.

GÖTZ: How do you mean that?

MARTIN: It is well for you that you do not understand it. Eating and drinking, I believe, are the life of man.

GÖTZ: True.

MARTIN: When you have eaten and drunk, you are as new born, you are stronger, more courageous, more fit for your work. Wine rejoices the heart of man, and joy is the mother of all virtues. When you have drunk wine you are everything twice over that you are supposed to be. You think twice as easily, you are twice as enterprising, twice as quick at execution.

GÖTZ: The way I drink it, that is true.

MARTIN: That is what I am talking about too. But we . . .

---

[1]Martin Luther was an Augustinian monk at Erfurt, but the present character seems to be an independent personage intended, apparently, only to suggest the *era* of the actual Luther.

(Enter Georg with water.)

GÖTZ *(aside to Georg)*: Go down to the Dachsbach road and put your ear to the ground and see if you don't hear horses coming. Then come straight back here.

MARTIN: . . . but we, when we have eaten and drunk, are precisely the opposite of what we are supposed to be. Our sleepy digestion attunes the head to the belly, and in the weakness of an over-copious repose desires are engendered which quickly grow higher than their mother's head.

GÖTZ: One glass, Brother Martin, won't disturb your sleep. You have done a lot of walking today.

(He raises a toast to him.)

All fighters!

MARTIN: In God's name! *(They clink glasses.)*

I cannot endure idle people. And yet I cannot say that all monks are idle; they do what they can. I have just come from St. Vitus', where I slept last night. The prior took me out into the garden; that is their beehive, you know. Excellent lettuce! Cabbage to warm your heart! Especially cauliflower and artichokes, like none in Europe!

GÖTZ: But that, of course, isn't your province.

(He gets up, looks for the boy, and returns.)

MARTIN: Would that God had made me a gardener or a worker in the laboratory! Then I could be happy. My abbot is fond of me—my monastery in Erfurt in Saxony—and he knows I cannot be still. So he sends me around wherever there is something to be looked after. I am on my way to the Bishop of Constance.

GÖTZ: Another one! Successful discharge of your business!

MARTIN: The same to you.

GÖTZ: Why do you look at me that way, Brother?

MARTIN: Because I am in love with your armor.

GÖTZ: You would like some like it? It is heavy and burdensome to wear.

MARTIN: What is not burdensome in this world? And nothing seems more burdensome to me than not to be allowed to be a human being. Poverty, chastity, and obedience—three vows, each one of which separately seems the most unbearable thing to Nature, and they are all three unbearable. And to pant meekly all one's life beneath this weight or beneath the far more oppressive burden of conscience! O Sir, what are the tribulations of your life compared to the miseries of a class which, out of misunderstood desire to get nearer to God, condemns the best impulses by which we exist and grow and thrive?

GÖTZ: If your vow were not so sacred, I should like to persuade you to put on a suit of armor. I'd give you a horse and we would set off together.

MARTIN: Would to God that my shoulders had the strength to bear the armor and my arm the power to thrust an enemy off his horse!—Poor weak hand that has never been accustomed to wielding anything but crucifixes and banners of peace or swinging anything but censers, how would you manage lance and sword! My voice, tuned solely to Aves and Hallelujahs, would herald my weakness to the enemy, while yours would overwhelm him. No vow would keep me from entering again the Order which my Creator Himself founded.

GÖTZ: Prosperous return journey!

MARTIN: To that I shall drink only for you. Return to my cage will be unhappy in any case. When you, Sir, return inside your walls with the consciousness of your bravery and strength which no weariness can affect, and for the first time after a long interval stretch out unarmed on your bed, safe from enemy at-

tack, and relax in sleep that tastes sweeter to you than drink
tastes to me after a long thirst—then you can talk about happiness.

Götz: On the other hand, that occurs only rarely.

Martin (more ardently): And when it does come, it is a foretaste of heaven.—When you return laden with booty from your
enemies and recall: this one I knocked off his horse before he
could shoot, and that one I ran down horse and all—and then
you ride up to your castle, and . . .

Götz: What are you thinking?

Martin: And your women folk! (He pours himself a drink.) To
the health of your wife! (He wipes his eyes.) You do have one?

Götz: A noble and excellent woman.

Martin: Blessed is the man who hath a virtuous wife, for the
numbers of his days shall be double.[1] I know no women, yet
woman was the crown of creation.

Götz: Forgive me. Farewell. (He extends his left hand to him.)

Martin: Why do you give me only your left hand? Am I not
worthy of the knightly right one?

Götz: Even if you were the Emperor, you would have to be
content with this one. My right one, although not useless in
warfare, is insensitive to the pressure of love. It is identical
with its glove. You see: it is made of iron.

Götz (to himself): I feel sorry for him. The feeling of his class
is eating his heart out.

Georg (running in): Sir, I hear horses at a gallop. Two of them.
It is surely they.

Götz: Lead out my horse. Hans shall ride. Farewell, dear Brother,
God be with you. Have courage and patience. God will make
room for you.[2]

Martin: May I ask your name?

---

[1]*Ecclesiasticus* 26:1.
[2]*Genesis* 26:22.

MARTIN: Then you are Götz von Berlichingen! O God, I thank Thee that Thou hast caused me to behold him, this man whom the princes hate and to whom the oppressed turn.

(He takes his right hand.)

Give me this hand, let me kiss it.

GÖTZ: That you shall not.

MARTIN: Let me do so! Thou, more precious than a reliquary hand through which the holiest blood has flowed, lifeless instrument animated by the noblest spirit's reliance upon God!

GÖTZ *(puts on his helmet and takes up his lance.)*

MARTIN: There was a monk of ours some time ago who visited you when it was shot off before the walls of Landshut. The way he told us about what you suffered and how greatly it pained you to be maimed in your profession, and how you recalled having heard about someone who had only one hand and yet served for a long time as a brave cavalier—I shall never forget it.

(Enter the two outriders.)

GÖTZ *(goes over to them; they speak in secret.)*

MARTIN *(continues speaking meanwhile)*: I shall never forget how he spoke in the simplest and noblest confidence in God: Even if I had twelve hands and Thy grace availed me not, what would they avail? Thus with one I can . . .

GÖTZ: To Haslach Forest then. *(He turns to Martin.)* Farewell. worthy Brother Martin. *(He kisses him.)*

MARTIN: Do not forget me! I shall not forget you!

(Exit Götz.)

How choked my heart became when I saw him! He said nothing, and yet my spirit was able to discern his. It is a delight to see a great man.

GEORG: Reverend Sir, will you sleep in our house?

MARTIN: Can I get a bed?

GEORG: No, Sir. I know about beds only from hearsay. At our lodge there is nothing but straw.

MARTIN: It will do. What is your name?

GEORG: Georg, reverend Sir.

MARTIN: Georg! There you have a brave patron saint.

GEORG: They say he was a horseman. That's what I want to be.

MARTIN: Wait a moment. *(He takes out a prayerbook and gives the lad a holy card.)* There you have him. Follow his example, be brave and fear God. *(Exit Martin.)*

GEORG: Oh, a beautiful white horse! If only I had one like that! —And the golden armor!—That's a nasty dragon.—I only shoot sparrows now.—Saint George, make me tall and strong, give me a lance like this one, and armor, and a horse. Then let me find the dragons!

*

[SCENE 3]

Jaxthausen. Götz's castle.
Elizabeth. Maria. Karl, his little son.

KARL: Please, Auntie dear, tell me again about the Worthy Child. That's such a nice story.

MARIA: You tell it to me, you little rogue. Then I will hear whether you pay attention.

KARL: Wait a bit, I want to think.—*Once upon a time* . . . yes: *Once upon a time there was a child and his mother was ill. Then the child went* . . .

MARIA: No, no. *Then his mother said, "Dear child* . . .

KARL: *I am ill* . . .

MARIA: . . . *and cannot go out." . . .*

KARL: *And she gave him money and said, "Go find yourself a breakfast." Along came a poor man . . .*

MARIA: *The child set out. And he came upon an old man who was . . .* Well, Karl?

KARL: *Who was . . . old . . .*

MARIA: That's right! . . . *who could scarcely walk any more, and he said, "Dear child, . . .*

KARL: . . . *give me something. I ate no bread yesterday nor yet today." Then the child gave him the money . . .*

MARIA: . . . *which was to have been for his breakfast.*

KARL: *Then the old man said . . .*

MARIA: *Then the old man took the child . . .*

KARL: . . . *by the hand and said . . . and he was seen to be a beautiful and radiant saint, and said, . . . "Dear child, . . .*

MARIA: . . . *for your charity Our Blessed Lady will reward you through me: What sick person soever you touch . . .*

KARL: . . . *with your hand"* . . . It was the right hand, I think . . .

MARIA: Yes.

KARL: *". . . he shall be made well."*

MARIA: *Then the child ran home and was unable to speak for joy . . .*

KARL: . . . *and fell upon his mother's neck and wept for joy.*

MARIA: *Then his mother cried out, "What thing is happening to me!" and was . . .* Well, Karl?

KARL: . . . *and was . . . and was . . .*

MARIA: But you're not paying attention! . . . *and was well. And the child cured king and emperor and became so rich that he built a great monastery.*

ELIZABETH: I cannot understand where my lord stays. It is already five days and nights that he has been away, and he hoped to carry out his exploit so soon.

MARIA: It has long worried me. If I had such a husband who

was forever exposing himself to dangers, I would die in the
first year.

ELIZABETH: I, on the contrary, thank God for having made me
of sterner stuff.

KARL: But must Father ride out if it's so dangerous?

MARIA: It is his will to do so.

ELIZABETH: Of course he must, Karl dear.

KARL: Why?

ELIZABETH: Do you remember how the last time he rode out he
brought back rolls for you?

KARL: Will he bring me some more?

ELIZABETH: I think so. You see, there was a tailor from Stuttgart,
and he was a splendid archer and had won first place in the
shooting match at Cologne.

KARL: Was it a lot?

ELIZABETH: A hundred thalers. And afterwards they wouldn't
give it to him.

MARIA: That was mean, wasn't it, Karl?

KARL: Mean people!

ELIZABETH: Then the tailor came to your father and asked him
if he would help him get his money. And so he rode out and
carried off a couple of merchants of the people in Cologne and
kept bothering them until they came across with the money.
Wouldn't you have ridden out too?

KARL: No! I would have to go through a deep, deep forest, and
there are gypsies and witches in it.

ELIZABETH: A fine fellow you are, afraid of witches.

MARIA: You will do better, Karl, just to live in your castle as a
good and Christian knight. There is opportunity enough for
good deeds right in one's own lands. The most upright knights
do more injustice than justice on their expeditions.

ELIZABETH: Sister, you don't know what you're saying. God grant
that our boy shall grow braver with time and that he won't

take after this Weislingen who has dealt so faithlessly with my husband.

MARIA: Let us not pass judgment, Elizabeth. My brother is very bitter, and you are too. I am more of a spectator in the whole matter and I can be more fair.

ELIZABETH: There is no excuse for him.

MARIA: What I have heard about him fascinates me. How many kind and good things your husband himself used to tell about him! How happy their boyhood was when they were pages of the Margrave together.

ELIZABETH: That may well be. But tell me, what good can there ever have been in a man who lays snares for his best and truest friend, sells his services to my husband's enemies, and tries to deceive our excellent Emperor, who is so gracious to us, by false and malicious representations!

KARL: There's Father! There's Father! The tower warder is blowing his call. Hey there, open the gate!

ELIZABETH: Here he comes with booty.

(*Enter an outrider.*)

OUTRIDER: We've been hunting and we've made a catch! God greet you, noble ladies!

ELIZABETH: Have you caught Weislingen?

OUTRIDER: Him and three horsemen.

ELIZABETH: What happened that kept you away so long?

OUTRIDER: We were lying in wait for him between Nürnberg and Bamberg but he just wouldn't come along; and yet we knew he was on his way. Finally we got on his trail. He had taken a side road and was sitting comfortably with the Count at Schwarzenberg.

ELIZABETH: They would like to make him too an enemy of my husband's.

OUTRIDER: That's just what I said right away to the master. Off he went, and rode into Haslach Forest. And then something curious happened. As we are riding along in the darkness, there happened to be a shepherd guarding his flocks right there and five wolves are attacking the flock and going stoutly to it. Then our master laughed and said, "Good luck, my hearties, good luck everywhere and to us as well!" And we were all cheered by the good omen. And meanwhile Weislingen comes riding along with four squires.

MARIA: My heart trembles within me.

OUTRIDER: I and my comrade, as the master had commanded, crept up close to him as if we had grown together so that he couldn't stir or budge, and the master and Hans attacked the squires and took them prisoners. One of them got away.

ELIZABETH: I am curious to see him. Are they coming soon?

OUTRIDER: They're riding up the valley. They will be here in a quarter of an hour.

MARIA: He must be downcast.

OUTRIDER: He looks grim enough.

MARIA: The sight of him will pain my heart.

ELIZABETH: Ah!—I will get supper ready at once. You must all be hungry.

OUTRIDER: Thoroughly.

ELIZABETH: Take the key to the cellar and fetch some of the best wine. They've earned it.

(Exit Elizabeth.)

KARL: I'll come with you, Auntie.

MARIA: Come, boy.

(Exeunt Maria and Karl.)

OUTRIDER: He won't be like his father, or he'd have gone to the stable.

(Enter Götz, Weislingen, and squires.)

GÖTZ *(laying his helmet and sword on the table)*: Unbuckle my armor for me and give me my jerkin. The comfort will feel good. Brother Martin, you were right . . . You gave us a run for our money, Weislingen.

WEISLINGEN *(does not reply, paces back and forth.)*

GÖTZ: Cheer up. Come, lay aside your arms. Where are your clothes? I hope none of them has got lost. *(to the outrider)* Ask his squires and open up the baggage, and take care that nothing goes astray. I could lend you some of mine, too.

WEISLINGEN: Leave me as I am, it makes no difference.

GÖTZ: I could give you a nice clean coat. It's only linen, of course. It's gotten too tight for me. I wore it to the wedding of my gracious lord the Count Palatine, on just the occasion when your Bishop waxed so poisonous about me. Two weeks before that I had captured two of his ships on the Main. And I'm just going up the steps with Franz von Sickingen in the Stag Inn in Heidelberg. Before you get all the way up there is a landing with an iron railing. There stood the Bishop and gave his hand to Franz as he passed and gave it to me too when I came along behind. I laughed to myself and walked over to the Landgrave of Hanau, who has been a very loving gentleman to me, and said, "The Bishop gave me his hand. I'll bet he didn't recognize me." The Bishop heard that, because I talked loud on purpose, and came over defiantly to us and said, "I did indeed give you my hand because I did not recognize you." Then I said, "Sir, I clearly saw that you didn't recognize me, and here you have your hand back again." Then the popinjay's neck got as red as a lobster with anger and he ran into the room to Count Palatine Ludwig and the Prince of Nassau and complained about it. We've had many a good laugh over it ever since.

WEISLINGEN: I wish you would leave me to myself.

GÖTZ: Why? I beg you, be cheerful. You are in my power, and

I won't misuse it.

WEISLINGEN: I wasn't worried on that score. That is your knightly duty.

GÖTZ: And you know that it is sacred to me.

WEISLINGEN: I am a captive. Nothing else makes any difference.

GÖTZ: You shouldn't talk that way. What if you had princes to deal with and they hung you up by chains in the depths of the dungeon and the guard had the task of whistling away your sleep?

(Enter the squires with the clothes.)

WEISLINGEN *(takes off garments and puts fresh ones on.)*

(Enter Karl.)

KARL: Good morning, Father.

GÖTZ *(kisses him.)*: Good morning, boy. How have you people passed the time here?

KARL: Very cleverly, Father. Auntie says I'm very clever.

GÖTZ: So!

KARL: Did you bring me something?

GÖTZ: Not this time.

KARL: I've learned a lot of things.

GÖTZ: Oh!

KARL: Shall I tell you about the Worthy Child?

GÖTZ: After supper.

KARL: I know something else too.

GÖTZ: What might that be?

KARL: Jaxthausen is a village and castle on the Jaxt. It has belonged for two hundred years to the lords of Berlichingen by hereditary right and by right of possession.

GÖTZ: Do you know the Lord of Berlichingen?

KARL *(looks at him fixedly.)*

GÖTZ *(to himself)*: For sheer erudition he doesn't know his own father.—To whom does Jaxthausen belong?

KARL: Jaxthausen is a village and castle on the Jaxt.

GÖTZ: I'm not asking you that.—*I* knew every path and road and ford before I knew the names of the river and village and castle.—Is your mother in the kitchen?

KARL: Yes, Father. She's cooking turnips and a roast of lamb.

GÖTZ: You know that too, Little Jack Chef?

KARL: And for dessert Auntie has baked me an apple.

GÖTZ: Can't you eat them raw?

KARL: They taste better this way.

GÖTZ: Always having to have something special.—Weislingen, I'll be right with you. I must see my wife a moment. Come along, Karl.

KARL: Who is the man?

GÖTZ: Speak to him. Tell him to be cheerful.

KARL: There, man, here is my hand. Be cheerful, supper will soon be ready.

WEISLINGEN *(picks him up and kisses him.)*: Fortunate child that knows no evil except supper is delayed. God grant you much joy of the lad, Berlichingen.

GÖTZ: Where there is much light there is also strong shadow— but I would welcome it. We shall see how it turns out.

(Exeunt Götz and Karl.)

WEISLINGEN: Oh, if I could wake up and all this were a dream! In Berlichingen's power, from whom I had hardly worked my way free, whose memory I shunned like fire, whom I hoped to conquer! And he—old, loyal-hearted Götz! Holy God, what will come of all this? Brought back, Adelbert, to the hall where we romped about as boys—when you loved him, hung upon him as on your own soul! Who can come near him and hate him? Oh, I am such a cipher here! Happy times, you are past and gone, when the elder Berlichingen used to sit here by the hearthside and we used to play around him and loved each

other as angels love. How worried the Bishop will be, and my
friends! I know the whole country will sympathize with my
misfortune. But what of that? Can they give me what I am
striving for?

Götz *(with a bottle of wine and glasses)*: Till supper is ready
we'll have a drink. Come, sit down, make yourself at home.
Think of it, you are back with Götz once more. It's a long time
since we have eaten together, a long time since we cracked a
bottle with each other.

(Raises a toast to him.)

A cheerful heart!

WEISLINGEN: Those times are past.

Götz: God forbid! To be sure, we won't find happier days again
than at the Margrave's court when we still shared a bed and
went around together. I remember my youth with joy. Do you
remember the trouble I got into with that Pole whose curled
and pomaded hair I accidentally ruffled with my sleeve?

WEISLINGEN: It was at table, and he lunged at you with a knife.

Götz: I gave him a thorough going over at the time, and later
you picked a fight with his friend. We always stuck solidly
together as good, stout lads, and everybody acknowledged that
of us.

(He pours another glass and offers a toast to Weislingen.)

Castor and Pollux! I always had a good feeling inside me when
the Margrave called us that.

WEISLINGEN: It was the Bishop of Würzburg that started it.

Götz: There was a learned gentleman, and yet affable too. I shall
never forget him as long as I live, the way he used to pet us,
praise our harmony, and always used to call any man fortunate
who was his friend's twin brother.

WEISLINGEN: No more of that!

Götz: Why not? I don't know of anything more pleasant after
work than to recall the past. In fact, when I think of how we

used to bear joys and sorrows together, used to be everything
to each other, and how I imagined things then, that's the way
it ought to be all our lives. Wasn't that my whole consolation
when this hand of mine was shot off before Landshut and you
nursed me and took more care of me than a brother? I hoped
that Adelbert would be my right hand after that. And now . . .

WEISLINGEN: O!

GÖTZ: If you had followed my advice then, as I urged you to do,
to go with me to Brabant, everything would have continued
to be all right. But that wretched court life kept you back, and
the flirting and dawdling after women. I always told you, if
you took up with those vain and nasty sluts and told them tales
about unsatisfactory marriages, seduced girls, and the harsh
skin of a third party, or whatever else they like to hear about,
you would turn out a scoundrel, as I used to say, Adelbert.

WEISLINGEN: What is all this leading up to?

GÖTZ: I would to God I could forget it or that it were otherwise!
Are you not as free, as nobly born as any man in Germany,
independent, subject only to the Emperor, and you cringe before vassals? What do you get from the Bishop? Because he is
your neighbor and could make trouble for you? Don't you have
arms and friends to trouble him back again? Do you under-
estimate the value of being a free knight who is subject only
to God, his Emperor, and himself! And you go crawling after
the first court lackey of a hoity-toity, envious priest!

WEISLINGEN: Let me speak.

GÖTZ: What have you to say?

WEISLINGEN: You look at princes the way the wolf looks at the
shepherd. And yet, can you blame them for defending the best
interests of their subjects and lands? Are they safe for a minute
from the unjust knights who attack their subjects on every
highway and lay waste their villages and castles? If now, on the
other hand, our beloved Emperor's lands are exposed to the

violence of the archenemy, and he requires aid from the estates, and they can scarcely defend their own lives, is it not a good spirit that counsels them to think of means of pacifying Germany, of administering right and justice, so that every man, great and small, may be allowed to enjoy the blessings of peace? And you find fault with us, Berlichingen, for entrusting ourselves to their protection when their help is close to us, when far-off Majesty cannot protect himself?

GÖTZ: Yes, yes, I understand you, Weislingen, if the princes were the way you describe them we would all have what we want. Order and peace! I believe it! That's what every bird of prey wants: to devour its quarry in comfort. Every man's welfare! If that were the only thing they're getting grey hair over! And they are toying with our Emperor in a disgraceful fashion. He means well and would gladly improve matters. Every day along comes some new tinker with this opinion and that opinion. And because our master grasps a thing quickly and has but to speak to set a thousand hands in motion, he thinks everything will be just that quickly and easily carried out. Then decrees follow decrees, and one after the other is forgotten. And whatever is grist for the princes' mill, they're right after it and glory in the order and security of the Empire until they've got the little fellows under their heels. I'll take my oath that many a one of them thanks God in his heart that the Turks counterbalance the Emperor.

WEISLINGEN: You see things from *your* side.

GÖTZ: So does every man. The question is on which side light and right are, and your movements at least shun the daylight.

WEISLINGEN: You can talk. I am the captive.

GÖTZ: If your conscience is clear, you are free. But how did it go with the Permanent Peace? I still remember, as a boy of sixteen I was with the Margrave at the Diet. How the princes opened their yaps then, and the ecclesiastical ones worst of all! Your Bishop yowled the Emperor's ear off, as if Justice had become O *so* dear! to his heart. And now he strikes down a page of mine at a time when our quarrels are composed and I don't have a wicked thought. Isn't everything straightened out between us? What business has he got with the lad?

WEISLINGEN: It happened without his knowledge.

GÖTZ: Why doesn't he let him go again?

WEISLINGEN: He hasn't behaved the way he should.

GÖTZ: Not the way he should? By my oath, he has done as he should, as sure as he was captured with your and the Bishop's knowledge. Do you think I was born yesterday, that I am not supposed to see where all this is leading?

WEISLINGEN: You are suspicious and do us an injustice.

GÖTZ: Weislingen, shall I talk to you straight from the shoulder? I am a thorn in your flesh, small as I am, and Sickingen and Selbitz no less so, because we are determined to die before we owe anyone but God for the air we breathe and before we pay loyalty and service to anyone but the Emperor. And now they're stalking me, blackening my reputation with His Majesty and His Majesty's friends and with my neighbors, and spying for some advantage over me. They want me out of the way, no matter what. That's why you took my page prisoner, because you knew I had sent him out to reconnoitre; and he didn't behave as he was supposed to because he didn't betray me to you. And you, Weislingen, are their tool!

WEISLINGEN: Berlichingen!

GÖTZ: Not another word about it! I am a foe of explanations; a man betrays himself or the other fellow, and usually both.

KARL: Come to dinner, Father.

GÖTZ: Good news!—Come! I hope my womenfolk will cheer you up. You used to be a gallant; young ladies had a lot to tell of you. Come!

*

[SCENE 4]

In the episcopal palace at Bamberg. The dining hall.
The Bishop of Bamberg. The Abbot of Fulda. Olearius.
Liebetraut. Courtiers.
At table. Dessert and the great wine cups are being brought in.

THE BISHOP: Are there many of the German nobility now study-
ing at Bologna?

OLEARIUS: Nobles and burghers. And boasting aside, they are
carrying off the highest honors. At the academy there is a saying that goes: "As industrious as a German nobleman." For
though the burghers bring a praiseworthy diligence to bear, in
order to make up through talent for their lack of birth, the
others exert themselves in a praiseworthy competition to enhance their inherent dignity by the most splendid accomplishments.

THE ABBOT: Ah!

LIEBETRAUT: What all doesn't a man live to hear! "As industrious
as a German nobleman!" *That* I've never heard in all my days.

OLEARIUS: Yes, they are the admiration of the whole academy. Before long several of the oldest and best skilled of them will be
coming back as *Doctores*. The Emperor will be fortunate in being able to fill the best posts with them.

THE BISHOP: No doubt about it.

THE ABBOT: Do you happen to know, for example, a squire . . . ?
He comes from Hesse . . .

OLEARIUS: There are numbers of Hessians there.

THE ABBOT: His name is . . . It's . . . Don't any of you know? . . .
His mother was a von . . . Oh! His Father had only one eye . . .
and he was a Marshal.

LIEBETRAUT: Von Wildenholz?

THE ABBOT: That's it. Von Wildenholz.

OLEARIUS: I know him well. A young gentleman of many capacities. He is especially renowned for his strength in debate.

THE ABBOT: He gets that from his mother.

LIEBETRAUT: Only her husband failed to praise that in her.

THE BISHOP: What did you say was that Emperor's name that wrote your *Corpus Juris?*

OLEARIUS: Justinian.

THE BISHOP: An excellent gentleman! Long may he live!

OLEARIUS: His memory!

(They drink.)

THE ABBOT: It must be a wonderful book.

OLEARIUS: You might call it the book of all books, a collection of laws, with the sentence ready for any case. And whatever is missing or obscure is supplied by the glosses with which the most learned men have adorned the supremely excellent work.

THE ABBOT: A collection of all laws! Thunderation! Then the Ten Commandments must be in it too.

OLEARIUS: *Implicite* to be sure, though not *explicite*.

THE ABBOT: That's what I mean, just put down without further explication.

THE BISHOP: And the best part of it all is, that, as you say, a state could live in the securest tranquillity and peace wherever it was fully introduced and properly administered.

OLEARIUS: Unquestionably.

THE BISHOP: All Doctors of Law!

OLEARIUS: To that I will drink with enthusiasm.

(They drink.)

Would God that people spoke that way in my homeland!

THE ABBOT: Where are you from, learned Sir?

OLEARIUS: From Frankfurt-on-the-Main, so please Your Eminence.

THE BISHOP: Aren't you gentlemen well thought of there? How does that happen?

OLEARIUS: Oddly enough. I was there to collect my inheritance from my father. The mob all but stoned me when they heard I was a lawyer.

THE ABBOT: God forbid!

OLEARIUS: But the reason for that is this: the Court of Sheriffs, which is held far and wide in great esteem, consists solely of men who are not acquainted with Roman Law. They think it is sufficient to acquire through age and experience a precise knowledge of the internal and the external condition of the city. Thus the citizens and the adjacent areas are ordered in accordance with ancient tradition and a few statutes.

THE ABBOT: Well, that's good.

OLEARIUS: But nowhere near sufficient. Human life is short, and not all cases turn up in one generation. Our book of laws is a collection of such cases over a period of several centuries. Besides, the will and the opinions of human beings fluctuate; what seems right today to one man is disapproved tomorrow by another, and in that way confusion and injustice are inevitable. This is all determined by laws, and laws are unchangeable.

THE ABBOT: That is better, to be sure.

OLEARIUS: The common people do not realize this. Greedy as they are for novelties, they still utterly despise anything new that gets them out of their rut, no matter how much they may be bettered by it. They consider a lawyer as bad as a disturber of the peace, or a pickpocket, and they are furious when one thinks of establishing himself there.

LIEBETRAUT: You're from Frankfurt! I am well acquainted there. At Emperor Maximilian's coronation we stole a march or two on your lover-swains. Your name is Olearius? I don't know anyone by that name.

OLEARIUS: My father's name was Ölmann. Merely to avoid misunderstanding on the title page of my Latin works I call myself Olearius, according to the example and advice of worthy professors of law.[1]

LIEBETRAUT: You did well to translate your name. A prophet is without honor in his fatherland, and you might have had the same experience in your mother tongue.[2]

OLEARIUS: That was not the reason.

LIEBETRAUT: Everything has more than one cause.

THE ABBOT: A prophet is without honor in his fatherland!

LIEBETRAUT: And do you know why, reverend Sïr?

THE ABBOT: Because he was born and brought up there.

LIEBETRAUT: True! That may be one reason. The other is because on closer acquaintance with the gentlemen the halo of venerability and holiness disappears which misty distance shed about them, and then they are nothing but little stubs of tallow.

OLEARIUS: It seems as though you are appointed to pronounce truths.

LIEBETRAUT: Since I have the heart for it, I don't lack for mouth.

OLEARIUS: But you do lack the knack of bringing them out appropriately.

LIEBETRAUT: Cupping-glasses are appropriately applied when they draw blood.

OLEARIUS: You can tell a barber-surgeon by his apron and you are not offended by anything in their trade. As a precaution, you would do well to wear a cap-and-bells.

LIEBETRAUT: Where did you graduate from? It's only by way of inquiry so that, if the notion ever took me, I could go straight to the right manufacturer.

---

[1]Ölmann and Olearius are German and Latin respectively for "oil man." Prominent sixteenth century Germans often translated their names into Latin or Greek. Goethe's maternal ancestors had thus Latinized their names of Weber ("weaver") as Textor.

[2]*Matthew* 13:57: "A prophet is not without honour, save in his own country . . ."

OLEARIUS: You are impudent.

LIEBETRAUT: And you are putting on a lot of airs.

(The Bishop and the Abbot laugh.)

THE BISHOP: Change of subject!—Not so hot, gentlemen. At table, anything goes.—Another topic, Liebetraut!

LIEBETRAUT: Opposite Frankfurt there's a thing called Sachsenhausen. . . .[1]

OLEARIUS *(to the Bishop)*: What are people saying about the Turkish campaign, Your Princely Grace?

THE BISHOP: The Emperor has no more urgent concern than, first, to pacify the realm, abolish feuds, and confirm the authority of the courts. Then, they say, he will proceed in person against the enemies of the empire and of Christendom. Right now his private affairs are still giving him plenty to do, and the empire, in spite of some forty proclamations of peace, is still a den of slaughter. Franconia, Swabia, the upper Rhine, and the adjacent territories are being laid waste by bold and insolent knights. Sickingen, Selbitz with his one leg, and Berlichingen with his iron hand make mockery of Imperial authority in those regions.

THE ABBOT: Yes, and if His Majesty doesn't do something about it soon, those fellows will wind up with someone in the bag.

LIEBETRAUT: That would have to be *some* fellow, to try to shove the Fulda wine-cask in the bag.[2]

THE BISHOP: That last one in particular has been my implacable enemy for many a year and annoys me beyond words. But that won't go on much longer, I hope. The emperor is now holding court in Augsburg. We have taken steps, and we cannot fail.— Doctor, do you know Adelbert von Weislingen?

OLEARIUS: No, Your Eminence.

---

[1] Sachsenhausen was proverbial for the rudeness of its inhabitants.

[2] "The Fulda wine-cask" is the obese Abbot himself. Liebetraut's remark must be an aside to the audience.

THE BISHOP: If you will wait for this man's arrival you will be delighted to see in one person the noblest, most intelligent, and most agreeable of knights.

OLEARIUS: He must be an excellent man to deserve such encomiums from such lips.

LIEBETRAUT: He was never at any academy.

THE BISHOP: We know that.

(The servants run to the window.)

What is the matter?

A SERVANT: Färber, Weislingen's squire, is just riding through the castle gate.

THE BISHOP: See what he brings. He must be announcing him.

(Exit Liebetraut.
They rise and drink another cup.)
(Reenter Liebetraut.)

THE BISHOP: What news?

LIEBETRAUT: I wish somebody else had to tell you. Weislingen has been captured.

THE BISHOP: O!

LIEBETRAUT: Berlichingen abducted him near Haslach, and three squires besides. One escaped to report it to you.

THE ABBOT: A regular Job's messenger.

OLEARIUS: I am heartily sorry.

THE BISHOP: I want to see the squire. Bring him up.—I want to talk to him myself. Bring him to my study.

(Exit.)

THE ABBOT *(sitting down)*: Another swallow.
(The servants pour wine for him.)

OLEARIUS: Would Your Reverence not desire to take a little stroll into the garden?

Post coenam stabis
Seu passus mille meabis.[1]

LIEBETRAUT: Quite true. Sitting isn't healthy for you. You will have another stroke.

(The Abbot rises.)

(to himself) If I can just get him outdoors I'll guarantee his exercise.

(Exeunt.)

*

[SCENE 5]

Jaxthausen.

Maria. Weislingen.

MARIA: You say you love me. I readily believe it, and I hope to be happy with you and to make you happy.

WEISLINGEN: I feel nothing except that I am yours entirely.

(He puts his arms around her.)

MARIA: I beg you, let me go. I allowed you a kiss as a pledge. But you seem to be trying to take possession already of what is yours only on certain conditions.

WEISLINGEN: You are too strict, Maria! Innocent love pleases the Deity instead of offending Him.

MARIA: Be it so. But I am not edified by such. I was taught that caresses were like chains, strong by dint of their interconnection, and that girls, when they are in love, are weaker than Samson after the loss of his hair.

WEISLINGEN: Who taught you that?

---

[1] After supper rise
  Or take a thousand paces exercise.

MARIA: The Abbess of my convent. I was with her until into my sixteenth year, and only with you do I feel the happiness that I enjoyed in her company. She had loved and could talk. She had a heart full of sensitivity. She was a wonderful woman.

WEISLINGEN: Then she was like you! (*He takes her hand.*) What will become of me if I have to leave you!

MARIA (*drawing back her hand*): You will be a little depressed, I hope, because I know how I will be. But you must go.

WEISLINGEN: Yes, Dearest, and I will. Because I realize what bliss I shall gain by that sacrifice. Blessed be your brother and the day when he set out to capture me!

MARIA: My heart was full of hope for him and for you. "Farewell," he said upon departure, "I will see that I find him again."

WEISLINGEN: He did. How I wish I had not neglected the management of my estates and their safety by my accursed life at court! You could be mine right away.

MARIA: Postponement too has its joys.

WEISLINGEN: Don't say that, Maria, or I shall have to be afraid that your feelings are less strong than mine. But I deserve the penance. And what hopes will accompany me at every step! To be all yours, to live only in you and in the sphere of the Good; far away, cut off from the world, to taste all delights that two such hearts can furnish to each other! What is the favor of princes, what is the world's approval, compared to this one simple happiness? I have hoped and wished for a great deal, but this befalls me beyond all my hopes and wishes.

(Enter Götz.)

GÖTZ: Your page is back. He could hardly speak a word for exhaustion and hunger. My wife is giving him something to eat. I understood this much: the Bishop won't release the lad; Imperial commissioners are to be named and a day set when the affair can be settled. Be that as it may however, you are free, Adelbert. I ask nothing further but your hand that in the future you will neither publicly nor secretly give aid to my enemies.

WEISLINGEN: Here I take your hand. From this moment on let friendship and trust be between us unalterably, like an eternal law of Nature! At the same time allow me to take this hand (*He takes Maria's hand.*) and possession of this noblest of girls.

GÖTZ: May I say Yes for you?

MARIA: If you will say it with me.

GÖTZ: We are fortunate in having advantages that go together this time. You need not blush. Your looks are sufficient proof. All right then, Weislingen! Take each other's hands, and I will say Amen.—My friend and brother!—I thank you, sister. You can do more than spin hemp. You have wound a thread to hold this bird-of-Paradise. You don't look quite free, Adelbert. What's the matter? I—am completely happy. What I had hoped for only in dreams I now behold, and I am as if in a dream. Ah! now my dream comes out. Last night I thought I gave you my right iron hand, and you held me so tight that it came out of the brassarts as if it had been broken off. I was terrified and woke up at that point. I would only have needed to go on dreaming and I would have seen how you grafted a new living hand upon me.—Now you must leave me to put your castles and estates in perfect condition. The accursed court has made you neglect both. I must call for my wife. Elizabeth!

MARIA: My brother is at the peak of joy.

WEISLINGEN: And yet I can challenge him for that rank.

GÖTZ: You will live delightfully.

MARIA: Franconia is a blessed land.

WEISLINGEN: And I can say that my castle lies in the most blessed and delightful of districts.

GÖTZ: That you can, and I will confirm it. Here flows the Main, and gently rises the hill clad in fields and vineyards and crowned with your castle. Then the river suddenly bends and disappears around the turn behind the cliffs of your castle. The windows of the great hall look steep down to the water with a view many hours into the distance.

(Enter Elizabeth.)

ELIZABETH: What is going on?

GÖTZ: You must lend your hand to this too, and say: "God bless you!" They are a couple.

ELIZABETH: So fast!

GÖTZ: But not unexpectedly.

ELIZABETH: May you always yearn for her as you have till now, while you were wooing her! And then! May you be as happy as you hold her dear!

WEISLINGEN: Amen! I desire no happiness except under that head.

GÖTZ: The bridegroom, my dear wife, is making a little journey, for the big change entails many small ones in turn. He is withdrawing first of all from the episcopal court in order to allow the friendship to cool little by little. Then he will wrest his lands out of the hands of selfish tenants. And. . . . Come, sister; come, Elizabeth. We shall leave him alone. Doubtless his page has private business with him.

WEISLINGEN: Nothing that you cannot hear.

GÖTZ: No need.—Franconia and Swabia, you are now closer of kin than ever. What a hold we shall keep on those princes!

(The three go out.)

WEISLINGEN: God in Heaven! Can it be that You have granted me such bliss in my unworthiness? It is too much for my heart. The way I hung upon those wretched people whom I fancied I controlled, and on the glances of the prince, and on reverential approval around me! Götz, dear old Götz, you have given me back to myself; and Maria, you make the transformation of my mind complete. I feel as free as if I were in the bright air. Bamberg I will not see again, I will cut all the shameful ties that held me beneath myself. My heart expands. Here is no toilsome straining after greatness denied. As sure as anything, only he is happy and great who has neither to command nor to obey in order to be something!

(Enter Franz.)

FRANZ: Greetings to my gracious lord! I bring you so many greetings that I don't know where to begin. Bamberg and everyone for ten miles around send you a thousand greetings.

WEISLINGEN: Welcome, Franz! What else do you bring?

FRANZ: You stand in such remembrance at court and everywhere else as it is impossible to express.

WEISLINGEN: That won't last long.

FRANZ: As long as you live. And after your death it will shine brighter than the brass letters on a tombstone. How they took your misfortune to heart!

WEISLINGEN: What did the Bishop say?

FRANZ: He was so eager to know that he held up my answer with the zealous speed of his questions. As a matter of fact, he already knew about it, because Färber, who had escaped from Haslach, brought him the news. But he wanted to know everything. He asked with such concern whether you were not injured. I said, "He is quite unharmed, from the tips of his hair to his little toe nail."

WEISLINGEN: What did he say to the proposals?

FRANZ: He wanted to turn over everything at once—the page, and money besides, just to get you free. But when he heard that you were going to get off without that and that your word alone was going to do as much as releasing the page, he absolutely insisted on having Berlichingen brought to trial. He told me a hundred things to say to you—but I have forgotten them again. There was a long sermon on the text: "I can't get along without Weislingen."

WEISLINGEN: He'll have to learn how!

FRANZ: How do you mean? He said, "Make him hurry! Everything waits for him."

WEISLINGEN: It will have to wait. I am not going to court.

FRANZ: Not going to court? Sir! How can you think of such a thing? If you knew what I know! If you could only dream of what I have seen!

WEISLINGEN: What has come over you?

FRANZ: Just the mere recollection of it sets me beside myself. Bamberg is Bamberg no longer. An angel in woman's form is making it the antechamber of Heaven.

WEISLINGEN: Nothing more than that?

FRANZ: I'll turn monk if you see her and are not beside yourself.

WEISLINGEN: Who is she?

FRANZ: Adelheid von Walldorf.

WEISLINGEN: Her! I've heard a good deal about her beauty.

FRANZ: Heard? That's as if you said, "I've seen music." It is just as impossible for the tongue to express a line of her perfection, because in her presence the eye itself is inadequate.

WEISLINGEN: You're out of your senses.

FRANZ: That may well be. The last time I saw her I had no more senses than a drunken man. Or rather I should say that at that moment I felt as saints must feel at the sight of celestial apparitions: all the senses keener, higher, more perfect, and yet the use of none of them.

WEISLINGEN: This is odd.

FRANZ: As I was taking leave of the Bishop she was sitting with him. They were playing chess. He was very gracious, held out his hand for me to kiss, and said a number of things of which I heard nothing. For I was looking at his companion. She had her eyes fixed on the board as if she were meditating a major move. A line of subtle watchfulness about her mouth and cheek! I might have been the white king. Nobility and kindliness prevailed upon her brow. And the dazzling light of her countenance and of her bosom, how it was set off by her dark hair!

WEISLINGEN: You've turned into a downright poet over it.

FRANZ: At that moment I felt what it is that makes a poet: a full heart, a heart totally filled with one emotion! As the Bishop concluded and I was bowing, she looked at me and said, "A greeting from me as well though I have not met him. Tell him to come soon. New friends are waiting for him, and he should not scorn them because he is already so rich in old ones."—I started to make some reply, but the channel from heart to tongue was choked. I made a bow. I would have given my entire fortune to be allowed to kiss the tip of her little finger. As I stood there the Bishop knocked a pawn off the table. I went after it and in picking it up I touched the hem of her garment. A shock went through all my limbs, and I don't know how I managed to get out the door.

WEISLINGEN: Is her husband at court?

FRANZ: She has already been a widow for four months. To divert her mind she is staying in Bamberg. You will see her. When she looks at anyone it's as though one were standing in spring sunlight.

WEISLINGEN: It would have a lesser effect on me.

FRANZ: I hear you are as good as married.

WEISLINGEN: I wish I were. My gentle Maria will create my life's happiness. Her sweet soul is mirrored in her blue eyes. And white as an angel of Heaven, composed of innocence and love, she guides my heart to rest and delight. Pack up! And then: to my castle! I will not see Bamberg, not if Saint Vitus in person wanted me to.

(Exit.)

FRANZ: Now God prevent that! We'll hope for the best. Maria is gracious and beautiful, and I can't take it amiss in a captive and a sick man for falling in love with her. In her eyes there is comfort, sympathetic melancholy.—But around you, Adelheid, there is life, fire, spirit.—I would . . . !—I am a fool . . . One glance from her made me so. My lord must go down there! I must go down there! And there I will gape myself sane again, or else completely insane.

ACT II

[Scene 1]

Bamberg. A hall.

The Bishop and Adelheid are playing chess. Liebetraut with a zither; ladies and courtiers gathered around him by the fireplace.
LIEBETRAUT (*plays and sings*):

> With arrow and bow,
> With torch aglow,
> Swept Cupid a-down
> To wage a brave war
> And triumph afar
> And conquer renown.
>> Up! Up!
>> On! On!
> His weapons, they stirred,
> His pinions, they whirred,
> And fierce was his frown.
>
> But there he found hearts
> So defenseless, alas—
> They took him so gladly
> Onto their laps—
> He flung down his arrows
> On the hearth in a heap;
> They kissed him and held him
> And rocked him to sleep.
>> Hei ei o! Popeio!

ADELHEID: Your mind is not on the game. Checkmate!
THE BISHOP: There's still a way out.

ADELHEID: You won't go on much longer. Checkmate!

LIEBETRAUT: If I were a great lord I wouldn't play this game, and
I would prohibit it at court and throughout the country.

ADELHEID: It's true, this game is a touchstone of the intellect.

LIEBETRAUT: That's not the reason! I would rather hear the howl
of a death-knell and of evil-omened birds, I would rather hear
the barking of the growling watchdog Conscience, and hear
them through the deepest slumber, than hear chess-bishops and
chess-knights and the rest of those animals with their everlasting "Checkmate!"

THE BISHOP: Who would ever think up such a thing?

LIEBETRAUT: Someone, for example, that was weak and had a
strong conscience, the way those two things usually go together.
They call it a royal game and say it was invented for a king
who rewarded the inventor with an ocean of abundance. If
that is true, I feel as though I saw him before me. He was a
minor either in brains or in years, under the tutelage of his
mother or his wife, he had baby-hair in his beard and flax at
his temples, he was pliant as a willow-shoot, and he liked to
play checkers with the ladies[1]—not out of passion, God forbid!—
but just as a pastime. His tutor, too active to be a scholar and
too stiff to be a man of the world, invented the game *in usum
Delphini*[2] because it was so like His Majesty—and so forth.

ADELHEID: Checkmate!—You ought to fill in the gaps in our history books, Liebetraut.

(They get up.)

LIEBETRAUT: The gaps in our genealogical trees, that would be
more profitable. Since the achievements of our ancestors and
their portraits serve one and the same purpose, namely to dec-

---

[1]"Checkers" and "ladies" are both *Damen* in German.

[2]*In usum Delphini*—(Latin) "for the use of the Dauphin," a phrase applied
to specially expurgated texts used in the education of the heir to the
throne of France.

orate the empty walls of our rooms and of our characters, there
would really be some point in that.

THE BISHOP: He will not come, you say?

ADELHEID: I beg you, dismiss it from your mind.

THE BISHOP: What can it be?

LIEBETRAUT: What? The reasons can be ticked off like rosary-
beads. He has fallen into a kind of contrition, of which I'd like
to cure him fast.

THE BISHOP: Do that. Ride over to see him.

LIEBETRAUT: My errand?

THE BISHOP: Anything whatsoever. Stop at nothing if you can
get him back.

LIEBETRAUT: May I also bring you into it, my Lady?

ADELHEID: With discretion.

LIEBETRAUT: That's a big order.

ADELHEID: Do you know me so little, or are you too young to
know in what tone you have to talk to Weislingen about me?

LIEBETRAUT: In the tone of a quail-call, I imagine.

ADELHEID: You will never learn sense.

LIEBETRAUT: Does anyone, my Lady?

THE BISHOP: Go, go. Take the best horse in my stable, choose
your squires, and bring him here to me.

LIEBETRAUT: If I don't charm him here, say an old woman that
cures warts and freckles knows more about sympathetic powers
than I do.

THE BISHOP: What good will that do? Berlichingen has taken
him in completely. If he does come here, he will only want to
leave again.

LIEBETRAUT: *Want*—that's no problem; but will he be *able?* The
hand-clasp of a prince and the smile of a beautiful woman—
no Weislingen will tear himself away from those. I go in haste
and take my leave of Your Grace.

THE BISHOP: Prosperous journey!

ADELHEID: Adieu.

(He leaves.)

THE BISHOP: Once he gets here, I will be counting on you.

ADELHEID: You intend to use me as a limed twig?

THE BISHOP: Oh no!

ADELHEID: As a decoy-bird, then?

THE BISHOP: No, Liebetraut will play that part. I beg you, do not refuse what no one else can provide!

ADELHEID: We'll see.

*

[SCENE 2]

Jaxthausen.
Hans von Selbitz. Götz.

SELBITZ: Everyone will praise you for declaring war on those Nürnberg people.

GÖTZ: It would have eaten my heart out if I had had to go on owing it to them for very long. It has come out that they betrayed my page to the Bambergers. They shall have reason to think of me!

SELBITZ: They have an ancient grudge against you.

GÖTZ: And I against them. It suits me fine that they have started something.

SELBITZ: The imperial cities and the clergy have always stuck together.

GÖTZ: They have reason to.

SELBITZ: We'll make things hot for them.

GÖTZ: I was counting on you. I wish to God the Mayor of Nürnberg with his gold chain around his neck would come our way: he'd be surprised, for all his cleverness.

SELBITZ: I hear Weislingen is on your side again. Will he join us?

Götz: Not yet. There are reasons why he can't openly give us
help yet. For a while it will be enough that he is not against
us. Without him, the priest is what the vestments are without
the priest.

Selbitz: When do we move out?

Götz: Tomorrow or the day after. Pretty soon now there will be
merchants from Bamberg and Nürnberg coming back from the
Frankfurt Fair. We'll make a good catch.

Selbitz: God willing.

(Exeunt.)

*

[Scene 3]

Bamberg. Adelheid's room.
Adelheid. Lady-in-waiting.

Adelheid: He is here, you say? I can hardly believe it.

Lady-in-waiting: If I hadn't seen him myself, I would say I
doubted it.

Adelheid: The Bishop can have Liebetraut mounted in gold. He
has achieved a masterpiece.

Lady-in-waiting: I saw him as he was about to ride in the castle
gate. He was on a white horse. The horse shied as it came to the
drawbridge and would not budge. The people had come running up out of all the streets to see him. They were delighted
at the horse's misbehavior. From all sides they hailed him, and
he thanked them all. He sat his mount with a pleasing com-
posure, and with coaxing and threatening he finally got it
through the gate, Liebetraut with him and a few attendants.

Adelheid: How do you like him?

Lady-in-waiting: As I have liked few men. He resembled the
Emperor here *(pointing to Maximilian's portrait)* as if he were

his son. Only his nose was somewhat smaller, just such friendly light brown eyes, just such fine blond hair, and built like a god. A half melancholy look on his face—I don't know—pleased me so much.

ADELHEID: I'm curious to see him.

LADY-IN-WAITING: There would be a gentleman for you.

ADELHEID: Silly fool!

LADY-IN-WAITING: Children and fools. . . .

(Enter Liebetraut.)

LIEBETRAUT: Well, my Lady, what do I deserve?

ADELHEID: Horns from your wife. For by her account you have lured many a neighbor's honorable housewife from her duty.

LIEBETRAUT: Not at all, my Lady! *To* her duty, you mean. For if it did happen, I lured her to her husband's bed.

ADELHEID: How did you manage to get him here?

LIEBETRAUT: You know perfectly well how fools are caught. Am I supposed to teach you *my* tricks besides?—First I pretended I knew nothing, understood nothing about his conduct, and thereby put him at the disadvantage of telling the whole story. Right away I saw it from a completely different angle from his, I could not agree—could not understand—and so on. Then I talked all sorts of stuff about Bamberg hit and miss, great things and small things, revived certain old memories, and when I had his imaginative powers engaged, I really tied up again a number of threads that I found broken. He didn't know what was coming over him, he felt a new urge toward Bamberg, he desired . . . without desiring. Then, when he got to consulting his heart and tried to sort all those things out and was much too concerned with himself to be on his guard, I threw a rope around his neck woven of three powerful strands: women's favor, princes' favor, and flattery—and with it dragged him here.

ADELHEID: What did you say about me?

LIEBETRAUT: The simple truth. That you were having unpleas-antnesses over your estates—that you hoped that since he had so much influence with the Emperor, he might easily put an end to these.

ADELHEID: Very well.

LIEBETRAUT: The Bishop will bring him to you.

ADELHEID: I will be waiting for them . . .

(Exit Liebetraut.)

. . . with such a heart as I have seldom waited for any visitor.

*

[SCENE 4]

In the Spessart Forest.
Berlichingen. Selbitz. Georg in squire's dress.

GÖTZ: You didn't find him, Georg?

GEORG: He had ridden to Bamberg the day before with Liebe-traut, and two squires along.

GÖTZ: I don't see what that will come to.

SELBITZ: I do. Your reconciliation was a little too sudden to be lasting. That Liebetraut is a sly rascal. He let himself to talked into it by him.

GÖTZ: Do you think he'll prove faithless to his alliance?

SELBITZ: The first step has been taken.

GÖTZ: I don't believe it. Who knows how necessary it may have been for him to go to court? People are still indebted to him. We shall hope for the best.

SELBITZ: Let's hope to God he deserves it and does the best!

GÖTZ: A stratagem just occurs to me. Let's put Georg into that smock we took from the Bamberg outrider and give him the safe-conduct pass. He can ride over to Bamberg and see how things stand.

GEORG: I've hoped for this for a long time.

GÖTZ: It will be your first mission. Be careful, lad! I'd hate to have you meet with an accident.

GEORG: Don't worry! It won't put me off if ever so many are crawling around me: to me they're like rats and mice.

(Exit.)

*

[SCENE 5]

Bamberg.
The Bishop. Weislingen.

THE BISHOP: You do not wish to be kept here any longer?

WEISLINGEN: You would not like to have me break my oath.

THE BISHOP: I would have liked not to have you swear it. What kind of a spirit possessed you? Was I not able to set you free without that? Do I count for so little at the Imperial court?

WEISLINGEN: It is done now. Forgive me if you can.

THE BISHOP: I don't understand what on earth obliged you to take that step! Give me up? Weren't there a hundred other terms on which to escape? Don't we have his page? Wouldn't I have given him money enough and quieted him? Our designs against him and his associates would have been dropped . . . Oh, I forget that I am talking with his friend who is now working against me and who can easily disengage the mines that he himself has set.

WEISLINGEN: My Lord!

THE BISHOP: And yet—now that I see your face again, hear your voice. . . . It is not possible, not possible.

WEISLINGEN: Farewell, my Lord.

THE BISHOP: I give you my blessing. Formerly when you used to go away I would say: Till we meet again! Now—God grant we never see each other again!

WEISLINGEN: Many things can change.

THE BISHOP: Perhaps I shall see you once more—as an enemy before my walls laying waste the fields that now have you to thank for their flourishing condition.

WEISLINGEN: No, my Lord.

THE BISHOP: You cannot say No. The secular estates, my neighbors, all have it in for me. As long as I had you. . . . Go, Weislingen! I have nothing more to say to you. You have undone many things. Go!

WEISLINGEN: And I don't know what I can say.

(Exit the Bishop.
Enter Franz.)

FRANZ: Adelheid is waiting for you. She is not well. And yet she does not want to let you go without farewell.

WEISLINGEN: Come.

FRANZ: Are we really leaving?

WEISLINGEN: This very evening.

FRANZ: I feel as if I were departing from the world.

WEISLINGEN: So do I. And what's more, as if I didn't know where I was going to.

*

[SCENE 6]

Adelheid's room.
Adelheid. Lady-in-waiting.

LADY-IN-WAITING: You look pale, my Lady.

ADELHEID: I do not love him and yet I wish he were staying. You

see, I could live with him although I would not like to have
him for a husband right away.

LADY-IN-WAITING: Do you think he will go?

ADELHEID: He is at the Bishop's to say good-bye.

LADY-IN-WAITING: He has another hard stand to make after that.

ADELHEID: How do you mean?

LADY-IN-WAITING: Can you ask, my Lady? You have his heart on
your hook, and if he tries to tear himself loose he will bleed to
death.

(Enter Weislingen. [The lady-in-waiting retires.])

WEISLINGEN: You are not well, my Lady?

ADELHEID: You cannot care about that. You are leaving us, leaving us forever. Why should you ask whether we live or die?

WEISLINGEN: You misjudge me.

ADELHEID: I take you as you present yourself.

WEISLINGEN: Appearances deceive.

ADELHEID: Are you a chameleon?

WEISLINGEN: If you could see my heart!

ADELHEID: Pretty things would meet my eye.

WEISLINGEN: Indeed they would! You would find your picture in
it.

ADELHEID: In some nook or other along with the portraits of extinct families. I beg you, Weislingen, to realize you are talking
with me. False words are most valid when they serve as masks
for our actions. A masker who is recognizable plays a sorry role.
You do not deny your actions and yet you say the opposite.
What is anyone to make of you?

WEISLINGEN: Whatever you will. I am so plagued with what I *am*
that I am not much concerned about what people may take
me for.

ADELHEID: You have come to say good-bye.

WEISLINGEN: Allow me to kiss your hand and I will say farewell.

You remind me. I didn't realize . . . I am being tiresome, my Lady.

ADELHEID: You misconstrue me. I wanted to help you on your way—for you do want to be on your way.

WEISLINGEN: O, say I must. If I were not compelled by my knightly obligation, by my solemn hand-clasp. . . .

ADELHEID: Go! Go! Tell that to girls that read *Teuerdank* and want a man like that.[1] Knightly obligation! Children's nonsense!

WEISLINGEN: You don't mean that.

ADELHEID: Upon my oath, you're pretending! What have you promised? And to whom? To a man who fails to recognize his obligation to the Emperor and to the empire you incur obligation at precisely the moment when he incurs the ban of outlawry by the act of taking you prisoner. Incur obligation that can be no more valid than the oath illegally obtained under duress! Don't our laws release us from such vows? Talk stuff like that to children that believe in Rübezahl.[2] There are other things behind this. To turn enemy of the state, enemy of civil peace and welfare! Enemy of the Emperor! A brigand's partner! You, Weislingen, with your gentle soul!

WEISLINGEN: If you only knew him . . .

ADELHEID: . . . I would do him justice. He has a lofty, intractable soul. For that very reason woe to you, Weislingen! Go and imagine you are his partner! Go and let yourself be dominated! You are affable, obliging. . . .

WEISLINGEN: So is he.

ADELHEID: But you are yielding and he is not. He will sweep you away unawares, you will be the slave of a nobleman when

---

[1]*Teuerdank* is an allegorical romance of chivalry outlined by Emperor Maximilian and composed by his secretary, depicting Maximilian's own suit for the hand of Maria of Burgundy; published 1517.
[2]Rübezahl—a waggish mountain sprite of the Riesengebirge, somewhat resembling Robin Goodfellow.

you could be master over princes.—But it is cruelty to spoil your taste for your future status.

WEISLINGEN: If you had only felt how graciously he treated me!

ADELHEID: Graciously! You credit him with that? It was his duty. And what would you have lost if he had been disagreeable? To *me* that would have been more welcome. A haughty man like him. . . .

WEISLINGEN: You're speaking about your enemy.

ADELHEID: I was speaking for your liberty—and I really don't know what advantage there is in that for me. Good-bye!

WEISLINGEN: Allow me one more moment.

(He takes her hand and remains silent.)

ADELHEID: Have you anything further to say to me?

WEISLINGEN: — — I must be going.

ADELHEID: Then go!

WEISLINGEN: My Lady! . . . I cannot.

ADELHEID: You must.

WEISLINGEN: Is this to be the last sight of you?

ADELHEID: Go. I am ill, most inopportunely.

WEISLINGEN: Don't look at me like that.

ADELHEID: You decide to be our enemy and we are supposed to smile? Go!

WEISLINGEN: Adelheid!

ADELHEID: I hate you!

(Enter Franz.)

FRANZ: My Lord, the Bishop is calling for you.

ADELHEID: Go on! Go on!

FRANZ: He begs you to come quickly.

ADELHEID: Go on! Go on!

WEISLINGEN: I will not say good-bye. I shall see you again!

(Exit.)

ADELHEID: See me again? We shall prevent that. Margarete, if he
comes, turn him away. I am ill, I have a headache, I am asleep
. . . Turn him away! If he is still to be won, that will be the
way to do it!

(Exit.)

*

[SCENE 7]

An antechamber.
Weislingen. Franz.

WEISLINGEN: She will not see me?
FRANZ: It is getting dark. Shall I saddle the horses?
WEISLINGEN: She will not see me?
FRANZ: For when does Your Grace order the horses?
WEISLINGEN: It is too late. We shall stay here.
FRANZ: Thanks be to God!

(Exit.)

WEISLINGEN: You're staying? Be on your guard. The temptation
is great. My horse shied as I was about to come in the castle
gate. My good angel blocked his way, knowing the perils that
awaited me here.—And yet it is not right not to put the many
affairs that I left unfinished for the Bishop into some order at
least, so my successor will be able to take up where I left off.
And I can do that much without harm to Berlichingen and
our alliance. For keep me here they shall not.—Would have
been better, though, if I hadn't come. But I will get off—tomorrow, or the day after.

(Exit.)

*

[SCENE 8]

In the Spessart Forest.
Götz. Selbitz. Georg.

SELBITZ: You see, it went just as I said.

GÖTZ: No! No! No!

GEORG: Please believe the news I bring you is true. I did as you ordered, took the Bamberger's smock and his safe-conduct pass, and to earn my food and drink besides, I escorted Reineck peasants up to Bamberg.

SELBITZ: In that disguise? That could have gone badly with you.

GEORG: I realize that now too, afterwards. A horseman that thinks ahead of time won't take any very broad jumps. I got to Bamberg, and the first thing I heard at the inn was that Weislingen and the Bishop had made up and that there was much talk of a marriage with von Walldorf's widow.

GÖTZ: Gossip.

GEORG: I saw him escorting her to table. She is beautiful, by my oath, she is beautiful! We all bowed. She thanked us all. He nodded his head and looked very pleased. They passed on, and the crowd murmured, "A handsome couple!"

GÖTZ: That may be.

GEORG: Listen further. The next day as he was on his way to Mass, I watched my chance. He was alone with a page. I was standing at the foot of the steps and I said to him softly, "A word or two from your Berlichingen!" He was startled; I saw the confession of his crime on his face. He scarcely had the heart to look at me—me, a mere squire.

SELBITZ: That was because his conscience was lower than your rank.

GEORG: "You're a Bamberger?" said he.—"I bring you greetings from Knight Berlichingen," said I, "and I am supposed to ask . . ."—"Come to my room tomorrow morning," said he, "and we'll talk further."

Götz: Did you go?

Georg: Of course I went, and it was a long, long while that I had to stand out in the antechamber. And the lads in silk eyed me front and back. I thought: "Go ahead and stare!" Finally I was ushered in. He seemed angry, but I didn't care. I stepped up to him and carried out my errand. He acted furiously angry, like someone that didn't have the stomach for it and didn't want it to show. He was amazed that you should take him to task through the intermediary of a squire. That made me mad. I said there were only two kinds of people, honest men and rascals, and I served Götz von Berlichingen. Then he started in and talked all kinds of silly stuff, which amounted to this: You had rushed him, he was under no obligation to you, and he didn't want to have anything to do with you.

Götz: You have that from his own lips?

Georg: That and more besides.—He threatened me . . .

Götz: That's enough! So he is lost now too! Faith and Trust, you have deceived me again. Poor Maria! How will I break the news to you!

Selbitz: I'd rather lose my other leg too than be a son of a bitch like that.

(Exeunt.)

*

[Scene 9]

Bamberg.
Adelheid. Weislingen.

Adelheid: The time begins to hang unbearably heavy. I don't

feel like talking and I am ashamed to play with you. Boredom, you are worse than a cold fever.

WEISLINGEN: Are you tired of me already?

ADELHEID: Not so much of you as your company. I wish you were where you wanted to go and we had not kept you back.

WEISLINGEN: Such is woman's favor! First she hatches out our fondest hopes with maternal warmth, then like a fickle hen she leaves the nest and abandons her already growing progeny to death and corruption.

ADELHEID: Blame it on women! The reckless gambler chews and stamps on the cards that made him lose in all innocence. But let me tell you something about men. Who are you to talk about fickleness? You, who are rarely what you claim to be and never what you ought to be. Kings in holiday robes, envied by the mob. What would a tailor's wife give to wear around her neck a string of pearls from the hem of your garment that is contemptuously kicked aside by your heels!

WEISLINGEN: You're bitter.

ADELHEID: It is the antistrophe of your ode. Before I knew you, Weislingen, I was like the tailor's wife. Rumor, hundred-tongued, and not metaphorically speaking, had so quack-doctor-touted you that I let myself be talked into wishing: "Wouldn't you just love to get a look at that quintessence of the male sex, that Phoenix Weislingen!" My wish was granted.

WEISLINGEN: And the Phoenix turned out to be an ordinary barnyard rooster.

ADELHEID: No, Weislingen, I was interested in you.

WEISLINGEN: It seemed so . . .

ADELHEID: And was. For you really did surpass your reputation. The mob prizes only the reflection of merit. Just as I have a way of not liking to think about people to whom I wish well, just that way we lived for a time side by side. Something was lacking, and I didn't know what it was I missed in you. Finally my eyes were opened. Instead of the active man who enlivened the affairs of a princedom, who did not lose sight of himself and his fame in so doing, who had climbed to the clouds over a hundred great enterprises as over mountains piled one on top of the other, I saw all of a sudden someone complaining like a sick poet, as melancholy as a healthy girl, and idler than an old bachelor. At first I attributed it to your misfortune, which lay fresh upon your heart, and excused you as well as I could. Now that it seems to be getting worse with you from day to day, you will have to forgive me if I tear my favor away from you. You possess it without right, I gave it to someone else for life who was unable to transfer it to you.

WEISLINGEN: Then set me free.

ADELHEID: Not before all hope is lost. In these circumstances solitude is dangerous.—Poor man, you are as dejected as one whose first girl has proven unfaithful, and just for that reason I will not give you up. Give me your hand, forgive me for what I have said out of love.

WEISLINGEN: If you could only love me, if you could only grant one drop of comfort to my ardent passion! Adelheid! Your accusations are terribly unjust. If you had any notion of the hundredth part of what has been seething within me all this time, you would not have mangled me so mercilessly this way and that way with favor and indifference and contempt . . . You smile! . . . Coming to terms with myself again after that overhasty step cost me more than *one* day. To struggle against the man whose memory is so vividly fresh in my love!

ADELHEID: Strange man, who can love someone whom you envy! It's as if I brought provisions to my enemy.

WEISLINGEN: I realize that delay will not do in this case. He is informed that I am once again Weislingen, and he will avail himself of his advantage over us. Besides, Adelheid, we are not so sluggish as you think. Our horsemen are reenforced and alert, our negotiations are proceeding, and we hope the Imperial Diet in Augsburg will bring our projects to fruition.

ADELHEID: You're going there?

WEISLINGEN: If I could take some hope with me!

(He kisses her hand.)

ADELHEID: O ye of little faith! Always signs and wonders![1] Go, Weislingen, and complete the work. The Bishop's advantage, yours, mine, they are so intertwined that, even if it were only for the sake of policy . . .

WEISLINGEN: You can jest.

ADELHEID: I am not jesting. The haughty Duke is holding my estates; Götz will not leave yours unharassed for very long; and if we do not stick together like our foes and do not get the Emperor over on our side, we are lost.

WEISLINGEN: I am not worried. The biggest share of the princes are of our opinion. The Emperor wants help against the Turks and for that reason it is proper for him to support us again. What a joy it will be for me to liberate your estates from haughty enemies, to lay the restless heads in Swabia back on their pillows, to restore the peace of the bishopric and of us all! And then . . . ?

ADELHEID: One day leads to another, and the future is in the hands of Fate.

WEISLINGEN: But we have to want it.

ADELHEID: Well, we do want it.

WEISLINGEN: You're sure?

ADELHEID: Why, yes. Go.

WEISLINGEN: Enchantress!

---

[1] *John* 4:48—"Except ye see signs and wonders, ye will not believe."

*

[SCENE 10]

An inn. A peasant wedding. Music and dancing outside.
The bride's father, Götz, and Selbitz at table. The bridegroom
steps up to them.

GÖTZ: The most sensible thing was that you brought your quarrel
to such a happy and fortunate end by means of a marriage.

THE BRIDE'S FATHER: Better than I had dared dream. Peace and
quiet with my neighbor, and a daughter well provided for
besides.

THE BRIDEGROOM: And I in possession of the disputed land, and
the prettiest Miss in the whole town as well. I wish to God you
had intervened sooner.

SELBITZ: How long have you been at this lawsuit?

THE BRIDE'S FATHER: Going on eight years. I'd rather have the
ague twice that time as start in again from the beginning. It's
a tussle, you wouldn't believe it, to drag a verdict out of those
curliwigs' hearts.[1] And what have you got when you're through?
Devil take that Assessor Sapupi![2] He's a damned black Italian.

THE BRIDEGROOM: Yes, he's a mad one. I was there twice.

THE BRIDE'S FATHER: And I three times. And see, Gentlemen,
we finally do get a verdict, one where I am as much in the right
as he is, and he as much as I am, and we stood there with our
mouths hanging open until the Lord God prompted me to
give him my daughter and the land too in the bargain.

GÖTZ *(drinking a toast)*: Good trials in the future.

THE BRIDE'S FATHER: God grant! Come what may, however, I'll
never go to law again as long as I live. What a pile of money
it takes! You have to pay for every bow the attorney makes you.

---

[1]The artificial curled wigs of lawyers were worn in Goethe's eighteenth,
but not in Götz's sixteenth, century.

[2]"Sapupi" is an anagram of Papius, a bribe-taking assessor discharged from
the Imperial Court in Wetzlar just before young lawyer Goethe arrived to
work there in 1772.

SELBITZ: Well, there *are* Imperial inspection tours annually.

THE BRIDE'S FATHER: Never heard of them. But many a sweet Thaler went for extras. Such bleeding you never heard of!

GÖTZ: How do you mean?

THE BRIDE'S FATHER: Oh, there they all hold out a hollow paw. The assessor alone, God forgive him! got eighteen Gulden in gold out of me.

THE BRIDEGROOM: Who?

THE BRIDE'S FATHER: Sapupi! Who else?

GÖTZ: It's a shame.

THE BRIDE'S FATHER: All right, I had to pay down twenty to him. And when I had counted them out for him in his garden house—which is magnificent—in the big main hall, my heart fairly broke for grief. For look, a man's house and home stand firm, but where is ready cash to come from? I stood there, God knows what came over me. I didn't have a red cent in my purse for travel money. Finally I worked up the courage and put it up to him. Then he saw my soul was turning to water and he threw two of them back down for me and sent me off.

THE BRIDEGROOM: That's not possible! Sapupi?

THE BRIDE'S FATHER: Why look that way! Of course! Nobody else!

THE BRIDEGROOM: Devil take him! He got fifteen Gulden in gold out of me too.

THE BRIDE'S FATHER: Damnation!

SELBITZ: Götz, *we* are robbers!

THE BRIDE'S FATHER: That's why the verdict came out so lopsided. You dog!

GÖTZ: You mustn't let this go unreported.

THE BRIDE'S FATHER: What are we supposed to do?

GÖTZ: Start out for Speyer. It's inspection time right now. Make a complaint. They have to investigate it and help you get what is yours.

THE BRIDEGROOM: Do you think we'll get it through?

GÖTZ: If I could get him by the ears, I'd promise you you would.

SELBITZ: The amount is well worth a try.

GÖTZ: I've ridden out before this for one fourth the amount.

THE BRIDE'S FATHER: What do you think?

THE BRIDEGROOM: We will, come what may.

(Enter Georg.)

GEORG: The Nürnbergers are on their way.

GÖTZ: Where?

GEORG: If we ride nice and gently, we'll grab them in the woods between Beerheim and Mühlbach.

SELBITZ: Fine!

GÖTZ: Come on, children! God be with you! Help us all to get what is ours!

THE PEASANT: Many thanks. You won't stay on for supper?

GÖTZ: We can't. Good-bye.

ACT III

[SCENE 1]

Augsburg. A garden.
Two Nürnberg merchants.

FIRST MERCHANT: Here we will stand, for here the Emperor has to pass by. He is just coming up the long path.

SECOND MERCHANT: Who is with him?

FIRST MERCHANT: Adelbert von Weislingen.

SECOND MERCHANT: Bamberg's friend! That's good.

FIRST MERCHANT: We'll fall on our knees, and I will do the talking.

SECOND MERCHANT: Good. There they come.

(Enter the Emperor and Weislingen.)

FIRST MERCHANT: He looks annoyed.

THE EMPEROR: I am depressed, Weislingen, and when I look back on my past life I could well turn despondent—so many enterprises half accomplished, so many that came to naught, and all because there is not a prince in the empire who is not so small but that he is more concerned about his own whims than about my ideas.

(The merchants cast themselves at his feet.)

THE MERCHANT: Serenest Highness! High and Mighty!

THE EMPEROR: Who are you? What is it?

THE MERCHANT: Poor merchants from Nürnberg, Your Majesty's servants, who implore your aid. Götz von Berlichingen and Hans von Selbitz have set upon thirty of our number in the Bamberg safe-conduct area as they were on their way back from

150

the Frankfurt Fair and robbed them. We beg Your Imperial
Majesty for help, for support; otherwise we shall all be ruined
men compelled to beg our bread.

THE EMPEROR: God in Heaven! God in Heaven! What is this?
One of them has only one hand, the other only one leg. If they
ever had two hands and two legs what would you do then?

THE MERCHANT: We most submissively request Your Majesty to
cast a compassionate eye upon our hard pressed circumstances.

THE EMPEROR: The way things go! If a merchant loses a bag of
pepper the whole empire is supposed to be called out, and if
there is business to be done of great moment to Imperial Majesty and to the empire, involving kingdoms, princedoms, duke-
doms, then there is not a soul to be rounded up.

WEISLINGEN: You come at an inopportune time. Go now and
wait here for a few days.

BOTH MERCHANTS: We commend us to Your Grace.

(Exeunt.)

THE EMPEROR: More troubles again! They keep growing like the
Hydra's heads.

WEISLINGEN: And they won't be exterminated except by fire and
sword and by an energetic campaign.

THE EMPEROR: You think so?

WEISLINGEN: I consider nothing more practicable, if Your Majesty and the princes could agree on other insignificant differences. It is by no means all of Germany that is complaining
about disturbance. Franconia and Swabia alone still show fire
in the ashes from what is left of the destructive internecine
civil war. And even there there are many nobles and freemen
who yearn for peace. If we could just get this Sickingen, this
Selbitz—this Berlichingen out of the way, the rest would soon
collapse of themselves. For *they* are the ones whose spirit stirs
up the rebellious crowd.

THE EMPEROR: I should like to spare those men; they are brave and noble. If I were fighting a war they would have to take the field with me.

WEISLINGEN: One could wish they had long since learned to respond to their obligations. Then, too, it would be extremely dangerous to reward their rebellious enterprises with positions of honor. For it is precisely this Imperial gentleness and clemency that they have so monstrously misused up to now; and their followers, who are setting their hope and trust on it, cannot be brought under control until we have annihilated them completely in the eyes of the world and cut off totally any hope they may have of ever getting back up again.

THE EMPEROR: You recommend severity, then?

WEISLINGEN: I see no other means of eliminating the giddy folly that grips whole provinces. Do we not already hear in this place and in that place the bitterest complaints of the nobles to the effect that their subjects, their serfs are revolting against them and disputing with them and threatening to diminish their traditional sovereignty, so that the most dangerous consequences are to be feared?

THE EMPEROR: This would be a fine opportunity to move against Berlichingen and Selbitz; only, I wouldn't want them to come to any harm. I would like to have them taken captive, and then they would have to swear their oath of truce to stay quietly in their castles and not to leave their jurisdictions. At the next session I will propose it.

WEISLINGEN: A joyous acclamation of approval will spare Your Majesty the end of the speech.

(Exeunt.)

❋

[SCENE 2]

Jaxthausen.
Sickingen. Berlichingen.

SICKINGEN: Yes, I have come to ask your noble sister for her heart and hand.

GÖTZ: Then I wish you had come sooner. I must tell you: during his captivity Weislingen won her love, sued for her hand, and I promised her to him. I let him loose, that caged bird, and he scorns the kindly hand that fed him in time of distress. He is flitting about, God knows on what hedge, looking for his food.

SICKINGEN: Is this true?

GÖTZ: As I say.

SICKINGEN: He broke a double bond. It's well for you that you did not become related any closer with the traitor.

GÖTZ: She sits there, the poor girl, grieving and praying her life away.

SICKINGEN: We'll make her sing.

GÖTZ: What? Can you make up your mind to marry a girl that has been deserted?

SICKINGEN: It is an honor for both of you to be betrayed by him. Is the poor girl supposed to enter a convent because the first man she knew was a good-for-nothing? Not at all! I insist on her becoming the queen of my castles.

GÖTZ: I tell you she was not indifferent to him.

SICKINGEN: Don't you think I'm capable of driving away the shadow of a scoundrel? Let's go and see her.[1]

(Exeunt.)

＊

---

[1]The historical Franz von Sickingen, 1481-1523, a champion of the Reformation and a friend of Martin Luther, was far more distinguished politically and militarily than Götz von Berlichingen, into whose family he did not marry.

[SCENE 3]

Camp of the Imperial Ban Enforcement.
A Captain. Officers.

THE CAPTAIN: We must go cautiously and spare our troops as much as possible. Besides, we have express orders to corner him and take him alive. That will take some doing, for who is going to tackle him?

FIRST OFFICER: Right! And he will fight back like a wild boar. Never in his life has he done us any harm, and every man will avoid risking arms and legs to please the Emperor and the empire.

SECOND OFFICER: It would be a shame if we didn't capture him. If I once get him by the collar he won't get away.

FIRST OFFICER: Just don't grab him with your teeth: he might rip your jaw off. My dear young Sir, people of that sort are not to be grabbed like runaway thieves.

SECOND OFFICER: We'll see.

THE CAPTAIN: He must have our letter by now. We mustn't put off sending out a patrol to observe him.

SECOND OFFICER: Let me lead it.

THE CAPTAIN: You're not familiar with the area.

SECOND OFFICER: I have a groom that was born and brought up here.

THE CAPTAIN: I'm satisfied with that.

(Exeunt.)

*

[SCENE 4]

Jaxthausen.
Sickingen.

SICKINGEN: Everything is going just as I hoped. She was a bit startled at my proposal and looked me over from head to foot. I'll bet she was comparing me with that whitefish of hers.[1] Thank God I can stand the comparison! Her answer was brief and confused. All the better! Let her simmer a while yet. With girls that are parboiled in unhappy love, a proposal of marriage cooks done fast.

(Enter Götz.)

What news, my friend?

GÖTZ: Proclaimed an outlaw!

SICKINGEN: What?

GÖTZ: Here, read this edifying letter. The Emperor has ordered activation of the ban against me, which is supposed to carve my flesh for the birds beneath the heaven and the beasts upon the field.

SICKINGEN: They'll go to them first. I'm here at just the right time.

GÖTZ: No, Sickingen, you must leave. Your great projects might be ruined if you started to turn enemy of the state at so inopportune a time. Besides, you will be of much more use to me if you appear to be neutral. The Emperor likes you, and the worst that can happen to me will be to be taken prisoner. *Then* come forward with your intercession and pull me out of the mess into which untimely help could plunge us both. What good would it do? The expedition is on its way to attack me. If they find you are with me, they will only send more men, and we will be no better off. The Emperor is at the source, and I would be irrevocably lost if bravery could be breathed into men as fast as a posse can be blown together.

SICKINGEN: At least I can secretly send over twenty horsemen or so to join you.

GÖTZ: Good. I have already sent Georg for Selbitz and my fol-

---

[1]A *Weisling* is a kind of small white fish.

lowers in the vicinity. When I get my men together, old boy, they will be a company the like of which few princes have ever seen gathered.

SICKINGEN: You will be few against their numbers.

GÖTZ: One wolf is too many for a whole flock of sheep.

SICKINGEN: But what if they have a good shepherd?

GÖTZ: Don't worry! They're nothing but hirelings. And then, the best knight can't do anything when he is not master of his actions. They came against me once before this way, when I had promised to serve the Count Palatine against Konrad Schotte. He handed me a memorandum from the Chancery about how I was supposed to ride and behave. I threw the paper back at the Councillors and said I wouldn't know how to follow its directions; I didn't know what I might run into, *that* wasn't in the memorandum; I had to keep my own eye peeled and see for myself what I had to do.

SICKINGEN: Good luck, Brother! I'll be off right away, and I'll send you whatever I can scare up in a hurry.

GÖTZ: See the ladies yet before you go. I left them together. I wanted you to have her word before you left. Then send me the horsemen and come back secretly to pick up Maria. For my castle, I fear, will soon be no place for women.

SICKINGEN: We'll hope for the best.

(Exeunt.)

✳

[SCENE 5]

Bamberg. Adelheid's room.
Adelheid. Franz.

ADELHEID: Then both enforcement expeditions have already started out?

FRANZ: Yes, and my lord has the pleasure of attacking your enemies. I wanted right away to go along, however glad I was to come to see you. And now I want to start right off again in order to come back soon with happier news. My lord has given me permission.

ADELHEID: How are things with him?

FRANZ: He is cheerful. He bade me kiss your hand.

ADELHEID: There . . . Your lips are warm.

FRANZ *(to himself, pointing to his bosom)*: It's still warmer here. *(Aloud)* My Lady, your servants are the most fortunate people under the sun.

ADELHEID: Who is the leader against Berlichingen?

FRANZ: The lord of Sirau. Farewell, best and gracious Lady. I must be off again. Do not forget me.

ADELHEID: You must eat and drink something, and rest.

FRANZ: What need? I have seen you. I am neither weary nor hungry.

ADELHEID: I know your faithfulness.

FRANZ: Oh, my Lady!

ADELHEID: You can't stand it. Take some rest and eat a little something.

FRANZ: Your concern for a poor youth!

(Exit.)

ADELHEID: There are tears in his eyes. I love him with all my heart. No one has ever been so genuinely and so warmly attached to me.

(Exit.)

*

[SCENE 6]

Jaxthausen.
Götz. Georg.

GEORG: He wants to talk to you himself. I don't know him. He is an imposing man with fiery black eyes.

GÖTZ: Bring him in.

(Enter Lerse.)

GÖTZ: God's greeting to you! What do you bring?

LERSE: Myself. That isn't much, but all there is I offer you.

GÖTZ: You are welcome, doubly welcome. A brave man, and just at this time when I didn't dare hope to gain new friends but rather feared the loss of old ones from hour to hour. Give me your name.

LERSE: Franz Lerse.

GÖTZ: I thank you, Franz, for making me acquainted with a brave man.

LERSE: I introduced myself to you once before, but that time you didn't thank me for it.

GÖTZ: I don't recall you.

LERSE: I'm sorry. Do you still remember how you became enemies with Konrad Schotte on account of the Count Palatine and started out to ride to Hassfurt for the Mardi Gras?

GÖTZ: I remember it well.

LERSE: Do you recall how on the way you encountered twenty-five horsemen near a village?

GÖTZ: Right. I thought at first there were only twelve of them and divided my band—there were sixteen of us—and stopped near the village behind the shed intending to let them go by. Then I was going to go after them, as I had arranged with the other group.

LERSE: But we saw you and rode up a hill near the village. You rode past and stopped down below. When we saw you weren't going to come up, we rode down.

GÖTZ: Only then did I notice that I had stuck my hand into the coals. Twenty-five against eight! There was no dilly-dallying then. Erhard Truchsess ran a squire of mine through, and for that I charged him right off his horse. If they had all held out

like him and one squire, it would have gone hard with me
and my little band.

LERSE: The squire of whom you said . . .

GÖTZ: He was bravest I had seen. He went after me hot and
heavy. Every time I thought I had beaten him off and was
about to take on some others, there he was at me again and
thrusting away furiously. He jabbed me through the vambrace
too so that he grazed my arm a little.

LERSE: Have you forgiven him?

GÖTZ: I liked him only too well.

LERSE: Well, I just hope you will be satisfied with me. I did my
demonstration performance on you yourself.

GÖTZ: Are you the one? O welcome!—Maximilian, can you say
that among the men serving you you enlisted a single one this
way!

LERSE: I'm surprised you didn't figure me out sooner.

GÖTZ: How was I supposed to imagine that anyone would offer
me his services who had tried like the worst of enemies to
conquer me?

LERSE: Just that very fact, Sir! From my youth up I have served
as a squire and I have pitted my strength against many a knight.
When we ran up against you I was glad. I knew your name
and then I came to know you. You know I didn't hold out, but
you saw it wasn't from fear, because I kept coming right back
again. In short, I got to know you, and from that time on I
made up my mind to serve you.

GÖTZ: How long do you want to serve with me?

LERSE: For a year. Without pay.

GÖTZ: No, you shall be maintained like anyone else, and what's
more, like the man that gave me such a rough time of it at
Remlin.

(Enter Georg.)

GEORG: Hans von Selbitz sends you his greetings. He will be here tomorrow with fifty men.

GÖTZ: Good.

GEORG: A detachment of Imperials is coming down along the Kocher,[1] doubtless to reconnoitre your position.

GÖTZ: How many?

GEORG: Fifty of them.

GÖTZ: Is that all? Come on, Lerse, we'll knock hell out of them so, when Selbitz comes, he'll find one job done.

LERSE: That'll be a plentiful early vintage.

GÖTZ: To horse!

(Exeunt.)

＊

[SCENE 7]

A forest at the edge of a swamp.
Enter two Imperials, meeting.

FIRST SQUIRE: What are you doing here?

SECOND SQUIRE: I got permission to answer the call of Nature. Since the false alarms of last night it's hit me in the bowels so I have to dismount every two minutes.

FIRST SQUIRE: Is the detachment stationed near by?

SECOND SQUIRE: A good hour up the woods.

FIRST SQUIRE: Then how do you come to be wandering down here?

SECOND SQUIRE: I beg you not to betray me. I want to get to the nearest village and see if I can't cure my trouble with warm compresses. Where do you come from?

FIRST SQUIRE: From the next village. I've picked up some wine and bread for our officer.

---

[1]The Kocher is a small river parallel to the Jaxt.

SECOND SQUIRE: So! He gets himself something good right before our faces and we're supposed to go hungry! A fine example!

FIRST SQUIRE: Come on back with me, you sneak!

SECOND SQUIRE: The fool I'd be! There are a lot more in the detachment that would be glad to go hungry if they were as far away from it as I am.

FIRST SQUIRE: Do you hear? Horses!

SECOND SQUIRE: O my God!

FIRST SQUIRE: I'll climb this tree.

SECOND SQUIRE: I'll hide among the reeds.

(Enter Götz, Lerse, Georg, and squires on horseback.)

GÖTZ: On past the pond here and left into the woods. That way we'll come around behind them.

(They ride on.)

FIRST SQUIRE *(climbs down from the tree.)*: It's no good there. Michel! He doesn't answer? Michel, they're gone! *(He walks over to the swamp.)* Michel! My God! He's sunk out of sight. Michel! He doesn't hear me, he's smothered. So you died anyway, you coward!—We're beaten. Enemies, enemies everywhere!

(Enter Götz and Georg on horseback.)

GÖTZ: Halt there, you, or you're a dead man!

THE SQUIRE: Spare my life!

GÖTZ: Your sword! Georg, lead him to the other captives that Lerse has down on the edge of the woods, I've got to overtake their fugitive leader.

(Exit.)

THE SQUIRE: What has become of our knight that was leading us?

GEORG: My master knocked him head over heels off his horse so his plume stuck in the mire. His horsemen lifted him onto his horse and off they went like mad!

(Exeunt.)

❋

[SCENE 8]

Camp.
The Captain. The first knight.

FIRST KNIGHT: They're fleeing toward camp from way out.

THE CAPTAIN: He must be at their heels. Have fifty men sent out as far as the mill. If he extends himself too far maybe you will catch him.

(Exit the knight.
Enter the second knight, led in.)

How are things with you, young Sir? Did you lose a couple of points off your antlers?

THE KNIGHT: Plague take you! The strongest antlers would have splintered like glass. You devil! He charged me and I felt as if a thunderbolt were driving me into the ground.

THE CAPTAIN: Thank God you got away at all.

THE KNIGHT: No thanks are called for. A couple of my ribs are in two. Where is the surgeon?

(Exeunt.)
∗

[SCENE 9]

Jaxthausen.
Götz. Selbitz.

GÖTZ: What do you say to the outlawry proclamation, Selbitz?

SELBITZ: It's Weislingen's doings.

GÖTZ: You think?

SELBITZ: I don't think, I know.

GÖTZ: From where?

SELBITZ: He was at the Imperial Diet, I tell you; he was around the Emperor.

Götz: All right, then we'll undo another of his plots.

Selbitz: Let's hope so.

Götz: We're off, and let the rabbit hunt begin.

*

[Scene 10]

Camp.

The Captain. Knights.

The Captain: We're getting nowhere this way, gentlemen. He will knock out one detachment after another for us, and everyone that doesn't get killed or captured will rather go running in God's name over to Turkey than back to camp. That way we'll get weaker every day. We must close in on him once and for all, and in earnest. I will be there myself and he shall see who it is he has to deal with.

A knight: That's satisfactory to all of us. Only, he is so familiar with the district, knows every path and trail in the mountains, that he's no more to be caught than a mouse in a granary.

The Captain: We'll get him just the same. First, on to Jaxthausen. Willy-nilly, he'll have to come up to defend his castle.

A knight: Is our whole detachment to march?

The Captain: Of course! Don't you know we're melted down by a hundred as it is?

A knight: Let's move fast then, before the whole ice-block thaws out. It's warm around here and we're like butter in the sun.

(Exeunt.)

*

[Scene 11]

Mountain and forest.

Götz. Selbitz. A detachment of soldiers.

Götz: They're coming in full force. It's high time Sickingen's horsemen made a junction with us.

SELBITZ: Let's divide up. I will go left around the hill.

GÖTZ: Good. And you, Franz, take the fifty up through the woods to the right. They'll come across the heath, and I will hold against them. Georg, you will stay with me. And when you see them attack me, don't lose any time hitting their flanks. We'll splash them. They don't think we can give them any opposition.

(Exeunt.)

∗

[SCENE 12]

The heath, with a hill on one side and a forest on the other.
The Captain. The Ban enforcement column.

THE CAPTAIN: He's stopping on the heath! That's impertinent. He'll pay for it. What! Not be afraid of the river rushing down on him?

THE KNIGHT: I wouldn't like to have you ride at the head of the column. He looks as if he'd plant the first man to hit him upside down in the ground. Ride behind.

THE CAPTAIN: I don't like to.

THE KNIGHT: I beg you. You are still the knot that holds this scourge of hazel rods together; untie it, and he will lop you off one by one like sedge grass.

THE CAPTAIN: Blow, trumpeter, and blow him away!

(Exeunt.)
(Enter Selbitz at a gallop from behind the hill.)

SELBITZ: Follow me! They're going to shout to their hands: "Be multiplied!"

(Exit.)
(Enter Lerse out of the forest.)

LERSE: To Götz's aid! He's almost surrounded. Brave Selbitz, you have already broken through. We'll strew the heath with their thistle-tops.

(He rides on.
Tumult.)

✳

[SCENE 13]

A hill with a watchtower.
Selbitz wounded. Squires.

SELBITZ: Lay me down here and go back to Götz.

FIRST SQUIRE: Let us stay, Sir! You need us.

SELBITZ: One of you climb the watchtower and see how things are going.

FIRST SQUIRE: How am I going to get up?

SECOND SQUIRE: Stand on my shoulders. Then you can reach the hole and boost yourself up through the opening.

FIRST SQUIRE *(climbs up.)*:   Oh, Sir!

SELBITZ: What do you see?

FIRST SQUIRE: Your horsemen are fleeing toward the hill.

SELBITZ: The damned scoundrels! I wish they were standing firm and I had a bullet through my head. One of you ride over and curse and damn them back!

(Exit a squire.)

Do you see Götz?

THE SQUIRE: I see his three black plumes in the midst of the turmoil.

SELBITZ: Swim, brave swimmer! *I* lie here!

THE SQUIRE: A white plume. Who is that?

SELBITZ: The Captain.

THE SQUIRE: Götz forces his way to him . . . wham! Down he goes.

SELBITZ: The Captain?

THE SQUIRE: Yes, Sir.

SELBITZ: Fine! Fine!

THE SQUIRE: Oh! I don't see Götz any longer.

SELBITZ: Then die, Selbitz!

THE SQUIRE: A terrific crush where he was standing. Georg's blue plume has disappeared too.

SELBITZ: Come down. You don't see Lerse?

THE SQUIRE: Nothing. Everything is all mixed up.

SELBITZ: No more! Come! How are Sickingen's horsemen holding up?

THE SQUIRE: Good.—There goes somebody fleeing toward the woods. Another one! A whole detachment! Götz is gone.

SELBITZ: Come down.

THE SQUIRE: I can't.—Good! Good! I see Götz! I see Georg!

SELBITZ: On horseback?

THE SQUIRE: High on their horses! We've won! We've won! They're running away!

SELBITZ: The Imperials?

THE SQUIRE: Their banner in the midst of them, and Götz after them. They're scattering. Götz overtakes the standard bearer . . . He has the banner . . . He's stopping. A handful of men around him. My friend has caught up with him . . . They're riding this way.

(Enter Götz, Georg, Lerse, and a detachment of soldiers.)

SELBITZ: Welcome, Götz! Victory! Victory!

GÖTZ *(dismounting)*: A costly one! A costly one! You're wounded, Selbitz?

SELBITZ: You are alive and victorious! I did very little. And those dogs of horsemen of mine! How did you get away?

GÖTZ: It was a hot one this time! And I have Georg here to thank for my life, and Lerse here to thank for it. I knocked

the Captain off his nag. They struck my horse down and rushed
at me. Georg cut his way through to me and jumped off; I
like a lightning flash was up on his nag, and he like a thunder-
clap was mounted again too. How did you come by that horse?

GEORG: I ran my dagger into the guts of some fellow that was
slashing at you, just as his armor was raised up. He went down,
and helped you free of a foe and myself to a horse.

GÖTZ: There we were, stuck, till Franz beat his way in to us, and
then we mowed ourselves out from the inside.

LERSE: Those dogs I was leading were supposed to mow their
way in from the outside until our scythe-blades met, but they
fled like Imperials.

GÖTZ: Friend and foe both fled. Only you, my little band, kept
the rear open. I had enough to do with the boys in front of
me. Their Captain's fall helped me shake them, and they ran
for it. I have their banner and a few prisoners.

SELBITZ: The Captain got away from you?

GÖTZ: They had rescued him in the meantime. Come on, children! Come on, Selbitz!—Make a stretcher out of boughs.—
You can't get on a horse. Come to my castle. They're scattered.
But we are few, and I don't know whether they have any troops
to send back. I'll put you up, my friends. A glass of wine will
taste good after a scrap like this.

*

[SCENE 14]

Camp.

THE CAPTAIN: I could kill you all with my own hands! What!
Run away! He didn't have a handful of men left! Run away
from one man! Nobody will believe it, except those that enjoy
laughing at us.—Ride around, you, and you, and you. Wherever
you find any of our scattered troops, bring them back or strike

them down. We've got to hone these stains off even if our swords are ruined in the process.

*

[SCENE 15]

Jaxthausen.
Götz. Lerse. Georg.

GÖTZ: We mustn't delay a single minute! Poor lads, I dare not offer you any rest. Hunt around quickly and try to scare up more horsemen. Have them all gather at Weilern. They will be safest there. If we delay, they'll move up before my castle.
(Exeunt Lerse and Georg.)
I've got to send out one on reconnoissance. Things are beginning to get hot. If they were brave fellows . . . ! But, as things stand, it's their numbers.

(Exit.)
(Enter Sickingen and Maria.)

MARIA: I beg you, dear Sickingen, do not leave my brother! His horsemen and Selbitz' and yours are all scattered; he is alone, Selbitz has been taken wounded to his castle, and I fear the worst.

SICKINGEN: Be calm. I won't leave him.

(Enter Götz.)

GÖTZ: Come to the church, the priest is waiting. In a quarter of an hour you shall be a married couple.

SICKINGEN: Let me stay here.

GÖTZ: Right now to the church with you.

SICKINGEN: Gladly.—And afterwards?

GÖTZ: Afterwards you shall go your way.

SICKINGEN: Götz!

Götz: You don't want to go to the church?
Sickingen: Come on! Come on!

*

[Scene 16]

Camp.
The Captain. The knight.

The Captain: How many are they all told?
The knight: A hundred and fifty.
The Captain: Out of four hundred! That's bad. Up now and straight to Jaxthausen before he gets his breath again and meets us on the road.

*

[Scene 17]

Jaxthausen.
Götz. Elizabeth. Maria. Sickingen.

Götz: God bless you and give you happy days, and may He keep for your children those that He takes away from you.
Elizabeth: And may He make them as you are: upright. Then let them be whatever they may.
Sickingen: I thank you. And I thank you, Maria. I have led you to the altar, and you shall lead me to happiness.
Maria: We shall make a pilgrimage together to that strange promised land.
Götz: Prosperous journey!
Maria: We didn't mean it that way, we are not going to leave you.
Götz: You must, sister.
Maria: You are very unkind, brother!
Götz: And you more tender than provident.

(Enter Georg.)

GEORG *(privately)*: I can't scare up anyone. Just one was so inclined; afterwards he changed his mind and wouldn't.

GÖTZ: Good, Georg. My luck is beginning to turn like the
weather. I suspected as much, though. *(Aloud)* Sickingen, I beg
you to leave yet this evening. Persuade Maria. She is your
wife. Make her realize that. When women cut across our enterprises our foes are safer in the open field than they would
otherwise be in their castles.

(Enter a squire.)

THE SQUIRE *(softly)*: Sir, the Imperial column is on the march
straight for here and very fast.

GÖTZ: I have stirred them up with whips. How many are they?

THE SQUIRE: About two hundred. They can't be more than two
hours from here.

GÖTZ: Still across the river?

THE SQUIRE: Yes, Sir.

GÖTZ: If I just had fifty men they wouldn't get across. You
didn't see Lerse?

THE SQUIRE: No, Sir.

GÖTZ: Have everybody stand by in readiness.—We must part, my
dear ones. Weep, my good Maria. Moments will come when
you will be glad. It is better to weep on your wedding day
than that too great joy should be the herald of future misery.
Farewell, Maria. Farewell, brother!

MARIA: I cannot leave you, sister. Dear brother, let us stay! Do
you think so little of my husband that you scorn his help in
this extremity?

GÖTZ: Yes, things have gone a long way with me. Perhaps I am
near my fall. You are beginning to live, and you must cut
yourselves off from my fate. I have ordered your horses saddled.
You must leave at once.

MARIA: Brother! Brother!

ELIZABETH *(to Sickingen)*: Do as he says. Go!

SICKINGEN: Dear Maria, let us go.

MARIA: You too? My heart will break.

GÖTZ: Then stay. In a few hours my castle will be surrounded.

MARIA: Alas! Alas!

GÖTZ: We shall defend ourselves as best we can.

MARIA: Mother of God, have mercy on us!

GÖTZ: And in the end we will either die or surrender.—You will have wept your noble husband into one fate along with me.

MARIA: You are torturing me.

GÖTZ: Stay! Stay! We will be taken prisoner together. Sickingen, you will fall into the pit with me. I was hoping you would help me out of it.

MARIA: We will go. Sister! Sister!

GÖTZ: Get her to safety, and then remember me.

SICKINGEN: I will not share her bed until I know that you are out of danger.

GÖTZ: Sister . . . dear sister! *(Kisses her.)*

SICKINGEN: Away! Away!

GÖTZ: Just one minute more . . . I will see you again. Be comforted. We shall meet again.

(Exeunt Sickingen and Maria.)

I drove her away, and now that she is going I would like to keep her here. Elizabeth, you will stay with me!

ELIZABETH: Till death!

(Exit.)

GÖTZ: Whom God loves, to him may He give a wife like that!

(Enter Georg.)

GEORG: They're near by, I saw them from the tower. The sun was rising and I saw their pikes gleaming. As I saw them I was no more frightened than a cat before an army of mice. We are playing the part of the rats.

Götz: Look after the bolts on the gate. Barricade it on the inside with beams and rocks.

(Exit Georg.)

We'll fool their patience, and their bravery they shall chew away on their own fingernails.

(A trumpeter from outside.)

Aha! Some red-coat scoundrel who is going to put the question before us whether we intend to show the white feather.

(He goes to the window.)

What's this?

(A voice is heard speaking in the distance.)

(in his beard) A noose around your neck!

(The trumpeter goes on speaking.)

Offender of Majesty!—A priest put in that provocation.

(The trumpeter concludes.)

(answering) Surrender? Unconditionally? Whom are you talking to! Am I a brigand? Tell your Captain this: Before Imperial Majesty I have, as always, all due respect. But as for him, tell him he can kiss my arse!

(He slams the window shut.)

＊

[SCENE 18]

Siege. The kitchen.
Elizabeth. Götz, entering.

Götz: You have a lot of work, my poor wife.

Elizabeth: I wish I had it for a long time to come. We can hardly hold out very long.

GÖTZ: We didn't have time to lay in provisions.

ELIZABETH: And all those people that you were always feeding.
We're already running low on wine too.

GÖTZ: If we can only hold out to a certain point, so they propose capitulation! We'll do them some fine damage. They'll
shoot all day long and wound our walls and smash our window-
panes. Lerse is a brave lad. He'll slip around with his gun, and
wherever one of them ventures too near . . . Bang! He's a
goner.

(Enter a squire.)

THE SQUIRE: Coals, my Lady.

GÖTZ: What's the matter?

THE SQUIRE: That was the last of the bullets. We're going to cast
some new ones.

GÖTZ: How are we on powder?

THE SQUIRE: So-so. We're spacing our shots nicely.

*

[SCENE 19]

The great hall.
Lerse with a bullet mold and the squire with coals.

LERSE: Set it there and see if you can find some lead in the house.
Meanwhile I'll help myself here.

(He lifts out a window and smashes the panes.)

Every advantage counts.—That's the way in this world, nobody
knows what use things can be turned to. The glazier that set
these panes certainly never thought the lead might give one
of his descendants a nasty headache. And when my father begot
me he never thought what bird under the sky or what worm
in the ground might eat me.

GEORG *(enters with an eaves-trough pipe.)*: There's lead for you.
If you hit them with just half of it, there won't one of them

get away to report to His Majesty: Lord, we made a poor showing.

LERSE *(cutting off a chunk)*: A nice piece.

GEORG: Let the rainwater look for a new path. I'm not afraid of it. A brave horseman and proper rain will get through anywhere.

LERSE *(pours.)*: Hold the ladle. *(He goes to the window.)* There's one of those Imperial boys going around with a gun. They think we're out of ammunition. He can sample this bullet hot off the griddle.

(He loads.)

GEORG *(lays the ladle up against the mold.)*: Let me see.

LERSE *(fires.)*: I got my sparrow.

GEORG: He was firing at me before . . . *(They pour.)* . . . as I was climbing out the attic window to get the eaves-trough. He hit a pigeon sitting not far from me; it dropped into the eaves-trough. I thanked him for the roast of fowl and climbed back in with double booty.

LERSE: We'll load up now and go around through the whole castle earning our dinner.

(Enter Götz.)

GÖTZ: Wait, Lerse, I've got something to tell you. I won't keep you, Georg, from your hunting.

(Exit Georg.)

They're offering me a truce.

LERSE: I'll go out to them and hear what it amounts to.

GÖTZ: It will be that I am supposed to enter knightly imprisonment on certain terms.

LERSE: That won't do. How would it be if they granted us free retreat, as long as you are not expecting relief from Sickingen? We would bury all the money and silver where they would never find it with a divining rod, then turn the castle over to them and get away in good style.

Götz: They won't let us.

Lerse: Let's give it a try. We'll call for a safe-conduct and I'll go
out and see.

(Exeunt.)

*

[Scene 20]

The great hall.
Götz, Elizabeth, Georg, squires at table.

Götz: This is the way danger brings us together. Enjoy it, my
friends! Don't forget the drinking. The bottle is empty. Another one, dear wife.

(Elizabeth shrugs her shoulders.)

No more left?

Elizabeth *(softly)*: *One* more. I put it aside for you.

Götz: Oh no, my dear. Bring it out. They need fortifying. I
don't. It's my affair, you know.

Elizabeth: Bring it in from the cupboard out there.

Götz: It's the last one. And I feel as though we had no cause to
be sparing. It's a long time since I have been so satisfied.

(He pours.)

Long live the Emperor!

All: Long may he live!

Götz: That shall be our second-last word when we are dying! I
love him, for we have one and the same fate. And I am more
fortunate than he. He has to catch mice for the estates of the
empire while the rats are gnawing away at his possessions. I
know he often wishes himself dead rather than be any longer
the soul of such a crippled body.

(He pours.)

There's just enough to go around once more. And when our

blood starts on its decline the way the wine in this bottle runs first feebly and then drop by drop . . . *(He lets the last drops fall into his glass.)* . . . what shall our last word be?

GEORG: Long live Freedom!

GÖTZ: Long live Freedom!

ALL: Long live Freedom!

GÖTZ: And if *she* survives us we can die in peace. For in our minds we see our grandchildren happy and our grandchildren's Emperor happy. If the servers of the princes served as nobly and freely as you serve me, if the princes served the Emperor as I would like to serve him . . .

GEORG: Then things couldn't help but be very different.

GÖTZ: Not so much as it might seem. Haven't I known excellent men among the princes, and can it be the stock has died out? Good men, who were happy in themselves and in their subjects, who could stand to have a free and noble neighbor beside them and neither fear him nor envy him, whose hearts rejoiced when they saw many of their equals around their tables, and who didn't first have to transform knights into court-toadies before they could live with them.

GEORG: Have you known such lords?

GÖTZ: Indeed I have! As long as I live I'll never forget how the Landgrave of Hanau gave a hunting party, and the princes and lords who were there ate under the open sky, and the countryfolk all hurried over to see them. It was no masquerade he had arranged in his own honor. But the full, round heads of the lads and lasses, all those red cheeks, and the prosperous men and stately oldsters, happy faces every one of them, and how they shared in the splendor of their master, who was enjoying himself on God's ground in their midst.

GEORG: That was a lord as perfect as you.

GÖTZ: Oughtn't we to hope that more such princes can some day rule, that reverence for the Emperor, peace and friendship

of neighbors, and love of subjects will be the most precious
heritage that can pass on to grandsons and great-grandsons?
Every man would keep what belonged to him and increase it
within itself, instead of the way they now think they are not
prospering if they are not destroying others.

GEORG: Would we have any missions to ride after that?

GÖTZ: Please God there wouldn't be any uneasy heads in all of
Germany! We would still find enough to do. We would clear
the wolves out of the mountains, we would fetch a roast out of
the forest for our peacefully tilling neighbor and in return
would eat soup with him. If that would not be enough, we
would emplace ourselves together with our brothers like cheru-
bim with flaming swords at the boundaries of the empire, against
those wolves the Turks, against those foxes the French, and at
the same time protect our dear Emperor's very exposed provinces and the tranquillity of the empire. What a life that
would be, Georg, when a man could risk his skin for the general welfare!

(Georg leaps up.)

Where are you going?

GEORG: Oh, I forgot we were hemmed in . . . and the Emperor
has hemmed us in . . . and to get away with our whole skins,
we will risk our skins.

GÖTZ: Be of good courage.

(Enter Lerse.)

LERSE: Freedom! Freedom! Those are bad men, indecisive, cautious asses. You are to withdraw with weapons, horses, and
armor. The provisions you will have to leave behind.

GÖTZ: They won't bring on a toothache chewing on them.

LERSE *(privately)*: Have you hidden the silver?

GÖTZ: No! Wife, go with Franz. He has something to say to you.

(Exeunt.)

*

[SCENE 21]

The castle courtyard.
Georg in the stable, singing.

GEORG: There was a bird caught by a boy
                        Hm! Hm!
              Who on the cage did gloat for joy.
                        Hm! Hm!
                        So! So!
                        Hm! Hm!
              So silly was his glee,
                        Hm! Hm!
              He grabbed so clumsily,
                        Hm! Hm!
                        So! So!
                        Hm! Hm!
              Out flew the tom-tit to a house
                        Hm! Hm!
              And laughed his fill at foolish louts.
                        Hm! Hm!
                        So! So!
                        Hm! Hm!

GÖTZ: How are things going?

GEORG *(leads his horse out.)*: They're saddled.

GÖTZ: You're fast.

GEORG: As the bird out of the cage.
                        (Enter all the besieged persons.)

GÖTZ: You have your guns? Oh, no! Go up and get the best ones
      out of the gun-racks. It won't cost any more. We'll ride ahead.

GEORG: Hm! Hm!
                        So! So!
                        Hm! Hm!
                        (Exeunt.)
                           *

[SCENE 22]

The great hall.
Two squires at the gun-rack.

FIRST SQUIRE: I'll take this one.

SECOND SQUIRE: I this one. There's a better one still.

FIRST SQUIRE: No, no! Hurry up and come on!

SECOND SQUIRE: Listen!

FIRST SQUIRE *(runs to the window.)*: Help, merciful God! They're murdering our master. He's down off his horse! Down goes Georg!

SECOND SQUIRE: Where shall we flee? Along the wall, down the walnut tree, and into the field.

(Exit.)

FIRST SQUIRE: Franz is still holding them off. I'll go help him. If they die, I don't care to live.

(Exit.)

ACT IV

[SCENE 1]

An inn at Heilbronn.
Götz.

GÖTZ: I feel like the evil spirit that the Capuchin conjured into a sack.[1] I wear myself out and accomplish nothing. The perjurors!

(Enter Elizabeth.)

What news, Elizabeth, of my beloved loyal men?

ELIZABETH: Nothing definite. Some were cut down, some are in prison. No one could or would name them more specifically for me.

GÖTZ: Is this the reward of loyalty, of childlike obedience?—Well may you fare and long may you live on earth!

ELIZABETH: Dear husband, do not chide our heavenly Father. They have their reward, it was born into them, a free and noble heart. Let them be captive: they are free! Heed the deputation of Councilors. Their great golden chains suit their countenances. . . .

GÖTZ: Like pearls on swine.—I'd like to see Georg and Franz shut up!

ELIZABETH: It would be a sight to make the angels weep.

GÖTZ: I wouldn't weep. I would clench my teeth and chew the cud of my fury. In chains, those apples of my eye! You dear lads, if you hadn't loved me!—I could not get my fill of gazing at them.—Not to keep their word given in the Emperor's name!

---

[1]Troublesome ghosts were trapped by monks in bags or boxes and deported by hand to remote places.

ELIZABETH: Dismiss these thoughts. Consider that you are about to appear before the Councilors. You are in no state of mind to meet them properly, and I fear the worst.

GÖTZ: What do they mean to charge me with?

ELIZABETH: The Court Summoner!

GÖTZ: Justice' jackass! Lugs their sacks to mill and their dung out to the field. What is it?

(Enter the Court Summoner.)

THE COURT SUMMONER: The Lords Commissioner are assembled at the City Hall and have sent for you.

GÖTZ: I'm coming.

THE COURT SUMMONER: I will accompany you.

GÖTZ: A big honor.

ELIZABETH: Restrain yourself.

GÖTZ: Have no fear.

(Exeunt.)

*

[SCENE 2]

The City Hall.
Imperial Councilors. The Captain. Aldermen of Heilbronn.

AN ALDERMAN: At your command we have assembled the strongest and bravest citizens. They are waiting close at hand for your signal to seize Berlichingen.

THE FIRST COUNCILOR: We shall not fail to praise, and with great pleasure, to His Imperial Majesty your readiness to comply with his supreme command.—They are artisans?

THE ALDERMAN: Smiths, wine draymen, carpenters, men with practised fists and well protected *(pointing to his chest)* here.

THE COUNCILOR: Good.

(Enter the Court Summoner.)

THE COURT SUMMONER: Götz von Berlichingen is waiting outside the door.

THE COUNCILOR: Show him in.

(Enter Götz.)

GÖTZ: God's greeting to you, gentlemen! What do you want with me?

THE COUNCILOR: First, that you reflect where you are and before whom!

GÖTZ: By my oath, I do not fail to recognize you, Sirs.

THE COUNCILOR: You do your duty.

GÖTZ: With all my heart.

THE COUNCILOR: Be seated.

GÖTZ: Down there? I can stand. That stool reeks of poor sinners,[1] just like the whole room.

THE COUNCILOR: Stand, then.

GÖTZ: To the point, if you will be so kind.

THE COUNCILOR: We shall proceed in proper order.

GÖTZ: That suits me. I wish it had always been the case.

THE COUNCILOR: You know how you passed into our hands unconditionally.

GÖTZ: What will you give me if I forget it?

THE COUNCILOR: If I could give you discretion I would help your cause.

GÖTZ: Help! If you only could! But that takes more doing than to harm it.

THE COURT CLERK: Shall I enter all this in the record?

THE COUNCILOR: Whatever has to do with the proceedings.

GÖTZ: As far as I'm concerned, you can have it printed.

THE COUNCILOR: You were in the power of the Emperor, whose paternal clemency took the place of Majesty's justice and by

---

[1]The poor sinners' stool or bench was a seat of public humiliation, usually at church, for persons convicted of certain wrongdoings.

way of abode for you designated, instead of a prison, Heilbronn, one of his beloved cities. You promised upon your oath
to appear, as beseems a knight, and to await further action
with humility.

GÖTZ: Quite so, and I am here and I am waiting.

THE COUNCILOR: And we are here to announce to you His Imperial Majesty's clemency and graciousness. He pardons your
transgressions, pronounces you free of the ban and of all well
deserved punishment, which pronouncements you will acknowledge with submissive gratitude, and in return you will repeat
the oath which shall herewith be read to you.

GÖTZ: I am His Imperial Majesty's loyal servant as always. One
word yet before you proceed. My men, where are they? What
is to be done with them?

THE COUNCILOR: That does not concern you.

GÖTZ: Then may the Emperor turn his face away from you when
you are in distress! They were my comrades and still are.
Where have you taken them?

THE COUNCILOR: We are not obliged to give you any account of
that.

GÖTZ: Ah! I forgot that you are not even bound to what you
promise, not to mention. . . .

THE COUNCILOR: Our commission is to present you with the oath.
Submit to the Emperor and you will find a way to plead for
your comrades' life and liberty.

GÖTZ: Your memorandum!

THE COUNCILOR: Clerk, read it out.

THE COURT CLERK: "I, Götz von Berlichingen, by means of this
document, publicly acknowledge that I have recently rebelled
in mutinous wise against Emperor and empire. . . ."

GÖTZ: That is not true! I am no rebel, I have committed no
crime against His Imperial Majesty, and the empire is no concern of mine.

THE COUNCILOR: Restrain yourself and listen further.

GÖTZ: I will listen to nothing further. Let any man step forth
and testify! Have I taken a single step against the Emperor,
against the house of Austria? Have I not demonstrated at all
times by all my acts that I realized better than anyone what
obligations Germany owes its ruler, especially what lesser persons, the knights and the freemen, owe their Emperor? I would
be a scoundrel if I allowed myself to be persuaded to sign that.

THE COUNCILOR: And yet we have express orders to persuade you
amicably, or, in event of failure, to put you in prison.

GÖTZ: In prison? Me?

THE COUNCILOR: And there you can wait your fate from the
hands of the law if you will not accept it from the hands of
clemency.

GÖTZ: In prison! You are misusing Imperial power. In prison!
That is not his command. What! First—the traitors—to set a
trap for me and to bait it with their oath, their knightly word,
then to promise me knightly imprisonment and break their
promise again!

THE COUNCILOR: We are under no obligation of good faith with
a brigand.

GÖTZ: If you were not wearing the Emperor's likeness which I
venerate in its meanest counterfeit, you would eat that word
"brigand" and choke on it! I am engaged in an honorable
feud. You could thank God and parade yourself large before
the world if you had ever in your life done a deed as noble as
that for which I now sit here captive.

> *(The councilor gestures to the alderman;*
> *the latter rings a bell.)*

Not for sorry gain, and not to grab territory and subjects away
from defenseless little people, did I ride out to war, but to
liberate my page and to protect my own skin! Do you see anything wrong in that? Neither Emperor nor empire would have

noticed our distress amid their pillows. I still have, thank God, *one* hand left and I did well to use it.

> *(Enter citizens with sticks in their hands*
> *and weapons at their sides.)*

What is the meaning of this?

THE COUNCILOR: You will not listen.—Seize him!

GÖTZ: Is that your intention? Whoever isn't a Hungarian ox better not come too close to me! He'll get such a box on the ears from this right iron hand of mine as will cure him once and for all of headache, toothache, and all the other aches of this world.

(They move toward him. He knocks one of them down and grabs
the weapon from the side of a second. They fall back.)

Come on! It would be a pleasure to get to know the bravest among you.

THE COUNCILOR: Surrender!

GÖTZ *(sword in hand)*: Do you realize that all I have to do now is to knock my way through this bunch of rabbit-chasers and gain the open field? But I am going to teach you how a man keeps his word. Promise me knightly imprisonment and I'll turn over my sword and be your prisoner as before.

THE COUNCILOR: You propose to bargain, sword in hand, with the Emperor?

GÖTZ: God forbid! Only with you and your noble company.— You can go home, good people. For the time you have lost you will get nothing, and there is nothing to be gotten here except lumps on your heads.

THE COUNCILOR: Seize him! Doesn't your love for your Emperor give you any more courage than this?

GÖTZ: Not any more than the Emperor gives them plasters to heal the wounds that their courage might bring them.

> *(Enter the Court summoner.)*

THE COURT SUMMONER: The tower watchman has just shouted a

column of more than two hundred men is moving on the city. They appeared unexpectedly from behind the vineyard and are threatening our walls.

THE COUNCILOR: Alas for us! What is this?

(Enter the watchman.)

THE WATCHMAN: Franz von Sickingen is at the gate and sends you word that he has heard how improperly the solemn promise to his brother-in-law was broken and how the men of Heilbronn have lent their full support. He demands an accounting, or else he will set fire to the city at all four corners within the hour and open it up to pillage.

GÖTZ: Good for my brother-in-law!

THE COUNCILOR: Withdraw, Götz.—What is to be done?

THE ALDERMAN: Have mercy on us and on our citizenry. Sickingen is ruthless in his anger, and he is the man to go through with it.

THE COUNCILOR: Are we to surrender our own and the Emperor's privileges?

THE CAPTAIN: If we only had the men to assert them. But this way we could be killed and the cause would only be that much worse off. We will gain by giving way.

THE ALDERMAN: We'll get Götz to put in a word for us. I feel as though I already saw the city in flames.

THE COUNCILOR: Show Götz in.

GÖTZ: What now?

THE COUNCILOR: You would do well to talk your brother-in-law out of his mutinous undertaking. Instead of rescuing you from destruction he will only plunge you deeper into it by putting himself in your position.

GÖTZ *(sees Elizabeth by the door and says privately to her)*: Go down and tell him to force his way in instantly and come here, only to do no harm to the city. If these rascals oppose him here,

he is to use force. I don't care if I get killed just so long as they
all get cut down with me.

*

[Scene 3]

A large room in the city hall.
Sickingen. Götz. *The entire city hall is occupied by Sickingen's
troops.*

Götz: That was help from Heaven. How did you happen to
come so unexpectedly and just when wanted, brother-in-law?

Sickingen: No magic to it. I had sent out two or three scouts to
hear how things were going with you. At the news of their
perjury I started out. And now we have them.

Götz: I'm not asking for anything but knightly imprisonment.

Sickingen: You are too honorable. Not even to avail yourself of
the advantage that the upright man has over perjurors! They
are in the wrong, and we're not going to put any pillows under
them. They have shamefully misused the Emperor's commands.
And if I know His Majesty, you can certainly insist on more.
This is too little.

Götz: I have always been satisfied with little.

Sickingen: And have always gotten the short end. My opinion is
that they should let your squires out of prison and let you and
them together withdraw to your castle on your oath. You can
promise not to go beyond your boundaries, and you will be
better off than here.

Götz: They will say my possessions are forfeit to the Emperor.

Sickingen: Then we will say you mean to live there and pay rent
until the Emperor confers them on you again in fief. Let them
squirm like eels in a basket, but they won't give us the slip.
They will talk about Imperial Majesty and about their commission. That will make no difference to us. I know the Em-

peror too, and count for something with him. He has always
wanted to have you in his army. You won't be at your castle
very long before you get called up.

GÖTZ: God make it soon, before I unlearn how to fight.

SICKINGEN: Courage is not unlearned any more than it is learned.
Don't worry about anything. Once your affairs are in order I
will go to court—for my enterprise is beginning to ripen. Favorable signs tell me: "Start!" All I have to do yet is to sound out
the Emperor's sentiments. Trier and the Palatine will be expecting the sky to collapse sooner than for me to descend upon
them. And I mean to descend like a hailstorm! And if we can
shape our destiny you will presently be the brother-in-law of
an Electoral Prince. I was counting on your fist in this enterprise.

GÖTZ *(looks at his hand.)*: O this was foreshadowed by the dream
I had when I promised Maria to Weislingen the following day.
He promised me loyalty and held so tight onto my right hand
that it came out of the vambrace as though it had been broken
off. Ah! I am more defenseless at this minute than I was when
it was shot off. Weislingen! Weislingen!

SICKINGEN: Forget the traitor. We will wipe out his schemes, undermine his esteem, and conscience and shame shall eat him
to death. I see, in my mind I see my enemies and your enemies
overthrown. Götz, just a half a year more!

GÖTZ: Your soul soars aloft. I don't know, for some time now
no joyous prospects seem to want to open in mine.—I've been in
more trouble before this, I've been a prisoner once before, and
I have never felt the way I feel now.

SICKINGEN: Luck brings courage. Come on in to the curliwigs.
They've had their say long enough; let us assume the burden
for a change.

(Exeunt.)

*

[SCENE 4]

Adelheid's castle.
Adelheid. Weislingen.

ADELHEID: That is odious!

WEISLINGEN: I clenched my teeth. Such a wonderful scheme, so neatly executed, and then to let him go to his castle after all! That damned Sickingen!

ADELHEID: They shouldn't have done it.

WEISLINGEN: They were caught. What could they do? Sickingen threatened them with fire and sword, that overbearing, hottempered man! I hate him. His prestige swells like a river that swallowed up a couple of brooks—the others will follow of themselves.

ADELHEID: Didn't they have an Emperor?

WEISLINGEN: My dear wife, he is only the shadow of one. He is getting old and peevish. When he heard what had happened and the other government councilors were getting excited, he said: "Leave them alone. I can afford to allow old Götz that little spot, and if he is quiet there, what do you have to complain about in him?" We spoke of the welfare of the state. "O!" said he. "If I only had advisors all along who would have directed my uneasy mind more toward the happiness of individual human beings!"

ADELHEID: He is losing the spirit of a ruler.

WEISLINGEN: We went after Sickingen.—"He is my loyal servant." said he, "and if he did not do it at my command, he nevertheless performed my will better than my authorized agents, and I can call it good before or after the fact."

ADELHEID: It's enough to make one tear one's hair.

WEISLINGEN: All the same, I have not yet given up all hope. He has been left in his castle on his knightly word to be quiet there. That is impossible for him. We will soon have grounds against him.

ADELHEID: And all the sooner because we can hope the Emperor
will soon be leaving this world, and Charles, his admirable
successor, shows promise of more majestic views.

WEISLINGEN: Charles? He has not yet been either elected or
crowned.[1]

ADELHEID: Who doesn't wish and hope for it?

WEISLINGEN: You have a high opinion of his qualities. One would
almost think you saw them with other eyes.

ADELHEID: You offend me, Weislingen. Do you know me to be
such?

WEISLINGEN: I said nothing to offend you. But I cannot remain
silent in the face of it. Charles's unusual attention toward you
makes me uneasy.

ADELHEID: And my conduct?

WEISLINGEN: You are a woman. You women hate no one who
pays court to you.

ADELHEID: While men. . . . ?

WEISLINGEN: It gnaws at my heart, this fearful thought. Adelheid!

ADELHEID: Can I cure your folly?

WEISLINGEN: If you wanted to! You could withdraw from court.

ADELHEID: Name ways and means. Aren't you at court? Am I
supposed to leave you and my friends in order to entertain
myself with owls at my castle? No, Weislingen, no good would
come of that. Be reassured. You know how I love you.

WEISLINGEN: The sacred anchor in this storm, as long as the
rope doesn't break.

(Exit.)

ADELHEID: So that's the way you're starting in! That's all I needed!
The enterprises of my heart are too great for you to stand in
their way. Charles! Great and excellent man, and Emperor be-

---

[1]Charles V, elected Holy Roman Emperor 1519, crowned 1520.

sides! And should he be the only one among men not to be
flattered by the possession of my favor? Weislingen, don't dream
of hindering me! Or else into the ground you go, for my path
goes over you.

(Enter Franz with a letter.)

FRANZ: Here, my Lady.

ADELHEID: Did Charles himself give it to you?

FRANZ: Yes.

ADELHEID: What is the matter? You look so woebegone.

FRANZ: It is your will that I am to languish away and die. In the
years of hope you make me despair.

ADELHEID: [*aside*]: I am sorry for him. And how little it costs
me to make him happy!—Be of good spirits, lad. I feel your
love and loyalty and I shall never be ungrateful.

FRANZ *(choked up)*: If you were capable of that I would surely
perish. My God, I haven't a drop of blood in me that isn't
yours, nor a thought except to love you and to do what pleases
you.

ADELHEID: Dear boy!

FRANZ: You're humoring me. *(Bursting into tears)* If this devotion deserves nothing more than to see others preferred to me,
to see all your thoughts directed toward this Charles. . . . .

ADELHEID: You don't know what you're asking, still less what
you're saying.

FRANZ *(stamping his foot in vexation and anger)*: I don't want
any more of it. I won't play the go-between any longer.

ADELHEID: Franz! You are forgetting yourself.

FRANZ: To sacrifice myself! My dear master!

ADELHEID: Leave my sight.

FRANZ: My Lady!

ADELHEID: Go, reveal my secret to your dear master. I was a fool
to take you for something you aren't.

FRANZ: Dear, gracious Lady, you know I love you.

ADELHEID: And you used to be my friend, so close to my heart. Go, betray me.

FRANZ: I'd sooner tear my heart out of my body! Forgive me, my Lady. My heart is too full, my senses cannot endure it.

ADELHEID: Dear, warm-hearted youth!

(She takes his hands, draws him to her, and their kisses meet.

He falls upon her neck weeping.)

Leave me!

FRANZ *(choked with tears at her neck)* : My God! My God!

ADELHEID: Leave me. The walls are traitors. Leave me! *(She disengages herself.)* Do not waver in your love and loyalty, and the most beautiful reward will be yours.

(Exit.)

FRANZ: The most beautiful reward! Just let me live till then! I would murder my father if he contested this place with me!

*

[SCENE 5]

Jaxthausen.

Götz at a table. Elizabeth with her work beside him. A lamp and writing materials are on the table.

GÖTZ: I just can't get the taste for idleness and my restriction becomes more oppressive every day. I wish I could sleep, or just be able to pretend that quiet is something pleasant.

ELIZABETH: Then go on writing your biography that you have started. Put into the hands of your friends a testimonial to shame your enemies. Provide a noble posterity with the joy of not misunderstanding you.

GÖTZ: Oh! Writing is busy idleness, I find it sour. While I am writing about what I have done, I am annoyed at the loss of the time in which I could be doing something.

ELIZABETH (*takes the written pages.*) : Don't be foolish. You are up to your first imprisonment at Heilbronn.

GÖTZ: That was always an unlucky place for me.

ELIZABETH (*reads*) : "In that place there were several members of the League who told me I had been foolish to confront my worst enemies when I could have guessed they would not deal forbearingly with me. Then I answered: . . ."— Well, what did you answer? Go on and write it.

GÖTZ: I said: "If I risk my skin for others' property and money, shan't I risk it for my word?"

ELIZABETH: You have that reputation.

GÖTZ: And they're not going to take it away from me! They've taken everything else, property, liberty, . . .

ELIZABETH: That was at the time when I encountered the lords of Miltenberg and Singlingen at the inn and they didn't know me. Then I had a pleasure as if I had borne a son. They were praising you among themselves and saying: "He is the model of a knight, brave and noble in his liberty and calm and loyal in misfortune."

GÖTZ: Let them show me one man to whom I have broken my word! And God knows that I have sweated harder to serve my neighbor than myself and that I have worked for the name of a brave and loyal knight and not to gain lofty riches and rank. And, thanks be to God, what I strove for has been granted me.

(*Enter Lerse and Georg with game.*)

Greetings to you, gallant huntsmen!

GEORG: From gallant horsemen that is what we have turned into. Boots are easily converted into slippers.

LERSE: Hunting is still something, and a kind of warfare.

GEORG: If only we didn't always have to be having something to do with Imperials around here! You remember, Sir, how you prophesied that if the world turned upside down we would become hunters? Here we are, without that.

GÖTZ: It amounts to the same thing, we are moved out of our sphere.

GEORG: These are critical times. For a week now there's been a fearful comet visible, and all Germany is in terror that it may mean the death of the Emperor, who is very ill.

GÖTZ: Very ill! Our road is coming to an end.

LERSE: And here in the vicinity there are still more frightful changes. The peasants have started a horrible rebellion.[1]

GÖTZ: Where?

LERSE: In the heart of Swabia. They're scorching the land and burning and murdering. I'm afraid they'll lay the entire province waste.

GEORG: There's a terrible war. Some hundred villages are already in revolt, and more every day. Recently a storm wind uprooted whole forests, and shortly after that, in the district where the rebellion began, two fiery swords were seen crosswise in the air.

GÖTZ: Then some of my good knights and friends must surely be suffering innocently along with others.

GEORG: A shame we are not allowed to ride out to war!

---

[1]Emperor Maximilian died January 12, 1519. The Peasants War occurred in 1525.

ACT V

[Scene 1]

The Peasants War. Tumult and pillaging in a village.
Women and old men with children and packs, in flight.

An old man: Get along, get along, so we escape from these murdering curs!

A woman: Merciful God! How blood-red the sky is! The setting
sun is blood-red!

A mother: That means a fire.

The woman: My husband! My husband!

The old man: Get along! Get along! Into the woods!

(They move on.)

Link: Whoever resists, mow him down! The town is ours. See
that none of the harvest is destroyed and none of it gets left
here. Plunder everything and fast! We're going to set fire
right away.

Metzler *(running down the hill)*: How're things going with
you, Link?[1]

Link: Topsy-turvily, as you see. You're here for the clean-out.
Where from?

Metzler: From Weinsberg. *There* was a party!

Link: How so?

Metzler: We mowed them down so it was a joy to see.

Link: Who all?

Metzler: Dietrich von Weiler led the dance.[2] The money! There

---

[1]Jörg Metzler, identical with the character in Act I, Scene 1, was an
actual historical personage, as was "Link," nickname of Hannes Bermetter.

[2]The last dance was called a "clean-out" (*Kehraus*).

195

we were in full pack howling like mad all around, and he was up there on the church tower wanting to deal with us nice-like. Bang! Somebody shot him through the head. Up we streaked like lightning, and out through the window came the fellow.

LINK: Ah!

METZLER *(to the peasants)*: Shall I put legs on you, you curs? The way they dawdle and hang back, the donkeys!

LINK: Set fire! Let's roast 'em inside! Come on! Go to it, you rascals!

METZLER: Then we led out Helfenstein, and Eltershofen, around thirteen of them nobles, eighty all told. Led them out on the plain toward Heilbronn. And then there was a jubilating and a tumult-making from our lads as that long line of poor wealthy sinners came along, gawking at each other, gawking at the ground and the sky! Before they knew it they were surrounded and mowed down with pikes, all of them.

LINK: And I had to miss that!

METZLER: Never had so much fun in all my born days.

LINK *(to a peasant)*: Get a move on! Out with you!

THE PEASANT: Everything is empty.

LINK: Then set fire at every corner.

METZLER: It'll make a cute little fire. D'you see how those fellows tumbled all over each other and squeaked like frogs! My heart ran over like a glass of brandy. There was a Rixinger there. When that fellow used to ride to the hunt with his plume on his hat and his nostrils wide, the way he would drive us on ahead of him with the dogs and like the dogs. I hadn't seen him since then, but I caught his monkey-face right away. Bash! and the pike was between his ribs, and there he lay and stretched out all fours across his companions. Those fellows went twitching down on top of each other like rabbits when the dogs run them down.

LINK: It's smoking nice already.

METZLER: It's burning over in back there. Let's amble down with the booty to the main force.

LINK: Where's it camped?

METZLER: This side of Heilbronn. They're hard up for a leader that all the people would have respect for; for *we*'re only their own sort, after all. They feel it and they're getting hard to handle.

LINK: Who're they thinking of?

METZLER: Max Stumpf or Götz von Berlichingen.

LINK: That'd be good. It'd give the thing a polish if Götz took it on; he's always passed for an upright knight. Come on! Come on! We're heading for Heilbronn. Pass the word along!

METZLER: The fire'll light our way for a good stretch. Have you seen the big comet?

LINK: Yes. That's a hideous, dreadful sign! If we march all night we'll see it all right. It rises around one.

METZLER: And stays only five quarters of an hour. It looks like a bended arm with a sword, kind of blood-yellow.

LINK: Have you seen the three stars at the tip and sides of the sword?

METZLER: And that broad cloud-colored tail with thousands and thousands of streamers like pikes, and in between like little swords.

LINK: I shuddered to look at it. The way it was all so pale red, and all those fiery bright flames around, and in between those cruel faces with shaggy heads and beards!

METZLER: Did you see them too? And the way it all keeps flashing higgeldy-piggeldy, as if it were lying in a gory sea and fermenting inside, till it makes your senses swim?

LINK: Come on! Come on!

(Exeunt.)

*

[Scene 2]

A field. In the distance two villages and a cloister
are seen burning.
Kohl. Wild. Max Stumpf. Bands of soldiery.

MAX STUMPF: You can't want me to be your leader. It wouldn't
be any good for you or for me. I'm a Palatine subject, so how
should I lead men against my master? You would always think
I didn't have my heart in it.

KOHL: We knew you'd find an excuse.

(Enter Götz, Lerse, and Georg.)

GÖTZ: What do you want of me?

KOHL: You're going to be our leader.

GÖTZ: Am I supposed to break my knightly word to the Emperor
and leave my district?

WILD: That's no excuse.

GÖTZ: Even if I were completely free, and you meant to go on
acting the way you did at Weinsberg with the nobles and gentry
and to keep carrying on this way, with the country all around
burning and bleeding, and I am supposed to help you in your
shameful, crazy doings—you'll have to kill me first like a mad
dog before I would be your head!

KOHL: If that hadn't happened, maybe it never would happen.

STUMPF: That was just the trouble, they didn't have a leader they
respected, one that could put a stop to their madness. Assume
this command, I beg you, Götz! The princes will be grateful
to you, all Germany will. It will be for the best interests of
everybody. Human beings and provinces will be spared.

GÖTZ: Why don't you take it over?

STUMPF: I've said I'd have no part of it.

KOHL: We don't have time for dillydallying and long pointless
speeches. Short and sweet: Götz, be our leader or else look out

for your castle and your skin. Two hours' time to think it over. Put a guard on him.

Götz: What's the good of that? I've got my mind made up as much now as later. Why did you start out on this expedition? To get back your rights and liberties? Why are you raging so and laying the land waste? If you are willing to cut out all these misdoings and act like proper people that know what they want, I'm willing to help you get your demands and be your leader for one week.

Wild: What happened, happened in the first flush, and it doesn't need you to hinder us in the future.

Kohl: You have to agree to it for a quarter of a year at least.

Stumpf: Make it four weeks. Then you will both be satisfied.

Götz: All right.

Kohl: Your hand!

Götz: And swear to me to send out this contract you have made with me in writing to all bands, and to live up to it strictly under penalty.

Wild: All right! We'll do that!

Götz: So I contract myself to you for four weeks.

Stumpf: Good luck! Whatever you do, spare our gracious master, the Count Palatine.

Kohl (softly): Watch him. See that no one talks to him outside your presence.

Götz: Lerse! Go to my wife. Stand by her. She will have news of me soon.

> (Exeunt Götz, Stumpf, Georg, Lerse,
> and several peasants.)
> (Enter Metzler and Link.)

Metzler: What's this we hear about a contract? Why a contract?

Link: It's a disgrace, entering into a contract like that.

Kohl: We know what we're doing as well as you do, and we're free agents.

WILD: This raging around and burning and murdering had to stop some time, tomorrow if not today. This way we've got ourselves a brave leader besides.

METZLER: What's this about stopping! You traitor! What are we here for? To take revenge on our enemies and help ourselves up!—Some princely lackey put this into your head.

KOHL: Come on, Wild, he's like an ox.

(Exeunt.)

METZLER: Go on! There won't a band stick with you. The rascals! Link, let's stir up the others to go and set fire to Miltenberg over yonder, and if there's any to-do on account of the contract, we'll knock all the contractors' heads off.

LINK: We've still got the bulk of the band on our side.

*

[SCENE 3]

A hill and a valley. A mill at the valley's bottom.
A troop of horsemen. Weislingen comes out of the mill
with Franz and a messenger.

WEISLINGEN: My horse!—You told the other gentlemen too?

THE MESSENGER: At least seven companies will join you in the forest behind Miltenberg. The peasants are moving around down there. Messengers have been sent everywhere, the whole League will soon be gathered. It can't fail. They say there's dissension among them.

WEISLINGEN: All the better.—Franz!

FRANZ: Sir?

WEISLINGEN: Carry out the instructions exactly. I lay the charge to your soul. Give her the letter. She is to leave the court and go to my castle. At once! You are to watch her ride away and then report to me.

FRANZ: It shall be done as you command.

WEISLINGEN: Tell her she *has to* want to!

(to the messenger)

Lead us by the shortest and best road.

THE MESSENGER: We have to go around. All the streams are in flood from the terrible rains.

*

[SCENE 4]

Jaxthausen.
Elizabeth. Lerse.

LERSE: Take comfort, my Lady!

ELIZABETH: Oh, Lerse, he had tears in his eyes as he took farewell of me. It is cruel, cruel!

LERSE: He will come back.

ELIZABETH: That isn't it. When he used to ride out to seek honorable victory there was no pain around my heart. I used to look forward to his return, which I am now uneasy about.

LERSE: Such a noble man. . . .

ELIZABETH: Do not call him that, it starts my sorrows afresh. The scoundrels! They threatened to murder him and set fire to his castle.—When he does come back—I will see him grim, grim. His enemies will fix up lying articles of accusation, and he will not be able to say "No!"

LERSE: He can and will.

ELIZABETH: He has left his assigned district. Say "No" to that!

LERSE: No! He was forced to it. Where are the grounds for condemning him?

ELIZABETH: Malice doesn't look for grounds, only excuses. He has joined up with rebels, evil-doers, murderers, he has marched at their head. Say "No" to that!

LERSE: Stop tormenting yourself and me. Didn't they solemnly promise him not to perpetrate any more actions like the ones at Weinsberg? Didn't I hear them myself saying half in remorse: "If it hadn't happened, perhaps it never would happen?" Wouldn't the princes and lords have to be grateful to him if he voluntarily became the leader of an unruly mob in order to put a stop to their madness and spare so many people and pieces of property?

ELIZABETH: You are a winning advocate.—If they took him prisoner and treated him as a rebel and misused his grey head. . . . Lerse, I would lose my mind.

LERSE: Grant her body sleep, dear Father of mankind, if Thou wilt not grant comfort to her soul!

ELIZABETH: Georg promised to bring word. But he won't be allowed either to do as he wishes. They are worse than prisoners. I know they are guarding them like enemies. Good Georg! He would not leave his master.

LERSE: My heart bled when he sent me away. If *you* had not needed my help, not all the perils of a shameful death could have parted me from him.

ELIZABETH: I don't know where Sickingen is. If I could only send Maria a messenger!

LERSE: Just write, and I will see to it.

(Exeunt.)

＊

[SCENE 5]

Near a village.
Götz. Georg.

GÖTZ: Quick, to horse, Georg! I see Miltenberg burning. So that's the way they keep a contract! Ride over and let them know my mind. The murderous arsonists! I resign from them. Let them make some gypsy their leader, not me. Quick, Georg!

(Exit Georg.)

I wish I were a thousand miles away in the deepest dungeon there is in Turkey! If I could only get away from them with honor! I drum it into them every day, I tell them the bitterest truths, so they will get tired of me and let me go.

(Enter a stranger.)

THE STRANGER: God's greeting to you, very noble Sir!

GÖTZ: God reward you! What do you bring? Your name?

THE STRANGER: That is not to the point. I come to tell you your head is in danger. The leaders are tired of taking such harsh words from you and they have decided to put you out of the way. Keep your temper or else look to your escape, and God be your guide!

(Exit.)

GÖTZ: To take leave of your life this way, Götz, to end like this! So be it! Then my death will be the surest sign to the world that I have nothing in common with these curs.

(Enter several peasants.)

THE FIRST PEASANT: Sir! Sir! They're beaten, they're taken prisoner!

GÖTZ: Who?

THE SECOND PEASANT: The ones that burned Miltenberg. A troop of Leaguists moved out from behind the hill and attacked them all of a sudden.

GÖTZ: Their reward awaits them.—O Georg! Georg!—They've captured him along with the scoundrels. . . . My Georg! My Georg. . . . !

(Enter the leaders.)

LINK: Up, Captain, up. There's no time to lose. The enemy is near by and in force.

GÖTZ: Who set fire to Miltenberg?

METZLER: If you want to make a fuss, we'll show you how no fuss is made.

KOHL: Look to your hide and ours. Come on! Come on!

GÖTZ (*to Metzler*): Are you threatening me? You good-for-nothing! Do you think you're more frightening to me because the Count of Helfenstein's blood is clotted on your clothes?

METZLER: Berlichingen!

GÖTZ: You can mention my name and my children will not be ashamed of it!

METZLER: You coward! Prince's lackey!

> *(Götz hits him over the head so he falls.*
> *The others intervene.)*

KOHL: You're insane. The enemy is breaking through on all sides, and you are feuding!

LINK: Come on! Come on!

> *(Battle and tumult.)*
> *(Enter Weislingen and horsemen.)*

WEISLINGEN: After them! After them! They're fleeing! Don't let rain and darkness keep you from them. Götz is among them, I hear. Put your hearts into it so you catch him. He's badly wounded, our men report.

> *(Exeunt the horsemen.)*

And once I get you. . . . !—It will still be mercy if we execute you secretly in prison.—Then his light will go out in the memory of men, and you can breathe more freely, foolish heart.

> *(Exit.)*

*

[Scene 6]

Night in the wild forest. A gypsy encampment.
A gypsywoman by the fire.

THE GYPSYWOMAN: Mend the thatch over the cave-door, daughter. There'll be rain a-plenty tonight.

(Enter a boy.)

THE BOY: A hamster, mother. There! Two field mice.

THE MOTHER: I'll skin them and roast them for you, and you shall have a cap from the pelts.—You're bleeding?

THE BOY: Hamster bit me.

THE MOTHER: Fetch me kindling to make the fire burn up. When your father comes he'll be wet through and through.

(Enter another gypsywoman with a child on her back.)

THE FIRST WOMAN: Did you make a good haul?

THE SECOND WOMAN: Little enough. The district is full of tumult all around so no one's life is safe. Two villages are blazing.

THE FIRST WOMAN: Is that a fire yonder, that glow? I've been looking at it for a long time. We've got so used to fiery signs in the sky lately.

(Enter the gypsy leader and three companions.)

THE LEADER: Do you hear the Wild Huntsman?[1]

THE FIRST WOMAN: He's passing right over us.

THE LEADER: How the dogs do bark! Bow! Wow!

THE SECOND GYPSY: The whips crack.

THIRD GYPSY: The huntsmen are shouting Holla Ho!

THE MOTHER: Well, you have brought in the devil's pack!

THE LEADER: We fished in troubled waters. The peasants themselves are plundering, so we may as well.

SECOND WOMAN: What have you got there, Wolf?

---

[1]The Wild Huntsman with his fellow-huntsmen and dogs is a folklore personification of the tempest. (Originally he was the god Wotan himself.)

WOLF: A rabbit—there—and a rooster, a roasting spit, a bundle of laundry, three cooking spoons, and a horse bridle.

STICKS: I've got a woolen blanket, a pair of boots, and tinder and powder.

THE MOTHER: All soaking wet. Let's dry it out, give it here.

THE LEADER: Hark, a horse! Go, see what it is.

(Enter Götz on horseback.)

GÖTZ: Thank God! Yonder I see a fire. They're gypsies. My wounds are gushing blood, the enemy is after me. Great God, Thou dost make a vile end of me!

THE LEADER: Is it peacefully you come?

GÖTZ: I implore you for help. My wounds have made me weak. Help me from my horse!

THE LEADER: Help him! A noble man in looks and speech.

WOLF *(softly)*: It's Götz von Berlichingen!

THE LEADER: Welcome! Everything we have is yours.

GÖTZ: I thank you.

THE LEADER: Come into my tent.

*

[SCENE 7]

The leader's tent.
The leader. Götz.

THE LEADER: Call Mother and have her bring blood-root and a plaster.

(Götz takes off his armor.)

Here is my Sunday jerkin.

GÖTZ: God reward you.

(The mother binds up his wounds.)

THE LEADER: It warms my heart to have you here.

GÖTZ: You know me?

THE LEADER: Who wouldn't know you! Götz, we'd give our lives and blood for you.

(Enter Schricks.)

SCHRICKS: Horsemen coming through the woods. They're Leaguists.

THE LEADER: Your pursuers! They shan't get to you. Come on, Schricks! Let the others know. We know the trails better than they do and we'll shoot them down before they sight us.

GÖTZ *(alone)*: O my Emperor, my Emperor! Robbers shield your children.

(A sharp exchange of firing is heard.)

Those wild lads, tough and true!

(Enter a gypsywoman.)

THE GYPSYWOMAN: Make your escape! The enemy is getting the upper hand.

GÖTZ: Where is my horse?

THE GYPSYWOMAN: Near by.

GÖTZ *(belts on his sword and mounts without armor.)*: For the last time they shall feel my arm. I'm not that weak yet.

(Exit.)

THE GYPSYWOMAN: He's galloping to our men.

(Flight.)

WOLF: Away! Away! All is lost. Our leader's shot. Götz is captured.

(Howling of women and flight.)

❋

[SCENE 8]

Adelheid's bedchamber.
Adelheid with a letter.

ADELHEID: He or I! What insolence! To threaten me!—We shall

anticipate you. What is that stealthy movement across the outer room?

(A knock.)

Who is out there?

FRANZ *(softly)*: Open the door, my Lady.

ADELHEID: Franz! He deserves to have me open the door.

(She lets him in.)

FRANZ *(falls on her neck)*: My dear Lady!

ADELHEID: Impudent! What if someone had heard you!

FRANZ: Oh, everybody is asleep, everybody!

ADELHEID: What do you want?

FRANZ: It gives me no rest. My lord's threats, your fate, my heart!

ADELHEID: He was very angry as you took leave of him?

FRANZ: As I had never seen him before. To her estates she shall go, he said; she *has to* want to!

ADELHEID: And we obey?

FRANZ: I don't know, my Lady.

ADELHEID: Foolish, betrayed youth, you don't see where this is leading. Here he knows I am safe. For he has long had designs on my freedom. He wants me on his estates. There he has the power to treat me as his hatred bids.

FRANZ: He shall not!

ADELHEID: Will you prevent him?

FRANZ: He shall not!

ADELHEID: I foresee my total misery. He will take me out of his castle by force and lock me up in a convent.

FRANZ: Hell and death!

ADELHEID: Will you rescue me?

FRANZ: Anything, anything but that!

ADELHEID *(in tears, embracing him)*: Franz, oh! to make our escape!

FRANZ: Down he shall go, I'll plant my foot on his neck.

ADELHEID: No temper! You shall have a letter to him, full of humility, saying that I obey him. And pour this little phial into his drink.

FRANZ: Let me have it! You shall be free!

ADELHEID: Free! When you will no longer come stealing to me on tiptoe and trembling . . . when I shall no more say anxiously to you: Go, Franz, the morning is near.

*

[SCENE 9]

Heilbronn, in front of the prison.
Elizabeth. Lerse.

LERSE: God lift your misery from you, my Lady! Maria is here.

ELIZABETH: Thanks be to God! Lerse, we are sunk into ghastly misery. Now it is all just as I foresensed. Captured, thrown into the deepest dungeon as a rebel and miscreant . . .

LERSE: I know all about it.

ELIZABETH: You know nothing, nothing. The grief is too great! His age, his wounds, a creeping fever, and more than all of that, the gloom of his soul to think it should end this way with him!

LERSE: Yes, and then to have Weislingen as the commissioner.

ELIZABETH: Weislingen?

LERSE: They have proceeded to unheard-of executions. Metzler was burned alive, hundreds broken on the wheel, impaled on pikes, beheaded, drawn and quartered. The countryside around looks like a shambles where human flesh is cheap.

ELIZABETH: Weislingen the commissioner! My God! A ray of hope. I'll have Maria go to him, he cannot refuse her anything. He always had a soft heart, and if he sees her whom

he loved so much, who was made so unhappy because of him.
. . . Where is she?

LERSE: Still at the inn.

ELIZABETH: Take me to her. She must start right away. I fear the
worst.

*

[SCENE 10]

Weislingen's castle.

WEISLINGEN: I am so sick, so weak. All my bones are hollow. A
miserable fever has eaten out the marrow. No rest or repose,
day or night. Poisonous dreams amid half-sleep. Last night I
met Götz in the forest. He drew his sword and challenged me.
I reached for mine and my hand failed me. Then he thrust it
into his sheath, looked at me contemptuously, and followed
me.—He is a prisoner, and I tremble before him. Wretched
man! Your word has condemned him to death, and you cower
like a miscreant before his dream-phantom! —And is he to die?
—Götz! Götz!—We human beings do not steer our own courses;
power over us is given to evil spirits to work their hellish mis-
chief to our destruction.

(*He sits down.*)

Feeble! Feeble! How blue my fingernails are! — A cold, cold,
consuming sweat paralyses my every limb. Everything spins
before my eyes. If I could only sleep! Oh. . .

(*Enter Maria.*)

Jesus and Mary!—Leave me in peace! Leave me in peace!—
That shape is all I needed! She is dying, Maria, she is dying
and she is appearing to me.—Leave me, blessed spirit! I am
miserable enough.

MARIA: Weislingen, I am not a ghost. I am Maria.

WEISLINGEN: That is her voice.

MARIA: I have come to beg you for my brother's life. He is innocent, no matter how much he seems to blame.

WEISLINGEN: Be still, Maria! You angel of heaven, you bring with you the torments of hell. Do not speak any more!

MARIA: And is my brother to die? Weislingen, it is monstrous that I should have to tell you he is innocent, that I have to show my grief in order to keep you from this horrible murder. Your soul is possessed to its uttermost depth by hostile Powers. And this is Adelbert!

WEISLINGEN: You see that the consuming breath of death has breathed upon me, my strength is sinking toward the grave. I would be dying as one in misery, and you come to plunge me into despair. If I could only speak, your utmost hatred would melt away to pity and sorrow. O Maria! Maria!

MARIA: Weislingen, my brother is wasting away in prison. His grievous wounds, his age! And if you were capable of harming his grey head . . . Weislingen, we would despair.

WEISLINGEN: Enough.

(*He pulls the bell-cord. Enter Franz in extreme agitation.*)

FRANZ: Sir?

WEISLINGEN: Those papers there, Franz!

(*Franz fetches them. Weislingen tears open a packet
and shows Maria a paper.*)

Here is your brother's death warrant, signed.

MARIA: God in heaven!

WEISLINGEN: Here: I tear it up. He lives. But can I recreate what I have destroyed? Don't weep so, Franz! Good youth, your misery touches my heart deeply.

(*Franz throws himself down before him
and embraces his knees.*)

MARIA (*to herself*) : He is very ill. The sight of him rends my heart. How I loved him once! And coming near him now, I realize how deeply.

WEISLINGEN: Get up, Franz, and stop your weeping. I can get well again. Hope is with the living.

FRANZ: You will not. You must die.

WEISLINGEN: I must?

FRANZ (*beside himself*) : Poisoned! Poisoned! By your wife! —I! I!

(He rushes away.)

WEISLINGEN: Maria, follow him! He is in despair!

(Exit Maria.)

Poisoned by my wife! Oh! Oh! I can feel it! Torment and death!

MARIA (*offstage*) : Help! Help!

WEISLINGEN (*tries to get up.*) : My God! I can't!

(Reenter Maria.)

MARIA: He is dead. He threw himself in a frenzy out of the window of the great hall into the Main.

WEISLINGEN: He is well off.—Your brother is out of danger. The other commissioners, Seckendorf especially, are his friends. They will allow him knightly imprisonment on the pledge of his word. Farewell, Maria, and go.

MARIA: I will stay with you, poor forsaken man.

WEISLINGEN: Forsaken and poor indeed! Thou art a dread avenger, God!—My wife . . .

MARIA: Give up these thoughts. Turn your heart to the All Merciful.

WEISLINGEN: Go, dear soul, leave me to my misery.—Monstrous! Even your presence, Maria, the last consolation, is torment.

MARIA (*to herself*) : Give me strength, O God! My soul succumbs with his.

WEISLINGEN: Alas! Alas! Poisoned by my wife!—My Franz corrupted by the vile woman! How she waits, listens for the messenger to bring the news: "He is dead." And you, Maria! Maria! Why did you come to weaken the sleeping memory of my sins! Leave me! Leave me, so I can die!

MARIA: Let me stay. You are alone. Imagine I am your nurse. Forget everything. May God forget everything about you as I forget everything about you!

WEISLINGEN: Soul full of love, pray for me, pray for me! My heart is shut.

MARIA: He will have mercy on you.—You are weak.

WEISLINGEN: I am dying, I am dying, and I can't die. And in this fearful struggle between life and death there are the torments of hell.

MARIA: Have mercy on him, have mercy on him! Cast just one glance of Thy love upon his heart so it may be opened to comfort and so his spirit may bring hope, the hope of life, into death!

*

[SCENE 11]

In a dismal, narrow, vaulted chamber.
The judges of the secret tribunal, all masked.[1]

THE ELDEST: Judges of the secret tribunal, swear by noose and by sword to be blameless, to judge in secrecy, to punish in secrecy like God! If your hearts and your hands are pure, then raise up your arms and over the wrongdoers cry out: Woe! Woe!

ALL: Woe! Woe!

---

[1]The historical secret tribunal (*Fehmgericht* or *Vehmgericht*) of the middle ages always met in the open air and by daylight, its members wore no masks, and women were not usually subject to its jurisdiction.

THE ELDEST: Summoner, begin the session.

THE SUMMONER: I the Summoner summon accusation against the wrongdoer. Whatever man whose heart is pure, whose hands are pure to swear by noose and by sword, let him accuse by noose and by sword, accuse, accuse!

THE ACCUSER (*steps up.*): My heart is pure of wrongdoing, my hands of innocent blood. May God forgive me evil thoughts and hinder the way of the will! I raise my hand aloft and I accuse, accuse, accuse!

THE ELDEST: Whom do you accuse?

THE ACCUSER: I accuse by noose and by sword Adelheid von Weislingen. She has committed adultery and poisoned her husband through her page. The page has condemned himself; the husband is dead.

THE ELDEST: Do you swear to the God of Truth that you accuse in truth?

THE ACCUSER: I swear.

THE ELDEST: If it is found false, do you offer your neck to the penalty of murder and of adultery?

THE ACCUSER: I so offer.

THE ELDEST: Your voices.

(*They speak secretly with him.*)

THE ACCUSER: Judges of the secret tribunal, what is your judgment on Adelheid von Weislingen who is charged with adultery and murder?

THE ELDEST: She shall die, die the bitter double death, and by rope and by dagger doubly atone for the double wrongdoing! Raise your hands aloft and cry woe upon her! Woe! Woe! into the hands of the Avenger!

ALL: Woe! Woe! Woe!

THE ELDEST: Avenger, Avenger, step forth!

(*The Avenger steps forth.*)

Take here this rope and this sword wherewith to exterminate her from the sight of Heaven within one week's time. Wheresoever you find her, down with her to the dust!—You judges who judge in secret and who punish in secret like God, keep your hearts from wrongdoing and your hands from innocent blood.

*

[SCENE 12]

The courtyard of an inn.
Maria. Lerse.

MARIA: The horses have rested enough. Let us go, Lerse.
LERSE: Rest rather till morning. The night is far too unfriendly.
MARIA: Lerse, I can have no rest until I have seen my brother. Let us go. The weather is clearing; we can expect a fine day.
LERSE: As you command.

*

[SCENE 13]

Heilbronn, in the prison.
Götz. Elizabeth.

ELIZABETH: Speak to me, dear husband, I beg you. Your silence troubles me. You are consumed with inner fire. Come, let us look to your wounds; they are much improved. I do not recognize you any longer in this despondent gloom.
GÖTZ: Were you looking for Götz? He is long since gone. Little by little they have maimed me—my hand, my freedom, my property, and my good name. My head, what is that worth?—What do you hear of Georg? Has Lerse gone for Georg?

ELIZABETH: Yes, my dear. Be of good cheer. Many things can change.

GÖTZ: Whom God strikes down does not rise again. I know best what lies upon my shoulders. Misfortune I am accustomed to endure. And now it's not Weislingen alone, not just the peasants alone, not the Emperor's death and my wounds—it is all these together. My hour has come. I had hoped it would be like my life. *His* will be done!

ELIZABETH: Will you not eat something?

GÖTZ: Nothing, wife. Look how the sun is shining outside.

ELIZABETH: A beautiful spring day.

GÖTZ: I wonder, my dear, whether you could persuade the jailer to let me out for half an hour in his little garden, so that I could enjoy the lovely sunlight and the clear sky and the pure air?

ELIZABETH: Right away, and he will surely do it.

*

[SCENE 14]

The little garden adjoining the prison.
Maria. Lerse.

MARIA: Go in and see how things stand.

(Exit Lerse.)
(Enter Elizabeth and the jailer.)

ELIZABETH: God reward you for your love and loyalty to my word.

(Exit the jailer.)

Maria, what do you bring?

MARIA: My brother's. safety. But, oh, my heart is torn. Weislingen is dead, poisoned by his wife. My husband is in danger.

The princes are getting too powerful for him. They say he is hemmed in and under siege.

ELIZABETH: Do not believe the rumor. And don't let Götz notice anything.

MARIA: How do things stand with him?

ELIZABETH: I was afraid he would not live to see your return. The hand of the Lord lies heavy upon him. And Georg is dead.

MARIA: Georg, the golden youth!

ELIZABETH: When those good-for-nothing rascals were burning Miltenberg, his master sent him to make them stop. Just then a troop of Leaguists attacked them.—Georg! If they had all acted as he did, they could not fail to have a good conscience. Many were cut down and Georg among them; he died a trooper's death.

MARIA: Does Götz know of it?

ELIZABETH: We are keeping it from him. He asks me ten times a day and ten times a day he sends me to find out what Georg is doing. I am afraid to deal that last thrust to his heart.

MARIA: O Lord, what are the hopes of this earth!

(Enter Götz, Lerse, and the jailer.)

GÖTZ: Almighty God! How good a man feels beneath Thy sky! How *free!*—The trees are putting out their buds and the whole world hopes. Farewell, my dear ones! My roots are cut away, my strength is sinking toward the grave.

ELIZABETH: Shall I send Lerse to the monastery to fetch your son so you can see him again and give him your blessing?

GÖTZ: Let him be, he is holier than I am, he does not need my blessing.—On our wedding day, Elizabeth, I didn't think I would die *this* way.—My old father gave us his blessing, and from his prayer welled forth a posterity of brave and noble sons.—Thou didst not hear him, and I am the last one.—Lerse, your face delights me more in the hour of death than in the bravest fight. Then my spirit guided yours; now you support me. Oh, if I could only see Georg once again and warm myself by his glance!—You cast down your eyes and weep . . . He is dead . . . Georg is dead . . . Then die, Götz!—You have outlived yourself, outlived the noble ones.—How did he die?— Oh, did they catch him among those murderous incendiaries, and has he been executed?

ELIZABETH: No, he was cut down at Miltenberg. He fought like a lion for his liberty.

GÖTZ: Thanks be to God!—He was the best lad under the sun, and brave.—Release my soul now!—Poor wife, I leave you in a vicious world. Lerse, do not forsake her!—Lock up your hearts more carefully than your doors. The times of Betrayal are coming, and to him free rein is given. The base will rule by cunning, and the noble man will fall into their snares. Maria, God give you back your husband again. May he not fall as low as he has climbed aloft. Selbitz is dead, and the good Emperor, and my Georg. Give me a drink of water.—Heavenly air . . . Freedom! Freedom!

(*He dies.*)

ELIZABETH: Only on high, on high with Thee. The world is a prison.

MARIA: Noble man! Noble man! Woe to the age that rejected you!

LERSE: Woe to the posterity that fails to appreciate you!

The "URFAUST"

(The first sketches, made probably in 1773–74, for a play
to be called *Faust* and never published by Goethe.)

The "URFAUST"

Readings in sixteenth-century German history and literature not only led Goethe to *Götz von Berlichingen* but also reawakened his interest in the figure of Doctor Faustus, that bizarre, self-styled magician who was almost the exact contemporary of Martin Luther. From childhood he had known the puppet plays in which the bombastic Faustus sold his soul to a devil named Mephistopheles for a life of pleasure and adventures. He also knew the old Faust Book of 1587, but not until years afterward did he discover Christopher Marlowe's English drama of 1589 or 1590.

At an unknown date a Faust drama of his own suggested itself to Goethe's mind. It was to be a serious and poetic stage work in which the fifty-year-old magician would somehow be restored to age twenty and granted the experience of a poignant love affair. The love story would be wholly of Goethe's invention, quite unlike the superficial amours of the traditional Faust. It is hazardous indeed to propose that any but these elementary ideas were in the author's original plans.

With inspiration running strong, the best-known passages in Goethe's entire career were written down just as they came to mind, in mixed order, on random sheets of paper, while other works were being composed in the intervals. The dramatic method was "modified Shakespearean," with some scenes in prose but with most scenes in the rough *Knittelvers* of the sixteenth-century Hans Sachs: tetrameter couplets and quatrains not too far removed from doggerel. The probable compositional dates fall between July of 1773 and early autumn of 1774, approximately the author's twenty-fifth year of life; further work into 1775 is less likely, and October 30, 1775 is a positive terminal date.

This "original *Faust*," or *Urfaust*, consists of twenty-two scenes, one wholly in prose, two others largely in prose, and the remainder in 1,441 lines of rhymed verse. Goethe never published it. The manuscript is lost. The indispensable scene in which the fifty-year-old is magically restored to age twenty was not composed until 1788. Certain other passages were written shortly after that. Disheartened then at the way his project was growing beyond all bounds, and with other works pressing him for time, Goethe published portions of a considerably amended version in 1790 under the title of *Faust. A Fragment,* excluding all lines after the cathedral scene. With still further changes, additions, and subtractions, *Faust, Part I* was published in 1808 as a text of 4,612 lines, more than triple the length of the *Urfaust* but still ending with the Dungeon scene. About *Faust, Part II,* which was composed in the years 1825–31, we speak briefly in the last pages of the present survey of Goethe's dramas.

In 1886, long after Goethe's death, the *Urfaust* was discovered among the effects of a person who had been dead since 1807, Fräulein Luise von Göchhausen, once a lady-in-waiting to Dowager Duchess Anna Amalia of Weimar. The manuscript is in the neat handwriting of Fräulein von Göchhausen herself, who must have copied it from the poet's own original, faithfully reproducing archaic spellings and sparse punctuation, doubtless to facilitate an oral reading such as Goethe sometimes gave in the 1780s.

The marginal numberings of the present *Urfaust* translation are for the use of readers who may wish to see correlations with the complete *Faust, Part I* of 1808. Since the three prefatory sections of the 1808 version were added later, our first number is 354, which was originally the opening line. A letter following a number indicates that a line was significantly modified later or that a different line was put in its place. Seventy *Urfaust* lines were deleted after line 1881, hence we number 1881-1, 1881-2, and so on through 1881-70. In the prose passages, numbers in parentheses key the text only approximately to the 1808 version.

The gaps are sometimes startling, as with the jump from line 605 to line 1868. The backwards-and-forwards of the count after line 3610 reveals the youthful author's uncertainty about how his material was yet to be ordered. The out-and-out cuts, such as 1881-1 through 1881-70, show what the same author found irrelevant or unacceptable in maturer years. A striking substantive difference shows the prank in

Auerbach's tavern as played by Faust himself in his traditional role as magician; in the final version Mephistopheles is the prankster, while Faust, with loftier purposes in mind, is merely disgusted and says nothing at all. Startling too is the *Urfaust* stage direction for the cathedral scene: "Funeral Mass for Gretchen's mother. . . . All relatives." In the 1808 version Goethe chose to eliminate that detail of anguish; the *Dies irae* hymn indicates a requiem Mass, but Gretchen is not seen at the funeral of the mother whose death is freshly and hideously upon her conscience.

While we stress that the *Urfaust* is the unfinished draft of a play, we find it an important work in Goethe's evolution as a dramatist. Its youthful ardor, as yet untempered by sober afterthought, also gives it poetic validity in its own right. By including a translation of it here we hope to clarify the differences between Parts I and II of *Faust* and thereby to establish a basis for the claims made about the total *Faust* at the end of the present book.

CHARACTERS

FAUST, an alchemist and magician
THE EARTH SPIRIT
WAGNER, Faust's famulus (graduate assistant
   to a university professor)
MEPHISTOPHELES, a devil
A STUDENT

Patrons of Auerbach's Tavern in Leipzig:
   FROSCH (a dialect word for "schoolboy")
   BRANDER (suggestive of *Brandfuchs,* "brant fox,"
      the term for a second-semester student)
   SIEBEL
   ALTEN (in the completed *Faust* "Altmayer,"
      approximately "Oldfellow")

MARGARET, a girl of the poorer classes, later
   called Gretchen (Margaretchen, "poor Margaret")
DAME MARTHA SCHWERDTLEIN, a neighbor woman
LIESCHEN, an acquaintance of Margaret's ("poor Lisa")
VALENTINE, Margaret's brother, a soldier
AN EVIL SPIRIT

The locale, as far as line 2050 is unspecified, though the implied university may be at Leipzig; Auerbach's Tavern was an actual tavern in Leipzig; from line 2605 the unspecified city may be thought of as the author's native Frankfurt-on-the-Main.

Time: around 1530.

NIGHT

Faust restless in his chair at his desk
in a narrow and high-vaulted Gothic room.

FAUST: I've read, alas! through philosophy,   354
 Medicine and jurisprudence too,
 And, to my grief, theology
 With ardent labor studied through,
 And here I stand with all my lore,
 Poor fool, no wiser than before.
 I'm Professor, and Doctor, and with my reading   360a
 These ten years now I have been leading
 My scholars on wild-goose hunts, out
 And in, cross-lots, and round about—
 To find that nothing can be known!
 This burns my very marrow and bone.
 I'm shrewder, it's true, than all the tribes
 Of Doctors, Professors, priests and scribes;   367a
 Neither doubts nor scruples now can haunt me,
 Neither hell nor devils now can daunt me—
 But by the same token I lose all delight.   370
 I don't pretend to know anything aright,
 I don't pretend to have in mind
 Things I could teach to improve mankind.
 Nor have I lands nor treasure hoards,
 Nor honors and splendors the world affords;
 No dog would want to live this way!
 And so I've yielded to magic's sway,
 To see if spirits' force and speech
 Might not bring many a mystery in reach;
 So I no longer need to go   380
 On saying things that I don't know;
 So I may learn the things that hold

The world together at its core,
So I may potencies and seeds behold,
And trade in empty words no more.

   O if, full moon, you did but shine
Your last upon this pain of mine,
Whom I have watched ascending bright
Here at my desk in mid of night;
Then over books and papers here,   390
Sad friend, you would come into view.
Ah, could I on some mountain height
Rove beneath your mellow light,
Drift on with spirits round mountain caves,
Waft over meadows your dim light laves,
And, clear of learning's fumes, renew
Myself in baths of healing dew!

   Am I still in this prison stall?
Accursed, musty hole-in-the-wall,
Where the very light of heaven strains   400
But dully through the painted panes!

   By these enormous book-piles bounded
Which dust bedecks and worms devour,
Which are by sooty charts surrounded
Up to the vaultings where they tower;
With jars shelved round me, and retorts,
With instruments packed in and jammed,
Ancestral junk together crammed—
Such is your world! A world of sorts!

   Do you still wonder why your heart   410
Is choked with fear within your breast?
Why nameless pain checks every start
Toward life and leaves you so oppressed?
Instead of Nature's living sphere
Wherein God placed mankind of old,
Brute skeletons surround you here
And dead men's bones and smoke and mold.

   Flee! Up! And out into the land!

Does not this mystic book indeed,
From Nostradamus' very hand,   420
Give all the guidance that you need?
Then you will recognize the courses
Of stars; within you will unfold,
At Nature's prompting, your soul's forces
As spirits speech with spirits hold.
In vain this arid brooding here
The sacred signs to clarify—
You spirits who are hovering near,
If you can hear me, give reply!
> (*He opens the book and glimpses*
> *the sign of the macrocosm.*)

Ha! Suddenly what rapture at this view   430
Goes rushing through my senses once again!
I feel a youthful joy of life course new
And ardent through my every nerve and vein.
Was it a god who wrote these signs whereby
My inward tempest-rage is stilled
And my poor heart with joy is filled
And with a mystic impulse high
The powers of Nature are revealed?
Am I a god? I feel so light!
In these pure signs I see the whole   440
Of operative Nature spread before my soul.
Now what the wise man says I understand aright:
"The spirit world is not locked off from thee;
Thy heart is dead, thy mind's bolt drawn!
Up, scholar, and bathe cheerfully
Thy earthly breast in rosy dawn!"
> (*He contemplates the sign.*)

How all things interweave to form the Whole,
Each in another finds its life and goal!
How each of heaven's powers soars and descends
And each to each the golden buckets lends;   450
On fragrant-blessed wings

From heaven piercing to earth's core
Till all the cosmos sweetly rings!
   O what a sight!—A sight, but nothing more!
Where can I grasp you, Nature without end?
You breasts, where? Source of all our lives,
On which both heaven and earth depend,
Toward you my withered heart so strives—
You flow, you swell, and must I thirst in vain?
       (Impatiently he turns pages of the book
       and glimpses the sign of the Earth Spirit.)
How differently I am affected by this sign!   460
You, Spirit of the Earth, are nearer me,
I feel more potent energy,
I feel aglow as with new wine.
I feel the strength to brave the world, to go
And shoulder earthly weal and earthly woe,
To wrestle with the tempests there,
In shipwreck's grinding crash not to despair.
Clouds gather over me—
The moon conceals its light—
The lamp has vanished!   470
Mists rise!—Red lightnings dart and flash
About my head—Down from
The vaulted roof cold horror blows
And seizes me!
I feel you hovering near,   475
Spirit implored.   475
Reveal yourself!
O how my heart is rent with fear!
With new emotion
My senses riot in wild commotion!
My heart surrenders to you utterly!   480
You must! You must! though it cost life to me!
       (He seizes the book and mystically
       pronounces the sign of the Spirit. A reddish

flame flashes. The Spirit appears in the
flame, hideous to behold.)

SPIRIT: Who calls me?

FAUST (*cowering*):   Ghastly shape!

SPIRIT: With might
  You have compelled me to appear,
  You long have sucked about my sphere,
  Now—

FAUST: No! I cannot bear the sight!

SPIRIT: You begged so breathlessly to bring me near
  To hear my voice and see my face as well;
  I bow before your strong compulsive spell,
  And here I am!—What childish fear
  Besets you, superman! Where is the soul that cried?   490
  Where is the heart that made and bore a world inside
  Itself and sought amid its gleeful pride
  To be with spirits equal and allied?
  Where are you, Faust, whose voice called out to me,
  Who forced yourself on me so urgently?
  Are you he who, at my mere breath,
  Now tremble to your being's depth,
  A terrified and cringing worm?

FAUST: Shall I give way before you, thing of flame?
  I am your equal. Faust is my name!   500

SPIRIT: In tides of life, in action's storm
  I surge as a wave,
  Swaying ceaselessly;
  Birth and the grave,
  An endless sea,
  A changeful life!   506
  I work in the hum of the loom of time   508
  Weaving the living raiment of godhead sublime.

FAUST: O you who roam the world from end to end,   510
  Restless Spirit, I feel so close to you!

SPIRIT: You are like the spirit you comprehend,
  Not me!

(Disappears.)

FAUST *(overwhelmed)*:
  Not you?
  Whom then?
  I, image of the godhead!
  Not even rank with you!

                    (A knock)

  God's death! I know who's there—my famulus—
  I topple from my heights of joy.
  To think this dry-bones should destroy   520
  The fullness of these visions thus!

            *(Enter Wagner in a dressing gown and nightcap, a
            lamp in his hand. Faust turns around impatiently.)*

WAGNER: Excuse me! I heard you declaiming;
  It surely was a Grecian tragedy?
  There I would like some more proficiency,
  Today it gets so much acclaiming.
  I've sometimes heard it said a preacher
  Could profit with an actor for a teacher.

FAUST: Yes, if the preacher is an actor too,
  As may on some occasions be the case.

WAGNER: Cooped up in one's museum all year through   530
  And hardly seeing folks except on holidays,
  One just can't learn the right persuasive knack   532
  Of setting people on the right track.   533

FAUST: Unless you feel it you will not succeed;
  Unless up from your soul it wells
  And all your listeners' hearts compels
  By utmost satisfaction of a need,
  You'll always fail. With paste and glue,
  By grinding others' feasts for hash,
  By blowing your small flame up too   540
  Above your paltry pile of ash,
  High praise you'll get in apes' and children's sight,
  If that's what suits your hankering—
  But heart with heart you never will unite

If from your heart it does not spring.

WAGNER: Delivery, though, can serve a speaker's turn.   546

FAUST: Delivery! That's a puppeteer's concern.   548a

  Young Sir, what you need is forcefulness!   548b

  Don't be a bell-loud fool! What good   549

  Are fine delivery and artifice   550a

  To friendship, love, and brotherhood?   551a

  If you have serious things to say,

  Why hunt for words out of your way?

  Your flashy speeches on which you have pinned

  The frilly cutouts of men's artistry

  Are unrefreshing as the misty wind

  That sighs through withered leaves autumnally!

WAGNER: Oh Lord! How long is art,

  How short our life! And ever

  Amid my work and critical endeavor   560

  Despair besets my head and heart.

  How difficult the means are to come by

  That get one back up to the source,

  And then before one finishes mid-course,

  Poor devil, one must up and die.

FAUST: Is that the sacred font, a parchment roll,

  From which a drink will sate your thirst forever?

  Refreshment will delight you never

  Unless it surges up from your own soul.

WAGNER: But what delight there is in pages   570

  That lead us to the spirit of the ages!

  In seeing how before us wise men thought

  And how far glorious progress has been brought.

FAUST: O yes, up to the furthest star!

  My friend, the eras and past ages are

  For us a book with seven seals.

  What you the spirit of the ages call

  Is only those men's spirits after all

  Held as a mirror that reveals

  The times. They're often just a source of gloom!   580

You take one look at them and run away.
A trash can and a littered storage room,
At best a plot for some heroic play
With excellent pragmatic saws
That come resoundingly from puppets' jaws.

WAGNER: But then the world! The mind and heart of man!
To learn about those things is our whole aim.

FAUST: Yes, call it learning if you can!
But who dares call a child by its right name?
The few who such things ever learned,   590
Who foolishly their brimming hearts unsealed
And to the mob their feelings and their thoughts revealed,
Were in all ages crucified or burned.
But it is late into the night, my friend,
We must break off now for the present.

WAGNER: I'd like to have stayed on till dawn to spend   596a
The time in talk so learned and so pleasant.   597
                         (*Exit.*)

FAUST: Why hope does not abandon all such brains   · 602
That cling forever to such shallow stuff!
They dig for treasure and are glad enough
To turn up angleworms for all their pains!   605

                         *

MEPHISTOPHELES IN A DRESSING GOWN
AND WITH AN ENORMOUS WIG. A STUDENT.

STUDENT: I've been here just a short time, Sir,   1868
And come to you with deference
To meet a man, and see and hear,   1870
Of whom all speak with reverence.

MEPHISTOPHELES: I must approve your courtesy.
A man like other men you see.
Have you inquired about elsewhere?

STUDENT: Take me, I entreat you, in your care.
I come with fresh blood, spirits high,

And money in tolerable supply.
My mother was loath to have me go,
But I would like to learn and know.

MEPHISTOPHELES: Then this is just the place to come.   1880

STUDENT: Frankly, I'd rather be back home.   1881
Things here all look so bleak and bare,   1881-1
Each home seems on starvation-fare.   -2

MEPHISTOPHELES: Just disregard that in your prudence;   -3
Here incomes all come out of students.   -4
But first off: where will you reside?   -5
That's quite important.

STUDENT: Be my guide!   -6
I'm very much the lamb that's lost.   -7
My aim is the Good at any cost,   -8
Also unlearning all the bad,   -9
But fun-time also must be had,   -10
And study so deep that after-years   -11
Will find it running out my ears.   -12
Oh, Sir, see to it that my soul   -13
Shall never miss its righteous goal!   -14

MEPHISTOPHELES (*scratching his head*):
You say you have no lodgings booked?   -15

STUDENT: I haven't yet so much as looked.   -16
My hostel-food will nicely do me,   -17
And nice waitresses to serve it to me.   -18

MEPHISTOPHELES: There—God forbid!—you might go
astray.   -19
Coffee and billiards! Curse that stuff!   -20
Those girls can flirt and ogle enough!   -21
You'll patterpiddle your time away.   -22
Besides, we rather like to call   -23
Our *studiosos* one and all   -24
Together once a week to feel   -25
The firm emplacement of our heel.   -26
And if one of them relishes our spittle-flavor,   -27
He sits at our right and enjoys our favor.   -28

STUDENT: The thought fills me with sheer alarm.   -29

MEPHISTOPHELES: That does the worthy cause no harm.   -30
  As to the question of where you live,   -31
  I have no better advice to give   -32
  Than Mrs. Beerbung's. Beyond a doubt   -33
  She knows *studiosos* in and out;   -34
  Her house is full from bottom to top   -35
  And she runs a very efficient shop.   -36
  True, Noah's Ark was cleaner swept,   -37
  But . . . there's tradition to be kept.   -38
  You'll pay what others paid before,   -39
  Who carved their names on the shit-house door.   -40
STUDENT: My heart feels just as choked as when   -41
  I was in school at home back when.   -42
MEPHISTOPHELES: There's lodgings settled. Now for
                                      board,   -43
  And at a price you can afford.   -44
STUDENT: But shouldn't this all follow, in effect,   -45
  The broadening of the intellect?   -46
MEPHISTOPHELES: Dear boy, there you might go astray.   -47
  You're strange to the Academic Way.   -48
  Forget home-cooking, and do not sputter   -49
  Against plain water and rancid butter.   -50
  No garden-greens, no fancy victuals: -51
  Be thankful for a dish of nettles;   -52
  They make you loose as a goose, it's true,   -53
  But then constipation's not for you.   -54
  Eat veal and mutton as world-without-end   -55
  As God's own starry firmament.   -56
  Your payments will make up the cost   -57
  Of what to dead-beats had been lost.   -58
  See that your purse is well provided,   -59
  That loans to friends are all avoided,   -60
  Pay landlords and tailors, but more than these   -61
  Be prompt to pay your Professor's fees.   -62
STUDENT: Quite so, dear reverend Sir, quite so,   -63
  But give me guidance before I go!   -64

Yonder Wisdom's field lies open wide,	-65
And I would gladly rush inside,	-66
But it's a crazy-patterned maze,	-67
And barren and waste in many ways;	-68
To me its distant prospects seem	-69
A Vale of Tempe with rills agleam.	(1881)-70

MEPHISTOPHELES: First tell me, before we go on, — 1896
What course have you decided on? — 1897

STUDENT: It's medicine I'm slated for, — 1897a
But I would most like to explore — 1897b
What all there is on earth, in heaven as well, — 1900
In science and in Nature too. — 1901

MEPHISTOPHELES: You're on the right track, I can tell. — 1902
Just see that nothing distracts you. — 1903
And so, dear friend, I would advise — 1910
First off *collegium logicum.*
There you will get your mind well braced
In Spanish boots so tightly laced
That it will henceforth toe the taut
And cautiously marked line of thought
And not go will-o'-the-wisping out
And in, across, and round about.
They will spend days on teaching you
About how things you used to do—
Like eating, drinking—just like that, — 1920
Need One! Two! Three! for getting at.
For with thought-manufacturies
It's like a weaver's masterpiece:
A thousand threads one treadle plies,
The shuttles dart back to and fro,
Unseen the threads together flow,
A thousand knots one movement ties;
Then comes the philosopher to have his say
And proves things have to be this way:
The first being so, the second so, — 1930
The third and fourth are so-and-so;

If first and second were absent, neither
Would third and fourth be present either.
All scholars find this very clever,
None have turned weavers yet, however.
Whoever wants to know and write about
A living thing, first drives the spirit out;
He has the parts then in his grasp,
But gone is the spirit's holding-clasp.
Encheiresin naturae chemists call it now,   1940
Thumbing their noses, they know not how.   1941a
STUDENT: I don't just get all you imply.
MEPHISTOPHELES: It will go better by and by,
    Once you have all these things principified
    And properly classified.
STUDENT: I feel as dazed by all you've said
    As if a mill wheel spun inside my head.
MEPHISTOPHELES: Above all else you next must turn
    To metaphysics. See that you learn
    Profoundly and with might and main   1950
    What does not fit the human brain.
    For what fits in—or misfits—grand
    Resounding phrases are on hand.
    But this semester most of all
    Keep schedule, be punctual.
    You'll have five classes every day;
    Be in there on the stroke of the bell.
    See that you are prepared as well,
    With paragraphs worked up in such a way
    That you can see with just a look   1960
    There's nothing said but what is in the book;
    And take your notes with dedication
    As if the Holy Ghost gave the dictation!   1963
STUDENT: Forgive me for so importuning you,   2001
    But I must trouble you again.
    Would you just say a telling word or two
    About the course in medicine?
    Three years is a short time, and O my God!

The field itself is far too broad.
With just a little hint alone
One feels it would not seem so great.

MEPHISTOPHELES (*aside*):

I've had enough of this dry tone,
I've got to play the Devil straight. 2010

(*aloud*)

The gist of medicine is grasped with ease;
You study through the great world and the small
To let it go on after all
As God may please.
In vain you'll go a-roving scientifically,
There each learns only what he can;
But one who grasps the moment, he
Is truly the right man.
You've got a good build on the whole,
And you won't lack for impudence; 2020
If you just have self-confidence
You'll have the trust of many a soul.
And learn to manage women, of that make sure;
For all their endless Ah!'s and Oh!'s
And thousand woes
Depend on One Point only for their cure,
And if you're halfway decent about that,
You'll have them all under your hat.
First, by a title win their confidence
That your skills many skills transcend, 2030
Then you can finger every little thing and be
Welcome where others wait for years on end.
Know how to take her little pulse, and grasp her
With slyly passionate glances while you clasp her
Around her trim and slender waist
To see how tightly she is laced.

STUDENT: I think that beats philosophy. 2037

MEPHISTOPHELES: Grey, my dear friend, is all of theory,
And verdant is life's golden tree.

STUDENT: I swear it's all just like a dream to me. 2040

Might I come back another time to sound
Your wisdom to its depths profound?
MEPHISTOPHELES: I'll gladly do anything I may.
STUDENT: It's just impossible to go away
Unless you take my album here and sign.
Would you do me the honor of a line?
MEPHISTOPHELES: With pleasure.
           (*He writes and gives the album back.*)
STUDENT (*reads*):   *Eritis sicut Deus, scientes bonum et*
                                        malum.
(*He respectfully closes the book and takes his leave.*)
MEPHISTOPHELES: Just follow that old saying of my   2049
                              cousin, the snake,
And you will surely tremble for your God's-likeness'   2050
                              sake!

                              *

        AUERBACH'S TAVERN IN LEIPZIG

        A drinking bout of jolly cronies.

FROSCH: Will no one drink? Will no one laugh?   2073
I'll snap you out of your gloomy daze!
Today you're all like sodden chaff
And usually you're all ablaze.
BRANDER: It's your fault, you've been keeping mum,
No horseplay and no jokes with sour scum.
FROSCH (*pours a glass of wine over his head*):
There's both!
BRANDER: You pig! You donkey, you!   2079a
FROSCH: Don't I need to be both those things with you?   2080a
SIEBEL: In three devils' names come to order and sing   (2081)
chorus! And in between, swill 'em down, and in
between, bellow out "Holla, hey," Up! Hey, there!
ALTEN: Bring me some cotton, he's splitting our
eardrums!   (2083)

SIEBEL: Can I help it if the damned low ceiling echoes   (2085)
  like this? Sing!

FROSCH: Ah, tara! Tara, Lara! dee!—We're in tune! So   (2088)
  what do we sing?

> The good old Holy Roman Empire,
> How does it hold together?

BRANDER: Bah! A filthy song! A political song, an offen-   (2092)
  sive song. Thank God the Holy Roman Empire is no
  concern of yours. Let's elect a pope.

FROSCH: Rise, Lady Nightingale, and soar,   (2101)
> Greet my sweetheart ten thousand times and more.

SIEBEL: Death and damnation! Greet my sweetheart!—   (2108)
  A mouse-pie stuffed with dry oak-leaves from the
  Blocksberg and delivered to her by a skinned rabbit
  with a rooster's head, and no greeting from the nightingale. Didn't she [jilt] me—? Throw my twirled
  mustache and all appurtenances behind the door like a
  worn-out broom, and all so—In three devils' names, no
  greeting for her, I say, except smashing her windows
  for her!

FROSCH (*pounding his drinking-mug on the table*): Come
  to order!—A new song, comrades, an old song if you
  will.—Pay attention now and come in on the chorus.
  Loud and clear!

> In a cellar once there lived a rat   2126
> And all he ate was lard and butter;
> He grew a gut so sleek and fat
> He looked like Doctor Luther.
> The cook, she put some poison out,   2130
> And then the world closed in about,
> As if he had love inside him.

CHORUS (*shouting*):   As if he had love inside him!

FROSCH:

> He traveled forth, he traveled to,
> He swilled from every puddle,
> He gnawed, he scratched the whole
>   house through
> In fury all befuddled.

He jumped for pain to beat the band,
But soon had all that he could stand,
As if he had love inside him.   2140

CHORUS: As if he had love inside him!

FROSCH: Into the kitchen by light of day
He ran in agony,
Dropped on the hearth and twitched and
    lay
And snuffled piteously.
The poisoneress, she laughed and said,
"One more squeak and then he's dead,
As if he had love inside him."

CHORUS: As if he had love inside him!

SIEBEL: And a good big dose of rat-poison in the cook's   (2150)
soup too! I'm not tender-hearted, but a rat like that
would move a stone to pity.

BRANDER: Rat yourself! I'd like to see the lard-gut there
by the hearth and blowing his little soul out of him!
          (*Enter Faust and Mephistopheles.*)

MEPHISTOPHELES: Now look at how they're carrying on   (2158)
here. If you like it, I'll furnish you company like this
night after night.

FAUST: Good evening, gentlemen.   (2183)

ALL: Thanks a lot!

SIEBEL: Who's the sideshow man?

BRANDER: Sh-h! They're some high-ups or other,
incognito. Their faces have that mean, dissatisfied look.

SIEBEL: Bah! Strolling players at best.

MEPHISTOPHELES (*softly*):   Observe: these fellows don't
suspect the Devil no matter how near he gets to them.

FROSCH: I'll worm it out of their noses, where they're   (2189)
from!— Is the road over from Rippach so bad that you
had to ride so late into the night?

FAUST: We didn't come that way.

FROSCH: I thought maybe you had dinner over there
with the famous Jack.

FAUST: I don't know him.

> (*The others all laugh.*)

FROSCH: Oh, he's from an old family. He has lots of relatives.

MEPHISTOPHELES: You must be one of his cousins.

BRANDER (*aside to Frosch*): Put *that* in your pocket! He got the point.

FROSCH: At Wurzen there, it's such a nuisance having to wait so long lots of times for the ferry.

FAUST: It is?

SIEBEL (*under his breath*): They're from the old part of the country, you can tell. Let them jolly up a bit.—Are you friends of a cordial dram? Come join us!

MEPHISTOPHELES: Why not?

> (*They clink glasses and drink.*)

FROSCH: Now gentlemen, a little song. One little song for a can of drink is cheap enough.

FAUST: I don't have a singing voice.

MEPHISTOPHELES: I'll sing one for me, two for my (2205) comrade, a hundred if you like. We've just come from Spain, where as many songs are sung at night as there are stars in the sky.

BRANDER: I won't have it! I hate that strumming, unless I'm drunk and sleeping so the world could come to an end and not wake me up.—It may be all right for little girls that can't sleep and that stand by the window sucking in the coolness of the moon.

MEPHISTOPHELES: A king once was, they tell, 2207
> Who had a big pet flea—

SIEBEL: Quiet! Listen! A pretty rarity! A pretty piece of (2209) gallantry!

FROSCH: Start over!

MEPHISTOPHELES: A king once was, they tell, 2211
> Who had a big pet flea;
> He loved him passing well,
> Just like a son, they say.

His tailor he then bade,
And up the tailor goes;
"Here measure me this lad
To make a suit of clothes."

SIEBEL: Measure him right, now! That's it.   (2219)
           (*They all guffaw with laughter.*)
           Make sure no creases bulge!

MEPHISTOPHELES: In silks and velvet dressed   2223
           He stood now in his pride,
           With ribbons on his chest
           And many a cross beside.
           Prime Minister by station,
           He wore a star of state,
           And all his flea relation
           Were numbered with the great.   2230

           The gentlemen and ladies
           At court were much distressed,
           Both queen and maid were harried
           Along with all the rest,
           Yet didn't dare to scratch
           However they might itch.
           When we are bit, we catch
           And squash them as they twitch.

CHORUS (*shouting*):   When we are bit, we catch
           And squash them as they twitch.   2240

ALL (*in medley*):   Bravo! Bravo! Fine and excellent!   (2241)
    Another one! A couple more cans of drink! A couple
    more songs!

FAUST: Gentlemen! This wine is going sour. Sour, the
    way all wines in Leipzig have a way of going sour. But
    I fancy you would permit tapping a different vat for
    you.

SIEBEL: Do you have your own supply? Are you a dealer
    in wines? Would you happen to be one of those shysters
    from the old part of the country?

ALTEN: Wait a minute! (*He stands up.*) I have a sort of test to see whether I should drink any more. (*He closes his eyes and stands still for a while.*) Hm, hm, my little head is bobbling as it is.

SIEBEL: Bah! One bottle! I'll bear the consequences before God and before your wife.—Bring on your wine!

FAUST: Bring me a gimlet.   (2257)

FROSCH: The host has a kind of basket with tools over in the corner.

FAUST (*taking the gimlet*): Good! What kind of wine would you like?

FROSCH: Hey!

FAUST: What would you like to have in your glass? I'll get it for you!

FROSCH: Hey! Hey! A glass of Rhine wine, maybe. Genuine Niersteiner.

FAUST: Right! (*He bores a hole into the table next to Frosch.*) Now some wax!

ALTEN: Here's the stub of a candle.

FAUST: Good! (*He plugs the hole.*) Hold in there now!—And you?

SIEBEL: Muscatel! Spanish wine or nothing! But I want to see where it comes out.

FAUST (*boring and stoppering*): What will you have?

ALTEN: Red wine, a French kind!—I can't stand the French, but I do have a great respect for their wine.

FAUST (*as before*): Now what's your preference?

BRANDER: Do you take us for fools?

FAUST: Quickly, Sir, name your wine!

BRANDER: Tokay, then!—Is it going to come out of the table wood?

FAUST: Quiet, young Sir!—Just watch! Hold your glasses underneath. Each of you pull out his wax plug, but see that not a drop spills on the floor, or there will be a mishap!

ALTEN: I feel creepy. He's got the Devil in him.

FAUST: Pull out the plugs!
>   (*They pull out the plugs and each man receives
>   the wine of his choice in his glass.*)

FAUST: Plugs back in! And now taste!

SIEBEL: Good! Very good!

ALL: Good! Regally good!—Welcome among us!
>   (*They drink repeatedly.*)

MEPHISTOPHELES: They're on board now.

FAUST: Let's be going.   (2296)

MEPHISTOPHELES: One moment yet.

ALL (*singing*):   We've got more fun than cannibals   2293
>   Or than five hundred sows!   2294
>   (*They drink repeatedly. Siebel drops a cork,
>   liquid flows onto the stone floor, then turns
>   to flame which darts up Siebel's body.*)

SIEBEL: Hell and devils!

BRANDER: Witchcraft! Witchcraft!

FAUST: Didn't I tell you so?
>   (*He plugs the opening and pronounces a
>   few words, whereupon the flame vanishes.*)

SIEBEL: Master and Satan! Do you think you can come
into honest company and practice your infernal hocus-
pocus!

FAUST: Quiet, fattened porker!

SIEBEL: Call me a pig, will you? You broomstick!
Brothers! Beat him up! Knock him down! (*They draw
knives.*) Wizards are outlaws! By the law of the realm,
outlaws!

>   (*They start to attack Faust; he waves his hand,
>   and suddenly they stand in joyous astonishment
>   gazing at each other.*)

SIEBEL: What do I see! Vineyards!   (2316)

BRANDER: Grapes at this time of year?

ALTEN: And ripe! How beautiful!

FROSCH: Wait, here's the nicest!

(*They reach out and take hold of each
other's noses; they raise their knives.*)

FAUST: Stop!—Go and sleep it off!
           (*Faust and Mephistopheles leave.*)
           (*The others come to their senses and
           disperse with cries of dismay.*)

SIEBEL: My nose! Was that your nose? Was that the   (2322)
  grapes? Where is he?

BRANDER: Gone! It was the Devil himself.

FROSCH: I saw him ride out on a vat.

ALTEN: Did you! Then it's certainly not safe out on the
  marketplace—. How are we going to get home?

BRANDER: Let Siebel go first.

SIEBEL: I'm not that much of a fool!

FROSCH: Come on, let's rouse the constables down in the
  City Hall basement. For a tip they'll probably do their
  duty. Come on!

SIEBEL: I wonder if the wine is still flowing?
                (*He inspects the plugs.*)

ALTEN: Not a chance! Dry as wood.

FROSCH: Come on, you fellows! come on!
              (*Exeunt.*)   (2336)

*

HIGHWAY

(*A wayside cross. An old castle on the
hill to the right; in the distance a
peasant hut.*)

FAUST: Why rush, Mephisto, and hurry so?   2336a
  Why from the cross avert your eyes?   2336b

MEPHISTOPHELES: It's nothing but a prejudice, I know,   2336c
  But it repels me, you must realize.   2336d

*

A STREET

Faust. Margaret passing by.

FAUST: Fair lady, may I be so free   2605
   As offer my arm and company?
MARGARET: I'm neither a lady nor fair, and may
   Go unescorted on my way.
            (She disengages herself and goes on.)
FAUST: That girl was mighty pretty, now,   2609a
   And she struck fire in me somehow.   2610a
   So virtuous and modest, yes,
   But with a touch of spunkiness.
   Her lips so red, her cheek so bright,
   I never shall forget the sight.
   The shy way she cast down her eye
   Has pressed itself deep in my heart;
   And then the quick and short reply,
   That was the most delightful part!
            (Enter Mephistopheles.)
   You must get me that girl, your hear?
MEPHISTOPHELES: Which one?   2620
FAUST: She just went by me here.
MEPHISTOPHELES: That one? She just came from the
      priest,
   He absolved her from her sins and all;
   I stole up near the confessional.
   She's just a simple little thing,
   Went to confession just for nothing.
   On such as she I have no hold.
FAUST: And yet she's past fourteen years old.
MEPHISTOPHELES: Why, you talk just like Jack the Rake
   Who wants all flowers to bloom for his sake
   And fancies that no honor is,   2630
   Or favor, but the picking's his.
   It doesn't always work that way.

FAUST: Dear Master Laudable, I say
   Don't bother me with your legality!
   And I am telling you outright,
   Unless that creature of delight
   Lies in my arms this very night,
   At midnight we part company.

MEPHISTOPHELES: Remember there are limits! I
   Need fourteen days at least to try   2640
   And find an opportunity.

FAUST: Had I but seven and they were clear,   2642a
   I wouldn't need the Devil near
   To lead that girl astray for me.

MEPHISTOPHELES: You're talking like a Frenchman.
                                  Wait!
   And don't be put out or annoyed:
   What good's a thing too soon enjoyed?
   The pleasure is not half so great
   As when you first parade the doll
   Through every sort of folderol   2650
   And knead and pat and shape her well,
   The way that all French novels tell.

FAUST: I've appetite enough without it.

MEPHISTOPHELES: With no more joking now about it:
   I'm telling you that pretty child
   Will not be hurriedly beguiled.
   There's nothing to be gained by force;
   To cunning we must have recourse.

FAUST: Get me some of that angel's attire!
   Lead me to her place of rest!   2660
   Get me the kerchief from her breast,
   A garter for my love's desire!

MEPHISTOPHELES: Just so you see that I do heed
   Your pain and serve your every need,
   We shall not waste a single minute.
   I'll take you to her room and put you in it.

FAUST: And I shall see her? Have her?

MEPHISTOPHELES: No!
   She'll be at a neighbor's when we go.
   And all alone there you can dwell
   Upon the fragrance of her cell   2670
   And hope for future joys as well.
FAUST: Can we go now?
MEPHISTOPHELES: It's too soon yet.
FAUST: Get me a gift for her, and don't forget.
               (*Exit.*)
MEPHISTOPHELES: He's acting like a prince indeed.   2674a
   Give Lucifer a dozen such   2675a
   And soon hell wouldn't lack for much   2676a
   Of having its income garnisheed.   2677a
               (*Exit.*)

*

EVENING

*A small, neat room. Margaret braiding
her hair and doing it up.*

MARGARET: I'd give a good deal if I knew
   Who was that gentleman today!
   He had a very gallant way   2680
   And comes of noble lineage too.
   That much I could read from his face—
   Or he'd not be so bold in the first place.
              (*Exit.*)
     (*Enter Faust and Mephistopheles.*)
MEPHISTOPHELES: Come on! But softly. In you go!
FAUST (*after a silence*):   I beg you, leave me here alone.
MEPHISTOPHELES (*peering about*):
   Not every girl's this neat, you know?
              (*Exit.*)
FAUST (*looking all around*):

Welcome, lovely twilight gloom
That hovers in this sacred room!
Seize on my heart, sweet love pangs who
Both live and languish on hope's own dew.   2690
How everything here is imbued
With stillness, order, and content!
Here in this poverty, what plenitude!
Here in this prison, what ravishment!
        (*He throws himself into the leather
        armchair beside the bed.*)
O you who have both joy and sorrow known
From times gone by, clasp me too in your arms!
How often at this patriarchal throne
Children have gathered round about in swarms!
Perhaps my sweetheart, plump-cheeked, used to stand
Here grateful for a Christmas present and   2700
Devoutly kiss her grandsire's withered hand.
I feel your spirit, maiden, playing
About me, breathing order, plenitude,
And every day in mother-fashion saying
The cloth upon the table must be fresh renewed
And underfoot clean sand be strewed.
Dear hand! so godlike! In it lies
What turns a cottage to a paradise.
And here!
        (*He lifts the bed curtains.*)
            What chill of rapture seizes me!
Here I could linger on for hours.   2710
Here, Nature, you with your creative powers
From light dreams brought the angel forth to be;
Here lay the child, her bosom warm
With life; here tenderly there grew
With pure and sacred help from you
The godlike image of her form.

    And you? What purpose brought you here?
How I am touched with shame sincere!

What do you want? Why is your heart so sore?
O sorry Faust! I know you now no more.   2720

    Does magic haze surround me everywhere?
I pressed for pleasure with no least delay,
And in a love dream here I melt away!
Are we the toys of every breath of air?

    If she this moment now were to come by,
What punishment your impudence would meet!
The loud-mouth lummox—O how small!—would lie
Dissolved in shame before her feet.
        (Enter Mephistopheles.)
MEPHISTOPHELES: Quick now! I see her at the gate.
FAUST: Away! And never to come back!   2730
MEPHISTOPHELES: Here is a casket of some weight,
   I took it elsewhere from a rack.
   Just put it in her clothespress there,
   It'll make her head swim, that I'll swear.
   I promise you the things inside   2735a
   Would win a princess in her pride.   2736a
   A girl's a girl and play is play.
FAUST: I wonder . . . should I?
MEPHISTOPHELES: You delay?
   You wouldn't maybe want to keep the baubles?
   In that case I advise Your Lust   2740
   To save my pretty daytime, just
   Don't bother me with further troubles.
   You are not miserly, I trust!
   I scratch my head, I rub my hands—
        (He puts the casket in the clothespress
        and pushes the lock shut again.)
   Off and away now!
   To get that lovely child to play now
   Into your heart's desires and plans.
   And you stand all
   Poised to proceed to lecture hall,

And as if in the flesh, and gray,   2750
Physics and Metaphysics led the way.
Come on!
                        (*Exeunt.*)
                    (*Enter Margaret with a lamp.*)
MARGARET: It's close in here, there is no air.
                    (*She opens a window.*)
And yet it's not so warm out there.
I feel so odd, I can't say how—
I do wish Mother would come home now.
I'm chilled all over, and shivering!
I'm such a foolish, timid thing!
            (*She begins to sing as she undresses.*)
                    There was a king of Thule
                    True even to the grave,   2760
                    To whom a golden goblet
                    His dying mistress gave.

                    Naught did he hold more dear,
                    He drained it every feast;
                    And from his eye a tear
                    Welled each time as he ceased.

                    When life was nearly done,
                    His towns he totaled up,
                    Begrudged his heir not one,
                    But did not give the cup.   2770

                    There with his vassals all
                    At royal board sat he
                    In high ancestral hall
                    Of his castle by the sea.

                    The old toper then stood up,
                    Quaffed off his last life-glow,
                    And flung the sacred cup
                    Down to the flood below.

He saw it fall, and drink,
And sink deep in the sea; 2780
Then did his eyelids sink,
And no drop more drank he.
(*She opens the clothespress to put her clothes
away and catches sight of the jewel casket.*)
How did this pretty casket get in here?
I locked the press, I'm sure. How queer!
What can it have inside it? Can it be
That someone left it as security
For money Mother has provided?
Here on a ribbon hangs a little key—
I think I'll have a look inside it!
What's this? O Lord in heaven! See! 2790
I've never seen the like in all my days!
A noble lady with such jewelry
Could walk with pride on holidays.
I wonder how this chain would look on me?
Such glorious things! Whose could they be?
    (*She puts it on and steps up to the mirror.*)
If just these earrings could be mine!
One looks so different in them right away.
What good does beauty do, young thing? It may
Be very well to wonder at,
But people let it go at that; 2800
They praise you half in pity.
Gold serves all ends,
On gold depends
Everything. Ah, we poor!

*

A WALK

*Faust pacing up and down in thought. Mephistopheles
comes to him.*

MEPHISTOPHELES: Now by the element of hell! By love
                                                refused!
  I wish I knew a stronger oath that could be used!
FAUST: What's this? What's griping you so badly?
  I've never seen a face the like of this!
MEPHISTOPHELES: Why, I'd surrender to the Devil
                                                gladly
  If I were not the Devil as it is!   2810
FAUST: Have you gone off your head? I grant
  It suits you, though, to rave and rant.
MEPHISTOPHELES: Just think, those jewels for Gretchen
                                                that I got,
  Some priest has made off with the lot!   2814
  If all your veins ran angel-juice   2814a
  You'd still turn fish-wife and howl abuse.   2814b
  Her mother got to see the things,
  Off went her dire imagings;
  That woman's got some sense of smell,
  She has prayerbook-sniffing on the brain,
  A whiff of any item, and she can tell
  Whether the thing is sacred or profane.   2820
  That jewelry she spotted in a minute
  As having no great blessing in it.
  "My child," she cried, "ill-gotten good
  Ensnares the soul, consumes the blood.
  Before Our Lady we will lay it,
  With heaven's manna she'll repay it."
  Margretlein pulled a pouty face,
  Called it a gift horse, and in any case
  She thought he wasn't godless, he
  Who sneaked it in so cleverly.   2830
  The mother had a priest drop by;
  No sooner did he the trick espy
  Than his eyes lit up with what he saw.
  "This shows an upright mind," quoth he,
  "Self-conquest gains us victory.

The church has a good healthy maw,
She's swallowed up whole countries, still
She never yet has eaten her fill.
The church, dear ladies, alone has health
For digestion of ill-gotten wealth."   2840
FAUST: That's nothing but the usual game,
    A king and a Jew can do the same.
MEPHISTOPHELES: Then up he scooped brooch, chain,
                                                and rings
    As if they were just trivial things
    With no more thanks, if's, and's, or but's
    Than if they were a bag of nuts,
    Promised them celestial reward—
    All edified, they thanked him for it.
FAUST: And Gretchen?
MEPHISTOPHELES: Sits lost now in concern,
    Not knowing yet which way to turn;   2850
    Thinks day and night about the gems,
    But more of him from whom the present stems.
FAUST: I hate to see the dear girl worry.
    Get her a new set in a hurry.
    The first one wasn't too much anyway.
MEPHISTOPHELES: My gentleman finds this mere child's
                                                play.
FAUST: And here's the way I want it. Go
    Make friends there with that neighbor. Show
    You're not a devil made of sugar water,
    Get those new gems and have them brought her.   2860
MEPHISTOPHELES: Sir, I obey with all my heart.
                    (*Exit Faust.*)
    This fool in love will huff and puff
    The sun and moon and stars apart
    To get his sweetheart pastime stuff.
                    (*Exit.*)

                              *

THE NEIGHBOR'S HOUSE

Martha [alone.]

MARTHA: Now God forgive my husband, he
    Has not done the right thing by me.
    Way off into the world he's gone,
    And leaves me on the straw alone.
    Yet he surely had no cause on my part,
    God knows I loved him with all my heart.   2870
                    (*She weeps.*)
    He could be dead!—If I just knew for sure!   2871
    — — — — — —   2871a
    — — — — — —   2872a

    Or had a statement with a signature!
                    (*Enter Margaret.*)
MARGARET: Dame Martha!
MARTHA: What is it, Gretelchen?
MARGARET: My knees are sinking under me.
    I've found one in my press again,
    Another casket, of ebony,
    And this time it's a gorgeous set
    Far richer than the first one yet.
MARTHA: This time you mustn't tell your mother,
    Off it would go to church just like the other.   2880
MARGARET: O look at them! Just see! Just see!
MARTHA (*putting them on her*): You *are* a lucky
                    creature!
MARGARET: Unfortunately
    In church or on the street I do not dare
    Be seen in them, or anywhere.
MARTHA: You just come over frequently,
    Put on the jewels in secret here,
    Walk by the mirror an hour or so in privacy,
    And we'll enjoy them, never fear.
    There'll come a chance, a holiday, before we're done,

Where you can show them to the people one by one,   2890
A necklace first, pearl ear-drops next; your mother
Won't notice it, or we'll make up some thing or other.   2892
            (*A knock*)
MARGARET: Could that be Mother? Look and see.   2895
MARTHA (*looking through the blinds*):
    It's a strange gentleman.—Come in!
          (*Enter Mephistopheles.*)
MEPHISTOPHELES: I'm so free as to step right in,
    The ladies must excuse my liberty.
      (*stepping back respectfully before Margaret*)
    I wish to see Dame Martha Schwerdtlein, if I may.
MARTHA: Right here! What might the gentleman have   2900
                          to say?
MEPHISTOPHELES (*aside to her*):
    I know you now, that is enough for me.
    You have distinguished company.
    Forgive my freedom, I shall then
    Return this afternoon again.
MARTHA (*aloud*):   Child, think of it! The gentleman
                               takes
    You for some lady! For mercy's sakes!
MARGARET: I'm just a poor young girl; I find
    The gentleman is far too kind.
    These gems do not belong to me.
MEPHISTOPHELES: Oh, it's not just the jewelry.   2910
    She has a quick glance, and a way!
    I am delighted I may stay.
MARTHA: What is your errand then? I'm very—
MEPHISTOPHELES: I wish my tidings were more merry.
    I trust you will not make me rue this meeting:
    Your husband is dead and sends you greeting.
MARTHA: He's dead! That faithful heart! Oh, my!
    My husband's dead! Oh! I shall die!
MARGARET: Dear lady, oh! Do not despair!
MEPHISTOPHELES: Now listen to the sad affair.   2920

MARGARET: I hope I never, never love.
　Such loss as this I would die of.
MEPHISTOPHELES: Glad must have sad, sad must have
　　glad, as always.
MARTHA: O tell me all about his dying!
MEPHISTOPHELES: At Padua, by Saint Anthony's
　They buried him, and he is lying
　In ground well sanctified and blest
　At cool and everlasting rest.
MARTHA: And there is nothing else you bring?
MEPHISTOPHELES: Yes, one request and solemn enter-　　　　2930
　　　　　　　　　　　　　　　　　　prise:
　Three hundred Masses for him you should have them
　　　　　　　　　　　　　　　　　　sing.
　My pockets are quite empty otherwise.
MARTHA: What, not a luck-piece, or a trinket such
　As any journeyman deep in his pack would hoard
　As a remembrance token stored
　And sooner starve or beg than use it!
MEPHISTOPHELES: Madam, it grieves me very much;
　Indeed he did not waste his money or lose it.
　And much did he his failings then deplore,
　Yes, and complained of his hard luck still more.　　　　2940
MARGARET: To think that human fortunes so miscarry!
　Many's the Requiem I'll pray for him, I'm sure.
MEPHISTOPHELES: Ah, you deserve now very soon to
　　　　　　　　　　　　　　　　　marry,
　A child of such a kindly nature.
MARGARET: It's not yet time for that. Oh, no!
MEPHISTOPHELES: If not a husband, then meanwhile a
　　　　　　　　　　　　　　　　　beau.
　It's one of heaven's greatest graces
　To hold so dear a thing in one's embraces.
MARGARET: It's not the custom here for one.
MEPHISTOPHELES: Custom or not, it still is done.　　　　2950
MARTHA: But tell me more!

MEPHISTOPHELES: I stood at his bed-
                                            side—
  Half-rotten straw it was and little more
  Than horse manure; but in good Christian style he
                                            died,
  Yet found he had still further items on his score.
  "How I detest myself!" he cried with dying breath,
  "For having left my business and my wife!
  Ah, that remembrance is my death.
  If she would just forgive me in this life!"—
MARTHA (*weeping*):   The good man! I long since for-
                                            gave.
MEPHISTOPHELES: "God knows, though, she was more   2960
  to blame than I."
MARTHA: It's a lie! And he with one foot in the grave!
MEPHISTOPHELES: Oh, he was talking through his hat
  There at the end, if I am half a judge.
  "I had no time to sit and yawn," he said,
  "First children and then earning children's bread,
  Bread in the widest sense, at that,
  And could not even eat my share in peace."
MARTHA: Did he forget my love, how I would drudge
  Both day and night and never cease?
MEPHISTOPHELES: No, he remembered that all right.   2970
  "As I put out from Malta," he went on,
  "I prayed for wife and children fervently;
  Then heaven too disposed things favorably
  So our ship took a Turkish galleon
  With treasure for the great Sultan aboard.
  The bravery came in for reward
  And I got, as was only fair,
  My own well calculated share."
MARTHA: What! Where? Do you suppose he buried it?   2980
MEPHISTOPHELES: Who knows where the four winds
                                            have carried it?
  A pretty girl took him in tow when he

Was roaming Naples there without a friend;
She showed him so much love and loyalty
He bore the marks right to his blessed end.
MARTHA: The rogue! He robbed his children like a
                                               thief!

And all that misery and grief
Could not prevent the shameful life he led.
MEPHISTOPHELES: But that, you see, is why he's dead.
Were I in your place now, you know,
I'd mourn him for a decent year and then   2990
Be casting round meanwhile to find another beau.
MARTHA: Oh Lord, the kind my first man was,
I'll never in this world find such again.
There never was a fonder fool than mine.
Only, he liked the roving life too much,
And foreign women, and his wine,   2996a
And then, of course, those devilish dice.
MEPHISTOPHELES: Well, well, it could have worked out
                                                        fine
If he had only taken such
Good care on his part to be nice.   3000
I swear on those terms it is true
I would myself exchange rings with you.
MARTHA: Oh, the gentleman has such joking ways!
MEPHISTOPHELES (aside):   It's time for me to be pushing
                                                   onward!

She'd hold the very Devil to his word.
(to Gretchen)
How are things with your heart these days?
MARGARET: What do you mean, Sir?
MEPHISTOPHELES (aside):   O you innocents!
(aloud) Ladies, farewell!
MARTHA: One word yet! What I crave is   3008a
Some little piece of evidence
Of when and how my sweetheart died and where his   3010
                                          grave is.

I've always been a friend of orderliness.
I'd like to read his death note in the weekly press.
MEPHISTOPHELES: Good woman, what two witnesses
report
Will stand as truth in any court.
I have a friend, quite serious,
I'll bring him to the judge with us.
I'll go and get him.
MARTHA: Do that! Do!
MEPHISTOPHELES: This lady will be with you too?
A splendid lad, much traveled. He
Shows ladies every courtesy.   3020
MARGARET: The gentleman would make me blush for
shame.
MEPHISTOPHELES: Before no earthly king that one could
name.
MARTHA: Out in the garden to the rear
This afternoon we'll expect both of you here.
(*Exeunt*.)

*

[AN UNTITLED SCENE, LATER MARKED "A STREET"]

Faust. Mephistopheles.

FAUST: How is it? Will it work? Will it succeed?
MEPHISTOPHELES: Ah, bravo! I find you aflame indeed.
Gretchen is yours now pretty soon.
You meet at neighbor Martha's house this afternoon.
The woman is expressly made
To work the pimp and gypsy trade!   3030
FAUST: I welcome her.
MEPHISTOPHELES: But not without some bother: 3031a
One good turn deserves another.   3032a
We will depose some testimony or other

To say her husband's bones are to be found
In Padua in consecrated ground.
FAUST: Fine! First we'll need to do some journey-going.
MEPHISTOPHELES: *Sancta simplicitas!* For that we need
not fuss.

Just testify, and never mind the knowing.
FAUST: Think of a better plan, or nothing doing.
MEPHISTOPHELES: O saintly man! and sanctimonious!   3040
False witness then you never bore
In all your length of life before?
Have you not with great power given definition
Of God, the world, and all the world's condition,
Of man, man's heart, man's mind, and what is more,   3045
With no more knowledge of them than   3048a
Of the decease of this Schwerdtlein man.   3049a
FAUST: You are a liar and a sophist too.   3050
MEPHISTOPHELES: Or would be, if I didn't know a thing
or two.

Tomorrow will you not deceive
Poor Gretchen and then make her believe
The vows of soul-felt love you swear?
FAUST: And from my heart.
MEPHISTOPHELES: All good and fair!
Then comes eternal faith, and love still higher,
Then comes the super-almighty desire—
Will that be heartfelt too, I inquire?
FAUST: Stop there! It will!—If I have feeling,
And for this feeling, for this reeling   3060
Seek a name, and finding none,
With all my senses through the wide world run,
And clutch at words supreme, and claim
That boundless, boundless is the flame
That burns me, infinite and never done,
Is that a devilish, lying game?
MEPHISTOPHELES: I still am right!
FAUST: Mark this and heed it,

And spare me further waste of throat and lung:
To win an argument takes no more than a tongue,
That's all that's needed. 3070
But come, this chatter fills me with disgust,
For you are right, primarily because I must.

*

A GARDEN

Margaret on Faust's arm, Martha with
Mephistopheles, strolling up and down.

MARGARET: I feel, Sir, you are only sparing me
And shaming me by condescending so.
A traveler, from charity,
Will often take things as they go.
I realize my conversation can
Not possibly amuse such an experienced man.
FAUST: One glance of yours, one word delights me more
Than all of this world's wisdom-store 3080
 (*He kisses her hand.*)
MARGARET: How can you kiss it? It must seem to you
So coarse, so rough a hand to kiss.
What kinds of tasks have I not had to do!
You do not know how strict my mother is.
 (*They pass on.*)
MARTHA: And so, Sir, you are traveling constantly?
MEPHISTOPHELES: Business and duty keep us on our
way.

Many a place one leaves regretfully,
But then one simply cannot stay.
MARTHA: It may well do while in one's prime
To rove about the world as a rolling stone, 3090
But then comes the unhappy time,
And dragging to the grave, a bachelor, alone,
Was never good for anyone.

MEPHISTOPHELES: Ah, such with horror I anticipate.
MARHTA: Then act, dear Sir, before it is too late.
                    (*They pass on.*)
MARGARET: But out of sight is out of mind!
    Your courtesy comes naturally;
    But you have friends in quantity
    Who are more clever than my kind.
FAUST: Dear girl, believe me, clever in that sense   3100
    Means usually a close self-interest.
MARGARET: Really?
FAUST: To think simplicity and innocence
    Are unaware their sacred way is best,
    That lowliness and sweet humility
    Are bounteous Nature's highest gifts—
MARGARET: Think only for a moment's time of me,
    I shall have time enough to think of you.
FAUST: Then you are much alone?
MARGARET: Yes, our house is a little one,
    And yet it must be tended to.   3110
    We have no maid, hence I must cook and sweep and
                                                  knit
    And sew, and do the errands early and late;
    And then my mother is a bit
    Too strict and straight.
    And yet she has no need to scrimp and save this way;
    We could live better far than others, you might say;
    My father left a sizeable estate,
    A house and garden past the city gate.
    But I have rather quiet days of late.
    My brother is a soldier,   3120
    My little sister died;
    The child did sometimes leave me with my patience
                                                  tried,
    And yet I'd gladly have the trouble back again,
    She was so dear to me.
FAUST: An angel, if like you.
MARGARET: I brought her up; she dearly loved me too.

She was born following my father's death.
Mother we thought at her last breath,
She was so miserable, but then
She slowly, slowly got her strength again.
It was impossible for her to nurse　　　　　　3130
The little mite herself, of course,
And so I raised her all alone
On milk and water; she became my own.
In my arms, in my lap she smiled,
Wriggled, and grew up to be a child.

FAUST:　You must have known the purest happiness.

MARGARET:　But many trying hours nonetheless.
At night her little cradle used to stand
Beside my bed, and she had but to stir
And I was there at hand,　　　　　　　　3140
Sometimes to feed her, sometimes to comfort her,
Sometimes when she would not be well, to rise
And pace the floor with her to soothe her cries,
And yet be at the washtub early, do
The marketing and tend the hearth fire too,
And every morrow like today.
One's spirits are not always cheerful, Sir, that way;
Yet food is relished better, as is rest.　　　　3148

(*They pass on.*)

MARTHA:　But is there no one, Sir, that you have found?　3153
Speak frankly, is your heart in no wise bound?

MEPHISTOPHELES:　The proverb says: A wife and one's
own household
Are worth their weight in pearls and gold.

MARTHA:　But I mean, have you felt no inclination?

MEPHISTOPHELES:　I have met everywhere with much
consideration.

MARTHA:　But has your heart in no case been impressed?

MEPHISTOPHELES:　With ladies one must not presume to　3160
jest.

MARTHA:　Oh, you misunderstand me!

MEPHISTOPHELES: What a shame!
I find
    I understand—that you are very kind.
        (*They pass on.*)
FAUST: And so you did, my angel, recognize
    Me in the garden here at the first look?
MARGARET: Did you not see how I cast down my eyes?
FAUST: And you forgive the liberty I took
    And all my impudence before
    When you had just left the cathedral door?
MARGARET: I was confused, the experience was all new.
    No one could say bad things of me. 3170
    Ah, thought I, could he possibly
    Have noted something brazen or bold in you?
    He seemed to think here was a girl he could
    Treat in just any way he would.
    I must confess that then I hardly knew
    What soon began to argue in your favor;
    But I was angry with myself, however,
    For not becoming angrier with you.
FAUST: My darling!
MARGARET: Wait!
      (*She picks a star flower and plucks
      the petals off it one by one.*)
FAUST: What is it? A bouquet?
MARGARET: No, just a game. 3180
FAUST: What?
MARGARET: You'd laugh at me if I
                should say.
    (*She murmurs something as she goes on plucking.*)
FAUST: What are you murmuring?
MARGARET (*half aloud*): He loves me—loves
                me not.
FAUST: You lovely creature of the skies!
      (*He takes both her hands.*)
MARGARET: I'm trembling!

FAUST: O do not tremble! Let this glance
  And let this pressure of my hands
  Say what is inexpressible: 3190
  To yield oneself entirely and to feel
  A rapture that must be everlasting!
  Eternal!—Its end would be despair.
  No! Without end! Without end!

  (*Margaret presses his hands, disengages
  herself, and runs off. He stands in thought for
  a moment, then follows her.*)

MARTHA: It's getting dark.

MEPHISTOPHELES: We must be on our way.

MARTHA: I'd ask you gentlemen to stay,
  But this is such a wicked neighborhood.
  It seems that no one has a thing to do
  Or put his mind to
  But watch his neighbor's every move and stir. 3200
  No matter what one does, there's always talk.
  What of our couple?

MEPHISTOPHELES: They've flown up the arbor
                                    walk.

  The wanton butterflies!

MARTHA: He seems to take to her.

MEPHISTOPHELES: And she to him. Such is the world's
  old way.

*

A SUMMER HOUSE

*Margaret comes running in, hides behind the
door, puts her finger to her lips, and peeps
through the crack.*

MARGARET: He's coming!

FAUST: Little rogue, to tease me so!

I'll catch you!
>   (*He kisses her.*)
MARGARET (*embracing him and returning his kiss*):
>   From my heart I've long loved you so!   3206a
>   (*Mephistopheles knocks.*)
FAUST (*stamping his foot*):
>   Who's there?
MEPHISTOPHELES: A friend!
FAUST: A beast!
MEPHISTOPHELES: It's time for us to go.
MARTHA: Yes, it is late, Sir.
FAUST: May I escort you, though?
MARGARET: My mother would—Farewell!
FAUST: Ah, must I leave you then?
>   Farewell!   3210
MARTHA: Adieu!
MARGARET: But soon to meet again!
>   (*Exeunt Faust and Mephistopheles.*)
>   Dear Lord! What things and things there can
>   Come to the mind of such a man!
>   I stand abashed, and for the life of me
>   Cannot do other than agree.
>   A simple child, I cannot see
>   Whatever it is he finds in me.   3216
>   (*Exit.*)

*

GRETCHEN'S ROOM

Gretchen at her spinning wheel, alone.

GRETCHEN: My peace is gone,   3374
>   My heart is sore,
>   I'll find it never
>   And nevermore.

When he does not come
I live in a tomb,
The world is all   3380
Bitter as gall.

O, my poor head
Is quite distraught,
And my poor mind
Is overwrought.

My peace is gone,
My heart is sore,
I'll find it never
And nevermore.

I look from my window   3390
Only to greet him,
I leave the house
Only to meet him.

His noble gait
And form and guise,
The smile of his mouth,
The spell of his eyes,

The magic in
Those words of his,
The clasp of his hand,   3400
And oh!—his kiss.

My peace is gone,
My heart is sore,
I'll find it never
And nevermore.

My bosom aches
To feel him near,
Oh, could I clasp
And hold him here
And kiss and kiss him   3410

Whom I so cherish,
Beneath his kisses
I would perish!

*

MARTHA'S GARDEN

Margaret. Faust.

GRETCHEN: But tell me, Henry!   3414a
FAUST: Tell what, then?
GRETCHEN: About religion, what do you feel now, say?
　You are a good, warmhearted man,
　And yet I fear you're not inclined that way.
FAUST: Leave that, my child! That I love you, you feel;
　For those I love, my flesh and blood I'd give,
　And no one's church or feelings would I steal.   3420
MARGARET: But that is not enough! One must believe!
FAUST:.   Must one?
MARGARET: O, if I had some influence!
　You do not even revere the sacraments.
FAUST: I do revere them.
MARGARET: But without desire.
　It's long since you have gone to Mass or to confession.
　Do you believe in God?
FAUST: My darling, who can say:
　I believe in God?
　Ask priest or sage you may,
　And their replies seem odd
　Mockings of the asker.   3430
MARGARET: Then you do not believe?
FAUST: My answer, dear one, do not misconceive!
　Who can name
　Him, or proclaim:
　I believe in Him?

Who is so cold
As to make bold
To say: I do not believe in Him?
The all-embracing,
The all-sustaining,
Does He not hold and sustain   3440
You, me, Himself?
Does heaven not arch high above us?
Does earth not lie firm here below?
And do not everlasting stars
Rise with a kindly glance?
Do I not gaze into your eyes,
And do not all things crowd
Into your head and heart,
Working in eternal mystery
Invisibly visible at your side?   3450
Let these things fill your heart, vast as they are,
And when you are entirely happy in that feeling,
Then call it what you will:
Heart, Fortune, Love, or God!
I have no name for it.
Feeling is everything,
Names are sound and smoke
Obscuring heaven's glow.

MARGARET: That is all very good and fair;
The priest says much the same, although   3460
He used a different wording as he spoke.

FAUST: It is said everywhere
By all hearts underneath the sky of day,
Each heart in its own way;
So why not I in mine?

MARGARET: It sounds all right when you express it so;
There's something not quite right about it, though;
You have no Christianity.

FAUST: Dear child!

MARGARET: It has this long time troubled me
To find you keep the company you do.   3470

FAUST: How so?

MARGARET: The person whom you have with you
   In my profoundest being I abhor,
   And nothing in my life before
   So cut me to the heart
   As this man's face when he came near.

FAUST: My darling, have no fear.

MARGARET: His presence roils my blood, yet for my
                       part,
   People otherwise win my heart;
   Much as I yearn to have you near,
   This person inspires in me a secret fear,   3480
   And if I take him for a scoundrel too,
   God forgive me for the wrong I do!

FAUST: Such queer fish also have to be.

MARGARET: To live with him would never do for me!
   Let him but so much as appear,
   He looks about with such a sneer
   And half enraged;
   Nothing can keep his sympathy engaged;
   Upon his brow it's written clear
   That he can hold no person dear.   3490
   In your embrace I feel so free,
   So warm, so yielded utterly;
   His presence chokes me, chills me through and through.

FAUST: O you intuitive angel, you!

MARGARET: This so overwhelms me, that when
   He joins us, be it where it may,
   It seems that I no longer love you then.
   With him there, I could never pray.
   This eats my very heart; and you,
   Henry, must feel the same thing too.   3500

FAUST: This is a matter of antipathy.

MARGARET: I must be going.

FAUST: O, when will it be
   That I may for a little hour rest
   In your embrace in quiet, breast to breast?

MARGARET: If I but slept alone, this very night
    I'd leave the door unbolted, you realize,
    But Mother's sleep is always light,
    And if she took us by surprise,
    I would die on the spot, I think.
FAUST: There is no need for that, my dear!   3510
    Here is a little phial. A mere
    Three drops into her drink
    Will shroud up Nature in deep sleep.
MARGARET: What will I not do for your sake?
    It will not harm her, though, to take?
FAUST: Would I propose it, Love, if that were so?
MARGARET: I look at you, dear man, and do not know
    What so compels me to your will;
    Already I have done so much for you
    That there is little left for me to do.   3520
                (*Exit.*)
        (*Enter Mephistopheles.*)
MEPHISTOPHELES: The little monkey's gone?
FAUST: You spied again?
MEPHISTOPHELES: I could
    Not help but hear it word for word:
    Professor had his catechism heard;
    I hope it does you lots of good.
    Girls have a way of wanting to find out
    Whether a man's conventionally devout.
    They think: he gave in there, he'll truckle to us, no
                       doubt.
FAUST: You, monster, do not realize
    How this good loyal soul can be
    So full of faith and trust—   3530
    Which things alone suffice
    To make her bliss—and worry holily
    For fear she must look on her best beloved as lost.
MEPHISTOPHELES: You supersensual sensual wooer,
    A girl has got you on a puppet wire.
FAUST: You misbegotten thing of filth and fire!

MEPHISTOPHELES: She's mighty clever too at physi-
                                      ognomy:
  When I am present, she feels—how, she's not just sure,
  My mask bodes meaning at a hidden level;
  She thinks beyond a doubt I'm a "Genie,"   3540
  And possibly the very Devil.
  Tonight, then—?
FAUST: What is that to you?
MEPHISTOPHELES: I have my pleasure in it too!

*

AT THE WELL

Gretchen and Lieschen with pitchers.

LIESCHEN: About Barbie, I suppose you've heard?
GRETCHEN: I get out very little. Not a word.
LIESCHEN: Why, Sibyl was telling me today.
  She's finally gone down Fools' Way.
  That's what grand airs will do!
GRETCHEN: How so?
LIESCHEN: It stinks!
  She's feeding two now when she eats and drinks.
GRETCHEN: Ah!   3550
LIESCHEN: Serves her right! And long enough
  She hung around that fellow. All that stuff!
  It was walk and jaunt
  Out to the village and dancing haunt,
  And everywhere she had to shine,
  Always treating her to pastry and wine;
  She got to think her good looks were so fine
  She lost her self-respect and nothing would do
  But she accepted presents from him too.
  It was kiss and cuddle, and pretty soon   3560
  The flower that she had was gone.
GRETCHEN: O the poor thing!

LIESCHEN: Is it pity that you feel!
  When our kind sat at the spinning wheel
  And our mothers wouldn't let us out at night,
  There she was with her lover at sweet delight
  Down on the bench in the dark entryway
  With never an hour too long for such play.
  So let her go now with head bowed down
  And do church penance in a sinner's gown!
GRETCHEN: But surely he'll take her as his wife!   3570
LIESCHEN: He'd be a fool! A chipper lad
  Finds fun is elsewhere to be had.
  Besides, he's gone.
GRETCHEN: O, that's not fair!
LIESCHEN: If she gets him, she'll find it bad.
  The boys will rip her wreath, and what's more,
  They'll strew chopped straw around her door!
                     (*Exit.*)
GRETCHEN (*walking home*):   How firmly I could once
                                              inveigh
  When any young girl went astray!
  For others' sins I could not find
  Words enough to speak my mind!   3580
  Black as it was, blacker it had to be,
  And still it wasn't black enough for me.
  I thanked my stars and was so game,
  And now I stand exposed to shame!
  Yet all that led me to this pass
  Was so good, and so dear, alas!

                     *

                     ZWINGER

        *In a niche of the wall, a statue of the
        Mater Dolorosa with jugs of flowers in
                     front of it.*

Gretchen bends down to fill the jugs from the
nearest well-basin, then puts into them
the fresh flowers that she has brought.

GRETCHEN: O deign
   Amid your pain
   To look down now upon my grief.   3589a

    With sword thrust through   3590
   The heart of you,
   You gaze up to your Son in death.

    To Him on high
   You breathe your sigh
   For His and your distressful grief.

    Who knows
   What throes
   Wrack me, flesh and bone?
   What makes my poor heart sick with fear
   And what it is I plead for here,   3600
   Only you know, you alone!

    No matter where I go,
   I know such woe, such woe
   Here within my breast!
   I am not quite alone,
   Alas! I weep, I moan,
   My heart is so distressed.

    The flowerpots at my window
   Had only tears for dew '
   When early in the morning   3610
   I picked these flowers for you.

    When bright into my room
   The early sun had come,

Upon my bed in gloom
I sat, with sorrow numb.

Help! Rescue me from shame and death!
O deign
Amid your pain
To look down now upon my grief!   3619a

*

CATHEDRAL

Funeral Mass for Gretchen's mother.
Gretchen. All relatives. Service, organ,
and choir.

EVIL SPIRIT (*behind Gretchen*):
  How different, Gretchen, it was   3776
  When still full of innocence
  You approached this altar
  And from your little dog-eared prayer book   3779a
  You murmured your prayers,   3780a
  Half childish play,
  Half God in heart!
  Gretchen!
  Where are your thoughts?
  Within your heart
  What deed of crime?
  Are you now praying for your mother's soul   3787a
  That slept away to pain because of you?   3788a
  —And beneath your heart   3790
  Does not a new life quicken,   3791
  To be born with shame's brand-mark?   3791a
  Tormenting itself and you
  With its premonitory presence?
GRETCHEN: Alas! Alas!
  If I could be rid of the thoughts

That rush this way and that way
Despite my will!

CHOIR: *Dies irae, dies illa*
Solvet saeclum in favilla.
        (*The organ sounds.*)

EVIL SPIRIT: Wrath seizes you!   3800
Trumpets ring out!   3801a
The graves shudder!
And your heart
From ashen rest,
For flames of torment
Once more reconstituted,
Quakes forth.

GRETCHEN: If I were out of here!
I feel as if the organ were
Stifling my breath,   3810
As if the choir dissolved
My inmost heart.

CHOIR: *Judex ergo cum sedebit,*
Quidquid latet adparebit,
Nil inultum remanebit.

GRETCHEN: I cannot breathe!
The pillars of the wall
Imprison me!
The vaulted roof
Crushes me!—Air!   3820

EVIL SPIRIT: You seek to hide?   3821a
Your sin and shame,   3821b
Would they be hidden?   3822
Air! Light!   3823
Woe to you!

CHOIR: *Quid sum miser tunc dicturus?*
Quem patronum rogaturus?
Cum vix justus sit securus.

EVIL SPIRIT: The clarified avert
Their countenances from you.
The pure shudder to reach   3830

Out hands to you   3831
In their purity!   3831a
Woe!

CHOIR: *Quid sum miser tunc dicturus?*

GRETCHEN: Neighbor! Your smelling-bottle!   3834
                    (*She falls in a faint.*)

*

NIGHT

In front of Gretchen's house.
Valentine, a soldier, Gretchen's brother.

VALENTINE: When I used to be in a merry crowd   3620
    Where many a fellow liked to boast,
    And lads in praise of girls grew loud
    And to their fairest raised a toast
    And drowned praise in glasses' overflow,
    Then, braced on my elbows, I
    Would sit with calm assurance by
    And listen to their braggadocio;
    Then I would stroke my beard and smile
    And take my brimming glass in hand
    And say: "To each his own! Meanwhile   3630
    Where is there one in all the land
    To hold a candle or compare
    With my sister Gretel anywhere?"
    Clink! Clank! the round of glasses went;
    "He's right!" some shouted in assent,
    "The glory of her sex!" cried some,
    And all the braggarts sat there dumb.
    But now!—I could tear my hair and crawl
    Right up the side of the smooth wall!—
    Now every rascal that comes near   3640
    Can twit me with a jibe or sneer!

With every chance word dropped I sweat
Like one who has not paid a debt.
I'd knock the whole lot down if I
Could only tell them that they lie. 3645
   (*Enter Faust and Mephistopheles.*)
FAUST: How from the window of that sacristy 3650
  The vigil lamp casts forth its flickering light
  Sidewise faint and fainter down the night,
  And darkness closes around totally.
  So in my heart the darkness reigns.
MEPHISTOPHELES: And I feel like a cat with loving-pains
  That sneaks up fire escapes and crawls
  And slinks along the sides of walls;
  I feel so cozy at it, and so right,
  With a bit of thievery, a bit of rutting to it. 3659
  Come on, then! What a shame this is! 3342
  You're going to your sweetheart's room 3343
  And not off to your doom. 3344
FAUST: What if I do find heaven in her arms? 3345
  Or if intense emotion my spirit warms? 3346a
  It's still undone by that poor soul's distress. 3347a
  Am I not still the fugitive, the homeless, 3348
  The monster without rest or purpose sweeping 3349
  Like a cataract from crag to crag and leaping 3350
  In frenzy of desire to the abyss? 3351
  While at one side, she, with her childlike mind, 3352
  Dwells in a cottage on the Alpine slope 3353
  With all her quiet life confined 3354
  Within her small world's narrow scope. 3355
  And I, the God-detested, 3356
  Had not enough, but wrested 3357
  The crag away and scattered 3358
  Its ruins as they shattered 3359
  To undermine her and her peace as well! 3360
  The victim you demanded, fiend of hell! 3361
  Help, Devil, make this time of anguish brief! 3362

Let it be soon if it must be!	3363
Let her fate crash in ruins over me,	3364
Together let us come to grief.	3365
MEPHISTOPHELES: Ah, now it seethes again and glows!	3366
Go in and comfort her, you lout!	3367
A head like yours beholds the close	3368
Of doom as soon as he sees no way out.	3369

*

N.B.—*The following prose scene has no title in the "Urfaust". In the completed poem it is placed after line 4398 and assigned the heading: "Gloomy Day. A field," but it is left as prose, with tiny changes from the following.*

Faust. Mephistopheles.

FAUST: In misery! Desperate! Long wandering pitifully upon the earth! Locked up as a wrongdoer for ghastly torments in a jail, that lovely, unfortunate creature! To come to this! Perfidious, worthless Spirit, and this you kept from me! Stand there! Stand there! Roll those devilish eyes furiously in your head! Stand and defy me with your unbearable presence! In prison! In irrevocable misery delivered over to evil spirits and to judging, heartless humanity! And meanwhile you lull me with insipid joys, conceal her increasing misery from me, and let her go helpless to destruction!

MEPHISTOPHELES: She is not the first!

FAUST: Cur! Monster of abomination! Turn him, Infinite Spirit, turn the worm back into his canine form, the way he used to like to trot along in front of me often in time of night, and roll at the feet of the harmless traveler, and cling to the shoulders of one who fell. Turn him back into his favorite shape, so he can crawl on his belly in the sand up to me and I can kick him, the reprobate!—Not the first!—Grief! Grief beyond the grasp of any human soul, that more than one creature has sunk to the depths of such misery, that the first did not atone for the guilt of all the others in her writhing and deathly agony before the eyes of the Eternal! It grinds through my marrow and my life, the misery of this one alone, and you grin over the fate of thousands.

MEPHISTOPHELES: Booby! Now you are once again at the end of your wits, where you gentlemen lose your heads. Why do you make common cause with us if you can't go through with it? You want to fly and your heads swim. Eh? Did we force ourselves on you, or you on us?

FAUST: Do not bare your ravening fangs at me that way! I loathe it!—Great and glorious Spirit who didst deign to appear to me, who knowest my heart and my soul, why dost thou forge me together with this infamous associate who gloats on harm and revels in destruction?

MEPHISTOPHELES: Are you through?

FAUST: Save her! Or woe to you! The ghastliest curses upon you unto millennia! Save her!

MEPHISTOPHELES: I cannot loose the avenger's bonds, nor open his locks. Save her—? Who was it plunged her into ruin? I or you?

(Faust gazes wildly about.)

So you reach for thunderbolts? Lucky they were not given to you miserable mortals! In your distraction is that the only trick you have to relieve your feelings, to pulverize the innocent party in your way?

FAUST: Take me there! She shall be free!

MEPHISTOPHELES: And the risk you run? Remember: upon the city still lies the blood-guilt that you brought upon her, and over the site of one slain there hover avenging spirits in wait for the returning murderer.

FAUST: This yet from you? A world of murder and death upon you, monster! Take me there, I say, and set her free!

MEPHISTOPHELES: I will take you, and what I *can* do: hear! Do I have all power in heaven and on earth? The jailer's senses I will becloud, *you* get possession of his keys and lead her out yourself with your human hand. I will stand watch and hold the magic horses in readiness. That much I can do.

FAUST: Up and away!

*

NIGHT. OPEN COUNTRY

Faust, Mephistopheles rushing on black horses.

FAUST: What are they doing yonder on Gallows Rock?   4399
MEPHISTOPHELES: I don't know what they're brewing or   4400
    doing.
FAUST: They soar and swoop, bending and stooping.
MEPHISTOPHELES: A crew of witches.
FAUST: They strew and bless.
MEPHISTOPHELES: On past! On past!   4404

*

DUNGEON

Faust in front of a little iron door,
with a bunch of keys and a lamp.

FAUST: A horror long unfamiliar seizes me. Inmost hor-   (4405)
    ror of humanity.
    Here, Here!—Up!—Your delay coaxes death up!
    (*He seizes the lock. Singing is heard from inside.*)
                    My mother, the whore,   4412
                    She murdered me!
                    My father, the rogue,
                    He has eaten me!
                    Little sister has laid
                    My bones away
                    In a place of cool, cool shade.
                    And I am turned into a woodland bird;
                    Fly away! Fly away!   4420

(Faust shrinks back, trembling, then summons courage and unlocks the door. He hears the chains rattle and the straw rustle.)

MARGARET *(cowering on her pallet)*: Alas! Alas! (4423)
They're coming. O bitter death!

FAUST *(softly)*:   Be still! I've come to set you free.
(He starts to unlock her chains.)

MARGARET *(resisting)*: Get away! At midnight!
Headsman, isn't tomorrow morning soon enough for
you?

FAUST: Don't!

MARGARET *(rolling away from him)*: Have pity on me (4432)
and let me live! I am so young, so young, and I used to
be pretty, and I am a poor young girl. Just look at my
flowers, just look at my wreath. Have pity on me!
What have I done to you? I never saw you in my life
before!

FAUST: Her mind is wandering and I can't do anything
about it.

MARGARET: See my baby! I must nurse it. There I had
it. There! I have nursed it! They took it away from me
and said I killed it, and they sing songs against me!—It
isn't true—it's just a story that ends that way, they
weren't singing it about me.

FAUST *(throwing himself on his knees beside
her)*: Gretchen!

MARGARET *(jumping up)*: Where is he? I heard him (4461)
call! He cried "Gretchen!" He called to me! Where is
he! Ah, through all the howling and gnashing of teeth I
recognize him, he called to me: "Gretchen!"
(throwing herself down in front of him)
Man! Man! Give him to me! Get him for me! Where
is he!

FAUST *(Wildly putting his arms around her)*: My Love!
My Love!
(Margaret buries her head in his lap.)

Up, my Love! Your murderer has become your deliverer. Up!

> (*While she remains insensate he undoes
> the chains on her arms.*)

Come, let's escape this horrible fate!

MARGARET (*leaning against him*): Kiss me! Kiss me!

FAUST: A thousand times! Only, hurry, Gretchen! Hurry!

MARGARET: Kiss me! Can you no longer kiss? What! (4484) What! You are my Henry, and you have unlearned how to kiss? How an entire heaven used to sweep over me with might at your embrace. The way you used to kiss as if you meant to suffocate me in pleasureful death. Henry, kiss me, or else I'll kiss you. (*She embraces him.*) Alas! your lips are cold! Death! You do not answer!

FAUST: Follow me and I'll hearten you with warmth a (4498) thousandfold. Only, follow me!

MARGARET (*sitting down and remaining silent for some time*): Henry, is it you?

FAUST: It is. Come with me.

MARGARET: I don't understand it! You? My chains removed? You set me free. Who is it you set free? Do you know?

FAUST: Come! Come!

MARGARET: I sent my mother to her death! I drowned (4507) my child. Your child! Henry!—Great God in heaven, can that not have been a dream! Your hand, Henry! It is moist—Wipe it off, I implore you! There is blood on it—Put up your sword! My head is awry.

FAUST: You are killing me.

MARGARET: No, you must stay alive, survive all the others. Who would look after the graves? All in a row, I implore you. My brother there, next to my mother! Me over there, and my baby at my right breast. Give me your hand on it, you are my Henry.

FAUST (*trying to pull her away*): Do you feel me? Do you hear me? Come, it is I, and I will set you free.

MARGARET: Out there.

FAUST: Freedom!

MARGARET: Out there? Not for the whole world! But if the grave is out there, come! If Death is lying in wait, come! From here to my eternal bed and not one step more. O Henry, if only I could go with you to the ends of earth!

FAUST: The dungeon is open, do not delay!

MARGARET: They're lying in wait for me on the road past the woods.

FAUST: Away! Away!

MARGARET: Not for the life of me!—Do you see it (4552) struggling! Save the poor mite, it's still struggling!— Away! Quick! Just across the bridge and straight on into the woods, left by the pond, where the plank is. Away! Save it! Save it!

FAIST: Save yourself!

MARGARET: If only we were past the hill! There sits my mother on a stone and wags her head. She doesn't beckon, she doesn't nod, her head is heavy. She had to sleep so we might stay awake and take delight together.

(*Faust seizes her and tries to carry her away.*)

I'll scream and wake them all up!

FAUST: The day shows grey. O my Love, my Love!

MARGARET: Day! It's getting daylight. The final day! My wedding day! Don't tell anyone that you had spent the night with Gretchen before.—My wreath!—We'll meet again!—Do you hear the citizens stealing through the streets? Do you hear? No word above a whisper. The bell summons!—Snap! The staff breaks!—Every neck senses the whetted blade that seeks my neck!— Hark, the bell tolls.

MEPHISTOPHELES (*stepping in*): Up! Or you are lost! (4597) My horses shudder, the dawn is breaking.

MARGARET: He! He! Leave him! Send him away! He comes for me! No! No! Judgment of God be mine, I am Thine! Save me! Never! Nevermore! Farewell forever! Farewell, Henry!

FAUST (*clasping her*):   I will not leave you!

MARGARET: You blessed angels protect my soul—I shudder at the sight of you, Henry.

MEPHISTOPHELES: She is condemned!

(*He disappears with Faust. The door clatters shut.*)

A VOICE (*growing fainter*):   Henry! Henry!   (4612)

*

EGMONT

In 1772, with his juristic credentials in order, Goethe had taken a position with the ancient Imperial law court in the town of Wetzlar and served there from May to September. He came away dissatisfied and still looking for a suitable appointment, but those same months had witnessed his famous love for Charlotte Buff, the young lady already engaged to be married to another. That hopeless passion became the principal substance of his novel, *The Sorrows of Young Werther,* which enormously enhanced his fame upon publication in the summer of 1774.

The following December "the author of *Werther*" was presented, at Mainz, to the seventeen-year-old Charles Augustus, Duke Apparent of Weimar. Impressions must have been favorable, for, ten months later Charles Augustus, his majority attained, invited the famous writer to enter Weimar service. Even with duties unspecified, this seemed to be the opportunity Goethe was waiting for. The offer was accepted on that September 22nd of 1775, and arrangements were made for Chamberlain von Kalb to come and escort Goethe to Weimar. Days and weeks passed, and no word came. In his chagrin Goethe decided to travel to Italy instead. With luggage packed, he had gotten as far as Heidelberg when Kalb, detained by circumstances beyond his control, overtook him on October 30th and Weimar became the destination after all.

In the interval of waiting *Egmont* was begun. How much of the play was written in those five uneasy weeks is a disputed point, but even if it was no more than Acts I and II, the author surely had the total scenario in mind. The necessary historical readings would alone imply that the subject had been contemplated for some time. Again the matter was drawn from sixteenth-century history, with focus on Dutch Count Egmont in his support of national and Protestant rights against his overlord in the Spanish Netherlands, King Philip II of Spain. In

287

the summer of 1567 the Duke of Alba occupied Brussels with an army of twenty thousand men and, in the king's name, began to enforce the Spanish and Catholic will. On September 9th he lured Egmont to his headquarters and arrested him. After a nine-month trial for high treason Egmont was found guilty and beheaded in the public square.

The unfinished play traveled to Weimar. From Goethe's diary and letters we hear mentions of *Egmont* in 1776, in 1778, and in 1782, but consecutive writing had apparently to wait until the leisure time of the author's Italian journey. Completion was noted on September 5, 1787, twelve years after inception, and publication followed that same year.

Reception was hostile. The pronouncements about "democracy" were deemed outrageously radical. The hero's sentimental liaison with a bourgeois girl was not only socially shocking but recklessly immoral, and denunciations were heard from pulpits warning the faithful away from such a corrupting work. To the author's much-reverenced Frau von Stein that bourgeois girl was a "hussy," whom the playwright had the bad taste to exalt as a goddess at the end of his play. Moderns who find *Egmont* stately to excess and even dull have no idea of how alarmingly unconventional it was in 1787. But these were small tempests which Goethe could endure. Far more serious was the thoughtful and, in the main, antagonistic review of the play published on September 20, 1788 by Schiller, who, at that point, was an acquaintance but not yet a friend.

By coincidence, 1787 was also the year when Schiller had published his own *Don Carlos,* a play set in the same era as *Egmont* and with even some of the same characters. No rivalry was involved in the review, but there was a question of radically different temperaments. Schiller had a very sure sense of theater, whereas Goethe tended to allow reflective thought to obscure the purely dramatic. There was the basis of reproach against the first three Acts of *Egmont.* All characters and all scenes existed solely to reveal the complex personality of the hero; the characters had no dramatic life of their own, the scenes were separate and detached "paintings," and the action was slow, jerky, and unclear, at least on the stage; in a quiet study it might be clear enough. About Act IV, where Schiller's own method is approximated, the review had little to say, but it had much to say against the dream vision with which the play ends. There the author had abandoned human feelings to make a *salto mortale*—a leap of desperation—into the world of opera. Nor did Schiller quite properly apprehend the nature of the "fatal flaw" in the hero's character.

Earlier in these pages, in the remarks about *The Lover's Whim,* there was mention of how Goethe tended to recur to that uncommon theme of the clash between somber and cheerful spirits. Goethe had conceived of his hero as one of those sunny dispositions that cannot believe in the malignity of any human being, not even when he has had warning of such, as Orange here warns Egmont. Here the normally good quality of "trustingness" is carried to the extreme where it becomes a fault; Egmont trusts the humanity of Alba, and Alba is wholly malign. The result is Egmont's destruction, as surely as Hamlet allowed reflective thought to interfere with action, as surely as Macbeth carried ambition too far. Schiller inclined, as many do, to put Egmont down as frivolous and even irresponsible.

The strictures against Acts I, II, and III are, on the whole, justified. On the other hand, Schiller admired the crowd scenes, unjustifiedly in our opinion. He admired the subplot centered on Klärchen, but he did not mention that it was wholly fictional within a main plot which was historically factual. He recognized that the overall method was "Shakespearean," but he failed to point out that one conspicuously Shakespearean factor was the combination of a main plot and a subplot that had only one point of contact, in Egmont himself. Nor did he mention the surprising innovation of having one plot aristocratic and the other bourgeois. But what really distressed him was that *salto mortale* into opera at the end.

Goethe's purpose ought to have been clear enough. Egmont is "a good man" in Aristotle's definition, and because of "good actions" he is utterly destroyed by "evil men," an outcome which Aristotle had termed intolerable in a drama. But by a markedly Christian turn of thought Egmont in his prison becomes "double": his mortal body is destroyed and killed, but his "spirit," the "spirit of liberty," survives. In token thereof, the "goddess of liberty" appears to him in a dream vision, first offering the crown of immortal patriot, then withholding the crown, because Dutch independence is still eighty years and several wars into the future. To signify those struggles there are blood-stains on the goddess's robe. By an exquisitely poetic touch the goddess has the features of the beloved Klärchen.

When, in 1794, friendship finally developed between the two dramatists, one of Goethe's first suggestions was to have Schiller prepare a stage version of *Egmont,* and Schiller accepted the idea with alacrity. The "collaborative version" was given its première in April 1796, without the Regent (of I, 2) and without the dream vision, and it was this "collaborative version" that held the stage until the middle of the following century. There is reason to think that Goethe was never quite reconciled to it, and that, for all his veneration of Schiller as man and as artist, this taking over of his work rankled with him. It would be strange if he had not felt so. His masculine, secular martyr had died for a cause, and at the moment of martyrdom *his* heaven had granted him a view into the future, where his cause would triumph and his own death would not have been in vain; in the "collaborative version" he perishes hopeless. Where Goethe intended a play of hope, Schiller had made a play of stark despair—as his own *Don Carlos* was.

Beethoven perceived Goethe's purpose and heartily supported it, so that when he came to compose the incidental music for *Egmont* in 1812 he included a setting of the dream vision. But where Beethoven understood Goethe, Goethe failed to understand Beethoven, although late in life he spoke in approval of the "melodrama," that is to say the background music for Liberty's epiphany to Egmont.

On several counts this play remains a curiously controversial one, but that dream vision is the prime bone of contention. Realists side with Schiller and form a majority opinion; romanticists side with Beethoven and plead the minority's point of view. The present writer is emphatically with Goethe, Beethoven, and the minority.

It is tempting to define *Egmont* as a Storm-and-Stress work compromised by twelve years of waiting to be finished; a youth began it, a sobered and somewhat troubled thirty-eight-year-old completed it. Yet even that claim is guesswork and without concrete evidence to support it. In any case, the work straddles two distinct eras in the author's life, and before hurrying ahead to the Weimar years after 1775 we shall need to consider some twenty dramas and fragments of dramas prior to 1775. To those works we devote a subsequent chapter.

EGMONT

A Tragedy in Five Acts

(Ein Trauerspiel in fünf Aufzügen)
1775–1787

CHARACTERS

MARGARET OF PARMA, daughter of Emperor Charles V and Regent of the Netherlands
COUNT EGMONT, Prince of Gaure
WILLIAM OF ORANGE
THE DUKE OF ALBA
FERDINAND, Alba's illegitimate son
MACHIAVELL, an officer of the Regent
RICHARD, Egmont's secretary
SILVA ⎱ officers serving under Alba
GOMEZ ⎰
KLÄRCHEN, Egmont's beloved
KLÄRCHEN'S MOTHER
BRACKENBURG, a burgher's son
SOEST,* a merchant ⎫
JETTER, a tailor ⎪ citizens of Brussels
A MASTER CARPENTER ⎬
A SOAP-BOILER ⎭
BUYCK,* a soldier under Egmont
RUYSUM,* a retired veteran, deaf
VANSEN, a scribe
CROWDS, RETINUES, GUARDS, ETC.

Place: Brussels, capital of the province of Brabant, now capital of Belgium.
Time: Early summer, 1568.

* Pronounce Soest approximately as "Soost"; Buyck as "Boik"; Ruysum as "Roizum."

ACT I

[SCENE 1]

[The annual Brussels] crossbow match.
Soldiers and citizens, with crossbows. Jetter, a citizen of Brussels, a
tailor by trade, steps up and draws the bow. Soest, a citizen of
Brussels, a merchant.

SOEST: Go on and shoot! Shoot the works! You still won't do me out
of it. You've never shot three rings inside the black in your life.
That pretty well makes me Master for *this* year.

JETTER: Master and King besides. Who begrudges you? Just for that
you'll pay the chit double; it's no more than right to pay for your
skill.

BUYCK (*a Hollander and a soldier under Egmont*):   Jetter, I'll buy
this shot from you, split the profit, and treat the gentlemen. I've
been here for a long while as it is and I'm indebted for a lot of
favors. If I miss, it'll be the same as if you had shot.

SOEST: I ought to have some say here, because I'm really the one
that stands to lose by it. But . . . go ahead, Buyck.

(*Buyck shoots.*)

BUYCK: All right, Scoremaster, bow![1]—One! Two! Three! Four!

SOEST: Four rings? Let it stand at that!

ALL: Long live our king! Hurrah! And again: Hurrah!

BUYCK: Thanks, gentlemen. "Master" would be too much! Thanks
for the honor.

JETTER: You have yourself to thank for it.

RUYSUM (*a Frisian, a wounded veteran and deaf*): Let me tell you!

SOEST: What, old fellow?

---

[1] The Scoremaster is a man in clown's costume and armed with a thin wooden
sword. He bows four times to show that Buyck has hit inside the fourth ring
of the target.

RUYSUM: Let me tell you! He shoots like his master, he shoots like Egmont.

BUYCK: Compared to him I'm just a bungler. With a gun he hits the mark like nobody else in this world. Not just when he's playing in luck or has a good day. No! He no sooner aims but what he always hits right inside the black. He's the one I learned from. Anybody'd have to be quite a fellow to serve with him and not learn something from him.—Let's not forget, gentlemen: a king takes care of his people. And so, on the king's bill, bring us wine!

JETTER: It was settled among us that every man—

BUYCK: I'm a stranger and a king, and I don't care about your laws and customs.

JETTER: Why, you're worse than the Spaniard. He, at least, has had to leave them alone up to now.

RUYSUM: What?

SOEST (*shouting*):   He wants to treat us. He won't have us chipping in and the king just paying double.

RUYSUM: Let him!—but without prejudice to our customs! That's his master's way too: do the grand thing and let things go so they do the most good.

(*Wine is brought in.*)

ALL: Your Majesty's health! Hurrah!

JETTER (*to Buyck*):   That's *your* Majesty, of course.

BUYCK: Thank you kindly, if that's how it has to be.

SOEST: Good! Because no Dutchman is likely to drink from his heart to the health of our Spanish Majesty.

RUYSUM: Who?

SOEST (*shouting*):   Philip the Second, King of Spain.

RUYSUM: Our most gracious king and lord! God grant him long life!

SOEST: Didn't you like his father, Charles the Fifth, better?

RUYSUM: God be his comfort! There was a master! He had his hand out over the whole world and he was all things in all. And when he met you, he would greet you the way one neighbor greets another; and if you were scared, he could put on such a kindly manner—Oh, you know—he used to walk out or ride out just as the fancy took him, with very few attendants. How we all did weep when he turned over the government here to his son—as I was saying, you know—*he* is different somehow, he is more majestical.

JETTER: He never showed himself when he was here except in splendor and royal state. He doesn't talk much, they say.

SOEST: He is no master for us Dutchmen. Our princes have to be cheerful and open like us, and live and let live. We don't want to be scorned and oppressed, even if we are good-natured fools.

JETTER: The king, I think, would doubtless be a gracious master if only he had better advisers.

SOEST: No, no! He has no feeling for us Dutchmen, his heart does not favor the people, he does not love us, so how can we love him in return? Why is everybody so fond of Count Egmont? Why would we all do our utmost for him? Because you can tell by looking at him that he wishes us well; because you can see his cheerfulness, his easy way, and his good intentions in his eyes; because he owns nothing but what he would share with the needy—or even with somebody that didn't need it. Long live Count Egmont! Buyck, it's up to you to propose the first toast: make it to your master's health!

BUYCK: With all my heart, then: to Count Egmont!

RUYSUM: Victor at St. Quentin!

BUYCK: To the hero of Gravelingin![2]

ALL: Hurrah!

RUYSUM: St. Quentin was my last battle. I could hardly keep going, hardly drag my heavy gun along. But I put one last one into the Frenchmen's hide, and then, for a goodbye, I got one more grazing bullet in my right leg.

BUYCK: Gravelingen! Friends, there was some lively going! We got that victory by ourselves.[3] And did we ever burn and scorch those French dogs all the way down through Flanders! And I mean: we knocked 'em off. Their rugged old fellows held out for a long time, but we pushed and shot and jabbed till they twisted their big mouths and their lines wavered. Then Egmont had his horse shot

[2] Battles against the French, at St. Quentin in 1557, at Gravelingen (Gravelines) in 1558.

[3] I.e., without the help of the English, as Buyck goes on to say.

out from under him, and we fought back and forth for a long time, man to man, horse to horse, troop to troop, down the broad flat sand by the sea. All of a sudden, out of a clear sky, from the mouth of the river: wham! bang! with cannon right into the thick of the French. It was Englishmen under Admiral Malin passing by from over Dunkirk way. Of course they didn't help us much; they couldn't get in except with their smallest ships, and that wasn't enough—besides, they fired in among us too. But it did help some. It broke the French and raised our spirits. Then there was some doing! Smack! Smack! this way, that way! The lot of them knocked dead or driven into the sea—and those fellows drowned as soon as they tasted the water. And every last Hollander of us right in after them. Land-and-water animals that we are, we didn't really get going till we were in the water like frogs. And in the river the enemy kept getting mowed down regularly, picked off like ducks. Such as got away, the peasant women mowed down in flight with hatchets and manure-forks. Then the French Majesty[4] had to hold up his little paw right quick and make peace. And the peace you have us to thank for, to thank great Egmont for.

ALL: Hurrah for great Egmont, hurrah! And hurrah again! And hurrah again!

JETTER: If they had just put *him* in as regent, instead of Margaret of Parma!

SOEST: Not at all! True is true! I won't have Margaret abused. Now it's my turn: long live our gracious Lady!

ALL: Long may she live!

SOEST: There are excellent women in that family, for a fact. Long live the regent!

JETTER: She is sensible and moderate in everything she does. If only she didn't stick so tight and fast to the clergy. She's partly to blame too, after all, for our having these fourteen new bishops' hats in the province. What are *they* supposed to accomplish, I ask you! Isn't it so foreigners can be shoved into good positions, where they used to have abbots elected from the chapter-houses? And we're supposed to believe it's for religion's sake. Oh, yes, we'll believe that. We

---

[4] Henri II (1547–59).

used to have enough with three bishops; then things went along decently and properly. But now each one has to make it look as if he were needed; and there's hard feelings and scraps spawned every minute. And the more you jiggle and joggle the sack, the dirtier it gets.

(*They drink.*)

SOEST: That was the king's will, I suppose; she can't do less nor more about it.

JETTER: And now we're not supposed to sing the new psalms.[5] They're really quite prettily rhymed and have quite edifying tunes. We're not to sing *them,* but bawdy songs to our hearts' content. Why? Because there's heresy in them, they say, and God knows what. But I've sung a few of them myself; they're something new now, and *I* didn't see anything in them.

BUYCK: I'd like to ask "them!" In our province we sing what we like. That's on account of how Count Egmont is our *Stadhouder;* he doesn't ask into things like that.—In Ghent, Ypres, all through Flanders, anybody sings them that feels like it. (*shouting*) There can't be anything more harmless than a hymn-tune, isn't that right, old fellow?

RUYSUM: No, Sir! Why, it's divine service, uplifting.

JETTER: But they say it's not the right kind, not *their* kind. And it's dangerous, after all and better left alone. The agents of the Inquisition are sneaking around and keeping an eye out; many an honest man has already come to grief. Intolerance was all we needed! As long as I can't *do* as I like, they might let me think and sing as I like.

SOEST: The Inquisition won't last. We're not made the way the Spaniards are, to let our consciences be tyrannized. And the nobility will soon have to clip its wings.

JETTER: It's a bad business. If those fine fellows take it into their heads to come storming into my house, and I'm sitting at my work and just happen to be humming a French psalm and not thinking anything about it, either good or bad—I'm humming it just because it's going through my head—then and there I'm a heretic and they

[5] Protestant versions of the Psalms in contemporary language and in rhymed verse.

throw me in jail. Or I'm walking along and stop by a crowd of people listening to a new preacher, one of those that have come from Germany: then and there I'm called a rebel and I stand to lose my head. Did you ever hear one of them preach?

SOEST: Upstanding men. I heard one speak lately in a field before thousands and thousands of people. It was another kettle of fish from when ours pound the pulpit and choke people with gobs of Latin. This one talked straight from the shoulder; told us how they've been leading us around by the nose up till now and keeping us in ignorance, and how we ought to have more enlightenment.— And he proved everything right out of the Bible.

JETTER: There may be something *to* that. I always said so myself and I used to kind of rack my brains over the matter. It's been running through my head for a long time.

BUYCK: And all the people are running after them, too.

SOEST: I can believe it—anywhere there's something good to be heard, and something new.

JETTER: And what is there to it? Anyone can be allowed to preach in his own way.

BUYCK: Come, gentlemen! With all this chatter, you're forgetting the wine—and Orange.

JETTER: *He*'s not to be forgotten. He's a regular wall: you no more than think of him, and right away you think of how you could hide behind him and the very Devil wouldn't get you out. To William of Orange: hurrah!

ALL: Hurrah! Hurrah!

SOEST: Now, old fellow, propose *your* toast too.

RUYSUM: To all soldiers! To all soldiers! Hurrah for war!

BUYCK: Good for you, old fellow! To all soldiers! Hurrah for war!

JETTER: War! War! Do you know what you're shouting? It falls easily from your lips—that's natural—but how miserable the likes of us feel about it, I can't tell you. Hearing the drum all year long; and listening to nothing but how one company comes marching one place and another one another place, how they got over a hill and halted by a mill, how many were killed here and how many were killed there, and how they push on, and how one loses and the other wins, without a man's understanding in all his born days who wins or loses what; how a city is captured and the civilians slaughtered, and how things go with the poor women and the innocent children. It's a worry and fret, and every minute you think: "There they come. It'll go the same with us."

SOEST: That's why a civilian must always be trained in weapons.

JETTER: Yes, men with wives and children train. But I'd rather hear about soldiers than see them.

BUYCK: I *could* take that the wrong way.

JETTER: I didn't mean you, countryman. When we got rid of the Spanish occupation troops we breathed easily again.[6]

SOEST: I'll bet they weighed heaviest on you, didn't they?

JETTER: Clown for yourself!

SOEST: They had pretty strict quarters in your house?

JETTER: Shut up!

SOEST: They drove him out of his kitchen, out of his cellar, out of his living room—out of his bed.

(Laughter)

JETTER: You're a nincompoop.

BUYCK: Peace gentlemen! Is it up to a soldier to cry peace?—Well, since you won't hear of *us*, propose your own toast, a civilian toast.

JETTER: For that we're ready! To security and peace!

SOEST: Order and freedom!

BUYCK: Fine! We're satisfied with that too.

(*They clink glasses and cheerfully repeat the words, but in such a way that each man cries out a different word, so the whole thing turns into a kind of "round." The old man listens and then winds up by joining in.*)

ALL: Security and peace! Order and freedom!

[SCENE 2]

The Regent's palace.

Enter Margaret of Parma in hunting costume. Courtiers, pages, servants.

---

[6] In 1561 Margaret of Parma had persuaded the king to withdraw three thousand Spanish troops.

REGENT: The hunt is countermanded. I shall not ride today. Tell
   Machiavell to report to me.

(All withdraw and leave the Regent to herself.)

The thought of these dreadful happenings gives me no peace! Nothing can delight me, nothing afford me diversion. Always these
images, these words, are before me. Now the king will say these are
the consequences of my kindness, of my leniency, and yet at every
step my conscience tells me I have done the best and most advisable
thing. Should I have fanned these flames and spread them with a
storm of fury? I had hoped to contain them, to turn them back
upon themselves. Yes, what I tell myself, what I very well know,
excuses me to myself, but how will my brother take it? Can it be
denied that the insolence of these foreign preachers has increased
daily? They have desecrated our sanctuaries, confounded the dull
wits of the common folk, and conjured madness into them. Impure
spirits have mingled with the insurgents, and dreadful things have
happened, horrifying to imagine, and which I now have to report in
detail to the court, quickly and in detail, so common rumor does
not anticipate me and so the king won't think that still more things
are being covered up. I see no way, strict or mild, to check this evil.
Oh, what are we great ones on the wave of humanity? We fancy we
control the wave, but it sweeps us up and down, backwards and
forwards.

(Enter Machiavell.)

Have the letters to the king been drafted?

MACHIAVELL: Within the hour you will be able to sign them.

REGENT: Did you make the report detailed enough?

MACHIAVELL: In full detail, the way the king likes. I tell how the
   frenzy of the image-breakers showed itself first around St. Omer.
   How a raging mob, armed with sticks, axes, hammers, ladders, and
   ropes and accompanied by a few armed men, first attacked chapels,
   churches, and monasteries, drove the worshipers away, broke open
   locked doors, wrecked everything, overthrew altars, pounded
   statues of the saints to bits, defaced all paintings, and smashed, tore
   to pieces, and trampled underfoot everything consecrated or
   sanctified that they came upon. How the mob gathered force as it
   went along and how the citizens of Ypres opened their gates to

them. How they devastated the cathedral with incredible speed and burned the Bishop's library. How a great crowd of people, caught up in the same madness, swarmed over Menin, Comines, Verwich, and Lille, meeting no resistance anywhere, and how the monstrous conspiracy burst forth and was carried out through almost the whole of Flanders all at the same moment.

REGENT: Oh, how the anguish seizes me anew at your recollection! And with it the fear that the evil will only become greater and greater. Tell me what you think, Machiavell.

MACHIAVELL: Forgive me, Your Highness. My ideas seem mere whims, and though you have always been satisfied with my services, you have seldom seen fit to take my advice. You have often said in jest: "You see too far ahead, Machiavell. You ought to be a historian. One who acts must look out for the present." And yet, did I not foretell this story? Did I not foresee it all?

REGENT: I foresee many things myself—without being able to change them.

MACHIAVELL: In briefest words: you will not suppress the new teaching. Leave them alone, segregate them from the right believers, grant them churches, include them in the civic order, hem them in: thay way you will pacify the insurgents immediately. All other methods are useless, and you will devastate the country.

REGENT: Have you forgotten the abhorrence with which my brother himself rejected the question of whether the new teaching could be tolerated? Don't you know how in every letter of his he most insistently recommends maintaining the true faith? How he will not hear of restoring peace and unity at the expense of religion? Doesn't he maintain spies in the province himself—spies we don't know—in order to find out who is inclined to the new way of thinking? Hasn't he, to our astonishment, named this one and that one who, while close to us, was secretly incriminating himself of heresy? Doesn't he insist on severity and rigor? And I am supposed to be mild? I am supposed to propose that he be lenient and tolerant? Would I not forfeit all confidence and trust with him?

MACHIAVELL: I realize. The king gives orders, he lets you know his intentions. You are supposed to restore peace and tranquility by means which will only embitter people more, which will inevitably sound the call to war from one end of the country to the other. Consider what you are doing. The big merchants have caught the infection; so have the nobles, the common folk, and the military. What is the use of sticking to our ideas if everyone around us is changing? Would that some benign spirit would inspire Philip with the notion that it better becomes a king to rule over citizens of two faiths than to have them destroy each other!

REGENT: Never speak like this again! I am aware that politics can rarely keep faith and trust, that it excludes frankness, charity, and compliancy from our hearts. In worldly affairs that is unfortunately only too true, but are we to trifle that way with God too, as we do among ourselves? Are we to be indifferent with regard to our attested teachings, for which so many have laid down their lives? Are we to surrender them for stray, unsure, mutually contradictory innovations?

MACHIAVELL: But do not think the worse of me for it.

REGENT: I know you and I know your loyalty, and I realize that one may be an honorable and sensible man even if he has missed the one true path to his soul's salvation. There are others, Machiavell, men whom I must esteem and condemn.

MACHIAVELL: Whom do you have in mind?

REGENT: I confess that Egmont roused a heartfelt and deep vexation in me today.

MACHIAVELL: By what behavior?

REGENT: By his usual, by insouciance and frivolousness. I received the dreadful news just as I was leaving church in the company of him and numerous other persons. I did not check my grief, I cried aloud, turning to him: "See what has come about in your province! *You* tolerate this, Count, by whom the king set such great store?"

MACHIAVELL: And what did he say?

REGENT: As if it was nothing at all, as if it was a nonessential matter, he replied: "If only the Dutch had their minds at ease over their form of government, the rest would follow of itself."

MACHIAVELL: He may have spoken more truthfully than shrewdly and piously. How is confidence to be developed and maintained when the Dutchman sees that his possessions are of more concern than his welfare or his soul's salvation? Have the new bishops saved more souls, or have they rather battened on fat benefices? and aren't they mostly foreigners? All *stadhouter* incumbencies are still occupied by Dutchmen: don't the Spaniards make it all too plain that they have the greatest, most uncontrollable desires for those incumbencies? Would a people not rather be governed in its own fashion by its own kind, rather than by foreigners who are seeking to acquire possessions at everybody's expense, and who bring in a foreign standard, and who rule hostilely and without sympathy?

REGENT: You array yourself with the opposition.

MACHIAVELL: Not with my heart, surely; and I wish I could be wholly on our side with my mind.

REGENT: If you did, I would need to resign my regency to them, for Egmont and Orange are getting up high hopes of taking over this position. They used to be opponents; now they are allied against me and have become friends, inseparable friends.

MACHIAVELL: A dangerous pair.

REGENT: Speaking frankly, I am afraid of Orange and I am afraid *for* Egmont. Orange is up to no good. His ideas reach far out; he is secretive, he seems to accept everything, he never contradicts, and, with profoundest respect, with utmost caution—he does as he pleases.

MACHIAVELL: Just the opposite, Egmont walks with a jaunty step as if he owned the world.

REGENT: He carries his head so high, as if the hand of Majesty did not hover over him.

MACHIAVELL: The people's eyes are all upon him and their hearts cling to him.

REGENT: Never has he avoided appearances, as if no one could require an accounting from him. He still goes by the name of Egmont; he likes to hear himself called Count Egmont, as if he didn't want to forget that his forebears were the owners of Gelderland. Why doesn't he call himself the Prince of Gaure, as befits him? Why does he do this? Does he mean to revive extinct claims?

MACHIAVELL: I consider him a loyal server of the king.

REGENT: If he wanted to, how much he might deserve of the government, instead of causing us untold annoyance—without gaining any advantage for himself. His parties, banquets, and revels have united and knit the aristocracy together more than the most dangerous secret assemblies. His guests are perpetually drunk from drinking his health, so that they have created themselves a condition of never-ending intoxication. How often his jesting talk gets people's minds stirred up, the way the lower classes were agog over those new liveries and those silly emblems of the servants![7]

MACHIAVELL: I am convinced it was unintentional.

REGENT: Bad enough. As I say, he harms us and doesn't help himself. He takes serious things as jokes, and we, so as not to appear idle and careless, have to take joking matters seriously. Each goads the other on, and what we try to avert is precisely what occurs. He is more dangerous than a determined leader of a conspiracy, and I would be in great error if he is not credited at court with the worst. I cannot deny that very little time passes without his offending me, very deeply offending me.

MACHIAVELL: To me he seems to act according to his conscience in all matters.

REGENT: His conscience consults an obliging mirror. His behavior is often offensive. He often acts as if he were fully convinced that he is the master and as if, from sheer courtesy, he didn't want us to realize that, as if he wouldn't exactly drive us out of the country, because that would happen of itself in due time.

MACHIAVELL: I beg you not to construe as over-dangerous his frankness and his happy disposition that takes all serious things lightly: you only harm him and yourself.

REGENT: I am not construing anything. I am speaking only about the unavoidable consequences, and I know him. His Netherlandish aristocracy and his Golden Fleece on his chest reenforce his confidence and his audacity. Both may protect him from a sudden arbitrary ill-will of the king. Look carefully into it and you will find

[7] At a banquet in December 1563 at the home of a Dutch baron all the young noblemen agreed to dress all their servants in liveries of coarse cloth with armbands bearing a device that resembled both a monk's cowl and a fool's cap, in mockery of Cardinal Granvelle, King Philip's minister to the Low Countries.

that he alone is to blame for the whole misfortune that besets
Flanders. He was the first to indulge the foreign preachers,
wouldn't be too strict about them, and perhaps was secretly pleased
that we had something to do. No, let me speak! What I have on my
heart shall, with this opportunity, be disburdened. And I do not
want to use up my arrows for nothing. I know where his weak spot
is—and he does have a weak spot, too.

MACHIAVELL: Have you ordered the council to assemble? Will
Orange be coming also?

REGENT: I have sent to Antwerp for him. I plan to thrust the burden
of responsibility close enough to him. Either they shall join me in
seriously opposing the evil or else they shall declare themselves as
rebels also. Hurry those letters to conclusion and bring them to me
for signature. Then quickly dispatch the trusty Vasca to Madrid—
he is tireless and faithful—so that my brother gets the news from
him first and so rumor doesn't outrun him. I want to speak to him
myself before he starts.

MACHIAVELL: Your commands shall be swiftly and precisely
followed.

[SCENE 3]

A middle-class household.
Klara, Klara's mother, Brackenburg.

KLARA: Won't you hold the yarn for me, Brackenburg?

BRACKENBURG: I beg you to excuse me, Klärchen.

KLARA: What's wrong again? Why do you refuse me this little
service of love?

BRACKENBURG: You cast such a spell on me with the thread that I
can't look away from your eyes.

KLARA: Foolishness! Come and hold it!

MOTHER (*in an armchair, knitting*): Why not sing something?
Brackenburg takes the second part so nicely.

BRACKENBURG: I used to.

KLARA: We'll sing.

BRACKENBURG: As you will.

KLARA: Something lively, though, and start right off! It's a soldier's
song, my favorite.

> *(She winds yarn and sings with Brackenburg.)*
>
>> Set drumrolls a-clatter,
>> Set fifes at the shrill!
>> My dearest in armor,
>> Troops march at his will.
>> His spear is raised high,
>> His soldiers file by.
>> My heart is near bursting
>> Beholding all that.
>> Would *I* had a doublet
>> And hose and a hat!
>> With him I'd strike outward
>> With stout-hearted tread
>> And march through the provinces
>> Wherever he led.
>> The foe are near capture,
>> We fired, and they ran.
>> It must be sheer rapture,
>> Just being a man!

*(Brackenburg keeps glancing at Klärchen during the song.
Finally he chokes up, tears come to his eyes, he drops the
skein and goes to the window. Klärchen finishes the song
by herself. Her mother motions to her angrily. She gets
up, advances a few paces toward him, then half-undecided
she turns back and sits down again.)*

MOTHER: What's going on out in the street, Brackenburg? I hear
marching.

BRACKENBURG: It's the Regent's bodyguard.

KLARA: At this hour? What can it mean?

> *(She gets up and goes over to
> the window where Brackenburg is.)*

That's not the regular guard, there are many more of these. Almost
all her squadrons. Oh, Brackenburg, go out and see what's going

on! It must be something special. Go, good Brackenburg, as a favor
to me.

BRACKENBURG: I'll go. I'll be right back!

> (*He holds out his hand to her as*
> *he leaves and she gives him hers.*)

MOTHER: You've sent him away again.

KLARA: I'm curious. And don't blame me; it's painful having him
here. I never know how to act with him. I wrong him, and it
bothers me that he feels it so sharply.—But I can't do otherwise!

MOTHER: He's such a faithful lad.

KLARA: I can't help but be friendly to him, either. Sometimes my
hand clenches of itself when his hand touches me so gently, so lov-
ingly. I reproach myself for betraying him, for encouraging a hopeless love in his heart. I feel bad about it. God knows I'm not
betraying him. I don't want him to get his hopes up, and yet I can't
let him despair, either.

MOTHER: It isn't good.

KLARA: I was fond of him and I still wish him well in my heart. I
could have married him, yet I think I was never in love with him.

MOTHER: You would always have been happy with him.

KLARA: I would have been well provided and I would have had a
quiet life.

MOTHER: And all that is thrown away, of your own fault.

KLARA: I'm in an odd situation. When I think of how things have
gone, I realize it and I don't realize it. Then let me but see Egmont
again and everything becomes perfectly understandable—in fact,
would be far more understandable. Ah, what a man he is! All the
provinces adore him, so how should I not be the happiest creature
in the world?

MOTHER: How will it be later on?

KLARA: Oh, my only question is whether he loves me; and whether
he loves me: is there any question?

MOTHER: There's nothing from children but heart's sorrow. How
will it end? Nothing but worry and trouble! It won't turn out well.
You have made yourself unhappy and made me unhappy!

KLARA (*calmly*):   You went along with it at the beginning, though.

MOTHER: Unfortunately I was too easy. I'm always too easy.

KLARA: When Egmont rode by and I ran to the window, did you scold me then? Didn't you go to the window yourself? When he looked up, smiled, nodded, waved to me, did you mind? Didn't you find yourself honored in your daughter?

MOTHER: Go on, blame me.

KLARA (*touched*):   Then when he kept coming up this street and we thought he was coming this way on account of me, didn't you notice it with secret joy yourself? Did you call me away when I stood behind the panes waiting for him?

MOTHER: Did I ever think it would go so far?

KLARA (*with a catch in her voice and with suppressed tears*):   And when, one evening, wrapped in his cloak, he surprised us beside our lamp, who bestirred herself to make him welcome, while I seemed chained to my chair and went on sitting there in astonishment?

MOTHER: And how could I have feared that this unfortunate love would so quickly sweep my sensible Klärchen off her feet? Now I have to put up with my daughter's being—

KLARA (*her tears welling forth*):   Mother! You're saying that on purpose! You take pleasure in tormenting me.

MOTHER (*weeping*):   Weep all you want! Make me still more miserable with your mourning! Isn't it sorrow enough for me to have my only daughter a reprobate?

KLARA (*rising; coldly*):   Reprobate! Egmont's beloved a reprobate?—What princess would not envy poor Klärchen her place at his heart! Oh, mother—my own mother, you didn't use to talk like this. Dear mother, be kind!—The people who think *that*, the neighbor women, whatever *they* babble—This room, this little house is a paradise since Egmont's love dwells here.

MOTHER: No one can help loving him, it's true. He is always so friendly, so frank and open.

KLARA: There isn't a false hair in his head. See, mother, and he is still the great Egmont. And when he comes to me, he is so loving, so kind! The way he would like to conceal his status from me, conceal his bravery from me! The way he is concerned about me! The way he is only a human being, only a friend, only a beloved.

MOTHER: Will he be coming today?

KLARA: Haven't you noticed me going to the window again and again? Haven't you noticed how I listen every time there's a rustling by the door? Even when I know he won't be coming before nightfall, I expect him any minute from the time I get up in the morning. If only I were a boy and could always go with him, to court and everywhere else! If I could carry his banner in battle!—

MOTHER: You always were a madcap; even as a small child, one minute wild, the next minute lost in thought. Won't you be putting on something a little nicer?

KLARA: Perhaps, mother, if I'm bored.—Just think: yesterday men of his went by singing songs in praise of him. At least his name was mentioned in the songs—the rest I couldn't quite understand. My heart came up in my mouth—I would have called them back, only I was too shy.

MOTHER: Beware! Your impetuous way will ruin everything yet. You betray yourself in front of people, the way you did in front of your cousin lately when you found the woodcut and the wording underneath, and suddenly out you came with the cry of "Count Egmont!"—I turned red as fire.

KLARA: Didn't I have reason to cry out? It was the battle of Gravelingen. In the upper part of the picture I found the letter C, so I looked down below in section C of the printing, and there it said: "Count Egmont with his horse being killed out from under him." I felt a chill of horror—and afterwards I had to laugh at the Egmont in the woodcut, because he was as tall as the tower of Gravelingen right next to him and as the English ships at the side.—Sometimes when I remember the way I used to picture a battle, and how I used to imagine Count Egmont when I was a little girl and they told me about him, and how I imagined all Counts and Princes—and then the way I see it now!

(Brackenburg comes back in.)

What's going on?

BRACKENBURG: Nobody knows anything for sure. In Flanders there's supposed to have been some rioting, and they say the Regent is concerned that it may spread here. The palace is under heavy guard, citizens are crowded around the gates, and people are buzzing in the streets.—I must hurry to my aged father.

(*He moves as if to leave.*)

KLARA: Will we be seeing you tomorrow? I want to dress up a bit. Our cousin is coming, and I look so disgraceful. Help me a minute, mother.—Take the book along, Brackenberg, and bring me another story like that one.

MOTHER: Goodbye now.

BRACKENBURG (*extending his hand*): Your hand!

KLARA (*refusing*): When you come again.

(*Exeunt mother and daughter.*)

BRACKENBURG (*alone*): I meant to leave again right away, but when she takes me at my word and just lets me go, I could go wild.— Poor wretch! and you are not stirred by your country's fate, by the growing tumult? And is fellow-countryman and Spaniard all the same to you, and who rules, and who is in the right?

I was different when I was a boy in school. When they assigned an exercise: "Brutus's Speech in Defense of Freedom, for practice in oratory," then Fritz was always first, and the Rector used to say: "If only it were more orderly and things didn't go stumbling over one another so." In those days I felt a seething and driving!— Now I drag myself around by this girl's eyes. And yet I can't give her up! And she can't love me! Oh—no—she—she can't have thrown me over entirely—not entirely—by half, and nothing!—I won't stand for it any longer!—Might it be true, what a friend whispered recently? that she secretly admits a man at night, when she so coyly always sends me away before dark? No! It's not true, it's a lie, a disgraceful slandering lie! Klärchen is as innocent as I am unhappy.—She has thrown me over, driven me out of her heart—and I am supposed to go on living like this? I won't stand for it, I won't stand for it!

My country is violently racked with inner dissention, and I am merely withering away amid the turmoil! I won't stand for it!—

When the trumpet sounds or a shot is fired, I shudder to my very marrow, but it doesn't rouse me or challenge me to take a hand in it, to help save it, to venture anything.—Wretched, disgraceful condition!

It's better I ended it, once and for all. I threw myself into the water recently; I sank—but alarmed Nature proved the stronger; I realized I could swim and I rescued myself against my will.—If only I could forget those times when she loved me, or seemed to love me! Why did happiness penetrate my flesh and bone? Why did my hopes devour all pleasure in life by showing me a paradise from afar?—And that first kiss! That only one!—Here,

> (*He places his hand on the table.*)

here we were alone —she had always been so friendly and well-disposed toward me— then she seemed to soften—she looked at me—all my senses were in a whirl, and I felt her lips on mine.—And now?

Die, poor wretch! What are you waiting for?

> (*He brings a little bottle forth from his pocket.*)

Not for nothing did I steal you from my brother's medical case, you healing poison! It is for you to resolve and consume once and for all this fearfulness, these whirlings in my head, this deathly sweat.

ACT II

[SCENE 1]

A square in Brussels.
Enter Jetter and a master carpenter, in conversation.

CARPENTER: Didn't I predict this? A week ago, at the guild meeting, I said there would be bad trouble.

JETTER: Is it true they plundered the churches in Flanders?

CARPENTER: They completely gutted churches and chapels, left nothing standing but the four bare walls. The worst riff-raff! And that makes our good cause bad. What we should have done was to go, in orderly fashion and resolutely, and present our legitimate case to the Regent, and then stick to it. Now, if we talk, now, if we assemble, they'll say we're supporting the agitators.

JETTER: Yes, everybody's first thought is: why stick your nose in, when it's located so close to your neck?

CARPENTER: I'm worried: if the cry goes up from that gang, from the people that have nothing to lose, they'll plead as their excuse the very thing that *we* would have to cite, and they'll plunge the country into disaster.

(Soest comes up.)

SOEST: Good day, gentlemen. What's the news? Is it true the image-breakers are heading straight this way?

CARPENTER: They shan't touch one thing here.

SOEST: A soldier came into my shop to buy some tobacco, and I asked him some things. The Regent, gallant and shrewd lady that she is, is completely out of patience this time. It must really be bad, for her to duck behind her bodyguard right off. The fortress is heavily garrisoned. Some even think she may flee the city.

CARPENTER: She shan't go! Her presence protects us, and we'll provide her more security than those mustachios of hers.[1] And if

---

[1] Spanish guards.

312

she maintains our rights and liberties we'll carry her around on a chip.

(*A soap-boiler joins them.*)

SOAP-BOILER: Nasty business! Dirty business! Things are getting unsettled and it'll come to a bad end.—Better lie low, so you don't get taken for agitators.

SOEST: Here come the Seven Sages of Greece.

SOAP-BOILER: I know there are quite a few that hold secretly with the Calvinists, that revile the bishops, and don't stand in fear of the king. But a loyal subject, an upright Catholic—

(*Gradually a crowd of all sorts of people gather around and listen. Vansen joins them.*)

VANSEN: Greetings, gentlemen. What's the news?

CARPENTER: Don't have anything to do with him, he's a bad one.

JETTER: Isn't he Dr. Wiets's secretary?

CARPENTER: He's had several employers. He used to be a secretary, but as one patron after another fired him for underhanded tricks, he's taken to botching up notaries' and attorneys' jobs—and he's a brandy-bung, too.

(*More people gather and stand around in groups.*)

VANSEN: You've assembled too, and have your heads together. It's always worth mentioning.

SOEST: I think so too.

VANSEN: Now if one or the other of you had the heart and one or the other of you had the head as well, we could break the Spanish chains right off.

SOEST: Sir, you must not say such things! We swore an oath to the king.

VANSEN: And the king to us. Mark that.

JETTER: There's something to that. State your opinion.

SEVERAL OTHERS: Listen to him, he's got ideas!—He's up to sly tricks.

VANSEN: I used to have an elderly patron, and he owned parchment books and charters of institutions and contracts and claims from way, way back; he went in for the rarest books. In one of them there was our whole constitution: how first individual princes ruled us Netherlanders, all according to traditional rights and privileges and customs; and how our ancestors all respected their prince if he ruled the way he should, and how they took precautions when he went over the line. The Estates were right behind, for every province, no matter how small, had its Estates, its Parliament.

CARPENTER: You shut up! We knew all that long ago. Every proper citizen is informed about the constitution as much as he need be.

JETTER: Let him talk! You always find out something more.

SOEST: He's right!

SEVERAL VOICES: Tell us! Tell us! We don't get to hear this kind of thing every day.

VANSEN: So you are citizens! You just live from one day to the next, and just as you took over a business from your parents, in the same way you let the government do as they like with you, any way they can and may. You don't inquire about tradition, about history, about the rights of a regent; and what with your negligence, the Spaniards have pulled the wool over your eyes.

SOEST: Who gives that a thought, so long as he gets his daily bread?

JETTER: Damn! Why doesn't somebody step up in time and tell people a thing like that?

VANSEN: I'm telling you now. The King of Spain, who owns all these provinces from a stroke of luck, may not rule and govern them otherwise than as the small princes did, who owned them separately before him. Do you understand?

JETTER: Explain it for us.

VANSEN: It's as clear as day. Aren't you subject to trial according to your provincial laws? How does that come about?

A CITIZEN: True!

VANSEN: Doesn't a Brussels man have a different law from the Antwerp man? And the Antwerp man from the man of Ghent? Now, how does that come about?

ANOTHER CITIZEN: By God!

VANSEN: But, if you let things go on this way, they'll soon show you a different way of doing things. Bah! What Charles the Bold, Frederick the Warrior, and Charles the Fifth couldn't do, Philip is now doing through a woman.

SOEST: Yes! The princes of old tried this before.

VANSEN: Of course!—Our ancestors were on their guard. When they got mad at a lord, they maybe took his son and heir hostage, kept him among themselves, and gave him up only on the most favorable terms.[2] Our forefathers were men! They knew what was good for them! They knew how to take a hand and settle something! Real men! That's how our privileges came to be so clearly defined and our freedoms so assured.

SOAP-BOILER: What freedoms are you talking about?

VOICES OF THE PEOPLE: About our freedoms, about our privileges! Tell us some more about our privileges!

VANSEN: We Brabanters especially, although all the provinces have their advantages, we are magnificently provided for. I've read all about it.

SOEST: Tell us more.

JETTER: Let's hear!

A CITIZEN: I beg you.

VANSEN: In the first place it says: The Duke of Brabant shall be a good and faithful master to us.

SOEST: Good? Does it say that?

JETTER: Faithful? Is that so?

VANSEN: As I say. He is obligated to us as we are to him. Secondly: he is not to show, display, or think of permitting any coercion or arbitrary force toward us, in any way whatsoever.

JETTER: Wonderful! Wonderful! Not to show.

SOEST: Not to display.

ANOTHER: And not to think of permitting! There's the main point. Permit no one, in any way whatsoever.

VANSEN: Right there in so many words.

JETTER: Get us that book.

A CITIZEN: Yes, we've got to have it.

OTHERS: The book! The book!

ANOTHER: We'll go to the Regent with the book.

ANOTHER: You'll be our spokesman, Doctor.

[2] In 1488 the citizens of Bruges did precisely this with Frederick III of Germany by taking his son Maximilian hostage.

SOAP-BOILER: Oh, these fools!

OTHERS: What's some more from that book!

SOAP-BOILER: I'll knock his teeth down his throat if he says another word.

DIFFERENT VOICES: We'll see if anybody lays a hand on him! Tell us something about our privileges! Do we have some other privileges?

VANSEN: All sorts of them, and very good ones, very worthy ones. It also says: the ruler shall not promote or increase the clergy without the assent of the nobles and the estates. Note that! Nor change the national constitution.

SOEST: Is that so?

VANSEN: And we stand for these new bishops? The nobles must protect us or we'll make trouble!

OTHERS: And we let ourselves be backed into a corner by the Inquisition?

VANSEN: That's your fault.

VOICES: We still have Egmont! We still have Orange! They'll look out for our good.

VANSEN: Your brethren in Flanders have begun the good work.

SOAP-BOILER: You cur! (*He hits him.*)

OTHERS (*intervening and shouting*):   Are you another Spaniard?

ANOTHER: What! this honorable man?

ANOTHER: This scholar?
                    (*They attack the soap-boiler.*)

CARPENTER: For heaven's sake, be quiet!
                    (*Others get into the fight.*)
      Citizens! What will come of this?
      (*Boys whistle, throw stones, set dogs on. Citizens stand and gape. People come running up; others stroll calmly back and forth, others play all sorts of pranks, shout, and cheer.*)

OTHERS: Freedom and privileges! Privileges and freedom!
                    (*Enter Egmont with a retinue.*)

EGMONT: Quiet! Quiet, people! What's going on? Quiet down! Separate them!

CARPENTER: Noble Sir, you come like an angel from heaven. Quiet, there! Don't you see who's here? Count Egmont! Bow to Count Egmont!

EGMONT: Here too? What are you up to? Citizen against citizen! Doesn't the proximity of our royal Regent hold back this madness? Disperse! Go to your occupations. It's a bad sign when you turn workdays into holidays. What happened?

(*The tumult gradually subsides and they all stand around him.*)

CARPENTER: They're fighting over their privileges.

EGMONT: Which they will yet wantonly destroy.—And who are you? You look like respectable people.

CARPENTER: We aim to be.

EGMONT: Of what trade?

CARPENTER: Carpenter and guild-master.

EGMONT: And you?

SOEST: Merchant.

EGMONT: You?

JETTER: Tailor.

EGMONT: I remember you. You worked on the liveries for my servants. Your name is Jetter.

JETTER: Kind of you to remember that.

EGMONT: I don't readily forget anyone I've once seen and talked with.—Whatever you can do to keep peace, do it, people; you're in enough trouble as it is. Provoke the king no further; after all, the final power is in his hands. A law-abiding citizen that supports himself honorably and industriously has as much freedom as he needs anywhere.

CARPENTER: That's just our trouble! It's the idlers and drinkers and loafers—begging Your Grace's permission—that kick up rows for lack of something to do and make a fuss in their greed for privileges and talk lies to the curious and the credulous. To get treated to a tankard of beer they start trouble that makes thousands of people miserable. That just suits them. We keep our houses and coffers well protected, and so they'd like to drive us from them with firebrands.

EGMONT: All possible support shall be yours. Measures have been taken to meet these troubles forcefully. Stand firm against the foreign teachings, and don't you ever believe that privileges are secured by rioting. Stay in your homes. Don't let them gather on the streets. Sensible people can accomplish a good deal.

(*Most of the mob has by now dispersed.*)

CARPENTER: Thanks to Your Excellency, thanks for the good advice! Anything we can do.

(*Exit Egmont.*)

A gracious lord! A true Netherlander! Nothing Spanish about him.

JETTER: If only we had him for Regent! People would gladly follow him.

SOEST: The king sees to that. He always names his own people to that post.

JETTER: Did you notice his clothes? The latest fashion, and all cut Spanish.

CARPENTER: A handsome lord!

JETTER: His neck would be a feast for an executioner.

SOEST: Are you mad? What are you thinking of!

JETTER: Stupid enough to have such an idea.—It just seems that way to me. Whenever I see a nice long neck like that, right away I think in spite of myself: that is good beheading.—Damnable executions! You can't get them out of your mind. When lads go swimming and I see a naked back, right away dozens come to mind that I've seen under the lash. Let a real pot-belly meet me, and I seem to see it roasting at the stake. At night all my limbs twitch in my dreams; there isn't a cheerful hour. Any merriment, any joke, I've half forgotten, but the ghastliest shapes seem to be branded on my brow.

[SCENE 2]

Egmont's residence.

His secretary at a table strewn with papers; he rises in agitation.

SECRETARY: Still he doesn't come! Two hours I've been waiting, pen in hand and papers in front of me; and today is just the day when I'd like to get away early. The ground is burning under my feet. I'm so impatient I can hardly sit still. "Be there on the hour," he told me before he left—and now he doesn't come. There is so much to do I won't get done before midnight. I admit he sometimes winks at things, but it would be easier on me if he were strict and then dismissed me at the appointed time. That way you could make plans. He's already been gone two hours from the Regent's. Who knows whom he's caught up on the way?

(Enter Egmont.)

EGMONT: How do things look?

SECRETARY: I am ready, and three messengers are waiting.

EGMONT: I must have tarried too long: you look annoyed.

SECRETARY: I have been waiting for quite some time to carry out your orders. Here are the papers.

EGMONT: Donna Elvira will be angry at me when she hears I have held you up.

SECRETARY: You jest.

EGMONT: No, no. Don't be embarrassed. You show good taste. She is pretty; and it is quite all right with me for you to have a lady-friend at the palace. What do the letters say?

SECRETARY: A number of things, few of them pleasant.

EGMONT: Then it's a good thing we have pleasure at home and don't need to wait for it to come from outside. Has much come in?

SECRETARY: Enough. And three messengers are waiting.

EGMONT: Start in. The most essential.

SECRETARY: Everything is essential.

EGMONT: One at a time, but quickly!

SECRETARY: Captain Breda reports what further went on in Ghent and the surrounding area. The tumult has mostly died down.

EGMONT: He probably relates more of the separate incivilities and foolhardy doings.

SECRETARY: Yes! Many more are coming out.

EGMONT: Spare me.

SECRETARY: Six more have been hauled in of those that pulled down the Virgin's statue at Verwich. He inquires whether he should have them hanged like the others.

EGMONT: I am weary of hangings. Have them soundly flogged and let them go.

SECRETARY: There are two women among them; should he have them flogged too?

EGMONT: Have him put them on warning and turn them loose.

SECRETARY: Brink, in Breda's Company, wants to get married. The Captain hopes you will refuse him permission. There are so many women with the Company, he writes, that when we march, it looks more like a band of gypsies than a march of soldiers.

EGMONT: In this case: granted. He's a handsome lad, and he requested me urgently before I came away. But no more permissions after this one, much as it grieves me to prohibit the poor devils their best pleasure, when they are tormented enough without this.

SECRETARY: Two of your men, Seter and Hart, have misused a girl, an inn-keeper's daughter. They got her alone and the wench couldn't fend them off.

EGMONT: If she's an honest girl and they used force, he is to have them flogged three days in succession, and if they've got anything, he is to confiscate enough of it to make a dowry for that girl.

SECRETARY: One of the foreign preachers passed through Comines secretly and was caught. He swears he is just going to France. According to the order, he is to be beheaded.

EGMONT: Have them quietly escort him to the border and then guarantee him he won't get away a second time like that.

SECRETARY: A letter from your tax-collector. He writes that little money is coming in and he can hardly send the required amount in a week; the tumult, he says, has thrown everything into total confusion.

EGMONT: The money must be brought in; how he collects it is his affair.

SECRETARY: He says he will do his utmost, and that he wants at long last to bring action against that Raymond that's owed you for so long, and have him jailed.

EGMONT: But he did promise to pay.

SECRETARY: The last time he himself allowed him two weeks.

EGMONT: Then allow him another two weeks; then he can take action against him.

SECRETARY: That's nice of you. It isn't inability, it's ill-will. He will get down to business when he sees you're not joking.—The tax-collector says further: he would like to defer for half a month the alms-payments you issue to veterans, widows, and certain others;

meanwhile ways and means can be considered and arrangements can be made.

EGMONT: What is there to arrange? The people need the money more than I do. Tell him to leave that matter alone.

SECRETARY: Then where do you order him to get the money from?

EGMONT: That's up to him. He was told in the preceding letter.

SECRETARY: That is why he is making the suggestions.

EGMONT: They're of no use. He is to think of something else. He is to make suggestions that are acceptable, and above all he is to get the money.

SECRETARY: I have put Count Oliva's letter back in this batch. Forgive me for reminding you. The old gentleman deserves a circumstantial reply more than all the rest. You were going to write him yourself. He does, indeed, love you like a father.

EGMONT: I'll never get to it. Among many detestable things, writing is for me the most detestable. As long as you imitate my hand so well, write him in my name. I am expecting Orange. I won't get to it, and I would really like to have something written to him that will allay his worries.

SECRETARY: Give me some idea of what you have in mind and I will draft the reply and submit it to you for inspection. It shall be written so that it could stand up in court for your handwriting.

EGMONT: Let me have the letter. (*after glancing at it*) Good, honorable, old fellow! Were you this cautious in your youth? Did you never climb a wall? Did you hang behind the battle, as prudence counsels?—The true-hearted worrywart! He's concerned for my life and my happiness and he doesn't realize that a man who lives for his security is already dead.—Write him not to worry; I act as I must and I will take care of myself. He is to use his credit at court for my advantage and be assured of my total gratitude.

SECRETARY: No more than that? Oh, he expects much more.

EGMONT: What more should I say? If you want to put in extra words, that's up to you. It keeps coming back to one point: I am supposed to live the way I do not want to live. The fact that I am cheerful, that I take matters lightly, that I live headlong: that is my good luck—and I shall not exchange it for the security of a death-vault. For the Spanish way of life I don't have one single drop of blood in my veins, nor do I have any desire to pattern my steps on this new cautious court-cadence. Do I live simply to ponder about life? Am I to refuse to enjoy the present moment just so I can be sure of the next one? And then consume that one in turn with worries and fancies?

SECRETARY: I beg you, Sir, not to be so hard and harsh on the good man. You are friendly toward everybody else. Say me a gracious word that will soothe your noble friend. See how anxious he is, how delicately he alludes to you.

EGMONT: And yet he always touches the same chord. He has long known how I dislike these admonitions; they only confuse, they don't do any good. If I were a somnambulist walking on the perilous ridgepole of a house, would it be the friendly thing to do to call out my name as a warning and wake me up and kill me? Let everybody go his own path—and take care of himself.

SECRETARY: It befits you not to worry, but anyone knowing you and loving you—

EGMONT (*reading in the letter*):   Here he brings up once again those old fairytales about what we did and said one evening in the high jinks of sociability and wine, and about what deductions and proofs were made of that and dragged all through the realm.—All right, so we did have cap-and-bells and fools' cowls embroidered on our servants' sleeves, and later on we did change those crazy emblems into sheaves of arrows.[3] That was a still more dangerous emblem for all who try to interpret where there's nothing to interpret. So we did in a jolly moment give and take this folly and that folly. We are guilty of having had a whole crowd of nobles dress up in beggars' rags, and we did choose a ridiculous name for ourselves,[4] and under that name we did go in mock humility and remind the king of his obligation. We are guilty—what else does he say here? Is a

---

[3] At the protest of the Regent, Margaret of Parma.

[4] The party with the servants' emblems took place in December of 1563. At a more boisterous party held on April 3, 1566 the nobles chose for themselves the "ridiculous name" of Beggars, from a slurring remark about beggars (*gueux*) made by Baron Barlaymont to the Regent à propos of the three hundred noblemen who formally protested the Inquisition before the State Council that same day.

Mardi Gras prank right away high treason? Are we to be begrudged the brief motley tatters that youthful spirits and animated imagination may drape around the nakedness of our lives? If you take life all too seriously, what does it amount to? If morning doesn't waken us to new joys, and if at evening there is no joy left to look forward to, is it really worth dressing and undressing for? Does today's sun shine so I can brood over what happened yesterday? And puzzling and piecing together what cannot be puzzled out or pieced together, is that the destiny of a dawning day? Spare me these observations. Let's leave them to schoolboys and courtiers. Let them cogitate and excogitate, walk and creep, arrive where they may and creep up on what they can.—If you can use any of this, it's all right with me, only don't let your epistle turn into a book. The good oldster finds everything much too grave. It's the way a friend who has held our hand for some time gives it a harder squeeze when he is about to let go of it.

SECRETARY: Forgive me: a plodding wayfarer grows dizzy at seeing a man driving along at breakneck speed.

EGMONT: Child! Child! No more of this! As if whipped on by invisible spirits, the sun-steeds of time sweep the light chariot of our destiny along, and the most we can do is to maintain courage and calm, hold the reins tight, and steer the wheels to right or to left, here avoiding a stone and there avoiding a plunging crash. Where we are headed, who knows? We hardly recall whence we came.

SECRETARY: Sir! Sir!

EGMONT: I have climbed high, and I can and I must climb higher still. In me I feel hope and courage and vigor. I have not yet attained the summit of my growth, but once I do stand on that summit, I want to stand firmly, not timorously. If I am to fall, let it be a thunderbolt, a stormwind, yes, even a misstep of my own, that sends me hurtling to the abyss; there I shall lie with many thousands. With my good comrades in battle I have never shrunk from throwing the dice of blood for the sake of a small advantage, so why haggle when the whole free value of life is at stake?

SECRETARY: Oh, Sir! You do not realize what you are saying! God preserve you!

EGMONT: Gather up your papers. Orange is coming. Finish up the most essential of them so the messengers get off before the city gates are closed. The rest can wait. Leave the letter to the Count until tomorrow. Don't put off your visit to Elvira, and give her my good wishes.—Keep an ear open for how the Regent is. She is said not to be feeling well, although she conceals that fact.

(*The secretary leaves.*)
(*Enter Orange.*)

Welcome, Orange. You don't look exactly unpreoccupied.

ORANGE: What do you think about our interview with the Regent?

EGMONT: I found nothing extraordinary in the way she received us. I have seen her like that before. She seemed not to be quite well.

ORANGE: You didn't notice that she was more reticent? At first she quietly claimed to approve of our conduct in the face of the new uprising of the mob; afterwards she remarked on what a false light would be cast upon it, and then turned the subject to her usual line of talk: about how her good and kindly way of doing things and her friendship for us Dutchmen had never been sufficiently recognized, had been treated too lightly; about how nothing seemed to be turning out right; and how she couldn't help becoming weary at long last and the king would have to decide for other measures. Did you hear that?

EGMONT: Not all of it. My mind was on something else just then. She is a woman, my good Orange, and women always want everybody to cuddle down quietly beneath their gentle yoke and to have every Hercules lay aside his lion-skin and join their spinning-circle. Because *they* are peaceably disposed, the ferment that seizes upon a nation, the storm that powerful rivals raise against one another, these things are supposed to be adjusted by one friendly remark, and the most adverse elements are supposed to unite in sweet harmony at her feet. Such is her case; and since she cannot manage it, she has no recourse except to turn moody, bewail ingratitude and unwisdom, and with anticipation of dreadful things to come, to threaten and threaten that she will—resign.

ORANGE: Don't you think that this time she may carry out her threat?

EGMONT: Never! I've seen her ready to leave too many times! Where would she go? Here, she is Regent, Queen; do you think she could bear moping out useless days at her brother's court? or going to Italy and dragging herself around in old family feuds?[5]

ORANGE: You think her incapable of this decision because you have seen her vacillating, seen her backing down. Nevertheless she is quite capable of doing it. New circumstances are driving her to the long delayed decision. What if she did go? and the king sent someone else in her place?

EGMONT: Well, that person would come and would also discover that he had his hands full. He would come with great plans, projects, and ideas about how to set everything to rights, get everything under control and hold it all together. And today he would have to deal with this little problem and tomorrow with that little problem; day after tomorrow he would find another obstacle; he would spend a month on plans, another month in irritation over projects that didn't work out, and half a year in troubles with each individual province. He too will find time passing, and his head spinning, and things going their usual course, so that, instead of sailing across broad seas to a prescribed line, he will thank God if he can keep his ship off the rocks in this storm.

ORANGE: But what if the king were advised to make the attempt?

EGMONT: What attempt?

ORANGE: To see what the body could do without a head?

EGMONT: How do you mean?

ORANGE: Egmont, I have, these many years, borne all our relationships in my heart. I always stand as if over a game of chess, and I take no move of an opponent as being without significance. Just as idle people fuss with the greatest concern over the mysteries of Nature, I consider it the duty, indeed the vocation, of a ruler to know the opinions and advice of all parties. I have reason to fear an explosion. The king has long acted according to certain principles, and he sees they aren't getting him anywhere. What is more likely than that he should try a different way?

EGMONT: I doubt it. When people get older and have tried so many things, and still the world won't shape up, they finally have to make the best of it.

---

[5] Margaret was related to the feuding Medici and Farnese families.

ORANGE: There is one thing he hasn't yet tried.

EGMONT: Namely?

ORANGE: Sparing the people and destroying the leaders.

EGMONT: How many have feared just that, for a long time. It's nothing to worry about.

ORANGE: It might be. Little by little it became my suspicion, and finally a conviction.

EGMONT: Has the king any servers more loyal than we are?

ORANGE: We serve him in our own way; and between ourselves we can admit that we know how to trade off the king's rights and ours.

EGMONT: Who doesn't do just that? We are subject to him and at his disposition in matters that are his due.

ORANGE: But what if he were to go further and consider as treason what we call standing on our rights?

EGMONT: We can defend ourselves. Let him convoke the Knights of the Golden Fleece, and we will submit to judgment.

ORANGE: What about a sentence before the investigation? or an execution before the sentence?

EGMONT: An injustice that Philip would never be guilty of—and a folly I do not believe of him or of his counsellors.

ORANGE: What if they were unjust and foolish?

EGMONT: No, Orange, it isn't possible. Who would dare lay hands on us?—Arresting us would be a forlorn and futile undertaking. No, they don't dare raise the banner of tyranny that high. The breeze that wafted that news across the country would fan a monstrous conflagration. And where would it get them? The king cannot try and condemn on his sole authority. And would they set out to assassinate us?—They can't mean that. A terrible alliance would unite the nation in a single minute. Hatred and permanent separation from the Spanish name would be declared with violence.

ORANGE: The fire would then rage over our graves, and our enemies' blood would flow in an empty sacrifice of atonement. Let us consider plans, Egmont.

EGMONT: But how would they?

ORANGE: Alba is on his way.

EGMONT: I don't believe it.

ORANGE: I know it.

EGMONT: The Regent claimed she had no knowledge.

ORANGE: All the more reason for me to be convinced. The Regent will yield her place to him. I know his murderous mind, and he is bringing an army with him.

EGMONT: To burden down the provinces with again? The people will become very difficult.

ORANGE: They will arrest the leaders.

EGMONT: No! No!

ORANGE: Let's you and I each go to his own province. There let's strengthen our forces. He won't start out with open force.

EGMONT: Aren't we obliged to welcome him when he comes?

ORANGE: We'll put it off.

EGMONT: And what if he summons us in the king's name to his presence?

ORANGE: We'll think of ways to evade him.

EGMONT: And if he insists?

ORANGE: We make excuses.

EGMONT: And if he demands?

ORANGE: We're even less likely to come.

EGMONT: And war is declared and we are the rebels. Orange, don't be misled by cleverness—I know fear cannot make you give way. Consider this step.

ORANGE: I have considered it.

EGMONT: Consider what you are guilty of if you are wrong—the most destructive war that ever laid a country waste. Your refusal would be the signal that would call the provinces to arms instantly; it would justify every cruelty that Spain has long been seeking a pretext for. What we have quieted by protracted effort, you would stir up to horrible confusion with one gesture. Think of the cities, the nobles, the common people, business, agriculture, the trades! And think of the devastation, the slaughter!—The soldier may calmly see his comrade killed beside him on the battlefield, but downstream the corpses of citizens, children, and young girls will float to meet you until you stand there and won't know whose cause you are defending, as ruin overwhelms the very ones for whose liberty you took up arms. And how will you feel when you have to say to yourself: I took them up for *my* security?

ORANGE: We are not isolated individuals, Egmont. If it behooves us to sacrifice ourselves for the sake of thousands, it also behooves us to rescue ourselves for the sake of thousands.

EGMONT: Whoever rescues himself has to be suspicious of himself.

ORANGE: Whoever knows himself can advance and retreat in safety.

EGMONT: The evil you fear will, because of your own action, come to pass.

ORANGE: It is both wise and brave to face up to an unavoidable evil.

EGMONT: Before so great a peril the slightest hope must be considered.

ORANGE: There is no room left us for the slightest step; the abyss lies right before us.

EGMONT: Is the king's favor that narrow a space?

ORANGE: Not that narrow, perhaps, but slippery.

EGMONT: By God, you wrong him! I won't have him unfairly thought of! He is Charles's son and incapable of any baseness.

ORANGE: Kings never do anything base?

EGMONT: People should get to know him.

ORANGE: Precisely that acquaintance signifies we should not wait for the outcome of a dangerous test.

EGMONT: No test is dangerous if one has the courage for it.

ORANGE: You're getting all excited, Egmont.

EGMONT: I have to see it with my own eyes.

ORANGE: Oh, would that you saw with mine this time! Friend, because yours are open, you think you are seeing. I am leaving! You can wait for Alba's arrival, and God be with you! Maybe my refusal will save you. Maybe the dragon will think he's made no catch if he doesn't devour both of us at one gulp. Maybe he will delay so as to carry out his design the more surely, and maybe in the meantime you will see the matter in its true form. But then act fast! Save yourself! Save yourself!—Farewell. Let nothing escape your watchfulness: how big a force he is bringing, how he garrisons the city, what power the Regent retains, how your friends feel. Send me word—Egmont—

EGMONT: What?

ORANGE (*seizing his hand*):   Let yourself be persuaded! Come with me!

EGMONT: What's this: tears, Orange?

ORANGE: It is also manly to weep for a man lost.

EGMONT: You count me lost?

ORANGE: You are! Consider! You have only a little time left. Farewell.

(*Exit.*)

EGMONT: To think that other persons' thoughts should have such effect on us! It would never have occurred to me. And this man's anxiety carries over to me.—Away! This is an alien drop in my blood. Expel it, good Nature, again! And to wash away the brooding wrinkles from my brow there is still one kindly balm.[6]

---

[6] Namely, Klärchen.

ACT III

[Scene 1]

The Regent's palace.
Margaret of Parma [is discovered alone.]

REGENT: I should have expected it. Ha! When you work and toil away from day to day you always think you are doing your utmost; and someone that looks on from afar and issues orders, thinks he is asking no more than the possible.—Oh, these kings!—I would never have believed it could vex me so. It is such a wonderful thing, to rule!—And to abdicate?—I do not know how my father could do it, but I want to do that too.

(Machiavell appears at the rear.)

Come in, Machiavell. I am here pondering over my brother's letter.

MACHIAVELL: May I know what it says?

REGENT: As much tender notice of me as concern for his lands. He praises the steadfastness, the industry, and the loyalty with which I have hitherto watched over His Majesty's rights in these provinces. He is sorry that the unruly population has caused me so much trouble. He is so totally persuaded of the profundity of my views, so extraordinarily satisfied with the sagacity of my conduct, than I am forced to say the letter is too splendidly written for a king—and certainly for a brother.

MACHIAVELL: It is not the first time that he has expressed his justified satisfaction.

REGENT: But the first time it is a figure of speech.

MACHIAVELL: I don't quite understand.

REGENT: You will.—For after this preface he opines that, without troops, without a little army, I will always cut a poor figure here! We made a mistake, he says, in listening to the complaints of the inhabitants and pulling our soldiers out of these provinces. A garrison, he thinks, that weighs down citizens' necks will, by its very weight, prevent them from getting out of line.

MACHIAVELL: It would rouse tempers in the extreme.

REGENT: The king believes, however—you hear?—he believes that an efficient General, the kind that doesn't stand for any arguments, would very soon bring order among commoners and nobles, citizenry and peasantry—and therefore he is sending a strong army—commanded by the Duke of Alba.

MACHIAVELL: Alba!

REGENT: You are surprised?

MACHIAVELL: You say he "is sending." Surely he is asking whether he *may* send?

REGENT: The king is not asking, he is sending.

MACHIAVELL: Then you will have an experienced soldier in your service.

REGENT: In my service? Speak frankly, Machiavell.

MACHIAVELL: I would not like to anticipate you.

REGENT: You think I'm dissimulating! It is painful to me, very painful. I'd rather my brother said what he thinks, rather than sign formal epistles drawn up by a secretary of state.

MACHIAVELL: Might I have a look—?

REGENT: I know them inside and out. They'd like to have things cleaned and swept up, and since they don't take a hand themselves, anybody with a broom in hand is confident. Oh, I can see the king and his council as clearly as if they were embroidered on this tapestry.

MACHIAVELL: That vividly?

REGENT: Not a feature is missing. There are good men among them. The honorable Roderich, who is so experienced and moderate, who doesn't aim too high and yet lets nothing get by him; the upright Alonzo, the diligent Freneda, the solid Las Vargas, and several others that go along when the good faction gains power. But there sits hollow-eyed Toledo[1] with the brow of bronze and his glance of sunken fire, muttering between his teeth about women's kindliness, untimely relaxation, and about how ladies may be carried by well-broken horses but are themselves poor riding-masters, and other such jokes that I have had to put up with in former times from political gentlemen.

MACHIAVELL: You have chosen a vivid palette for your painting.

[1] Alba's name was Ferdinand Alvarez of Toledo, Duke of Alba.

REGENT: You must admit, Machiavell, that in my whole range of color gradations that I could possibly paint with, there is no hue so yellowish-brown, so gall-black, as Alba's complexion or as the color in which *he* paints things. To him, everyone is guilty of blasphemy against God and of *lèse-majesté,* and on these scores everybody deserves right now to be broken on the wheel, impaled, drawn and quartered, and burned at the stake.—The good I have done here surely looks, from a distance, like nothing at all, precisely because it is good.—He clings to every prank that is over and done with, recalls every agitation that has been quieted, and to the king's eyes it will all seem so full of mutiny, rioting, and foolhardiness that he will imagine that people here are eating each other alive, whereas a fleeting rudeness of a rough-and-ready nation is long forgotten among us. Then he develops a cordial hatred for the poor people; they seem loathsome to him, like beasts and monsters; and he reaches for fire and sword, fancying that human beings are to be tamed thereby.

MACHIAVELL: You seem overvehement, you are taking it too seriously. Will you not still be Regent?

REGENT: I know how it will go. He will bring along an "instruction."—I have grown old enough in affairs of state to know how a person is forced out without their withdrawing his appointment. First, he will bring along an "instruction," which will be vague and indirect; he will gain ground, because ne has the power; and if I complain, he will hide behind a secret "instruction"; if I ask to see it, he will shift ground; if I insist, he will show me some document that contains something else entirely; and if I am still not satisfied, he will simply let me go on talking.—Meanwhile he will do the very things I dread and divert afar the things I wish.

MACHIAVELL: I wish I could gainsay you.

REGENT: What I have assuaged with patience beyond words to tell, he will stir up again with harshness and cruelties. I will see my work undone before my eyes and have to bear the blame for it besides.

MACHIAVELL: Your Highness should wait and see.

REGENT: I have enough self-control to keep still. Let him come. I will yield place to him with all grace—before he forces me out.

MACHIAVELL: So quick to take this important step?

REGENT: It is more difficult than you think. Anyone who is accustomed to ruling, for whom it is second nature to hold the fates of thousands in his hand every day, descends from the throne as if into the grave. But better that than to remain like a ghost among the living and loftily claim a position that somebody else has inherited and now possesses and enjoys.

[SCENE 2]

Klärchen's house.

Klärchen[2] *and her mother.*

MOTHER: A love like Brackenburg's I have never seen. I thought that kind of thing happened only in hero-tales.

KLÄRCHEN (*walking back and forth and humming a song*):

> Happiness lives
> In the lover alone.

MOTHER: He suspects your association with Egmont. But I think that, if you would be a little friendly toward him, and if you wanted to, he would still marry you.

KLÄRCHEN (*sings*):   Joyful
> And rueful,
> Far off in a thought;
> Yearning
> And burning,
> With sorrow distraught;
> Sky-high exulting,
> To death burdened down;
> Happiness lives
> In the lover alone.

MOTHER: Do stop you tra-la-la-ing.

KLÄRCHEN: Don't scold me for it; it's a song that gives strength. More than once I've sung it to lull a grown child to sleep.

MOTHER: You have nothing on your mind but your love. If only you

[2] Beginning here, the author terms the heroine Klärchen, rather than Klara.

didn't forget everything else for that one thing. You should esteem
Brackenburg, I'm telling you. He can make you happy once more.

KLÄRCHEN: He?

MOTHER: Oh, yes. The time will come!—You young people don't
look ahead at all and you just won't listen to our experience. Youth
and fine loving come to an end like everything else, and a time will
come when you thank God for some place to crawl into.

KLÄRCHEN (*shuddering, falling silent, and then suddenly crying
out*):   Mother, let time and death come in their own good time.
Thinking of them in advance is horrible!—what if the time does
come? When we have to—then—we'll act whatever way we can.—
Give you up, Egmont! (*in tears*) No, it isn't possible, it isn't possible.

(*Enter Egmont in a riding cloak, with his hat pulled
down over his eyes.*)

EGMONT: Klärchen!

KLÄRCHEN (*with a cry, falling back*):   Egmont! (*rushing toward him*)
Egmont! (*embracing him and nestling close to him*) Oh, my kind,
sweet beloved! Have you come? Are you here?

EGMONT: Good evening, mother.

MOTHER: God greet you, noble Sir! My little girl is almost wasted
away from your staying away so long. She has been talking about
you and singing about you again this whole livelong day.

EGMONT: You will give me a bit of supper, won't you?

MOTHER: You are too kind. If only we had something.

KLÄRCHEN: Of course! Don't you trouble, mother, I have everything
arranged. I have some things ready. Don't betray me, mother.

MOTHER: Slim enough.

KLÄRCHEN: Just wait! And then I think: when he is with me I am
not hungry at all, so he shouldn't have any great appetite when I
am with him.

EGMONT: You think so?

(*Klärchen stamps her foot and angrily turns her back.*)
What is the matter?

KLÄRCHEN: How cool you are today! You haven't even offered me a
kiss yet. Why have you got your arms all bundled up in your cloak

like a baby in swaddling clothes? It's not becoming for a soldier or a lover to have his arms all bundled up.

EGMONT: In due time, my darling, in due time. When a soldier is lying in wait to trick the enemy out of something, he gathers himself together, clasps his arms around himself, and chews his idea thoroughly. And a lover—

MOTHER: Won't you have a seat? Make yourself comfortable? I must go to the kitchen: Klärchen thinks of nothing else when you are here. You'll have to make do.

EGMONT: Good will is the best sauce.

(*The mother goes out.*)

KLÄRCHEN: What would my love amount to then?

EGMONT: As much as you wish.

KLÄRCHEN: Make an estimate if you have the heart to do so.

EGMONT: First of all, then.

(*He throws off his cloak and stands in magnificent garb.*)

KLÄRCHEN: Oh-h-h!

EGMONT: Now I have my arms free. (*He sweeps her into his arms.*)

KLÄRCHEN: Let me go! You're spoiling your clothes.

(*She steps back.*)

How magnificent! I don't dare touch you.

EGMONT: Are you satisfied now? I promised you to come some time all in Spanish garb.

KLÄRCHEN: Since then I haven't asked any more about it; I thought you didn't want to—Oh! and the Golden Fleece!

EGMONT: Yes, now you get to see it.

KLÄRCHEN: The Emperor hung it around your neck?

EGMONT: Yes, child. And the chain and emblem confer the noblest liberties upon anyone that wears them. I acknowledge on earth no judge of my actions except the Grand Master of the Order in the assembled chapter of the knights.

KLÄRCHEN: Oh, you could afford to have the whole world judge you.—The velvet is simply magnificent. And the braiding! and the embroidery work!—I don't know where to start.

EGMONT: Look your fill.

KLÄRCHEN: And the Golden Fleece! You told me the story and you said: it is a symbol for all that is great and rare that anyone can earn and win with labor and effort. It is very precious—I dare to compare it to my love. I wear *that* at my heart the same way—and beyond—

EGMONT: What were you going to say?

KLÄRCHEN: Beyond that there are no more comparisons.

EGMONT: How so?

KLÄRCHEN: I won it with labor and effort, but I did not earn it.

EGMONT: In love it is different. You earn it because you do not seek for it—and it is chiefly won by people who do not strive for it.

KLÄRCHEN: You do make an exception in your own case? Did you make that proud remark about yourself? You, whom the whole nation loves?

EGMONT: If only I had done something for them! If only I could do something for them! It is their good pleasure to love me.

KLÄRCHEN: Surely you were at the Regent's today?

EGMONT: Yes, I was there.

KLÄRCHEN: Do you stand well with her?

EGMONT: I seem to. We are friendly in an official way.

KLÄRCHEN: And in your heart?

EGMONT: I wish her well. Each of us has his own objectives. But that is nothing to the point. She is an excellent woman; she knows her people, and she would see deep enough if she just wouldn't be suspicious. I cause her a great deal of bother because behind my actions she is always looking for secrets, and I haven't any.

KLÄRCHEN: None at all?

EGMONT: Well . . . a slight reserve. With time, any wine leaves a sediment in the vats. Now, Orange is even better conversation for her, constantly posing a new problem. He has acquired a reputation for always having some secret, and now she keeps staring at his brow to see what he can be thinking, and at his steps to see which way he may be heading.

KLÄRCHEN: Does she dissemble?

EGMONT: She is Regent, and you ask?

KLÄRCHEN: I'm sorry. What I meant to ask was: is she treacherous?

EGMONT: No more and no less so than anybody that's trying to achieve his own objectives.

KLÄRCHEN: I could never be at home in that world. But she also does have a masculine spirit. She is a different woman from us cooks and seamstresses. She is great, stouthearted, decisive.

EGMONT: Yes, when things don't get out of hand. This time, however, she is a bit out of patience.

KLÄRCHEN: How so?

EGMONT: She also has whiskers on her upper lip, and sometimes she gets a twinge of the gout. A regular amazon!

KLÄRCHEN: A majestical lady! I would be scared to step into her presence.

EGMONT: But you're not usually timid.—It wouldn't be fear, but maidenly shyness.

> (*Klärchen lowers her eyes, takes his hand,*
> *and nestles against him.*)

I understand you, my dear girl. You can lift your eyes.

> (*He kisses her eyelids*)

KLÄRCHEN: Let me be silent. Let me hold you. Let me look into your eyes and find everything in them—comfort and hope and joy and shyness.

> (*She puts her arms around him and gazes at him.*)

Tell me, tell me! I don't understand! Are you Egmont? Count Egmont? the great Egmont who makes such a great stir, on whom the papers say the provinces rely?

EGMONT: No, Klärchen, I am not.

KLÄRCHEN: What?!

EGMONT: You see, Klärchen—Let me sit down.

> (*He sits down; she kneels before him on a stool;*
> *rests her arms on his lap, and gazes at him.*)

That Egmont is a peevish, stiff, cold Egmont who has to keep himself in check and make now one sort of face and now another; tormented, misunderstood, and perplexed, when people think he is happy and cheerful; loved by a nation that doesn't know what it wants; honored and exalted by a mob that nothing can be done with; surrounded by friends to whom he doesn't dare entrust himself; watched by persons who would like to do him in, if they could; working and toiling often without purpose, usually without reward.—Oh, let me say no more about how he fares and how he feels. But *this* one, Klärchen, *this* one is serene, open, happy, loved and known by the best of hearts, which he too knows and with all the love and trust in the world presses to his own. (*He embraces her.*) This one is *your* Egmont!

KLÄRCHEN: Let me die like this! The world has no joys after these!

ACT IV

[Scene 1]

A street.

Jetter and the Master Carpenter.

JETTER: Hey! Pst! Hey, neighbor, a word!

CARPENTER: Go your way and keep still.

JETTER: Just a word. Anything new?

CARPENTER: Nothing except that they forbid us to talk about the news.

JETTER: What?

CARPENTER: Come up close by this house here. Be careful! The Duke of Alba issued an order as soon as he arrived, that people talking together in twos or threes on the street shall be considered guilty of high treason without investigation.

JETTER: Oh, Lord!

CARPENTER: It's life imprisonment to be talking about matters of state.

JETTER: Oh, our liberty!

CARPENTER: And the death penalty for disapproving actions of the government.

JETTER: Oh, our heads!

CARPENTER: And with high inducements fathers, mothers, children, relatives, friends, and servants are invited to disclose to specially constituted tribunals what goes on in the inmost recesses of homes.

JETTER: Let's go home.

CARPENTER: And cooperative persons are guaranteed they will suffer no injuries to life, honor, or property.

JETTER: There's mercy for you! As soon as the Duke entered the city I felt awful. Since then I've felt as if the sky was draped with a black pall that hung so low you have to stoop in order not to run your head into it.

CARPENTER: And how did you like his soldiers? *They*'re a different kettle of fish, eh? from what we've been used to.

339

JETTER: Ugh! It makes your heart sink down to your shoes to see a troop like that marching down the streets. Stiff as ramrods, don't look right or left, all in step, every last man of 'em. And when they stand guard and you go past one of 'em, it's as if he was trying to look right through you, and he looks so stiff and sullen you think you're seeing a corrections officer at every corner. They make me ill. Our militia was a jolly bunch, after all. They'd venture a thing or two and didn't stand around straddle-legged; they cocked their hats over one ear and lived and let live. But these fellows are machines, with a devil inside.

CARPENTER: If one of them shouts "Halt!" and puts his gun to his shoulder, do you think people would stop?

JETTER: I'd die right there.

CARPENTER: Let's go home.

JETTER: No good will come of this. Goodbye.

(Soest steps up and joins them.)

SOEST: Friends! Comrades!

CARPENTER: Quiet! Let's go.

SOEST: Have you heard?

JETTER: Too much already.

SOEST: The Regent has left.

JETTER: Now God have mercy on us!

CARPENTER: She still stuck up for us.

SOEST: All of a sudden and all on the quiet. She couldn't get along with the Duke. She left word for the nobles that she would be back,—but nobody believes it.

CARPENTER: God forgive the nobles for hanging this new scourge over us. They could have averted it. Our privileges are over.

JETTER: For God's sake, don't say anything about privileges! I can smell an execution morning: the sun can't come out, the clouds stink.

SOEST: Orange is gone too.

CARPENTER: Then we're completely abandoned!

SOEST: Count Egmont is still here.

JETTER: Thank God! May all the saints strengthen him to do his best. He is the only one that can do anything.

(Vansen comes up.)

VANSEN: Do I finally find a couple that haven't yet taken cover?

JETTER: Do us a favor and keep going.

VANSEN: You're not very polite.

CARPENTER: This is no time for compliments. Is your back itching for another flogging? Are you already over the last one?

VANSEN: Ask a soldier about his wounds! If I had ever worried about floggings, I would never have amounted to anything in all my born days.

JETTER: It may get more serious.

VANSEN: It seems you feel pretty weak in the knees from the storm that's brewing.

CARPENTER: Your knees will soon be making motions somewhere else, if you don't keep still.

VANSEN: Poor little mousies! In despair right away because the master of the house is getting a new cat! Just a wee bit different, but we'll go on as before, rest assured.

CARPENTER: You're a good-for-nothing idiot!

VANSEN: All right, cousin fool! Let the Duke have his way. The old tomcat looks as if he's swallowed devils instead of mice and couldn't digest them. Let him alone; he has to eat and drink too, and sleep, like other people. I'm not worried, if we just take our time. At the start, there's a great rush; later on, he too will find out it's nicer to live in the pantry among the sides of bacon and to sleep at night than to go sneaking up on mice, one at a time, in the grain storage. Go on, I know the *stadhouter*.

CARPENTER: What a man like you gets by with! If I had ever said a thing like that in all my life, I wouldn't feel safe for a minute.

VANSEN: Take it easy! God in heaven won't find out anything about worms like you, much less the Regent.

JETTER: Foul-mouth!

VANSEN: I know some others that would be better off if they had a streak of tailor in them instead of their hero's courage.[1]

CARPENTER: What do you mean by that?

VANSEN: Mmm, I have the Count in mind.

JETTER: Egmont! What does he have to be afraid of?

[1] Jetter is a tailor.

VANSEN: I'm a poor devil and I could live a whole year on what he
loses in one evening. And yet he could give me a whole year's
income of his to have *my* head on his shoulders for a quarter of an
hour.

JETTER: You think you're something special. The hairs on Egmont's
head have more sense in them than you have in your brain.

VANSEN: *You* say! But not shrewder. The nobles deceive each other
first. He shouldn't trust them.

JETTER: The stuff he talks! A great lord like that!

VANSEN: Just because he isn't a tailor.

JETTER: You filth!

VANSEN: I could wish your spirit into him for just an hour, till it
upset him and irked him and pestered him enough to make him
leave the city.

JETTER: What you say doesn't make sense. He's as safe as a star in
the sky.

VANSEN: Have you ever seen one get snuffed out? It's gone!

CARPENTER: Who's going to do anything to him?

VANSEN: Who? Maybe you'd try to stop it? Are you going to start
an uproar when they arrest him?

JETTER: Ah!

VANSEN: Would you risk your ribs for him?

SOEST: Eh!

VANSEN (*imitating them*):   Eh! Oh! Uh! Goggle right down the
alphabet. That's how it is and that's how it's going to stay. God
protect him!

JETTER: I am horrified at your impudence. A noble, upright man
like that has to be afraid of something?

VANSEN: Rascals have the upper hand everywhere. In the dock they
make a fool of the judge; in the judge's seat they enjoy making a
criminal out of the defendant. I once had to write up the minutes of
a case where the prosecutor got a bundle of money and praise from
the court because he went after a poor devil they wanted to get and
made him out to be a scoundrel.

CARPENTER: That's an outright lie again! Why should they want to
make somebody out a scoundrel when he's innocent?

VANSEN: Sparrow-brain! When there's nothing to be made out of somebody they make him into something. Uprightness makes a man reckless, maybe even defiant. So they start out by asking away gently, and the prisoner is proud of his innocence as they call it, and tells everything straight out that a sensible man would conceal. Then out of the answers the prosecutor makes new questions and is on the lookout for the least little contradiction to turn up; that's where he sets his trap. And if the stupid devil lets himself step into it by letting on that here he said a little too much and there a little too little, or maybe, from God knows what whim, passed over some circumstance in silence, or maybe even got scared at some point: *then* we're on the right track! And I guarantee you that beggar-women don't sort out rags from the junk-heap with more care than a scoundrel-manufacturer like that pieces together his rags-and-tatters scarecrow out of twisted, squinched-up, misplaced, mangled, private, public, disavowed depositions and particulars, so he can at least get his victim hanged in effigy. And the poor devil can thank God if he can see himself hanged.

JETTER: This one certainly has a running tongue.

CARPENTER: It may work with flies, but wasps laugh at your web.

VANSEN: Depending on the spiders. You see, the lanky Duke is the very picture of your garden-spider; not one of those bulgy-paunched ones—they are not so bad—but one of those long-legged, pinch-bellied ones that eat and never get fat and that spin a very fine thread that is all the tougher.

JETTER: Egmont is a knight of the Golden Fleece: who can lay a hand on him? He can be tried only by his peers, only by the full Order in convocation. Your loose tongue and your bad conscience mislead you to this kind of chatter.

VANSEN: Do I mean him any harm by it? I don't mind. He is an excellent lord. A couple of good friends of mine that would have been hanged anywhere else got off with backs full of whip-scars from him. Now go along, go along, I advise you myself. I see another patrol coming there, and they don't look as if they'd be drinking brotherhood with us right away. Let's wait and just quietly see. I have a couple of nieces and a tavern-keeper cousin; if they get a taste of them and don't get tamed, they've got to be pretty seasonsed wolves.

[SCENE 2]

The Duke of Alba's residence at the Eulenberg Palace.
Enter Silva and Gomez, meeting.

SILVA: Have you carried out the Duke's orders?

GOMEZ: Precisely. All day patrols have instructions to report at various points at a particular time as designated; meanwhile they go their usual rounds through the city to maintain order. None of them knows about the others; each thinks the order concerns his group alone, and so the cordon can be set up in one minute and all approaches to the palace can be manned. Do you know the reason for this order?

SILVA: I am accustomed to obeying blindly. And who is easier to obey than the Duke? The outcome soon shows he has given the right commands.

GOMEZ: Good, good. To me it's no wonder that you are getting to be as close-mouthed and laconic as he is, since you have to be around him all the time. It strikes me a bit odd because I'm used to the easy-going Italian service. In loyalty and obedience I am the same as I always was, but I've gotten used to chattering and arguing. You all keep still and never enjoy yourselves. To me the Duke seems like a tower of bronze without an entrance-gate the garrison had wings to reach. Recently I heard him talking at table about a cheerful, friendly fellow and saying he was like a miserable tavern-keeper with a brandy sign stuck up to attract idlers, beggars, and thieves.

SILVA: Didn't he lead us here in silence?

GOMEZ: Nothing against *that*. Sure! Anybody that witnessed his cleverness in bringing the army here from Italy, really saw something. The way he wound his way, so to speak, through friends and foes, through the royal and Huguenot French, through the Swiss and their Geneva allies, keeping the strictest disciplines and bringing up easily and without any offense a column when everybody thought it was so dangerous!—We saw something there, we could learn something.

SILVA: Here too! Isn't everything here as calm and still as if there had been no rebellion?

GOMEZ: Well, it was already mostly quiet when we arrived.

SILVA: In the provinces it's gotten much quieter. And if anybody is doing any more stirring, it's to escape. But he will soon block those ways too, I think.

GOMEZ: Now he will really gain the king's favor.

SILVA: That leaves us with nothing more important to do than to gain his. If the king comes here, the Duke will stay on, and nobody he recommends will go unrewarded.

GOMEZ: Do you think the king will come?

SILVA: They're making so many arrangements that it is very likely.

GOMEZ: They don't convince me.

SILVA: At least don't talk about it, then. For if it is the king's intention not to come, it certainly is for people to think that he will.

(Enter Ferdinand, Alba's illegitimate son.)

FERDINAND: Hasn't my father come out yet?

SILVA: We are waiting for him.

FERDINAND: The princes will soon be here.

GOMEZ: Are they coming today?

FERDINAND: Orange and Egmont.

GOMEZ *(aside to Silva)*:   I understand something.

SILVA: Then keep it to yourself.

(Enter the Duke of Alba. The others step back.)

ALBA: Gomez!

GOMEZ *(stepping forward)*:   Sir!

ALBA: Have you divided up the guard and issued them orders?

GOMEZ: Most precisely. The day patrols—

ALBA: Enough. You will wait in the gallery. Silva will tell you the moment when you are to bring them together and man the approaches to the palace. The rest you know.

GOMEZ: Yes, Sir!

(Exit.)

ALBA: Silva!

SILVA: Here I am.

ALBA: Everything I have always valued in you: courage, decisiveness, unceasing carrying out of commands: show those things today.

SILVA: I thank you for giving me the opportunity of showing you that I am the same as of old.

ALBA: As soon as the princes are in my presence make haste to arrest Egmont's private secretary. You did make all the arrangements for seizing the others who are on the list?

SILVA: Rely on us! Their fate will overtake them punctually and fearfully, like a well-calculated eclipse of the sun.

ALBA: You've had them closely observed?

SILVA: All of them; Egmont above all others. He is the only one that has not altered his behavior since you have been here. All day long off of one horse and onto another, he invites guests, is always jolly and entertaining at table, plays at dice, goes shooting, and by night slips away to his sweetheart. The others, however, have marked a notable pause in their way of living. They stay home; at their doors it looks as if people were sick in their houses.

ALBA: Then act fast, before they get well against our will.

SILVA: I'll bring them to bay. At your orders we are heaping them with gratifying honors; for reasons of policy they return us anxious thanks and feel the wisest thing is to make their escape. Not one of them dares to move; they hesitate, can't agree; and common opinion keeps them from taking any bold step individually. They would dearly like to escape any suspicion and simply make themselves all the more suspicious. With delight I already see your whole plan realized.

ALBA: I am delighted only by what has already happened, and not readily even by that, for there constantly remains what cannot but cause us to think and to worry. Luck is fickle and will often ennoble what is base and worthless while dishonoring well-considered deeds with a base outcome. Wait here until the princes arrive, then give Gomez the order to occupy the streets, and hurry yourself to arrest Egmont's secretary and the others that have been indicated to you. When that is done, come back here and report it to my son so he can bring me the news in council.

SILVA: I hope I may stand before you this evening.

(Alba goes over to his son, who has

meanwhile been standing in the gallery.)

I don't dare say it, but my hopes are wavering. I fear it will not
turn out the way he thinks. Before me I see spirits silently and pen-
sively weighing the fates of the princes and of many thousands in
the balance. Slowly the pointer wobbles back and forth. The judges
seem deep in thought. Finally one scale sinks lower and the other
rises, touched by the breath of Fate's caprice, and the matter is
decided.

(Exit.)

ALBA (*returning with Ferdinand*):   How did you find the city?

FERDINAND: They have all given in. I rode, as though for pastime,
up streets and down streets. Your well distributed patrols have
strained fear to the point where people don't dare whisper. The city
looks like an open field when lightning is flashing in the distance
and not a bird or beast is to be seen except as they are hurrying to
take cover.

ALBA: You had no further encounter?

FERDINAND: Egmont and several others came riding to the market;
we greeted each other; he had an unbroken horse that I couldn't
help admiring. "Let's hurry and break in some horses; we'll soon
be needing them!" he called over to me. He would see me again
today, he said, because he was coming at your request to discuss
matters with you.

ALBA: He will see you again.

FERDINAND: Of all the knights I know here, I like him best. It looks
as though we will be friends.

ALBA: You are still too impulsive and uncautious. In you I always
see that levity of your mother's that delivered her unconditionally
into my arms. Appearances have overhastily led you into more than
one dangerous alliance.

FERDINAND: Your will finds me tractable.

ALBA: I forgive your youthful blood this thoughtless good will, this
heedless cheerfulness. Just do not forget what business I have been
sent on and what part I might want to assign of it to you.

FERDINAND: Remind me and do not spare me in whatever you
consider necessary.

ALBA (*after a pause*): My son!

FERDINAND: My father!

ALBA: The princes will soon be coming, Orange and Egmont. It is not mistrust that I have not diclosed to you until now what is to take place. They will not be leaving here again.

FERDINAND: What is in your mind?

ALBA: The decision has been made to hold them prisoner.—You are astonished? Now here is what you have to do; the reasons for it you will know when it has taken place. There is no time to explain them now. With you alone I should like to discuss greatest and most secret things. A strong bond unites us; you are precious and dear to me; on you I would like to heap all things. In you I would like to inculcate not merely the habit of obedience, but also the habit of reasoning out intentions, of commanding and executing, and to transmit these qualities to you, thereby leaving you a mighty heritage, that of being the king's most useful servant. I would like to fit you out with the best that I have, so you need not be ashamed of appearing alongside your brothers.

FERDINAND: How much I shall be indebted to you for this love that you show me, since a whole kingdom trembles before you.

ALBA: Now here is what must be done. As soon as the princes have come in, every access to the palace will be manned with guards. Gomez has the orders for that. Silva will hurry to seize Egmont's secretary along with the most suspicious persons. You will control the guards at the gate and in the courtyards. Above all, you are to post-the most reliable men in the rooms here adjacent; then wait in the gallery until Silva comes back, and when he does, bring in to me some insignificant paper or other as a signal that his mission has been carried out. After that, remain in the anteroom until Orange leaves. Follow him. I will detain Egmont here, as if I had something further to say to him. At the far end of the gallery demand Orange's sword, call the guard, and quickly secure that more dangerous man; I will seize Egmont here.

FERDINAND: I shall obey, father—for the first time with heavy heart and with anxiety.

ALBA: I forgive you for that. It is the first great day of your life.

(*Enter Silva.*)

SILVA: A messenger from Antwerp. Here is a letter from Orange. He isn't coming.

ALBA: Does the messenger say so?

SILVA: No, my heart tells me so.

ALBA: In you my evil genius speaks.

(After reading the letter he motions the other two away. They retire into the gallery, while he remains alone downstage.)

He isn't coming! He puts off declaring himself until the last moment. He dares *not* to come! So this time, contrary to my surmise, the prudent one was prudent enough not to be prudent!

The clock advances. A small distance yet for the hand to move, and a great work is either done or missed, missed beyond recall; for it can neither be made up for nor concealed. Long and ripely I had pondered all chances, including this chance, and settled on what I would do even in this chance; and now that it is to be done, I can hardly keep the pros and cons from going alternately through my mind again. Is it advisable to seize the others if *he* gets away from me? Shall I put it off and let Egmont and his many followers elude me, who are now in my hands, and perhaps only for today? Does Fate compel you too, you who are proof to compulsion? How long thought out! How well prepared! How great and fine the plan! How close hope was to its goal! And now at the moment of decision you are placed between two evils. You reach into the dark future as into an urn of lots, and what your hand takes is still rolled up, unknown to you, a winner or a loser, as the case may be.

(He listens like someone who has heard a noise, and goes over to the window.)

There he is! Egmont! Did your horse carry you so readily in, without shying at the smell of blood or the spirit with the naked sword that meets you at the door?—Dismount! Now you have one foot in the grave—and now you have both.—Yes, go on and caress it, pat its neck for the last time in appreciation for its valiant service.—And I am left with no choice. Blinded as Egmont comes here now, never will he play into your hands this way a second time.—You two there, ho!

(Ferdinand and Silva hurry over to him.)

You will do as I commanded; I am not changing my plan. Come what may, I will detain Egmont until you bring me the report from Silva. Then stay close by. Fate robs you also of the great service of capturing the king's greatest enemy with your own hand. (*to Silva*) Hurry! (*to Ferdinand*) Go and welcome him.

(*Alba is left briefly alone; he paces silently up and down.*)

(*Enter Egmont.*)

EGMONT: I have come to receive the king's orders and to hear what service he desires of our loyalty, which is eternally devoted to him.

ALBA: He desires primarily to hear your advice.

EGMONT: On what subject? Is Orange coming too? I expected him here.

ALBA: I regret he is not with us at precisely this important hour. The king desires your advice, your opinion, about how these territories are to be pacified again. Indeed, he hopes for your powerful cooperation in quieting these turmoils and in establishing total and durable order in the provinces.

EGMONT: You are in a better position than I to know that things are already sufficiently pacified, indeed, were even more pacified before the arrival of the new troops stirred people's minds anew with fear and worry.

ALBA: You seem to imply that the wisest thing would have been for the king not to have put me in the position of asking you.

EGMONT: Forgive me. Whether the king ought to have sent the army, or whether the might of His Majesty's presence would perhaps, of itself, have had greater effect, these are not matters for me to decide. The army is here, *he* is not. We would, however, have to be very thankless, very thoughtless, if we did not recall what we owe the Regent. Let us acknowledge that by conduct as shrewd as it was brave she pacified the rebels by force and authority, by persuasion and astuteness, and to the world's astonishment guided a mutinous nation back, in a few months' time, to its duty.

ALBA: That I do not deny. The tumult has been stilled, and each man seems to have been charmed back within the confines of obedience. But does it not depend on the caprice of each, not to abandon them? Who is to stop the population from bursting forth? Where is the power to halt them? Where is the guarantee that they will be faithful and submissive in the future? Their good will is all the security we have.

EGMONT: And is a people's good will not the safest, the noblest security? By God! How can a king feel safer than when they all support one and one supports all? Safer against foes from inside and outside?

ALBA: We shall hardly be persuaded that such is the case here now, shall we?

EGMONT: Let the king proclaim a general amnesty, let him calm down excited minds, and it will soon appear that loyalty and love have returned with confidence.

ALBA: And let everybody go free and move about without hindrance, who has desecrated the majesty of the king and the holiness of religion! Let each live as a ready example to others, of how monstrous crimes go unpunished!

EGMONT: And is a crime of madness, of drunkenness, not rather to be excused than cruelly punished? Especially where there is definite hope, certainty, in fact, that the evils will not recur? Would kings not be the safer for it? Will present and future times not praise the ones who forgive an offense to their dignity, the ones who could deplore such, disdain such? Will they not on that account be deemed more like God, Who is far too great for a blasphemy to touch Him?

ALBA: All the more reason for the king to fight for the dignity of God, and for us to fight for the dignity of the king. What the higher power scorns to resent, is our duty to avenge. No guilty party, if I am to do the advising, shall enjoy impunity.

EGMONT: Do you fancy you will catch them all? Don't we hear daily that fear is driving them this way and that way, and out of the country? The wealthiest will rescue themselves and possessions in flight, their children and friends as well, while the poor will offer helpful hands to their neighbors.

ALBA: They will, if no one can prevent them. That is why the king is asking for the advice and support of every prince and seriousness from every *stadhouter*; not just telling about how things are, or about what might happen if everything were allowed to go on as it's going. Being a spectator of a great evil, flattering oneself with hopes, trusting to time, maybe even intervening, as in a Mardi Gras sport, so that there is a smacking sound and one seems to be doing something after all when all the time one would like to do nothing: doesn't that amount to incurring suspicion, as if the observer enjoyed watching the mutiny which he did not start but which he would like to encourage?

EGMONT (*flaring up, then checking himself, after a brief pause*):   Not all intentions are evident, and many a man's intention may be misconstrued. On all sides it is also being said that the king's intention is less concerned with ruling the provinces according to uniform and clear laws, with assuring the majesty of religion, with providing his people with universal peace, than it is concerned with subjecting them unconditionally to his yoke, with robbing them of their rights of old, with making himself master of their possessions, with curbing the splendid rights of the nobles, on whose account alone a noble man is willing to serve him and dedicate life and limb to him. Religion, they say, is only a magnificent tapestry behind which people only hatch the more easily any and all dangerous plots. The population is on its knees in adoration of the sacred symbols embroidered there, while back of it lurks the bird-catcher who is trying to befool them.

ALBA: Must I listen to this from *you*?

EGMONT: They're not *my* ideas! Only what is being said and loudly circulated, now here, now there, by great and small, sages and fools. The Dutch fear a double yoke, and who is going to guarantee their liberty for them?

ALBA: Liberty! A grand word—for whoever rightly understands it. What kind of freedom do they want? What is the freest of freedoms?—To do the right!—And the king will not prevent them from that. No! No! They consider themselves not free when they can't harm themselves and others. Would it not be better to abdicate than to rule a people like that? When foreign enemies crowd up, unthought of by the citizen because he is concerned only with his own affairs, and the king wants support, then they fall out with each other and conspire, as it were, with their enemies. It is far better to restrict them, so they may be kept like children and like children be guided to their own good. Believe me, a people does not grow up, does not become wise; a people remains forever like a child.

EGMONT: How rarely does a king attain the age of discretion! And are many not rather to trust in many than in one? Not even the one, at that, but the few around the one, that group that comes to wisdom by watching its master's glances. They are about the only ones to have the right to grow wise.

ALBA: Perhaps for the very reason that they are not left to their own devices.

EGMONT: And for that reason nobody wants to leave them to their own devices. Do as you will; I have answered your question and I say again: it won't work! It can't work! I know my fellow countrymen. They are men worthy of walking God's earth, each one an entity unto himself, a small-scale king, solid, agile, capable, loyal, and clinging to old customs. It is hard to win their confidence, but easy to retain it. Solid and stubborn! They can be oppressed, but not suppressed.

ALBA (*who keeps glancing around*): Would you repeat all this in the king's presence?

EGMONT: I would be worse off if his presence scared me off from it! It would be better for him and for his people if he encouraged me, if he gave me the confidence, to say a great deal more.

ALBA: What is useful *I* can hear as well as he.

EGMONT: I would say to him: the shepherd can drive a whole herd of sheep along ahead of him, the ox pulls the plow without resisting, but with a noble horse that you intend to ride, you have to learn his thoughts; you must not unwisely ask anything unwise of him. That's why the citizen wants to hold fast to his old constitution and be ruled by his fellow countrymen: because he knows how he will be led, because he can expect disinterestedness from them and sympathy with his fate.

ALBA: And should the ruler not have the power to change those old customs? Should that not be, in fact, his fairest privilege? What is lasting in this world? And should a system of government be able to endure? Must not every relationship change in the course of time, and by that token must an old constitution not become the source of a thousand evils, simply because it does not make provision for the present-day condition of a nation? I am afraid these old rights are so acceptable because they offer loopholes where the clever and powerful can hide, or through which they escape, to the detriment of the people.

EGMONT: And these arbitrary changes, these unchecked encroachments by supreme power, are they not indications that one man is trying to do what thousands may not do? He wants to make himself the only free man, so that he may satisfy his every wish and be able to carry out his every idea. And if we were to trust him entirely as a good and wise king, does he offer us a guarantee for his successors? giving assurance that none of them will rule without consideration or regard for us? Who will rescue us from total arbitrariness when he sends us his servers or his closest associates who, without knowledge of the country or of its needs, propose and dispose just as they please, meet no resistance, and realize they are free of any accountability?

ALBA (*repeatedly glancing around again*): Nothing is more natural than that a king should intend to rule by his own will and that he should prefer to entrust his orders to those who best understand him and try to understand him and who carry out his will unconditionally.

EGMONT: And it is quite as natural that a citizen wants to be ruled by someone who was born and brought up with him, who has the same conceptions of right and wrong, whom he can look upon as his brother.

ALBA: And yet the nobles have shared very unequally with these brothers of theirs.

EGMONT: That came about centuries ago and is still not begrudged. But if new persons were sent here unnecessarily and tried a second time to get rich at the expense of the nation, and if people saw themselves as the victims of a harsh, ruthless, uncontrolled greed— that would cause a ferment that would not readily dissolve by itself.

ALBA: You are saying things I ought not to listen to. I too am a foreigner.

EGMONT: The fact that I am saying them to you shows that I don't mean you.

ALBA: Even so, I would not want to hear them from you. The king sent me here in the hope of finding support from the nobility. The king *will* have his will. After profound deliberation the king has seen what is good for the people; things cannot continue the way they have been going. The king's intention is to curb them for their own good, to force their own welfare, if necessary, upon them, to sacrifice the injurious citizens so the others can find peace and enjoy the happiness of a wise government. Such is his decision, which I have orders to announce to the nobles, and in his name I solicit advice about *how* it is to be done, not about *what* is to be done, because *that* has been decided by *him*.

EGMONT: Unfortunately your words justify the people's fear, the universal fear! This way he has decided what no ruler should decide. The strength of a nation, its spirit, the conception it has of itself: these things he wishes to weaken, to suppress, to destroy, so as to be able to rule the people at his ease. He wants to ruin the essence of their self-identity—of course with the intention of making them happier. He wants to annihilate them so they can become something else. Oh, if his intention is good, it is misguided! The resistance is not against the king, but only against the king who has taken the first unhappy steps down a wrong road.

ALBA: Given your attitude, it seems futile for us to try to reach an agreement. You think meanly of the king and scornfully of his advisers if you doubt that all this has not already been pondered, tested, and weighed. I have no commission to go through every pro and con once again. I demand obedience of the people—and of you, you highest and noblest ones, I demand words and deeds in warranty of this absolute obligation.

EGMONT: Demand our heads; that way it can be done at one stroke. Whether necks are bowed to this yoke or whether they are bowed beneath the ax, is the same thing to noble souls. I have said so much—for nothing; all I have accomplished is to stir up the air.

(*Enter Ferdinand.*)

FERDINAND: Excuse me for interrupting your conversation, but here is a letter requiring urgent reply by messenger.

ALBA: Allow me to see what it says.

(*He steps off to one side.*)

FERDINAND (*to Egmont*):   That's a fine horse your men have brought to fetch you away with.

EGMONT: It's not the worst. I've had it quite a while; I'm thinking of disposing of it. If you like, perhaps we can make a deal.

FERDINAND: Good. We shall see.

(*Alba beckons to his son, who goes over to join him.*)

EGMONT: Farewell. Allow me to withdraw, because, by God!, there is nothing more I could say.

ALBA: Happily, chance has prevented you from betraying your thoughts any further. You have incautiously unfolded the pleats of your heart, thereby accusing yourself much more harshly than a hateful adversary could do.

EGMONT: This reproach leaves me unaffected. I know myself sufficiently and I know in what way I support the king—far more than many who in his service serve themselves. I am sorry to leave this argument unsettled, and my only wish is that service to our master and the welfare of the country may soon bring us into agreement. Perhaps if we resume this topic at a more propitious moment and in the presence of the other princes who are absent today, we will effect what seems impossible today. In that hope I withdraw.

ALBA (*giving Ferdinand a signal*):   Halt, Egmont!—Your sword!

(*The door at center-rear opens, revealing the gallery occupied by guards, who are standing motionless.*)

EGMONT (*silent, at first, from astonishment*):   This was intentional? You summoned me here for this? (*reaching for his sword as though to defend himself with it*) Am I defenseless?

ALBA: At the king's orders: you are my prisoner.

(*Armed guards enter from both sides.*)

EGMONT (*after a pause*):   The king?—Orange! Orange! (*surrendering his sword, after a moment's hesitation*) All right: take it! It has far more often defended the king's cause than this body of mine.

(*Exit by the center door, followed by the guards who are in the room and· by Alba's son. Alba stands motionless as the curtain falls.*)

ACT V

[SCENE 1]

A street at twilight.

Klärchen, Brackenburg, Citizens.

BRACKENBURG: Dearest, for heaven's sake, what are you trying to do?

KLÄRCHEN: Come with me, Brackenburg! You must not know these people: we will surely set him free. For what can be compared to their love for him? Every one of them, I swear, feels a burning desire to rescue him, to avert the danger from a precious life, and to give freedom back to the freest of men! Come! We lack only the voice to call them together. What they owe to him is still vivid in their hearts, and they know his powerful arm alone holds off their destruction. For his sake and for theirs we must dare anything. What do we risk? At most, our lives, which are not worth saving if he perishes.

BRACKENBURG: Unhappy girl, you fail to see the power that holds us in fetters of bronze.

KLÄRCHEN: It does not seem invincible to me. Let us not delay with useless words. Here come some of those old, honest, stout-hearted men! Friends, hear me! Neighbors, hear me!—Tell me, how do things stand with Egmont?

CARPENTER: What is that child doing? Make her be still!

KLÄRCHEN: Come closer, so we can talk softly until we come to an agreement and are stronger. We must not delay for a minute! The insolent tyranny that dares put him in chains already draws the dagger to murder him. Oh, friends, with every advance of the twilight I become more distressed. I dread this night. Come, let us divide up and quickly run from quarter to quarter of the city and rouse the citizens. Let every man seize his weapon of old. At the marketplace we will meet again and our tide will sweep everyone

357

along. Our enemies will see themselves surrounded and flooded, and they will be overwhelmed. How can a handful of slaves resist us? And in our midst *he* will return and find himself set free, and then he can thank *us* for once, who are so profoundly indebted to him. Perhaps he will see—surely he will see the dawn once more in the free sky.

CARPENTER: What is the matter, poor girl?

KLÄRCHEN: Can you possibly misunderstand me? I am speaking of the Count! I am speaking of Egmont.

JETTER: Don't mention that name. It is deathly.

KLÄRCHEN: Not mention that name! Not that name? Who does not mention it at every opportunity? Where does it not stand written? In those stars I have often read it with all its letters. Not mention it? How can that be, friends! Good, faithful neighbors, you are dreaming! Come to your senses. Don't stare at me so worriedly! Stop shifting glances away in embarrassment. I call out to you only the thing you each desire. Is my voice not the voice of your own hearts? Which one of you, before going to bed in this dread night, will not kneel down and with earnest prayer beseech Heaven to win him back? Ask each other! Ask yourselves! And who will not say after me: "Egmont's freedom or else death!"

JETTER: God save us! Here's a misfortune.

KLÄRCHEN: Wait! Wait, and do not turn away from his name to which you all once thronged so gladly!—When the cry went up: "Egmont is coming! He is coming from Ghent!" there was rejoicing by the inhabitants lucky enough to live in the streets where he had to pass. And when you used to hear his horse's hoofbeats, everybody dropped his work, and over the worried faces you thrust out the windows came a look of joy and hope like a sunbeam from his countenance. Then you would hold up your children in the doorways and point him out: Look! There is Egmont, there is the greatest of men! He's the one, he's the one from whom you can some day expect better times than your poor fathers knew." Do not let your children ask you some day: "What became of him! Where are those times you promised us?"—But we are wasting words this way! We are idle, we are betraying him.

SOEST: Shame on you, Brackenburg! Don't let her go on like this.

Prevent a misfortune!

BRACKENBURG: Dearest Klärchen, let's be going! What will your mother say? Maybe—

KLÄRCHEN: Do you think I'm a child? Or mad? What good is this "maybe?"—You will not divert me from this ghastly certainty by any hopes.—You must hear me, and you shall, because I see you are in dismay and cannot decide in your own hearts what to do. Amid the present peril cast but one glance at the past, the recent past. Turn your thoughts toward the future. Could you go on living then? *Will* you, if he is destroyed? With his breath the last gasp of liberty fails. What was he to you? For whose sakes did he face direst danger? His wounds bled and healed only for you. The great soul that supported you all is confined in a prison, and terrors of treacherous murder hover about it. He may be thinking of you, counting on you, *he*, whose way was only to give, only to grant.

CARPENTER: Neighbors, come along.

KLÄRCHEN: And I have no weapons like you, no mettle; but I do have what all of you lack: courage and scorn of danger. If only my breath could rouse you, if only I could warm you in my arms and put life into you! Come! I will go along in your midst!—The way a noble army of warriors keeps a helpless banner waving in its forefront, my spirit shall blaze about your heads, and love and courage shall unite a wavering and distracted people into a dread army.

JETTER: Take her away. I am sorry for her.

(*The citizens disperse.*)

BRACKENBURG: Klärchen, don't you see where we are?

KLÄRCHEN: Where? Beneath the sky that so often seemed to arch more grandly when that noble man passed beneath it. Out of those windows they have looked, four and five heads above each other; in these doorways they have scraped and bowed as he gazed down upon those cowards. Oh, I was so fond of them when they honored him! Had he been a tyrant, they might avoid his fall; but they loved him!—Oh, hands that touched caps in salute, why can't you reach for swords? Brackenburg, what of us? Should we revile them? These poor things who so often stood by him, what are they doing for him?—Guile has achieved so much in the world.—You know the streets and byways, you know the old palace. Nothing is impossible. Give me an idea.

BRACKENBURG: What do you say we go home?

KLÄRCHEN: Good.

BRACKENBURG: There at the corner I see Alba's patrol; let the voice of reason into your heart. Do you think I am a coward? Don't you believe I would die for you? Here we are both mad, I as well as you. Don't you see the impossibility? If only you would control yourself! You are beside yourself.

KLÄRCHEN: Beside myself! Abominable! Brackenburg, you are the one who are beside yourself. When you loudly honored the hero, called him friend and protector and hope, and shouted hurrah as he came along, there *I* was in my corner, half-opening the window, hiding but listening, and with my heart beating higher than all the rest of you. Now it is once again beating higher than all the rest of you—while you hide, now there's danger, deny him, and do not realize that you will be lost if he is destroyed.

BRACKENBURG: Come along home.

KLÄRCHEN: Home?

BRACKENBURG: Come to your senses! Look about you! These are the streets that you used to walk only in your Sunday best as you modestly went to church, where you used to get angry with excessive propriety if I joined you with a word of friendly greeting, and here you stand talking and carrying on in full view of the wide world. Come to your senses, my love! Where will it get us?

KLÄRCHEN: Home! Yes, I remember. Come, Brackenburg, let us go home. Do you know where my true home is?

(*They pass along.*)

[SCENE 2]

A prison.
A lamp casts its glow; there is a cot at the rear. Egmont is alone.

EGMONT: My friend of old, ever faithful sleep, do you too desert me like my other friends? How willingly you used to descend upon my free head, cooling my brow like a fair myrtle-crown of love. In

weapons' midst, upon the waves of life, I used to rest, soft-breath-
ing like a growing lad, in your embrace. While storms through
leaves and branches blustered, wrenching boughs and treetops in
creaking strain, the inmost core of my heart remained undisturbed.
What is it shakes you now? What is it shatters my firm, faithful
spirit? I feel it; it is the sound of the executioner's ax cutting my
roots away. I still stand upright, but an inner horror courses
through me. Yes, treacherous might well prevail; it undercuts the
stout and lofty tree, and then, before the bark has withered, down
will come the leafy crown with plunging crash. Why are you unable now, you who used to blow mighty cares away like soap bubbles, why are you unable now to banish the foreboding that looms
and subsides thousandfold within you? Since when does death seem
dreadful to you? Especially when you have so calmly lived amid its
changeful forms as amid other shapes of the accustomed earth?—
Oh, it is not the sudden foe against whom the sound heart rebels in
protest; it is prison, the grave's prefiguration, that is repugnant to
hero and coward alike. Even my cushioned chair used to be
intolerable to me when, in solemn assembly, the princes would
repetitively debate matters that were quite simple to decide, and
within the gloomy walls of the assembly chamber the ceiling beams
used to oppress me. Then I would hurry away as soon as possible
and fetch a deep breath as I swung myself astride my horse. Off I
would go to the regions where we rightfully belong, to open
country, where we are enveloped by every benison of Nature as it is
exhaled by earth and where all the blessings of the stars are wafted
across the skies; where, like that earth-born giant, we spring higher
aloft from every contact with our mother; where we sense humanity
to the full and human desires in all our veins; where through the
youthful huntsman's spirits glows the longing to press forward, to
overcome, to overtake, to use his strength, to possess, and to conquer; where with rapid step the soldier makes his claim upon the
whole wide world and in fierce freedom strides destructively like a
hailstorm through meadow, field, and forest, acknowledging no
boundaries set by human hand.

Remembered dream of happiness, you are but a picture I have
long possessed; to what has Fate treacherously reduced you? Does

Fate refuse to grant me never-shunned death swiftly before the countenance of the sun just to give me a foretaste of the grave amid this loathsome decay? How vilely this death breathes upon me out of these stones! Life already grows numb and my step avoids the sleeping-cot as it avoids the grave.

Oh, care, desist! care that begins murder ahead of time!—Since when is Egmont alone, completely alone, in this world? It is doubt, not happiness, that renders you helpless. The king's justice that you trusted all your life, the Regent's friendship which—you may admit it to yourself—was almost love: have these things vanished all of a sudden, like a glittering fiery image of the night and left you deserted upon your dark path? Will Orange not venture something at the head of your friends? Will a host not assemble and with gathering power rescue the friend of old?

You walls that close me in, do not hold back the well-intentioned thronging of so many spirits from me, and whatever valor was formerly cast upon *them* from my eyes, may it be reflected out of *their* hearts back into mine. Oh, yes! They stir now in their thousands! They are coming! They will stand at my side! Their heartfelt wish speeds urgently to Heaven, imploring a miracle. And if no angel will descend to me, I see them reaching for their swords and lances. The gates burst asunder, the iron palings snap, beneath their hands the wall gives way, and forth steps Egmont cheerfully into the freedom of the dawning day. How many familiar faces will greet me then with exultation! Ah, Klärchen, if you were a man, I would surely see you here first, and I would give you thanks for what a king can hardly give thanks for: freedom.

[Scene 3]

Klärchen's house.

Enter Klärchen from the chamber carrying a lamp and a glass of water. She sets the glass on the table, then goes over to the window.

KLÄRCHEN: Brackenburg? Is that you? What was it I heard, then?

Still no one? It was no one! I'll set the lamp in the window so he will see I am still up, still waiting for him. He promised to bring me news. News? Ghastly certainty! Egmont condemned!—What tribunal is empowered to summon him? And they condemn him! Is it the king that condemns him, or the duke? And the Regent withdraws! Orange and all his friends vacillate!—Is this the world I often heard was full of fickleness and untrustworthiness and never experienced it myself? Is this that world?—

Who would be evil enough to bear ill-will to that beloved man? Is evil powerful enough to plunge the universally acclaimed to such sudden ruin? But if so—It is!—Oh, Egmont, I would protect you from God and man, as in my arms! What was I to you? You called me *yours,* and I dedicated my whole life to your life.—What am I now? In vain I stretch out my hand toward the snare that holds you caught. You helpless, and I free!—Here is the key to my door. My going and coming are at my free choice, and I am useless to you!— Oh, bind me with chains so I will not despair! Cast me into the deepest dungeon so I may beat my head against dank walls, whimper for freedom, and dream of how I could help him, of how I would help him, if fetters did not paralyze me.—Now I am free! And in freedom lies the anguish of helplessness. Conscious, and unable to lift a hand to help him. Alas, your Klärchen, that tiny portion of your own being, is, like you, a captive also; divided from you in the throes of death, she is now making merely the final show of her forces.—I hear footsteps stealing along, and someone coughing—Brackenburg!—That's who it is! Wretched, kind man, your destiny remains ever the same; your sweetheart opens the door to you by night, and oh! for what an unhappy meeting!

(Enter Brackenburg.)

You come so pale and timidly, Brackenburg: what is the matter?

BRACKENBURG: Through byways and perils I seek you out. The main streets are garrisoned, and I had to steal my way here through alleyways and dark corners.

KLÄRCHEN: Tell me how things stand.

BRACKENBURG (*sitting down*): Oh, Klara, let me weep. I did not love him. He was that rich man who enticed the poor man's only lamb over to better pasture.[1] I never cursed him either; God created me loyal and weak. My life ebbed away in sorrows, and every day I hoped to pine away.

KLÄRCHEN: Forget all that, Brackenburg! Forget about yourself, and tell me of him! Is it true he is condemned?

BRACKENBURG: It is. I know it for sure.

KLÄRCHEN: And he is still alive?

BRACKENBURG: Yes, he is still alive.

KLÄRCHEN: How can you be sure? Tyranny murders that glorious man in the night! His blood flows hidden from all eyes. Restless in sleep lies the stunned nation and dreams of his rescue, dreams of its own desire's fulfillment, and meanwhile, above us, his indignant spirit is departing this world. He is gone! Do not deceive me, do not deceive yourself!

BRACKENBURG: No, most certainly he lives. And alas! the Spaniard is preparing a spectacle for the nation he intends to trample under foot, a hideous spectacle that will forever crush all hearts that stir for freedom.

KLÄRCHEN: Speak further and quietly pronounce my death sentence. My step moves ever closer to those blessed fields, and comfort wafts over to me from those regions of peace. Speak further.

BRACKENBURG: I could tell by the guards, and from bits of conversation in one place or another, that in the marketplace an object of horror is being readied. I slipped àlong through side-streets, through passageways I knew, to my cousin's house and looked out a back-window onto the marketplace. There was a movement of torches back and forth within a broad circle of Spanish soldiers. I strained my unaccustomed eyes, and out of the darkness a black structure met my sight, of considerable breadth, and high; seeing it made me shudder. All around numbers of men were busily engaged in masking over whatever woodwork was still white and visible with black cloth. The last thing they did was to cover the steps with

---

[1] An allusion to 2 Samuel 12:1–4, where Nathan speaks a parable to David about a rich man who had many flocks and herds, yet, when a traveler had to be entertained, slew the poor man's only lamb to furnish the banquet.

black cloth too—I saw them do it. They seemed to be preparing for some ghastly rite of sacrifice. A white crucifix that gleamed in the darkness like silver was reared aloft at one side. I gazed, and I saw the dreadful certainty becoming ever more certain. For some time longer the torches kept moving back and forth, then gradually they died out and were extinguished. All of a sudden the horrible offspring of night had returned into its mother's womb.

KLÄRCHEN: Be still, Brackenburg, be still! Let that covering rest upon my soul. The specters have vanished; may gracious night lend its mantle to the earth that is in inner ferment. No longer can earth bear its ghastly burden; she will open wide her profound gorges and snap the murderous scaffold up in her gnashing jaws. And the God Whom they have desecrated as witness of their fury will send one of His angels, and at that messenger's holy touch the bolts and fetters will fall off and around my friend he will cast a mild radiance; softly and gently he will guide him through the darkness to freedom.[2] My way too goes secretly amid that darkness to meet him.

BRACKENBURG (*interrupting her*): Where to, my child? What will you venture?

KLÄRCHEN: Speak softly, dear man, so no one is wakened, so we do not waken ourselves. Do you know this little bottle, Brackenburg? Jestingly I took it from you when you impatiently kept threatening overhasty death.—And now, my friend—

BRACKENBURG: In the name of all the saints!

KLÄRCHEN: You will not prevent me. Death is my lot. Grant me the soft and sudden death you planned for yourself. Give me your hand. At the moment when I open the dark portal from which there is no return, I could, with this touch of my hand, tell you how much I loved you and how sorry I felt for you. My brother died young, and you were the one I chose to take his place. Your heart opposed that and tormented itself and me; ardently and ever more ardently you sought what was not to be yours. Forgive me, and

---

[2] The allusion is to St. Peter's deliverance from prison by an angel in Acts 12: 1–4.

farewell. Let me call you "brother." It is a name that includes many other names. With faithful heart pick this last fair blossom of the departing one—receive this kiss. Death reconciles all things, Brackenburg—even us.

BRACKENBURG: Then let me die with you! Share it! Share it! It is enough to extinguish two lives.

KLÄRCHEN: Stay! You shall live. You can live. Help my mother, who would, without you, be consumed by poverty. Be to her what I can no longer be to her; live together and weep for me. Weep for our country and for him who alone could sustain it. The present generation will not be rid of this grief; the fury of revenge itself cannot obliterate it. Live out the time, poor people, which is no time any more. Today the world stands still all of a sudden, its orbit is suddenly arrested, and my own pulse will beat only a few minutes longer. Farewell.

BRACKENBURG: Oh, live with us, as we live for you alone! You kill us by killing yourself. Oh, live and endure. We will live inseparably at either side of you and love shall, with unfailing watchfulness, provide the sweetest comfort within her living embrace. Be ours! Ours! I dare not say "mine."

KLÄRCHEN: Softly, Brackenburg! You do not feel what it is you touch upon. Where you see hope, I see despair.

BRACKENBURG: Share the hope of the living! Pause at the brink of the abyss, gaze down, and then look back toward us.

KLÄRCHEN: I have conquered; do not call me back again into the fray.

BRACKENBURG: Your sense is numbed; shrouded in darkness, you seek the depths. Not every light is yet extinguished, there are many more days to come.

KLÄRCHEN: Woe to you for wrenching aside the veil from before my eyes! Yes, it will dawn, the day. In vain it will draw all clouds about itself and against its will it will dawn. Timorously the citizen will peer out of his window, the night has deposited a black spot; he continues to peer, and in the light there emerges horribly the execution scaffold. Suffering afresh, the desecrated image of God lifts His imploring eyes unto His Father. The sun does not venture forth, being averse to revealing the hour when he is to die. The clock-hands lag upon their path, one hour after the other strikes. Halt! Halt! The time has come! Intimation of the morning frightens me off to my grave.

>   (*She goes over to the window as though to look*
>   *out, and furtively drinks the poison.*)

BRACKENBURG: Klara! Klara!

KLÄRCHEN (*going over to the table and drinking the glass of water*):   Here is the rest. I do not lure you to follow. Do what you can. Farewell. Put out this lamp quietly and without hesitation: I am going to my rest. Slip away softly and pull the door to after you. Quietly! Do not wake my mother! Go, make good your escape! Make good your escape if you don't want to appear my murderer.

(Exit.)

BRACKENBURG: She leaves me this final time the way she always did. Oh, if only a human soul could feel how she can rend a loving heart. She leaves me standing here, abandoned to myself; and death and life are equally loathsome to me.—To die alone! Weep, you lovers! There is no harder fate than mine. She shares the deadly drops with me and then sends me away, away from her side. She draws me after her and thrusts me back into life. Oh, Egmont, what a precious lot falls to you! She goes on ahead; yours is the victory wreath from her hand, and she will bring all heaven to welcome you!

And am I to follow? To stand off to one side once again? To carry my unquenchable envy over into those abodes of the blessed? On earth there is no place for me any more, and heaven and hell afford me equal torment. How welcome the dread hand of annihilation would be to me in my misery!

(Exit.)

For a time the stage remains unchanged. Music begins, signifying Klärchen's death. The lamp, which Brackenburg has forgotten to put out, flares up a few times and then goes out.

The stage is transformed to represent the prison.

Egmont lies asleep on the cot. A rattling of keys is heard, and the door opens. Men enter with torches. They are followed by Alba's son Ferdinand and by Silva, escorted by armed guards. Egmont starts up from sleep.

EGMONT: Who are you that unkindly shake sleep from my eyes? What do your haughty, uncertain glances bode for me? Why this dread procession? What dream of terror have you come to pass off on the half-wakened spirit?

SILVA: We are sent by the Duke to anounce your sentence to you.

EGMONT: Have you brought along the executioner too, to carry it out?

SILVA: Hear it, and you will know what awaits you.

EGMONT: It suits you well and it suits your infamous conduct! Hatched by night and by night carried out. That is how this insolent deed of injustice chooses to hide! Step right forward, you there, carrying your sword concealed under your cloak! Here is my head, the freest that ever tyranny tore from its body.

SILVA: You are mistaken. What upright judges decide, they will not conceal from the face of day.

EGMONT: By so doing, impudence outranges every concept and notion.

SILVA (*taking the sentence from an attendant, unfolding it, and reading*): "In the king's name and by virtue of a special power vested in us by His Majesty, all subjects of His, of whatever rank, together with the Knights of the Golden Fleece, to judge, we deem—

EGMONT: Can the king deputize such power?

SILVA: —we deem you, Henry[3] Count Egmont, Prince of Gaure, after close preliminary investigation according to law, guilty of high treason, and we pronounce sentence as follows: that at the dawn of the coming day you shall be led from prison to the marketplace and there, in the sight of the people and by way of a warning to all trai-

---

[3] The historical Egmont's given name was Lamoral. (Goethe also gave the name Heinrich to the historical Dr. Georg—or possibly Johann—Faustus.)

tors, you shall be parted from your life and done to death by the sword. Given at Brussels—

> (*The day and year are read indistinctly so that the audience does not hear them.*)

signed: Ferdinand, Duke of Alba,
President of the Council of Twelve."

You now know your fate. You have but little time to acquiesce in the matter, to put your house in order,[4] and to make your farewells.

> (*Silva and his escort withdraw. Ferdinand remains behind with two torch-bearers, whose torches illumine the stage to some degree.*
>
> *Egmont has remained standing, lost in thought, without looking at Silva as the latter departed. He thinks he is alone, but as he lifts his eyes he notices Alba's son.*)

EGMONT: You stay behind? Is it your wish to increase my astonishment, my horror, still further by your presence? Or do you wish perhaps to bring your father a complete report of my unmanly despair? Go tell him—tell him he is deceiving neither me nor the world. Greedy for glory as he is, people will first whisper softly behind his back, then say outright louder and louder, and once he has stepped down from this pinnacle, a thousand voices will cry out: not the welfare of the state, not the dignity of the king, not the tranquillity of the provinces, led you to do this! For his own advantage he advised war, so the warrior could have the advantage in war. He stirred up this monstrous turmoil so he would be needed. And I die as a sacrifice to his base hatred, his petty envy. Yes, I know and I make bold to say—for a dying man, a mortally wounded man, *can* speak out—that the conceited man envied me, that he long planned and plotted to exterminate me.

Even back at the time when we were younger and playing at dice, and the piles of gold, one after another, passed quickly over from his side to me, he stood there furious, forcing the appearance

---

[4] This set phrase is from Isaiah 38:1: "Thus saith the Lord, 'Set thine house in order: for thou shalt die, and not live.'"

of calm, but inwardly devoured by anger, more at my luck than at his own losses. I still remember his glittering look, his tell-tale pallor, when we were competing in a shooting contest at a public festival in full view of many thousands of people. He challenged me, and both nations were standing there; Spaniards and Dutchmen were betting and making wishes. I beat him; his shot went awry and mine hit; a loud cry of joy went up from my people. Now his shot has hit me. Tell him I know it, that I know him, and that the world despises any symbol of victory that a small mind may sneakily set up. And you! If it is possible for a son to abandon his father's ways, cultivate shame in good time by being ashamed of the father you would like to respect with all your heart.

FERDINAND: I listen without interrupting you. Your reproaches fall like blows of a club upon a helmet; I feel the shocks, but I am in armor. You strike me but do not deal me a wound; the only thing I feel is the grief that tears me apart. Alas! Alas! that I should have grown to manhood for such a sight as this, for being sent to such a spectacle as this!

EGMONT: You burst out in lamentation? What has touched you, what has troubled you? Is it belated regret for lending your service to this shameful conspiracy? You are so young and you have a happy look. You were so confiding, so friendly to me. As long as I could see you I was reconciled with your father. And yet so cunningly, more cunningly than he, you lured me into the net. You are the loathsome one! Anyone trusting *him* does so at his own peril, but who would fear peril in trusting you? Go! Go! Do not rob me of my few moments left! Go, so I can compose myself and forget the world—you first of all.

FERDINAND: What can I say? I stand here looking at you, and I don't see you and I don't feel aware of myself. Shall I make excuses? Shall I assure you that I learned of my father's intentions only late, only at the last minute? That I have been treated as a lifeless instrument of his will, under compulsion? What difference does it make what opinion you may have of me? You are lost, and I, unlucky creature, can only stand here and assure you that it is so and that I pity you.

EGMONT: What a curious voice, what an unexpected consolation

looms up before me on my way to the grave? You, the son of my
first and almost my only enemy, you pity me, you are not one of my
murderers? Tell me, tell me, what am I to make of you?

FERDINAND: Oh, my cruel father, I recognize you in this order. You
knew my heart, my convictions, which you often used to inveigh
against as my heritage from a weak mother. You sent me here to
mold me in your image. By seeing this man on the edge of his
yawning grave and in the grip of an arbitrary murder, you force me
to feel the deepest sorrow so I may become deaf to all destiny, feelingless, befall me what may.

EGMONT: I am amazed! Control yourself! Stand and talk like a man.

FERDINAND: Oh, if only I were a woman! so people could say to me
"What is the matter? What is troubling you?" Cite me a greater, a
more monstrous evil, make me the witness of a more horrible deed,
and I will thank you and say: this was nothing.

EGMONT: You are losing your thread of thought. Where were you?

FERDINAND   Let this passion rage itself out, let me lament without
restraint! I do not want to appear steadfast when everything within
me is collapsing. I have to see you here? You! It's horrible! You
don't understand me! How should you understand me? Egmont!
Egmont!

        (*He throws himself into Egmont's arms.*)

EGMONT: Clear up this mystery to me.

FERDINAND: No mystery.

EGMONT: How is it that a strange man's fate stirs you so deeply?

FERDINAND: Not a strange man! You are not a stranger to me. It
was your name that shone upon me like a star of heaven in my
earliest youth. How often I listened for news of you, asked about
you! A child's hope is the youth, the youth's hope is the man. Thus
you walked before me, on and on, and with no envy I looked to you
and walked in your steps, on and on. Now I had hoped to see you
finally, and I saw you, and my heart sprang toward you. I had
fixed upon you for my own and I chose you anew when I saw you.
Then I hoped to be with you, to live with you, to embrace you,
to—Now all that is cut away before me and I see you here!

EGMONT: My friend, if it can help you any, rest assured that my
feelings went out to you at the very first moment. Listen to me. Let

us exhange a quiet word or two between ourselves. Tell me: is it your father's strict and serious intention to kill me?

FERDINAND: It is.

EGMONT: This sentence wouldn't be an empty bugbear to scare me, to punish me with fear and threats, to humiliate me, and then to lift me up again by the king's grace?

FERDINAND: No, oh, unfortunately, no. At first I consoled myself with that elusive hope, and even then I felt anguish and grief at seeing you in this condition. Now it is real, definite. No, I cannot control myself. Who will give me help, who will give me counsel as to how to escape the unavoidable?

EGMONT: Then listen to me. If your soul so pressingly urges you to rescue me, if you abominate the overweening power that holds me in chains, then rescue me! The moments are precious. You are the son of the all-powerful man and powerful in your own right—let us flee from here! I know the routes, you cannot help but know the means. Nothing but these walls, nothing but a few miles separate me from my friends. Undo these bonds, take me to them, and be one of us. Surely the king, in times to come, will thank you for rescuing me. Right now he has been taken by surprise, and perhaps not everything is known to him. Your father is taking a bold step, and Majesty must approve the deed once it is done, even if horrified by it. You pause to think? Oh, think up a way to freedom for me! Speak, foster the living soul's hope.

FERDINAND: Be still, oh, be still! With every word you intensify my despair. Here there is no escape, no hope, no flight. That torments me, that clutches and holds my heart as though with claws. I myself have drawn the net shut; I know its tight, strong knots; I know the ways are barred to all daring and to all cunning; I feel as if I were in chains along with you and all the others. Would I lament if I had not tried everything? I have knelt at his feet, talked and pleaded, and he sent me here to destroy whatever joy and pleasure in life may still be in me.

EGMONT: And no possibility of rescue?

FERDINAND: None!

EGMONT (*stamping his foot*): No possibility of rescue!—Sweet life! Fair, kindly habit of existence and action, I must part with you.

Part so tamely. Not in battle's tumult amid the clangor of weapons, not in the distraction of the fray do you bid me a hasty farewell, you do not take leave suddenly, you do not abridge the moment of separation. I am to take your hand, gaze once more into your eyes, feel your beauty and your value keenly, and then with determination tear myself away and say: farewell!

FERDINAND: And I must stand there beside you, looking on, and not be able to support you or stop them. Oh, what voice would be equal to this grief! What heart would not melt away out of its containing body at sorrow like this!

EGMONT: Control yourself!

FERDINAND: You may control yourself, you may renounce and hero-ically take that heavy step hand in hand with Necessity, but what can *I* do? What am I to do? You conquer yourself and us; you over-come; but I survive you and myself. Amid the joy of the banquet I have lost my light, amid the fray of battle I have lost my banner. Flat, dull, and confused the future lies before me.

EGMONT: Youthful friend, whom by a curious destiny I gain and lose together, who feel my death pangs for me, look upon me at this moment: you are not losing me. If my life has been a mirror in which you gladly beheld yourself, let my death be such also. Human beings are not together merely when they are in each other's presence, but the distant and the departed also live for us. I shall live for you, I have lived sufficiently for myself. I have delighted in every day, and every day I have, with rapid action, performed my obligations, as my conscience revealed them to me. Now this life is ending, as it could have ended earlier, earlier, say, upon the beach at Gravelingen. I cease to live, but I have lived. Live thus also, my friend, gladly and with joy, and do not shun death.

FERDINAND: You could and should have preserved yourself for us. You brought about your own death. I often heard, when shrewd men used to speak about you—and friend and foe used to debate your worth at length, but all agreed on one point that none of them would deny: "Yes," they all admitted, "he walks a dangerous path." How often I wished I could warn you! Didn't you have any friends?

EGMONT: I was warned.

FERDINAND: And point for point I found all those accusations, and your answers as well, in your trial. Good enough to excuse you, not cogent enough to free you from guilt—

EGMONT: Be that as it may. A man imagines he is conducting his life, guiding himself, but his inmost heart is irresistibly drawn on by his destiny. Let us not ponder that. Thoughts of that kind I can easily put aside—but not so easily my concern for this country. But that too will be taken care of. If my blood can be shed for the sake of many, if it can win peace for my people, it is willingly shed. Unfortunately it will not be so. But it befits a man not to fret about matters he can no longer take a hand in. If you can put a stop to your father's destructive power, if you can direct it, do so. Who will be able to do that?—Farewell.

FERDINAND: I cannot go.

EGMONT: Let me most cordially recommend my people to you. I have good men among my servers; see they are not dispersed and made unhappy. How do things stand with Richard, my secretary?

FERDINAND: He has preceded you. As an accessory to high treason, they have beheaded him.

EGMONT: Poor soul!—One more thing and then farewell, I cannot stand any more. However the mind may be compelled to function, Nature still makes her irresistible demands, and as a child enjoys refreshing sleep even in the coils of the serpent, the weary man will once more lie down before the gates of death and take deep repose, as if he had a long road to travel.—One more thing. I know a girl; you will not disdain her, for she was mine. Now that I have recommended her to you, I shall die easy. You are a man of lofty principles; a woman who finds such is well provided for.—Is my old Adolph still alive? Is he free?

FERDINAND: The lively old fellow that always rode with you?

EGMONT: The same.

FERDINAND: He is alive and he is free.

EGMONT: He knows her house; have him guide you, and reward him to the end of his days for showing you the way to that jewel.— Farewell.

FERDINAND: I cannot go.

EGMONT (*forcing him toward the door*):   Farewell!

FERDINAND: Oh, let me stay!

EGMONT: Friend, no leave-taking!

> (*He accompanies Ferdinand as far as the door, then wrenches himself away. Ferdinand, in a state of shock, swiftly departs.*)

EGMONT: Malignant man, you little thought you would show me this kindness through your son. By him I am relieved of cares and sorrows, of fear, and of every sense of dread. Softly and urgently Nature demands her final debt. It is over, it is resolved. And what kept me awake last night upon my couch for sheer uncertainty now lulls my senses with a certainty that nothing more can overcome.

> (*He sits down on his cot. Music begins.*)

Sweetest sleep, you come most willingly unbidden, unimplored, like sheer good fortune. You untie the hard knots of thought and tumble together all the images of joy and sorrow; unhindered spins the round of inner harmonies, and wrapped in pleasant fancies, we sink down and cease to be.

> (*He falls asleep; music accompanies his slumber.*
>
> *Behind his cot the wall seems to open up and a radiant apparition is seen: Liberty, in heavenly raiment and with a brilliance of light shed around her, rests upon a cloud. She has the features of Klärchen as she bends over the sleeping hero. She strikes an attitude of pity and seems to be lamenting for him. Presently she composes herself and with a cheering gesture shows him the sheaf of arrows, then the stave with the hat. She bids him be of good cheer, and, as she signifies to him that his death will achieve the liberation of the provinces, she hails him as victor and holds out a laurel crown toward him. As the crown approaches his head, Egmont moves like someone stirring in his sleep, so that he comes to lie face-upwards towards her. She holds the crown just above his head.*
>
> *In the far distance is heard a martial music of fifes and drums, at the very first sound of which the apparition vanishes. The music grows louder. Egmont awakes. Some morning light now*

illuminates the prison. His first gesture is to feel of his head; he
rises and peers about, still holding his hand on his head.)

The wreath has vanished! Fair image, the light of day has frightened you away! Yes, it was the two of them together, the two sweetest joys of my heart: the goddess Liberty, and bearing the features of my beloved; the lovely girl was clad in the heavenly raiment of my dear one. In this solemn moment they appear as one, more grave than kind. With bloodstained feet she stood before me, and the swaying folds of her skirt-hem were stained with blood. It was my blood and the blood of many noble persons. Nor was it shed in vain. March on, brave people, the victory-goddess is your leader! And as the sea bursts through your dikes, burst through the wall of tyranny and break it down and flood them drowning from the soil they have presumed to take!

(Drumrolls come closer.)

Hark! Hark! How often that sound has summoned me with free step to the field of battle and of victory! How lively my comrades strode to the path of peril and of fame! I too am about to stride forth from this prison to an honorable death. I die for the liberty I lived for and fought for, and to which I am now a passive sacrifice.

(A file of Spanish soldiers, armed with
halberds, occupies stage-rear.)

Yes, gather in there, close ranks, you do not frighten me. I am in the habit of standing in front of spears and against spears, and with menacing death all around me, I only feel courageous life at doubled tempo.

(Drumrolls)

The enemy hems you in on all sides. Swords flash. Friends, yet higher valor! At your backs you have parents, wives, children! *(pointing to the guards)* And these act upon the hollow word of a despot, not of their own wills. Defend your possessions! And to preserve the most cherished thing of all, die gladly, as I now set the example.

(Drumrolls. As he moves toward the guards and toward the rear
door, the curtain falls. The music strikes up and concludes the
work with a victory symphony.)

OTHER DRAMAS AND DRAMATIC PROJECTS
TO 1775
Juvenilia, 1765–67

After the miraculous feeding of five thousand persons on five loaves and two fishes, all four evangelists report that twelve basketfuls of bread fragments were collected from the green grass where the Galilean multitude had satisfied their hunger. Taking the five dramas just presented in translation as parallel to those five loaves, the purpose of the present chapter is to account for the leftover fragments, which is to say the lesser plays and parts of plays written by Goethe, chiefly in the years 1773–75, from age twenty-four to age twenty-six.

The merits of these works vary widely, from trivial to sublime. Few of the completed ones are likely to tempt modern producers, and the fragments are, by definition, useless to the practical stage, yet the slightest of them affords some glimpse into the mind of a perennially fascinating genius. By including three scraps of juvenilia we bring the count of such pieces to twenty, and even that number does not include the sketches for a dramatic *Caesar* and a dramatic *Socrates* which the author himself destroyed. Such a scale of production is astounding, but our wonder arises from the sheer profusion of ideas for dramatic creation, from the surprising variety of those ideas, and from the abounding vitality that gave rise to all of them collectively.

The three scraps of juvenilia stand as evidence for a teenager's eagerness to become a dramatist. The first dates probably from 1765 and age sixteen; the second followed within a year or so; the third is the work of a student at the University of Leipzig, probably in 1767.

1. ***The Royal Hermitess (Die königliche Einsiedlerin)***
    a monologue in fourteen creditably turned pentameter couplets (twenty-eight lines)
    scenario unknown
    An unnamed lady has fled from the splendor and falsity of a court to find solace in the shade of a favorite tree; alone

amid the beauties of nature, she avows that her heart feels redoubled pain.

2. **Belshazzar (Belsazar)**

a conspirator's speech in ten hexameter couplets (twenty lines) from "I, 1," and Belshazzar's monologue in twenty-two hexameter couplets (forty-four lines) from "II, 1."

scenario from the first five chapters of the Old Testament Book of Daniel.

3. **The Mirror of Virtue (Der Tugendspiegel)**

one and one-half pages of dialogue, in prose

a night scene by a roadside: two young merchants, Melly and Dodo, are discussing how Melly has ruined himself financially for a frivolous sweetheart named Nelly; as a result, the two young men are now in flight from the scene of the disaster.

Each of these early fragments represents a type of drama current in the 1760s: heroic pastoral, grandiose baroque tragedy, both with French antecedents, and "realistic" prose comedy of English derivation.

More than twenty years later Goethe had Wilhelm Meister recite the Royal Hermitess's monologue "from memory" for a small company resting in a bucolic place and had a lady of that small company "recite from memory" the monologue of Belshazzar; some scenario details are cited to introduce the latter, and the monologue itself leads into a discussion of tragedy writing. Both quotations occur in chapter 4 of Book II of "Wilhelm Meister's Theatrical Mission," that vivid first draft composed 1777–84 and abandoned for the revised version of the novel, *Wilhelm Meister's Apprenticeship,* 1790–96. The "Theatrical Mission" remained unknown, however, until accidental discovery of the manuscript in Switzerland in 1910. Already in 1909 Max Morris had collected the three scraps of juvenilia from other sources and included them, along with many other unpublished items, in his six-volume *Young Goethe.* Morris's compilation is also the primary printed source for several of the dramatic fragments we are about to discuss.

Less than a year after the third juvenilium listed above, the author, aged eighteen to nineteen, was composing *The Lover's Whim* (1767–

68), which brought to culmination the minor genre of the German
dramatic pastoral. Late in 1768, three or four months past his
nineteenth birthday, he wrote *Fellow Culprits*, casting the bourgeois
subject in elegant aristocratic verse. Early in 1772, in the middle of his
twenty-third year, he completed the first draft of *Götz*, which he did
not publish. From May 25th to September 11th of the same year he
was working as a lawyer in Wetzlar and undergoing the experience
which was to constitute the subject matter of his novel, *The Sorrows of
Young Werther*. Near the close of that experience he passed his
twenty-third birthday. To 1773 belong the revision of *Götz von Berlichingen*, its publication in June, and its achievement of national fame
almost over night; *inter*national fame was to follow the 1774 publication of *Werther*. At unidentified intervals of the same period the scenes
of the *Urfaust* were put together, and to other intervals of the same
period, 1773–74, belong the spate of dramatic experiments which
constitute our present concern.

1771–1775

4. **Concerto Dramatico** (1772), a playlet in seventeen lyric
stanzas of varying pattern, was a private joke intended for a circle of
friends in Darmstadt who termed themselves "the Community of
Saints," and the superscription indicates that the little piece was to be
performed by them. Each set of lines has only a musical term in lieu of
a speaker's name, beginning with *Tempo giusto* and passing by way of
Arioso, Andantino, etc., to the final *Presto fugato*, the overall distribution being roughly parallel to a four-movement sonata. A
headnote in Italian names the author as "Sigr Dottore Flamminio
detto Panurgo secondo," in allusion to Goethe's nickname of "the
Doctor" among the group. Presumably, then, it was Goethe who was
to speak (or sing) the *Air* in neatly turned French verses (with a few
misspellings):

1. Une fille
    Gentille
    Bien soignée par Mama   Elle en gagna
    Toute échauffée   Un gros rhume, et bonne Mama
    Dans une Allée   S'écria
    Se promena.   De toute sa poitrine
                                   Medecin! Medicine!

2.   Un garcon
   Bel et bon   La bien choffa
   Par avanture se trouva   Que rhume bientot s'en vola.
   Et s'y preta   Le Divin! la Divine;
   Et la frotta,   Medecin! Medicine!

This charming Rococo doggerel vies with the gallant verse trifles by Voltaire or Parny.

5.   *The Annual Fair at Plundersville. A Masquerade* (*Jahrmarktsfest zu Plundersweilern. Ein Schönbartsspiel*) is a ninepage playlet composed in irregular short lines with irregular rhymes approximating the rough *Knittelvers* of sixteenth-century Hans Sachs. Again in allusion to his nickname "the Doctor," Goethe appears in the person of "Doctor Medicus." The scene is a fair, the speakers are numerous and motley, and the focus of attention is a playlet-within-a-playlet as actors present to the crowd a quasi-medieval drama on the biblical theme of Queen Esther, Mordecai, and the wicked Haman. Between the miniature Acts, out comes the traditional clown, Hans Wurst (Jack Sausage), to proclaim that "Act I" is over, with "Act II" following directly, and to jolly the audience along. By 1773 Hans Wurst was twenty years out of date, and his revival here is by way of picturesque and nostalgic recall, entirely without the gross indecencies that had been Jack's stock-in-trade in the old days. Nostalgic too is the biblical playlet-within-a-playlet, which imitates the serious efforts of Hans Sachs two hundred years before—but the nostalgia is laced with irony.

The total nine-page work stands as a fore-study to *Faust* in its use of *Knittelvers,* in its sixteenth-century atmosphere, in its crowd scenes, which anticipate "Before the City Gate" (lines 808–1177 of the completed *Faust*), and in the quips of Hans Wurst, which look forward to the more sardonic quips of Mephistopheles.

6.   *Pater Brey.* Likewise nine pages long and likewise in *Knittelvers,* but with a more clear-cut scenario, is the playlet of *Pater Brey.* The use of Latin *Pater* signifies a Catholic clergyman. The full title of the playlet reads: *A Shrovetide Play, also perhaps for tragedizing after Easter, about Pater Brey, the False Prophet* (*useful for the instruction and entertainment of Christendom in general, especially of ladies and young gentlewomen at the Golden Mirror*).

The butt of this good-natured satire was F. M. Leuchsenring, a member of the "Community of Saints" who was given to extravagant utopianizing. As the false prophet here, he is bookish and garrulous, a vegetarian, and a glib reformer. As a lodger at the widow Sibilla's he awes that lady by his saintliness, but he also pays gallant attention to her daughter Leonora, whose fiancé, Captain Balandrino, has these three years been off to the wars in Italy. The "saint" has also infuriated the local grocer by reorganizing that merchant's entire store of goods—and by his preaching. Unexpectedly Captain Balandrino comes home, disguises himself as an aged nobleman just long enough to explore the situation, and then, with gusto and determination drives the Pater out of town and claims his loyal Leonora for himself.

Again there are anticipations of *Faust*: the captain is a nontragic forerunner of Valentine, and the interlocking conversations in Sibilla's garden (scene 2) are preparations for the interlocking conversations in Dame Martha's garden (lines 3073–3204 of the completed *Faust*). There is wit and charm in *Pater Brey,* as there was in the "Plundersville Fair," and the use of *Knittelvers* in both is skillful. The next item to be mentioned, however, represents a venture in a wholly different direction.

7. *Mohammed (Mahomet)* derived from Goethe's enthusiastic reading of David Friedrich Megerle's 1772 translation of the Koran, the first ever made into German, although the translator still hewed to the traditional view of the Prophet of Islam as Antichrist. Inevitably Goethe was also familiar with Voltaire's *Le Fanatisme, ou Mahomet le prophète* (1741), of which he was to make a translation in 1799. In that French drama the Messenger of God to the Arabs was portrayed as a master-deceiver and heroic-sized Tartuffe, and all Moslem components were intended as cover-names for the components of Roman Catholicism. Quite in contrast, Goethe's bold new idea was to present Mohammed as a charismatic leader of his people and as intermediary between his people and God. With easy substitutions, we note, the concept could be made to fit Moses as readily as Mohammed. The total scenario is obscure, but, to judge by slight collateral information, the author intended no "rescue," in Lessing's sense of that term, of Mohammed's maligned character but rather the portrayal of a Renaissance-type overreacher who must inevitably fail.

The opening scene (two pages of prose) begins with Mohammed's monologue in "a field" beneath the starry sky. The substance of his speech is a paraphrase of Sura 6, verses 77–80, of the Koran, a passage acceptable to any monotheist, even to a deist. To the speaker then comes his foster mother Halima, who tries to coax the youthful visionary indoors and away from the unwholesome darkness.

The second scene, in so far as we have it, consists of a "duet" between the Prophet's daughter Fatema and her husband Ali, its subject being a great leader's life expressed in the extended metaphor of a river's course from its wellspring to the ocean. Quite possibly the projected drama was abandoned because the author realized he had communicated its very essence in this one passage. At any rate, the "duet" was hardly completed when Goethe removed the indications of dialogue form, made a few changes in wording, and published it in 1773 in the *Göttinger Musenalmanach* as the lyric poem well known under the title of *Mohammed's Hymm* (*Mahomets Gesang*). The original dramatic form goes as follows:

ALI:	See the mountain spring,
	Clear as joy,
	Flashing like a star;
FATEMA:	Above the clouds
	Blessèd spirits nourished
	His infancy
	Amid scrub growth between the crags.
ALI:	Through the cloud
	Down he dances, youthfully
	Agile, onto marble cliffs,
	Re-exulting
	Toward the sky.
FATEMA:	Down through summit runnels
	Speeds his chase for colored pebbles,
ALI:	And with youthful leader's tread
	He assembles brother rills
	To his course.
FATEMA:	In the valley down below
	Flowers form beneath his footfall,

                    And the meadow
                    From his breath draws life.
ALI: But no shady glen detains him,
                    Nor the flowers
                    Twining to embrace his knees,
                    Worshipping with loving eyes:
                    His course presses toward the plain
                    Meandering.
FATEMA: Brooklets fondly
                    Nestle up. Now to the flatlands
                    He advances, silver-shining,
ALI: And the flatlands shine with him!
                    And the rivers of the flatlands
FATEMA: And the brooklets from the mountains
                    Hail him with the cry of "Brother!"
(*together*):   "Brother, take your brothers with you,
FATEMA: With you to your ancient father,
                    To the everlasting Ocean
                    Who with arms outstretched is waiting,
                    Waiting for us—
                    Arms, alas!, outstretched in vain
                    To embrace his yearning children.
ALI: Us the ravening sands devour
                    In desert wastes; the sun above us
                    Sucks our blood away; a hill
                    Hems us back in ponds! Brother,
                    Lead your brothers from the flatlands,
FATEMA: Lead your brothers from the mountains,
(*together*):   Lead us, lead us to your father!"
ALI: "Come one and all!"
                    And now he swells
                    More grandly; now a race entire
                    Lifts the leader high aloft!
                    And in triumph as he flows
                    He gives names to countries, cities
                    Spring up where his foot has trod.

FATEMA: Ever in his onward sweep
           He leaves towers tipped with flame,
           Marble dwellings, a creation
           Of his bounty, in his wake.

ALI: Cedar dwellings bears this Atlas
           On his giant-shoulders, as
           Above his head a thousand banners
           Wave and clatter in the wind,
           Witnesses to his high splendor.
           Thus he bears his brothers onward,

FATEMA: And his riches, and his children,
(*together*):   Exuberant, unto the heart
           Of their begetter, who awaits them.

8. ***Prometheus.*** Similarly exalted strains mark the two Acts of a *Prometheus,* in free verse, to a total of eleven pages. Again the protagonist is an overreacher, like Mohammed, like Faust, but with no discernible similarities to the rebel Titan of Aeschylus. The scenario seems to be Goethe's independent invention, apart from some hints in Book I of Ovid's *Metamorphoses* about how Prometheus shaped the first human beings out of clay. In spirit, the new myth is akin to Jean-Jacques Rousseau and to William Blake, though the hero patently shares attitudes of the young Goethe.

Act I opens in "a grove," with expressions of defiance from Prometheus to Mercury, the scandalized messenger from Jupiter and "the Establishment." Roundly Prometheus declares that he owes nothing to his parents; Time, not they, reared him; Fate is the only power that exists, and the gods are merely Fate's vassals. When Mercury has departed to report this defiance aloft, the hero's brother Epimetheus comes to announce that the gods have now decided to turn Olympus over to him and allow him to rule the earth. To which Prometheus retorts that he will not be the gods' bailiff. Around him stand male and female statues shaped by him out of clay but as yet without life: these, he says, are his "children," and his children are everything to him. Epimetheus blames him for not understanding that happiness lies with harmonious cooperation. To the brothers comes Minerva, the goddess of wisdom—or of intellect—and remonstrates in turn with Prometheus. His reply is that "we are all eternal"; he does not remember birth, nor does he expect to die. The goddess says that, in return for obedience, Jupiter will allow Prometheus to bring all his statues to life. Better, answers Prometheus, that they never live at all than to submit to Jupiter's will.

In Act II (scene 1), *On Olympus,* Mercury protests to Jupiter that Minerva has perpetrated treason by enabling Prometheus to bring all his creatures of clay to life: why, he is like a god to those creatures! So it is, says Jupiter, and so be it! In their youthful exuberance those creatures will listen to no objections until they discover a need for gods.

II, 2 (*At the foot of Olympus*) presents a beautiful valley where Prometheus smiles upon his living "children" at work and at play. From Ovid we are able to identify the scene as within the Golden Age. Suddenly two men quarrel over a she-goat and one strikes the other down; but, unlike Abel in Genesis 4, the fallen man is not dead. Prometheus shows him how to cure his wound with an herb. Forget the she-goat, he bids, and as for the assailant: if his hand is against every man, every man's hand will be against him. These are the words of Genesis 16:12 about Ishmael. As the cured victim departs, Prometheus exclaims:

> You are not degenerate, my children!
> Be industrious and lazy,
> Cruel and kind,
> Generous and greedy!
> Be like all your brothers in fate,
> Be like the beasts and the gods!

Enter then Pandora, daughter of Prometheus, in perturbation at having witnessed a couple in passionate embrace. Sexual passion, her father explains, is a joy among other joys, but it betokens a culmination, a fulfillment, and—death. Instantly Pandora cries, "Let us die!" To which Prometheus replies, "Not yet!" As a second thought the girl inquires what comes after death. Her father answers that, after death, as after waking from a sleep, there follows a new life in which "to fear, to hope, and to desire anew." With those words the fragment breaks off.

The unfinished drama, we infer, aimed at nothing less than a basic myth for a new religion, a religion that would reconcile classical tradition with Genesis and thus be consonant with the optimistic idealism of the author and of his era. By comparing *Prometheus* with *Faust, Part II* in general, and more particularly with Faust's final speech (lines 11,559–86), we discern that the youthful Goethe, like the aged one, saw mankind as mixed of good and evil and as dedicated to striving forever toward higher knowledge and higher achievement. The purpose of life is living and growing, and after death there must be further living and further growing; the ultimate goal is inconceivable.

Inevitably this eleven-page fragment has been closely scanned for hints of a reconciliation between a youthful Prometheus and an older and wiser Jupiter, i.e., for hints of the author's ultimate acceptance of traditional religion. Yet in Book III of his autobiography Goethe says that the well-known, independent ode entitled *Prometheus* was to open the third Act, and that ode is all defiance, with no hint of reconciliation. Moreover, stanza 5 of the ode rephrases the hero's opening remarks to Mercury, and the final stanza of the ode rephrases the hero's six-line monologue at the beginning of "II, 2." The monologue reads as follows:

> Look down here, Zeus,
> Upon my world: it lives,
> And I have formed it after my own image,
> A race that shall resemble me,
> To grieve and weep, to enjoy and to delight,
> And heed you as little as I.

In the case of the fragmentary *Mohammed* we suggested that Goethe's dramatic impulse died away when he discovered that he had fully expressed his thought in the lyric poem, *Mohammed's Hymn*: we find an exactly parallel case in the *Prometheus* ode, which we translate as follows:

> Shroud up your sky there, Zeus, in murk
> Of cloudy vapor,
> And like a lad lopping off thistles
> Go vent your power
> On oak trees and mountain tops;
> You still can not but leave me

My earth as it stands,
And my cottage, which you never built,
And my good hearth,
The warmth of which
You envy me.

I know nothing sorrier
Under the sun than you, gods!
From tribute offerings
And breath of prayers
You eke out diet for
Your majesty,
And would famish but that
Children and paupers
Are deluded fools.

Back in my childhood
I knew not the simplest thing;
I would lift up my straying eyes
To the sun, as if there were up there
An ear to hear my lamentation,
A heart like mine
To take compassion on the oppressed.

Who helped me
Stand against the arrogance of Titans?
And who delivered me from death,
From servitude?
Was all that not your own achievement,
Holily burning heart?
And, young and good, you burned—
Betrayed—your gratitude
Up to that sleepyhead?

I revere you? For what?
Did you assuage the sorrows
Of sufferers ever?
Did you allay the tears

Of the anguished ever?
And was I not forged into manhood
By almighty Time
And eternal Destiny,
Both my masters and yours?

Do you perhaps
Imagine I should hate life,
Flee to the wilderness,
Because not all
Dream-blossoms came to ripeness?

Here I sit, shaping humans
In my own image,
A race that shall be like me,
To grieve, to sorrow,
To enjoy and to perceive delight,
And heed you as little
As I!

9. *Satyros, or The Deified Forest-Demon (Satyros oder der vergötterte Waldteufel)*, a complete five-act play in *Knittelvers*, occupies a mere fourteen pages. Its simple stage requirements and relatively small cast place it within the scope of amateurs, and it might indeed be best realized as house entertainment running little over an hour's performing time.

In Act I, a hermit, who has fled from the raucous and criminal city, accepts into his forest hut a stray satyr—a conscienceless child of nature having some affinities with Shakespeare's Caliban.

Act II consists solely of a twenty-six-line monologue by the satyr as he wakes, presumably the following morning, alone in the hut. He is disgusted with his host's living quarters and repelled by the hermit's object of worship: sooner would he adore an onion till his eyes ran tears than "open his heart's shrine to a whittled figurine and crossed sticks":

> *Als öffnen meines Herzens Schrein*
> *Einem Schnitzbildlein, Queerhölzlein.*

(For the crucifix Goethe had a lifelong aversion.) The satyr runs away.

In Act III, merrily singing for his own pleasure beside a forest spring, the satyr is discovered by two maidens, Arsinoë and Psyche. After a few questions Arsinoë goes to fetch her father, but Psyche readily accepts the satyr's sensual advances. When Arsinoë returns with her father, whose name is Hermes, and a crowd of excited neighbor folk, the satyr explains to them that they all live staid, stale, dull, profitless lives, whereas they should be living carefree in the greenwood, with raw chestnuts for food. The crowd finds this a delightful idea.

Act IV finds the satyr still sermonizing and his listeners munching chestnuts "like squirrels," when along comes the hermit in high dudgeon over the theft of his crucifix. Indignantly the people drive him away from their new god.

V, 1 is a brief scene in which Eudora, the wife of Hermes, is serving the fugitive hermit bread and milk. This new god, she complains in outrage, has already tried to ravish her, but she has a stratagem for his undoing: let the hermit be caught by the crowd and carried off to be sacrificed as they have threatened; *she* will contrive the proper conclusion. Uneasily the hermit agrees to serve as decoy.

The finale (V, 2) is captioned "The Temple," meaning apparently an out-of-doors scene with an altar in front of the closed sanctuary. The satyr sits in barbarian solemnity on the altar, accepting the worship of the kneeling crowd, when the hermit is led in as a captive. He is to be sacrificed immediately. Just as Hermes lifts the sacrificial knife, Eudora's voice is heard crying for help within the sanctuary. Hermes bursts the doors open, and there the satyr is seen by everyone in the very act of overpowering the faithful wife. The satyr drops his prey, denounces the lot of them as fools, and announces that he will "descend to nobler motals." He is allowed to leave, but, in a final line, the hermit remarks that some maiden—presumably Psyche—will doubtless go with him.

Half again as long as *Pater Brey,* and better constructed, *Satyros* is still concerned with the theme of the false prophet, except that this time there are two false prophets instead of one. The satyr is doubtless no more that the principle of license arbitrarily embodied in a type figure out of Greek mythology, but in the hermit some people have claimed to detect veiled allusions to the philosopher and theologian Johann Gottfried Herder. A mere four years before, Herder had been Goethe's mentor, and a few years later Goethe was to obtain for Herder the appointment as official (Lutheran) court preacher to the Duke of Weimar, while in 1773, when *Satyros* was written, Herder had reached the ripe age of twenty-nine. Brilliant, industrious, and cantankerous, Herder quarreled at one time or another with almost all of his friends and was to be, to the end of his days, a fretful and disappointed man. Whether or not traits of his are included in the figure of the hermit in this little play, it is more important to see the hermit as an embodiment of the puritan principle opposite to the principle of amoral sensuality represented by the satyr.

10. *Gods, Heroes, and Wieland* (*Götter, Helden und Wieland*), eleven pages long, in prose, and subtitled "A Farce," was composed as Goethe's *réplique* to a literary critic, Christoph Martin Wieland.

In September of 1772 the Duchess Regent of Weimar had imported to her court this distinguished man of letters to act as tutor for her teenage son, Hereditary Duke Charles Augustus. Aged forty, Wieland was famous for an astonishingly large quantity of works in various genres, and for forty more years he was to continue his vast and varied literary production. His fame was already in decline in 1813, when he died at the age of eighty, and the common opinion nowadays is that he is "only of historical interest." In 1773, however, he was considered a figure of towering importance. His was the idea of making Weimar the intellectual capital of German-speaking Europe, and to that end he launched his magazine, *The German Mercury.* One of his articles in that magazine was "Letters concerning the Lyric Drama," in which he disparaged the dramas of Euripides in favor of his own modernized version of *Alkestis.* The twenty-four-year-old Goethe found the article preposterous. His reply was this little farce.

On the bank of the Cocytus in the afterworld various shades of departed persons are met for an altercation: the three principals of the Euripidean play—Admetus, Alkestis, and Hercules—together with the ghost of Euripides, the god Mercury, the infernal ferryman

Charon, and others. Mercury is being blamed for statements in *The German Mercury*. The participants are joined by "Wieland's shade, in a nightcap," and then the argument rages. Literary values are disputed and jibes are sharply traded, as when Hercules says to Wieland: "If you hadn't sighed overlong under the bondage of your religion and moral philosophy, you might have amounted to something." At last the wrangling becomes so loud that Pluto "from within" calls out for order: "A man can't even lie in peace with his wife when she has no objection!" At that point Wieland—wakes up.

In his old age Goethe claimed he had composed the little dreamfarce under the influence of wine and at the instigation of friends. Wieland shrugged the satire off in a subsequent issue of *The German Mercury,* and thus friendly cooperation of the two authors was made possible when Goethe himself entered Weimar service some two years later.

11. *The Artist's Earthly Pilgrimage (Des Künstlers Erdewallen)* is a poetic gem deliberately cast as a miniature two-Act verse play of two-and-a-half printed pages. The rhymed couplets have lines of varying length and of irregular meters.

In the first Act, a painter is seen trying to force himself to work at the portrait of an ugly woman. Impatiently he lays his brush aside and contemplates a life-size picture of Venus Urania, his ideal, which he must sell to keep from starvation. From an inner room comes the wail of a waking infant. The wife rouses at the sound; immediately she bids the artist fetch wood and kindle the fire. An older boy comes running, barefooted, to help his father.

In the second Act, the ugly woman of the commissioned portrait arrives with her husband. Both make insipid remarks while inspecting various paintings. Unseen by them at the other side of the studio the painter's Muse appears and speaks words of reassurance to the harried artist.

11a. Under the title of *The Artist's Deification (Des Künstlers Vergötterung)*, there is a one-page pendant to the foregoing, signed "Goethe" and dated July 18, 1774. In a gallery a student contemplates with awe the painting of Venus Urania, which is magnificently framed and on display. His master, noting his awe, consecrates him to the true Art. The two of them talk with reverence of the deceased painter, whom the master had personally known.

11b. Approaching age forty, in 1788, Goethe recurred again to this theme in the somewhat longer miniature drama of *The Artist's Apotheosis (Des Künstlers Apotheose)*. Again a student is contemplating the Venus Urania in a gallery. Passers-by offer him advice on how to become a great painter. The gallery inspector announces that a princely connoisseur has bought the painting. Overhead, the Muse introduces the spirit of the deceased artist and bids him gaze upon the scene. The spirit replies: "I feel only the oppressiveness of air." The Muse delivers a noble speech about the immortality conferred by great art.

The third of these miniature dramas is self-conscious and didactic, the second is overbrief, but the first has about it the poetic freshness of the dew. Separately and together this trio of poems carried far-reaching influence. The German Romantiker admired them, as did the Russian Romanticists, who knew the first and the third in D. V. Venevitínov's fine translations (ca. 1825). In England Barry Cornwall (B. W. Procter) cultivated the miniature drama as a form; his pieces, in turn, inspired imitations by Pushkin and looked forward to dramatic poems by Browning. In Alfred de Musset's famous *Nuits* of 1835–37, the Muse delivers grand tirades of consolation in dialogues with a poet (rather than with a painter).

Early in 1774, perhaps in January, Goethe set about writing his novel, *Werther,* which was published the same year. Readers who imagine that work as an all-engrossing, even shattering, experience are startled to discover that he was simultaneously occupied with multiple activities and with composing poems of importance not at all related to his novel. To the same period belong the very minor dramatic squibs numbered 12, 13, and 14 here.

12. *Prologue to "The Latest Revelations of God" (Prolog zu den neuesten Offenbahrungen Gottes)*, a scant two pages in length, satirizes K. F. Bahrdt, professor of theology at Giessen, who, the previous year, had published sample translations from the New Testament in slick, up-to-the-minute prose under the title of "The

Latest Revelations of God in Letters and Tales." The professor's simplistic and hidebound orthodoxy was irritating enough, but what set Goethe's teeth on edge was the affront to Martin Luther's biblical prose. The *Prologue,* in *Knittelvers,* presents the professor under his own name and shows him intercepted by the four irate evangelists themselves just when he is about to join guests in his garden. He finds all four of them monstrously unfit for social introduction; they find him an incarnate outrage. Saint Luke even attacks him physically. In the final line the professor vows to take his revenge on the writings of these boors.

13. *The Wandering Jew (Der ewige Jude)* consists of eight pages of a narrative poem in *Knittelvers* dealing with the medieval legend of the Wandering Jew. As the by-product of a dramatic intention it need not be discussed here, except to remark that the intention was indignantly anticlerical but not antireligious.

14. *A Newly Inaugurated Moral-Political Puppet Play (Neueröfnetes moralisch-politisches Puppenspiel)* constitutes a sixty-line prologue to a small collection published by Goethe in 1774, containing *The Annual Fair at Plundersville, The Artist's Earthly Pilgrimage,* and *Pater Brey.* The sixty lines of *Knittelvers* make a kind of thematic index to the three playlets, treating them as if they were all composed for puppet theaters.

15. The enormous and immediate success of *The Sorrows of Young Werther* elicited parodies, the most notorious of which was Friedrich Nicolai's pamphlet-length *Joys of Young Werther.* According to this rather ill-natured spoof Albert furnished the sorrowful hero with a toy pistol which fired only chicken's blood, so that Werther's suicide miscarried. Subsequently Albert divorced Lotte so she could marry Werther and bring the story to a "joyous" conclusion. Goethe's reply to the satire was a three-page scene in prose dialogue entitled *Anecdote for "The Joys of Young Werther" (Anekdote zu den Freuden des Jungen Werthers),* which appeared in 1775.

Here we learn that the pistol was real but the hero's aim was bad, so that he was only temporarily blinded from the powder-flash. He is indeed married to Lotte, and she is bandaging his eyes as they discuss their story, citing episodes by page numbers. Their whole difficulty, says Lotte, began with Albert's cold-heartedness on page 23. Werther reminds his "little wifey" not to forget to start getting supper ready.

16. *Hanswurst's Wedding, or The Way of the World* (*Hanswursts Hochzeit oder der Lauf der Welt*) is an experiment with a startlingly different sort of drama. It was begun as an adaptation of a musical comedy called *Harlequin's Wedding Feast*, which in turn was based on a comedy of 1695 by Christian Reuter. Hans Wurst (Jack Sausage), as mentioned before, was the oafish clown who jollied audiences along in the interludes between the Acts of comedies, or even of tragedies, until around 1750. Indecencies were his stock-in-trade, and if he was not merely Harlequin under a different name, he was Harlequin's blood brother.

The present dramatic fragment extends to eleven printed pages: first come 133 lines of dialogue in *Knittelvers,* then two long and overlapping cast-of-characters lists, then jottings of disconnected verse passages, and finally jottings of disconnected "ideas" in prose. In the 133 lines of dialogue Jack is being urged to mend his ways, now that he is about to take a wife. Here the barnyard humor is strong, but the lists of characters were drawn up with a Rabelaisian abandon.

After dinner on March 6, 1831, the octogenarian Goethe fetched forth the manuscript "of 1775"—actually of 1774—for Eckermann to inspect, remarking that it was conceived in a mood of high jinx and could never have been brought to completion. In Paris, he felt, such a work might have a chance of success, but hardly in Weimar or Frankfurt. About the handwriting of the manuscript Eckermann says not a word, but when scholars came to look at those pages more than a hundred years after they had been composed, it was immediately evident that two different hands had written them. The second hand was that of Goethe's friend, Johann Heinrich Merck, whose personality was one of the many factors that went into the creation of Mephistopheles. One can picture the hilarity of the two young cronies as they concocted names of more and more characters, far beyond what any drama could accommodate. The first list has 140 of them, and although the second list reduces these to 49, plus 7 extras, the number is still excessive. Clearly the names were invented for their own sakes.

Besides Jack himself as bridegroom and Ursula Blandina as bride, there is Jack's tutor, Kilian Brustfleck: "Kilian" for an Irish saint who once labored for the conversion of the Germans to Christianity, "Brustfleck" meaning perhaps "bib-stain." All the rest are wedding guests. From the first list of 140 we select 22 names, suggesting English translations and giving the German originals in the odd spellings of 1774.

1	Ursel mit dem Kalten Loch Tante	Cold-hole Ursula, aunt
2	Hans Arsch von Rippach	Jack Arse from Rippach
3	Hans Arschgen von Rippach empfindsam	Jack Arselet from Rippach, sensitive
4	Tölpel von Passau	Booby from Passau
5	Reckärschgen ⎫ Nichten	Stretch-assie ⎫ Nieces
6	Schnuckfözgen ⎭	Cuddle-pussie ⎭
7	Jfr Kluncke Putzmacherin	Miss Draggletassle, milliner
8	(Hans) Maulaff	(Jack) Monkey-mug
9	Peter Sauschwanz	Peter Sowstail
10	Rotzlöffel ⎫ Pagen	Snot-spooner ⎫ Pages
11	Gelbschnabel ⎭	Greenhorn ⎭
12	Schwanz Kammerdiener	Prick, valet
13	Hundsfott wird extemporisiert als Gastrolle	Dogturd, to be extemporized by a guest actor
14	Simplizissimus kommt von der Reise um die Welt	Simplicissimus, back from his trip around the world
15	Quirinus Schweinigel bel esprit	Quirinus Foulmouth, *bel esprit*
16	Thoms (*sic*) Stinckloch Nichts geringes	Thomas Stinkhole, Nothing Trifling
17	Blackscheisser Poet	Drivelshit, poet
18	Hans Hasenfus	Jack Lilyliver
19	Hungerdarm	Hungergut
20	Fladen Candidat	Cowflop, Candidate (in Theology)
21	Mlle Firlefanz	Mlle Frippery
22	Dr. Bonefurz	Dr. Bonnyfart

The scene is the wedding banquet at "the Golden Louse." The scenario is unknown.

In the Auerbach's Tavern scene of *Faust,* lines 2189–94 make covert allusion to Master Hans from Rippach (no. 2 above), but the others are not heard of again. The pictorial counterpart of the Hanswurst project as a whole may be found in certain Flemish paintings. The plan reveals an important but little-known aspect of Goethe's human and artistic personality.

17. *Erwin and Elmire,* twenty-three pages long, is a charming two-Act prose play interspersed with nearly twenty lyrics intended to be set to music as solos, duets, and trios. Undertaken late in 1773 on commission from the composer Johann André, who wanted a libretto for a *Singspiel,* it was abandoned because of disagreements between the writer and the musician and then taken up again at the instigation of Goethe's fiancée, Lili Schönemann—the Belinde of the dedicatory quatrain. Thus the text spans two years, 1773–75.

Act I, somewhat too long at thirteen pages, introduces an upper-class mother (Olimpia) fretting at the melancholy of her daughter Elmire, at the mysterious disappearance of young Erwin, and at the complexities of young people in general nowadays. When Olimpia was young, everything was simpler. In a monologue Elmire regrets her coldness toward Erwin; through her own folly she has driven him away. To her comes Bernardo, formerly her tutor in French and an older man—he may be over thirty. Has he, Elmire inquires, any news of Erwin? None, replies Bernardo, but he has met a most fascinating person whose acquaintance Elmire must make: a saintly hermit, who keeps a cottage and tends his own garden in a beautiful valley among the mountains. Elmire agrees to the journey.

As Act II begins, Erwin is happily tending his roses in the mountain valley when his peace is disturbed by the arrival of Bernardo, who reports that Elmire is on her way here. In a large bundle he has the necessary hermit-accouterments for Erwin to put on. While Erwin is enrobing himself inside the cottage, Elmire arrives and is told that the hermit is at prayers: that much the hermit had conveyed by sign language, because he is temporarily under a vow of silence.

As Bernardo retires, Erwin emerges in a flowing robe and long white beard, and then, in a show-stealing aria, Elmire makes devout confession of having accepted Erwin's love while deliberately withholding all compassion and requital. Hastily the hermit writes some words on a tablet, gives Elmire the tablet, and signifies by gestures that she is not to read it until she has gone as far as that distant linden tree yonder. Once she is out of sight, Erwin throws off his disguise, the music strikes up, and Erwin begins a solo; the returning Bernardo makes it a duet, and the returning Elmire makes it a joyous trio-finale.

The source for this *Singspiel* libretto was the thirty-nine-quatrain ballad "sung" in chapter 8 of Oliver Goldsmith's *Vicar of Wakefield*. In the ballad, the contrite maiden Angelina, disguised as a youth, comes by chance upon a kindly hermit who is none other than her beloved Edwin. The confession takes the form of the visitor's life story told by the fireside after a frugal supper. Forgiveness is instantly granted and the lovers are happily united. Goethe's additions are the expository first Act, the figures of Olimpia and Bernardo, and the gentle spoofing of the hermit.

A headnote to the text states: "The setting is not in Spain." To this we might add that, pleasingly and successfully, the setting and characters are contemporary, as of 1773–75. Dramatically, the confession aria is the high point of the text, but the most memorable lyric is Elmire's song in Act I—*Ein Veilchen auf der Wiese stand.*

> A violet in the field had grown,
> Closed in itself and all unknown;
> It was a lovable violet.
> One day a shepherdess came by
> With youthful tread and spirits high,
> Came by, came by,
> A-singing on her way.
>
> Ah! (thinks the violet) would that I
> Were the fairest flower beneath the sky!
> I'm but a lowly violet.
> If she would pick me, hold me pressed
> Till I grew faint upon her breast,
> No more, no more
> Than a quarter of an hour!

> But ah! the girl came by indeed
> And paid the violet no slightest heed;
> She trod upon the violet.
> It sank in death, yet gladly cried:
> "Though here I perish, I have died
> Of her, of her,
> And at her very feet!"

18. *Claudine of Villa Bella* is a second *Singspiel* libretto, nearly twice as long as the first, using eight characters (plus extras) instead of four, and it *is* set in Spain. Effort was made to have the songs grow naturally out of the story situations, but the lyrics are undistinguished. The implausible story depends on a highwayman who, in the end, proves to be not so bad a fellow after all.

Lively music and gala procession open the work. It is Claudine's eighteenth birthday, and her father, Don Gonzalo of Villa Bella, has arranged a festival to which many people have come thronging to hail their young lady. His own friend Don Sebastian points out to him that there is mutual, if undeclared, love between Claudine and the young foreigner Don Pedro, who is said to have a wicked lost brother. Two spiteful nieces wish they could think up something that would distress Claudine, but, as it turns out, both wholly lack inventiveness. They are Cinderella's spiteful sisters borrowed from another story and then reduced to mere extras. One of them, however, has been flirting with a husky lady-killer named Crugantino in the near-by town.

In scene 2, set in a disreputable inn, we learn that this Crugantino has his eye on Claudine. Scene 3 brings him to the moonlit terrace of Villa Bella, where the heroine first answers his call, thinking he is Pedro, and then retires in haste. Pedro appears, the two brothers fight, unaware of their kinship, and Pedro is wounded. Crugantino's man, Basko, carries the injured man off to the inn. Just then the master of Villa Bella comes out onto the terrace, encounters Crugantino, and inexplicably invites him in. He makes an entertaining guest in scene 4 until he is identified as the dangerous highwayman wanted by the police. With sword and pistol he holds the entire company at bay and makes his escape.

In scene 5 Claudine comes, in male attire, to the inn, searching for the wounded Pedro. She is seized by Crugantino; the wounded Pedro intervenes; Basko arrives to support his master. When the melee is at its height, the night watch descends and hales the four parties off to jail. Scene 6, in the jail, brings all the principals together. Everything is rapidly settled, the brothers are reconciled, and the "chorus," including the jailers, hails the happy lovers Claudine and Pedro.

In the scene on the moonlit terrace there is one very striking effect. The man Basko, who can whistle in imitation of a nightingale, is concealed amid the branches of a near-by tree. By prearrangement with his master he uses the bird song to warn Crugantino when danger approaches. With the moonlight pouring down and the night-ingale song persisting ever more urgently, Crugantino scales the grille fence and advances up the terrace unheeding. For those few minutes the situation comes vividly to life. In the jail scene Crugantino suddenly pronounces the startling sentence: "I find middle-class society insufferable!" But no social protest follows. The rest of his speech dwindles into a mere admission that he has never been able to get along with ordinary people. The psychological possibilities are therewith smothered and Crugantino becomes a mere puppet, like the rest of the cast.

Aside from these two tiny details, the forty pages are without interest.

19. *Clavigo,* on the other hand, is a five-Act prose play with a stage history. In May of 1774, just after completing *Werther* and sending the manuscript off to the publisher, Goethe was not a suicide or even prostrate from grief. Rather, he was enjoying the Friday meetings of a club of young people who gathered for social and for literary purposes. To one meeting he brought along the just-published Part IV of Beaumarchais' *Mémoires,* from which he read aloud the episode of the journey to Madrid. The company was delighted, and the proposal was made that Goethe turn the episode into a play. The idea appealed to him. Then and there he promised to write the play and have it ready by the following Friday. And he did.

By 1774 the versatile Beaumarchais had indeed passed through enough adventures to warrant extensive mémoires, but his literary accomplishments were still minor ones. He was now forty-two years old, *Le Barbier de Séville* was still a year into the future and *Le Mariage de Figaro* ten years into the future, and he was to have another quarter of a century of adventurous life before his death in 1799. Born Pierre-Augustin Caron, his talents as clock-maker and as harpist gained him early notice at the court of Louis XV, where he obtained a managerial appointment. Marriage to a widow left him, at her early death, the owner of a small property called the Bos (Bois) Marchais. Soon, as "Caron de Beaumarchais," he was handling all sorts of delicate commissions, at home and abroad, for persons in high place. Among other things, he was later to be credited with privately persuading Louis XVI to furnish secret aid to the American Revolution. Enormously resourceful, witty, energetic, and not always strictly honest, he was a kind of superadventurer.

His journey to Madrid was made on behalf of his sister, who had been courted and then jilted by José Clavigo, a writer and self-promoting courtier not wholly unlike Beaumarchais himself. Enjoying the special favor of the Spanish king, Clavigo felt perfectly safe from any recriminations a foreign girl might make against him. But Beaumarchais, as the indignant brother, journeyed to Madrid, penetrated court circles, and, on unfamiliar terrain and despite the handicap of a foreign language, managed to effect his revenge and ruin Clavigo's career.

In Goethe's play Beaumarchais is presented under his real name, and, if Act I consists of rather talky exposition, Act II presents the gist of the *Mémoires,* Part IV, in a single, continuous scene of considerable power. Beaumarchais, as a gentleman on travels and accompanied by a second gentleman on this occasion, comes to pay a formal call at Clavigo's house. The host is all courtesy and charm. The guest is no less urbane. From elegant compliments the conversation passes to innuendo, to frank accusations couched in icy formality, to a duel of words that threatens from minute to minute to become a duel with swords, and ends with Clavigo's writing, at his caller's dictation, a statement exonerating the young lady completely and confessing himself contemptibly blameworthy in her regard. Signed and delivered into Beaumarchais' hands, this document shall be published to the world—unless Clavigo can immediately obtain the lady's personal forgiveness. It would be a rare theater audience that could resist the melodramatic spell of this scene.

Act III brings Clavigo on his mission of apology to the house of

Marie de Beaumarchais. His passionate avowal of affection and remorse is genuine, and by it Marie is so agitated that she has to be taken out of the room—before declaring just what she intends to do about his request.

In the long IV, 1, Clavigo's faintly Mephistophelean friend Carlos talks him into reversing his decision: these Beaumarchais and their relatives in Spain are insignificant people, Clavigo has influence at court, the king is on his side, it will not be difficult to best these foreigners, and then Clavigo's brilliant career will be disencumbered of a sentimental *mésalliance*. Like Weislingen in *Götz*, Clavigo is a weakling and succumbs to these false arguments. In IV, 2, we behold the consternation in Marie's circle upon receiving Clavigo's impudent letter of withdrawal from his commitment.

In Act V, Clavigo chances to pass Marie's house in the night. He is surprised to confront a funeral procession: Marie's corpse is being carried out to burial. By torchlight Clavigo kneels beside the bier to beg forgiveness, while her family denounce him furiously. There, with a kiss upon the dead girl's hand, he too dies. Beaumarchais flees to escape inculpation in what may well look like murder.

This final Act, faintly echoing *Romeo and Juliet,* is over-hasty and ill-prepared. (How much it resembles the future finale of Donizetti's *Lucia di Lammermoor!*) The chance encounter, like the deaths of the lovers, is "at the dramatist's convenience," and the supporting characters recede into stage shadows in order to permit a lyric conclusion to a play which, after all, is about two broken hearts. Apart from the open-air finale, the play alternates interior settings easy to stage. The dialogue is in the prose of the upper classes, and the costuming was contemporary, or nearly so. In short, *Clavigo* was an effective, low-budget drama, welcome to theater managers and to audiences alike.

And it was a resounding success. Three different cities had their theaters produce it as soon as the printed text was available that same year (1774), and successive years found the work in almost every repertory. With *Götz von Berlichingen* Goethe had endeared himself to literary people and to the younger generation; with *Clavigo* his name became a household word among the sober middle classes.

Friends, however, were dismayed by it. One friend found it so bad he refused to believe that Goethe had written it. Another remarked that such trash was beneath Goethe. Wieland, still annoyed by *Gods, Heroes, and Wieland,* said in a private letter that here was evidence that Goethe's genius was overrated.

In his heart of hearts Goethe could not help but know that *Clavigo* was glib and slick, verging on what our present age terms soap opera. Nor could his conscience have failed to tell him that great drama is not promised in an instant and delivered in seven days. For a long time he was to insist that the German repertory was so meager in the 1770s that any good acting piece was desirable. Fifty-two years later he was to remark to Eckermann that he could have written a dozen plays like *Clavigo* with no difficulty at all and that he was sorry he had not done so. Modern readers are less regretful about that.

20. *Stella,* a five-act prose play of 1775, was the last and oddest of the stage pieces that Goethe completed before entering upon his *vita nuova* at Weimar, though, as we have seen, *Egmont* was partially written before that. The subtitle in this case is "A Drama for Lovers," and perhaps only lovers can give it their full sympathy.

The stagecraft is elementary, as contemporaries said and as posterity agrees. Act I presents the arrival of Madame Sommer and her fifteen-year-old daughter Luzie (Lucia, Lucy) at an inn. There, the postmistress, a cheerful and loquacious widow, provides the excuse for questions and answers that establish the immediate situation. Mme Sommer is a gentlewoman of limited means; Luzie is to enter service with the Baroness Stella, whose mansion is just across the way from the inn; and the Baroness Stella is reported to be a lady of great kindness and affability. Her story is a sad one, however, and not clear on all points. At age sixteen she had moved here with her husband, apparently an army officer. A child was born to them but died in infancy. Abruptly the husband disappeared. Gossip has it that they were never married. For the past three years Stella has lived in exemplary seclusion.

Upon hearing this recital, Mme Sommer remarks, in an aside, that Stella's case is parallel to her own. *Her* husband had likewise disappeared when Luzie was a small child, and to this day she does not know whether he is alive or dead. At a convenient stage moment, when Luzie is left alone briefly, an army officer named Fernando arrives at the inn. He is, of course, the missing party, and Act I closes with a piquant conversation between father and fifteen-year-old daughter, neither being aware of the other's identity.

The remaining four acts take place in different rooms of Stella's mansion across the way. The three ladies find each other most congenial, but Mme Sommer's heart is sorely tried when Stella displays the portrait of her missing husband. It is Mme Sommer's missing husband also, and Luzie recognizes the officer with whom she conversed only a few minutes ago. Fernando is sent for at once. Act II closes with his arrival and his impetuous rush toward Stella's study, his fleeting glance passing without recognition over Mme Sommer and Luzie.

Act III presents, first, the passionately joyous reunion of Fernando and Stella in the study, then the confrontation of Fernando with his first wife, whom he comes only gradually to recognize. In Act IV, consternation strikes all parties as the truth and its implications become apparent. Mme Sommer, now called Cezilie, determines to leave at once with her daughter, though she has not a word of reproach for Stella, nor Stella for her. Rather, both ladies express sisterly affection amid their grief. In the fifth Act departures and suicides are proposed, but none of the three principals really desires either departure *or* suicide. Ten lines before the end of the text, Mme Sommer proposes that they all remain together. The final tableau is that of a tearfully happy trio, with Fernando clasping his two wives in either arm.

Contemporaries said, and again posterity agrees, that this startling conclusion is psychologically unacceptable—though anthropologists, Moslems, and others might find no hindrance. More seriously, Fernando's reasons for two abandonments are left unexplained except for a vague plea about his need for freedom. Nor does he explain where he has been all these years, though for a time he "helped suppress the dying freedom of the noble Corsicans," i.e., he was in French military service in the acquisition of Corsica from Genoa prior to 1768. He *had* tried to locate his first wife, but could find no trace of her or of Luzie.

Late in Act V Mme Sommer recalls at length "a German Count" who went on crusade, was captured and held as a slave, was liberated by his owner's daughter, who then shared all his perils of warfare and travel. Moreover, he had brought the girl home with him, bidding his wife "reward her." The parallel between Fernando and "the German Count" seems less than exact, yet Mme Sommer is so moved by her own narration that the strained parallel inspires her to propose the *ménage à trois* with which the play ends. We suspect that the *ménage à trois* was the first notion of the author's and that the rest of the play was invented for the sake of that moment.

Astonishingly enough, *Stella* was read and discussed and performed for decades, and many readers and audiences were charmed by the affectionate good will of the characters. There is no villain, the very servants are filled with spontaneous devotion, and nowhere is wickedness touched upon, or even the corruption of courts and cities. There is not even a pert soubrette, not even a genial scallywag, not even an avuncular *raisonneur*. Human life is presented as the domain of the human heart, and the goodness of the human heart can resolve any dilemma. In this play the world is a sinless park, and we would not be astonished to see the characters take up crooks to go herding beribboned sheep by glade and murmuring stream.

Yet, thirty years later, in 1805, Goethe provided the play with a new ending, not in the interests of human truth but in the interests of conventional morality. Just as Mme Sommer concludes her story about "the German Count," it is discovered that Stella has swallowed poison. Immediately Fernando walks away with a pistol in his hand, and soon a shot is heard "in the distance." Stella bids Mme Sommer and Luzie leave her, and the final curtain falls as she collapses, saying "And I die alone."

By this revised ending the play is converted into a dismal melodrama, and what had been seen as the charmingly unreal world of the heart is revealed as a bleak stage where puppets sin and pay the wages of sin. Goethe's second thoughts about his works were almost always wrong.

Collecting impressions of the twenty items reviewed, together with the five translated plays, we are struck by the movements of a vivid imagination over a great variety of subjects. Originality there is, and abounding energy, and, despite the fragmentary state of several pieces, more than a little of a writer's self-discipline. In general, we note certain persistent traits: a preponderance of weak-willed male characters over strong ones, a pervasive dignity in women, absence of unmitigated tragic qualities, and a prevailing climate of good will, with excessive harshness nowhere. Repeatedly there is the implication that the human heart can settle issues of religion and morals. Some of these fragments are more worth our while than whole plays of other authors—or, alas!, than some that Goethe himself was later to complete and stage.

PART II

DRAMATIC WORKS, 1776–1832

IPHIGENIA IN TAURIS

Within months of his arrival in Weimar Goethe conceived the notion of composing a drama based on the *Iphigenia in Tauris* (412 B.C.) of Euripides. He intended no revival of the ancient Athenian dramatic form as such. There would be neither chorus nor masks nor any grandiose epiphany of an immortal at the close. Human beings with viewpoints of their own time would enact the myth. There would be no artificial reconstruction of a remote age with alien ways and customs and religion. Significantly, his Euripidean model had a woman as its center of interest and its scenario was not genuinely tragic; rather, it was a serious play with a conciliatory outcome.

What directly prompted the choice of subject is unknown, but it is likely that the personality of Charlotte von Stein was, from the outset, identified in Goethe's mind with the title character. This lady, seven years older than he, was the wife of the Master Equerry of the Weimar court, with three growing sons (and more children to follow). To judge by her portrait, she was less than beautiful. On January 7, 1776, one month to the day since his coming to this new milieu, Goethe wrote her the first letter of what was to become a voluminous, almost daily, correspondence. As Iphigenia of old had calmed and steadied her brother Orestes whom the Furies tormented, so this new-found "sister" shed grace and balm upon the young poet's spirit, a spirit troubled, we are told, by remorse over years of recklessly squandered youthful energies. To posterity Frau von Stein is an enigma, but through the decade 1776–86 Goethe saw her as the wise preceptress of his anxious heart. The Iphigenia of his play is a representation of that vision—or illusion.

When, fifty-five years after the fact, in 1831, Goethe stated to his secretary Eckermann that he had conceived the idea for his Iphigenia play in 1776, he presumably was accurate in his recall. He must, then, have pondered the idea for three years without committing a syllable of it to paper. Suddenly, in 1779, however, it was composed in six weeks' time, between February 14th and March 28th. Nine days after that, on April 6th, its première was given before invited guests beneath the trees of the ducal garden. Goethe himself played Orestes to the Iphigenia of Corona Schröter, the attractive leading actress of the Weimar troupe. Costumes were patterned to resemble known pieces of ancient sculpture. With the youthful Duke Charles Augustus taking the role of Pylades, the ultimate of decorum and attention was guaranteed among the select viewers. It was a rare, indeed an immortal afternoon.

That text of 1779 was, however, in prose, and Goethe was not satisfied with it. In the spring of 1780 he recast it in "free iambics," and in the summer of 1781 he made a third draft of it. And still the text, hesitating between prose and poetry, was unsatisfactory. With other unfinished works it had to wait for the serenity of mind and the resurgence of spirits made possible by the author's Italian journey, and then, in latter 1786, in Rome, the fourth and final version was written in the limpidly pure blank verse, the practice of which Goethe had just mastered.

Despite these unrhymed pentameters in lieu of the French classical hexamater couplets, the dramatic procedures of this play come closer to Racine than to Euripides. In its overall effect it most nearly resembles Racine's *Bérénice,* save that there is no talk of *la belle passion.* King Thoas's suit to his beautiful prisoner is that of a lonely, middle-aged widower who has lost his only son; his love has about it a subdued urgency tempered by respect, even by awe. Necessarily retained from the ancient story are the elements of adventure in a strange land and hair-breadth escape, but these are relegated to the background in order to concentrate on an examination of conscience.

Among the five good persons who enact this drama no villain lurks. Each of the five is willing to harken to reason, to persuasion, and to the heart's prompting about what is humanly right. There are, however, five markedly different grades of capacity for such harkening. In the four males the moral sense is submerged under varying depths of self-will and violence. It is deepest buried within Pylades. Upward from him the reader may determine gradations, but, as is characteristic of Goethe, the perception of moral values is least obscured in the mind of the woman.

Crimes and passions of the past, together with the dark savagery still lingering in the people of Tauris, have combined to place these five good persons in a fearful dilemma. The play deals largely in alternate proposals as to what should be done in this dilemma. Toward the end of Act IV the priestess-sister is persuaded that the rescue of her brother and her own escape to her homeland are the objectives of supreme importance, to be achieved at all costs. She must and will deceive King Thoas, repaying his years of kindness and affection with a trick that will mortify him and all his nation. Expediency is all, since this barbarian king would never yield to the needs of strangers.

At that moment she recalls an ancient song of the Fates which tells of monstrous treachery perpetrated of old by her ancestor Tantalus and other Titans and of the eternity of punishment visited upon them. In Act V, rather than resort to the planned deceit and desperate action, she confesses the whole truth to King Thoas and calls upon his humanity to grant freely what she and her brother and her brother's friend most earnestly desire. In sadness and with suppressed anger the King sets his own will aside and holds back his unlimited power in order to give all three of them their liberty. Iphigenia's last plea is for forgiveness, and that plea the King also concedes.

Such is this drama which has never been welcome to box-offices and business managers, but which Thomas Mann ranked supreme among all the works of German literature.

IPHIGENIA IN TAURIS

A Play in Five Acts
(*Ein Schauspiel*)

1776–1787

CHARACTERS

IPHIGENIA
THOAS, King of the Taurians
ORESTES
PYLADES
ARKAS

The scene is a grove in front of the temple of Diana.
The time is a few years after the Trojan War.

THE HOUSE OF TANTALUS

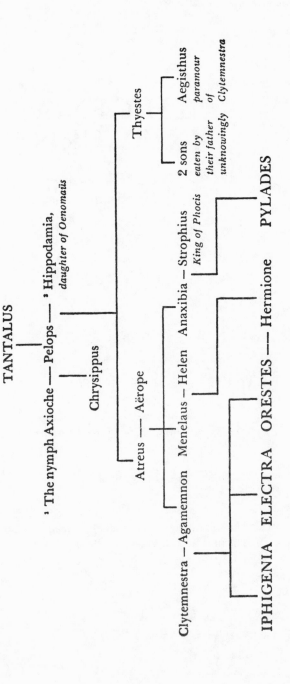

ACT I

IPHIGENIA: Out here into your shadows, stirring treetops
Of this thick-branching, ancient, sacred grove,
As in the goddess' own hushed sanctuary,
I even now step with a shuddering awe
As though my foot fell here for the first time,
And here my spirit cannot feel at home.
These many years I have been hidden here
By a high will unto which I submit,
Yet I am ever, as at first, a stranger.
For, ah! the sea divides me from my loved ones,   10
And by the shore I stand whole long days through
With my soul searching for the Grecian land,
And only muted tones amid its roaring
Does the wave bring in answer to my sighs.
Alas for one who far from parents, brothers,
And sisters leads a lonely life! From his
Lips grief will eat the closest joys away,
His thoughts forever go a-swarming off
Toward the halls of his father, where the sun
Revealed the heavens first to him and where   20
At play those born with him bound firm and firmer
The tender bonds that knit them to each other.
I do not argue with the gods; and yet
The lot of women is a piteous thing.
At home or in the wars a man commands,
And in far lands he still can make his way.
Possession gives him pleasure, victory crowns him.
A death with honor will be his at last.
How close restricted is a woman's joy!

415

Even obeying a harsh husband is   30
A duty and a comfort; but how wretched
If hostile fate drives her to alien lands!
Thus Thoas holds me here, a noble man,
In solemn, sacred bonds of slavery.
O with what shame it is that I acknowledge
I serve thee, Goddess, with a mute reluctance,
Who rescued me! My life was to have been
Consigned to thee in voluntary service.
I have, moreover, trusted in thee ever
And now trust in thee still, Diana, who   40
Didst take me in thy holy, gentle arm,
The outcast daughter of the mightiest king.
Yes, Zeus's daughter, if thou didst conduct
That lofty man whom thou didst plunge in anguish
Demanding his own daughter so that he,
The godlike Agamemnon, brought his dearest
Possession to thy altar, if thou didst
Guide him with fame from Troy's walls overthrown
Back to his fatherland, preserving for him
His spouse and treasures, Electra and his son:—   50
Then bring me too back to my own at last
And save me, whom thou once didst save from death,
From this life here as well, a second death!

[Enter Arkas.]

ARKAS: The king has sent me here with offer of
   His salutation to Diana's priestess.
   This is the day when Tauris thanks its goddess
   For freshly gained and wondrous victories.
   I hasten in advance of king and army
   To say that he and they are now approaching.

IPHIGENIA: We are prepared to meet them worthily.   60
   Our goddess too with favoring glance expects
   The welcome sacrifice from Thoas' hand.

ARKAS: Would that I also found the worthy and
   Most reverend priestess' glance as well, your glance,

O holy virgin, brighter and more radiant,
A good sign to us all. But grief still shrouds
Your inmost being up mysteriously.
In vain these many years we have been waiting
For one confiding word out of your heart.
As long as I have known you in this place,   70
This is the glance at which I always shudder,
And still your soul remains close riveted
As though with bonds of iron in your bosom.

IPHIGENIA: As best becomes an exile and an orphan.

ARKAS: Do you feel you are exiled here and orphaned?

IPHIGENIA: Can foreign lands become our native land?

ARKAS: Your native land is now quite foreign to you.

IPHIGENIA: And that is why my heart is never healed.
In earliest youth, when yet my soul was scarcely
Attached to father, mother, brother, sisters,—   80
Those newer scions, lovely and together,
Were seeking to grow skywards from the base
Of ancient trunks,—an alien curse descended
Unfortunately upon me, severing me
From those I loved and rending that fair bond
In twain with iron fist. Best joy of youth
Was therewith lost and all the thriving growth
Of early years. Even in rescue, I
Was but a shadow of myself, and joy
Of life will not bloom fresh in me again.   90

ARKAS: If you term yourself so ill-fortuned there,
Then I may also say you are ungrateful.

IPHIGENIA: My thanks were always yours.

ARKAS: But not true thanks,
For sake of which a kindly deed is done,
And not the cheerful glance that shows a host
A life contented and a willing heart.
These many years ago when a profoundly
Mysterious fate brought you here to this temple,
King Thoas came with favor and respect

To greet you as one whom the gods had sent   100
And these shores were then kind and friendly to you
Which formerly held terrors for all strangers
Because no one set foot within our kingdom,
Till you, who did not perish by old custom
A bloody victim on Diana's stairs.

IPHIGENIA: Life is not merely freedom to draw breath.
What kind of life is this which, like a shadow
By its own grave, I can but pine away
Here in this holy place? Am I to call it
A life of cheerful self-awareness when   110
Each day, once it is dreamed away in vain,
Prepares us for those dreary days spent by
The mournful throng of the departed dead
On Lethe's shore in self-forgetfulness?
A useless life is early death; this fate
Of women is, above all others, mine.

ARKAS: This noble pride in self-dissatisfaction
I can forgive, much as I pity you;
It robs you of the joy of life. You have
Accomplished nothing here since your arrival?   120
Who was it lightened the king's sombre mind?
And who from year to year has kept suspended
By soft persuasion that old cruel custom
Whereby all strangers lost their lives in blood
Upon Diana's altar and so often
Delivered captives from their certain death
To be returned to their own native lands?
Has not Diana, far from being angered
By lack of those old bloody sacrifices,
In generous measure heard your gentle prayer?   130
On joyous wings does Victory not attend
Upon the army? indeed, outfly its coming?
And do we not all feel a better lot
Now that the king, who so long led us wisely
And bravely, also finds a pleasure in

The mildness of your presence and has lightened
Our silent duty of obedience?
You term it to no purpose that a balm
Is shed on thousands from your very being?
That for a people, to whom a god brought you,   140
You are the fount of fresh good fortune and
On this inhospitable shore of death
You give the stranger rescue and return?

IPHIGENIA: This little soon fades from the view directed
Forward toward how much still is left to do.

ARKAS: You praise one who says what he does is naught?

IPHIGENIA: It is blameworthy to weigh out one's actions.

ARKAS: I too blame one too proud to grant true worth,
As much as one who idly vaunts false value.
Believe me and give ear to a man's word   150
Who is sincere in his devotion to you:
When the king speaks with you today, then make
What he desires to say more easy for him.

IPHIGENIA: Your every kindly word alarms me more.
I have eluded his proposal often.

ARKAS: Think what you do and what can profit you.
Since his son's death the king confides in few
Of his own people any more, and in
Those few no longer as he used to do.
He looks with envy on all sons of nobles   160
As his successor; and a lonely, helpless
Old age he stands in dread of, possibly
Bold insurrection and an early death.
Speech is not held in high esteem by Scythians,
By the king least of all. He, who is only
Accustomed to give orders and to act,
Has no skill in directing a discussion
With subtlety and slowly toward his purpose.
Do not then make it difficult for him
By a reserved denial or a willful   170
Misunderstanding. Go half way to meet him.

IPHIGENIA: Am I to speed the thing that threatens me?
ARKAS: Do you refer to his suit as a threat?
IPHIGENIA: It terrifies me more than all the others.
ARKAS: At least meet his affections with your trust.
IPHIGENIA: If he first sets my soul free of its fear.
ARKAS: Why do you hide your ancestry from him?
IPHIGENIA: Because a secret well befits a priestess.
ARKAS: Nothing should be a secret from the king.
   And though he does not ask it outright, still   180
   He feels it, feels it deep in his great soul,
   That you hold carefully aloof from him.
IPHIGENIA: He feels annoyance and ill-will toward me?
ARKAS: So it would almost seem. True, he says nothing
   Of you to me; yet certain random words
   Have shown me that his soul has firmly fixed
   On the desire of marrying you. O do
   Not, do not turn him back upon himself,
   Lest ill-will should mature within his bosom
   And horrify you and too late you think   190
   Regretfully of my well-meant advice.
IPHIGENIA: What? Can the king be planning to do what
   No noble man should think of doing if
   He loves his name and reverence for the gods
   Restrains his heart? Does he intend to drag
   Me from the altar to his bed by force?
   Then I will call on all the gods, and on
   Diana most of all, the strong-willed goddess,
   Who to her priestess, virgin unto virgin,
   Will surely lend protection readily.   200
ARKAS: Be still! Impetuous new blood does not
   Incite the king to perpetrate that sort
   Of youthful rashness. But, as his mind works,
   I fear a different harsh decision from him,
   Which he will carry out implacably,
   For his stern soul is not one to be swayed.
   Trust him, therefore, I beg you, and be grateful,

If there is nothing further you can give him.

IPHIGENIA: O tell me what else may be known to you.

ARKAS: Learn that from him. I see the king approaching.   210
　　You honor him, and your own heart bids you
　　Be friendly and confiding as you meet.
　　A kindly word from women goes a long
　　Way with a noble man.

IPHIGENIA (*alone*):　　　　I do not see
　　How I can follow this good man's advice,
　　Although I gladly do my duty in
　　Returning kind words to the king for his
　　Kind deed. I only hope that I can speak
　　With truthfulness and please the mighty man.
　　　　　　　　[*Enter Thoas.*]
　　May royal blessings be yours from the goddess!   220
　　And may she grant you victory and fame
　　And riches and well-being of your people
　　And the fulfillment of all proper wishes!
　　That, ruling providently over many,
　　You also know rare fortune more than many.

THOAS: It would suffice me if my people praised me;
　　Others enjoy what I accomplish more
　　Than I do. The most fortunate of men,
　　Be he a king or commoner, is he
　　Whose welfare is assured in his own home.   230
　　You shared in my profoundest sorrow when
　　My son, my last one and my best, was taken
　　Away from me by swords of enemies.
　　As long as vengeance occupied my mind,
　　I did not sense my house's emptiness;
　　But now that I have come back satisfied,
　　Their kingdom overthrown, my son avenged,
　　Nothing is left at home to give me pleasure.
　　The glad obedience which formerly
　　Would flash toward me from every eye is now   240
　　Dulled with displeasure and with discontent.

Each man thinks of the future, and obeys
Me, childless as I am, because he must.
Today I come into this temple where
I often came, to sue for victory
And to give thanks for victory. One wish
Of old I bear within my bosom, which
To you is neither strange nor unexpected:
I hope, both to my people's blessing and
My own, to take you home with me as bride.   250

IPHIGENIA: Too much you offer one you little know,
    O king. The fugitive stands here abashed
    Before you, who upon this shore asks nothing
    But rest and safety, which you have bestowed.

THOAS: This keeping secret of your origin
    From me and from the lowliest of mine
    Would not be right or good in any nation.
    This shore strikes fear in foreigners; the law
    Demands it and necessity. But you
    Who here enjoy a sacred privilege,   260
    Who are an alien well received by us,
    Passing your days at will and inclination,
    From you I hoped for such trust as a host
    May rightly look for in return for his.

IPHIGENIA: If I concealed my parents' names and my
    Descent, O king, it was embarrassment
    And not mistrust. For if, perhaps, you knew
    Who stands before you and what head curse-laden
    It is you feed and shelter, horror would
    Seize your great heart with an unwonted shudder   270
    And then, instead of offering me half of
    Your throne, you would drive me before the time
    Out of your kingdom, thrusting me perhaps
    Before the glad return among my own
    And the end of my wanderings are destined,
    Into the misery that everywhere
    With cold and alien hand of horror waits

For every wanderer exiled from home.

THOAS: No matter what the gods' plan for you is,
    Or what they destine for you and your house,   280
    Still, since you have lived here among us and
    Enjoyed the sacred privilege of a guest,
    I have not lacked for blessings from above.
    It would be difficult persuading me
    That in you I protect a guilty head.

IPHIGENIA: The good deed, not the guest, confers the blessings.

THOAS: Things done for wicked people bring no blessing.
    So put an end to silence and refusal;
    It is no unjust man who asks this of you.
    The goddess trusted you into my hands;   290
    To me you were as sacred as to her.
    Let her sign be in future my law also.
    If you can ever hope to go back home,
    I will pronounce you free of all demands.
    But if the way is closed to you forever,
    Or if your race is exiled or has been
    Wiped out by some immense calamity,
    By more than one law you belong to me.
    Speak freely! And you know I keep my word.

IPHIGENIA: Unwillingly the tongue is loosened from   300
    Its bonds of old in order to disclose
    At last a secret long kept silent. For,
    Once told, it leaves the deep heart's safe-kept dwelling
    Never to return, and then works harm,
    Or, as the gods may wish it, serves some end.
    Hear: I am of the race of Tantalus.

THOAS: How calmly you make that momentous statement.
    You call your ancestor one whom the world
    Knows as a man once highly honored by
    The gods? Can it be that same Tantalus   310
    Whom Jupiter once had at board and council,
    In whose age-tempered utterances fraught with
    Deep meaning gods themselves once took delight

As in the utterances of oracles?
IPHIGENIA: He is that very one. But gods should not
　Associate with men as with their peers.
　The race of mortals is too weak by far
　Not to grow dizzy at unwonted heights.
　Ignoble he was not, nor yet a traitor;
　But too great for a slave, and for a fellow　　　　　320
　Of the great Thunderer a mere mortal man.
　Thus his crime too was human, and their judgment
　Severe. The poets sing: Excess of pride
　And treachery cast him from Jove's own table
　In shame down into ancient Tartarus.[1]
　Alas, and all his kin then bore their hatred!
THOAS: For their ancestors' guilt or for their own?
IPHIGENIA: The mighty breast and vigorous strength of Titans
　Were, to be sure, the certain heritage
　Both of his sons and grandsons; but the god　　　　330
　Affixed a bond of bronze around their brows.
　Wisdom and patience, sense and moderation,
　These he concealed from their shy, sullen eyes,
　So each desire of theirs became a frenzy,
　And limitless their frenzy raged abroad.
　Already Pelops of the mighty will
　And Tantalus' beloved son, by murder
　And treachery had won the fairest wife,
　Hippodamia, Oenomaüs' child.[2]
　She to her spouse's joy bore him two sons,
　Atreus and Thyestes. Jealously
　They marked their father's love to his first son,[3]
　Who had sprung from an earlier marriage bed.
　United in their hatred, this pair then
　Committed fratricide as their first deed.
　The father thought Hippodamia was
　The murderess, and fiercely he demanded
　To have his son again from her, and she
　Took her own life—[4]

THOAS: You stop? Continue talking.
  Do not regret your confidences. Speak.   350
IPHIGENIA: Happy the man who can recall his fathers
  With joy, who with their deeds and greatness can
  Regale a hearer, and with quiet pleasure
  Beholds himself at the close of that fair
  Succession. For a house does not produce
  The monster or the demigod straight off;
  Only the evil or the good in series
  Will bring about the horror of the world
  Or the world's joy.—Upon their father's death
  The city was ruled jointly by Thyestes   360
  And Atreus. But that harmony could not
  Endure for long. Thyestes soon dishonored
  His brother's bed. In vengeance Atreus drove
  Him from the kingdom. Long before and slyly,
  Thyestes, plotting grievous deeds, had kidnapped
  One of his brother's sons and reared him as
  His own with fond cajolery. He filled
  His heart with rage and vengeance and then sent
  Him to the royal city so that he
  Might in his fancied uncle slay his father.   370
  The youth's intention was found out; the king
  Had the assassin fiercely punished, thinking
  It was his brother's son whom he was killing.
  Too late he learned who was expiring under
  The torture there before his glutted eyes;
  To clear the lust for vengeance from his bosom
  He silently thought up a deed unheard of.
  With feigned indifference, calmness, and appeasement
  He lured his brother with two sons of his
  Back to the kingdom, seized and slaughtered them,   380
  And set the loathsome, grisly dish before
  Their father at the first of their repasts.
  And when Thyestes had been sated with
  His own flesh, and there fell a gloom on him,

And he inquired about his children, thinking
He heard their voices and their footfall at
The doorway, Atreus, grinning, flung
The heads and feet of the slain lads before him,—
You turn away your face, O king, in horror!
So did the sun avert his countenance   390
And turn his car from its eternal track.
Such is your priestess's ancestral line;
And many are the dire fates of these men,
And many are the deeds of minds confused,
Which Night enfolds in heavy pinions so
That we peer only into dreadful twilight.

THOAS: Leave them concealed in silence too. Enough
Of horrors! Tell me by what miracle
It was that you sprang from that savage race.

IPHIGENIA: Atreus' eldest son was Agamemnon: 400
He is my father. I can say of him,
However, that from earliest times I have
Found him to be the paragon of men.
To him I was born as first fruit of love
By Clytemnestra, and Electra next.
Serenely ruled the king, and to the house
Of Tantalus was granted rest long missed.
But still my parents' happiness lacked for
A son, and scarcely was that wish fulfilled,
So that Orestes now, the favorite,   410
Was growing up between two sisters, when
Fresh evil came upon the carefree house.
Report has reached you of the war which brought
The total might of princes from all Greece
To camp about the walls of Troy avenging
Rape of the fairest woman. Whether they
Have won the city and attained their goal
Of vengeance, I have never heard. My father
Commanded the Greek army. But at Aulis
They waited for a favoring wind in vain;   420

Diana, angered at their mighty leader,
Held back the eager men, demanding through
The lips of Calchas the king's eldest daughter.
They lured me and my mother to the camp;
They dragged me to the altar and consigned
My head unto the goddess.—She was appeased;
She did not want my blood and wrapped me in
A cloud to rescue me;[5] inside this temple
I first regained my senses out of death.
I am that very same Iphigenia,   430
Grandchild of Atreus, Agamemnon's daughter,
The goddess' own, now speaking with you here.

THOAS: I give no greater preference or trust
To you as princess than to you as stranger.
I make my first proposal once again:
Come, follow me, and share in what I own.

IPHIGENIA: How can I venture such a step, O king?
Does not the goddess who delivered me
Have sole right to my consecrated life?
She chose this place of refuge for me here   440
And she preserves me for a father, whom
She punished quite enough by the mere semblance,
Perhaps for his old age's fairest joy.
Perhaps my glad return is close at hand;
And I, in disregard of her plan, should
Have entered into bonds against her will?
Were I to stay, I would ask for a sign.

THOAS: The sign is that you still are tarrying here.
Do not seek out excuses of that kind.
Much talk is useless to express refusal;   450
The other party only hears the No.

IPHIGENIA: Those were not words intended to deceive.
I have shown you my heart's profoundest depths.
Does your own heart not tell you how I must
Yearn with distressful feelings for my father,
My mother, and my sister and my brother?

So that amid the ancient halls, where sadness
Still sometimes whispers my name softly, joy,
As for a new-born child, may twine the fairest
Of garlands from one pillar to another?   460
O if you would but send me there in ships!
You would give me and all of us new life.

THOAS: Go back, then! Do as your heart bids you do,
  And pay no heed to the voice of good counsel
  And reason. Be a woman through and through,
  Yield to the impulse that without restraint
  Now takes and pulls you one way or the other.
  Once a desire has blazed up in their bosoms,
  No sacred bond will keep them from betrayers
  Who lure them from their fathers' or their husbands'   470
  Devoted arms, however long proved loyal;
  And if the swift fire in their bosoms dies,
  It is in vain with faith and power that
  Persuasion's golden tongue will urge them on.

IPHIGENIA: Remember, king, your noble word! Is this
  The way that you return my confidence?
  You did seem ready to hear anything.

THOAS: I was not ready for the unexpected;
  But I ought to have thought of that: was I
  Not dealing with a woman, after all?   480

IPHIGENIA: Do not find fault, O king, with our poor sex.
  Not glorious like yours, but still not wholly
  Ignoble are the weapons of a woman.
  I am superior to you, believe me,
  In seeing more than you, your happiness.
  You, unfamiliar with yourself or me,
  Think closer ties will bring us happiness.
  In all good courage, as in all good will,
  You urge me to submit to your decision.
  And I here thank the gods for giving me   490
  The firmness not to enter into this
  Alliance of which they have not approved.

THOAS: No god speaks; it is your own heart that speaks.
IPHIGENIA: Through our hearts only do they speak to us.
THOAS: Do I not have the right to hear them too?
IPHIGENIA: The storm of passion drowns out their soft voices.
THOAS: The priestess, I suppose, hears them alone?
IPHIGENIA: The king should note them more than anyone.
THOAS: Your sacred office and ancestral right
  To Jove's own table bring you closer to   500
  The gods than me, the earth-born savage.
IPHIGENIA: Thus
  I pay for confidence you forced me to.
THOAS: I am but human, and we had best stop.
  But let my word still hold. Be priestess of
  The goddess, as she has selected you;
  Diana must forgive me though, for having
  Quite wrongly up to now and with bad conscience,
  Withheld her ancient sacrifices from her.
  No stranger comes with safety near our shore;
  He could in all times past be sure of death.   510
  Only, you, with a certain friendliness
  That touched me deeply sometimes as a tender
  Daughter's love and sometimes as the quiet
  Affection of a bride, had so involved me
  In magic toils that I forgot my duty.
  You had lulled all my senses into sleep,
  I did not hear the murmuring of my people;
  They now are loudly crying down upon me
  The guilt and blame for my son's early death.
  I will no longer for your sake restrain   520
  The mob that clamors for a sacrifice.
IPHIGENIA: I never asked you, for my sake, to do so.
  He has misunderstood the heaven-dwellers
  Who fancies them a-thirst for blood; he merely
  Attributes his own cruel will to them.
  Did not the goddess save me from her priest?
  My service meant more to her than my death.

THOAS: It ill beseems us to interpret and
    Distort the sacred usages to suit
    Our minds by Reason's facile variations.   530
    Do your own duty, and I will do mine.
    Two strangers that we have found hidden in
    The caves along our shore and who bring to
    My country nothing good, are in my hands.
    With them your goddess shall receive once more
    Her former, rightful sacrifice so long
    Withheld. I'll send them here; you know your duty.

                    [Exit.]

IPHIGENIA *(alone)*: Thou hast clouds, O rescuing goddess,
    Wherein to enwrap the guiltless pursued
    And to waft them out of the arms of   540
    Iron destiny over the sea,
    Over the widest stretches of earth,
    Or wherever thou deemest fitting.
    Wise art thou, and thou seest the future;
    The past is for thee not past and done,
    And thy gaze rests upon thine own,
    Just as thy light, the life of the nights,
    Rests and prevails over the earth.
    O withhold then my hands from blood!
    Blessing and peace it never brings;   550
    And the shape of one murdered by chance
    Will with terror stalk the sombre
    Unwilled murderer's evil hours.
    For the Immortals bear love unto
    The good and far-flung races of men,
    And they gladly lengthen fleeting
    Life for a mortal, willingly granting
    To him some small share of the cheering
    View of their own everlasting sky
    For a certain measure of time.   560

ACT II

Orestes. Pylades.

ORESTES: It is the path of death that we are treading;
  With every step my soul becomes more silent.
  When I implored Apollo to remove
  The ghastly company of the avenging
  Spirits[1] from my side, he seemed to promise
  Aid and deliverance in the temple of
  His much-loved sister who rules over Tauris,
  In godlike words of hope and certainty.
  And now it is fulfilled that all distress
  Is to be ended wholly with my life.   570
  How easy it becomes for me, whose heart
  Was crushed, whose sense was numbed by a god's hand,
  To bid the fair light of the sun farewell.
  If an end crowned with victory in battle
  Is not vouchsafed to Atreus' son and grandson,
  If like my forebears, like my father, I
  Must like a beast of sacrifice die bleeding,
  So be it! Better here before the altar
  Than off in some abandoned corner where
  The nets of murderers close of kin are spread.   580
  Till then leave me in peace, ye Subterraneans,
  Who like loosed dogs pursue and snuff the scent
  Of blood that oozes with my every footfall
  To make my path a trail for you to follow!
  Leave me, I will come down among you soon;
  The light of day shall not see you or me.
  The fair green carpet of the earth must not
  Become a sporting ground for ghosts. Down there

431

Below I'll come to you; there all are bound
By one fate to a dull and endless night.   590
But you, my Pylades, you wholly guiltless
Companion in my guilt and ban of exile,[2]
How loath I am to take you to that land of grief
Before your time! The matter of your life
Or death alone still gives me hope or fear.

PYLADES: I am not ready yet, like you, Orestes,
   To go down to that realm of shades. Through all
   The tangled paths that seem to lead down to
   Black night, I still keep thinking of how we
   Can wind our way back up to life again.   600
   I do not think death; I keep pondering, listening
   To see whether the gods are not preparing
   Some way and means of glad escape for us.
   Death, whether feared or not feared, still will come,
   Beyond our powers to resist it. When
   The priestess lifts her hand to cut our locks
   Of hair in sign of consecration, my
   Sole thought will be of rescue for us both.
   Raise up your soul out of this gloominess;
   By doubting, you bring danger on. Apollo's   610
   Pronouncement was: a sister's sanctuary
   Contains your hope and comfort and return.
   The words of gods are not ambiguous,
   As downcast people in their gloom imagine.

ORESTES: It was already round my tender head
   My mother cast the darkling veil of life,
   And thus I grew to manhood, the image of
   My father, and my silent glance was bitter
   In its reproach to her and to her lover.
   How often, when beside the fire Electra,   620
   My sister, would be sitting in the hall,
   I used to crowd up sorrowing against
   Her lap and stare with great eyes up at her
   As she shed bitter tears. Then she would tell

Me many things about our noble father;
How much I longed to see him, be with him!
Now I would wish myself to Troy, now wish
Him home. The day came—
PYLADES: O, let hellish spirits
Converse nocturnally about that hour!
May recollections of fair times give us   630
New strength for fresh careers of heroism.
The gods have need of many a good man
To do their service on this earth. And they
Have reckoned on you also; they did not
Allow you to accompany your father
When he unwillingly went down to Orcus.
ORESTES: O would that I had clasped his garment-hem
And followed him.
PYLADES: They who saved you watched out
For me as well; for what would have become
Of me, had you not lived, I can't imagine,   640
Because since childhood I have lived and only
Care to live with you and for your sake.
ORESTES: Do not remind me of those splendid days[3]
When your house gave me sanctuary and
Your noble father wisely and with kindness
Took care of the young blossom half-benumbed;
When you, an ever blithe companion, like
A light and many-colored butterfly
Around a sombre flower, every day
Would dart in new and playful life about me   650
And put your merriment into my soul,
Till I, forgetting my distress, would revel,
Swept off with you into vivacious youth.
PYLADES: My life began when I began to love you.
ORESTES: Say rather: "my distress," and you speak truly.
That is the worrisome thing about my fate,
That I, like an infected outcast, bear
Death and a secret sorrow in my bosom;

Let me but come to the most wholesome place,
And straightway all around me blooming faces　　　　　660
Take on the painful traces of slow death.

PYLADES:　I would, Orestes, be the first to die
That death, if your breath ever spread contagion.
Am I not full of joy and spirit still?
And joyousness and love are wings that soar
To mighty deeds.

ORESTES:　　　　　To mighty deeds? Yes, I
Recall the time when we saw them before us!
When we together often coursed the game
Through hills and valleys, hoping some day we,
In breast and hand our lofty forebears' equal,　　　　670
Would hunt for monsters with our clubs and swords
And would pursue upon the trail of robbers;
Then in the evening we would sit beside
The broad sea gently leaning on each other
As waves came playing softly to our feet
And as the world so wide before us lay;
Then one of us would sometimes grasp his sword
And future deeds would come out thronging from
The night around us countless as the stars.

PYLADES:　The work is endless that the soul burns to　　680
Accomplish. We would like to do each deed
As grandly as it will grow and become
When after lapse of years through lands and races
The tongues of poets have increased and told it.
They sound so fine, the things our fathers did,
When, resting in the quiet evening shadows,
Youth drinks them in to the tones of a harp;
And what we do is, as it was for them,
Mere toil and idle botchwork.
Thus we pursue the thing that flees before us　　　　690
And give the path no heed that we are treading
And hardly see the footprints of our forebears
And traces of their earthly life before us.

It is their shades we always hasten after,
Which godlike in some further distance crown
The peaks of mountains on a golden cloud.
I set no store by any man who thinks
About how nations might perhaps exalt him.
But give thanks to the gods, O youth, for their
Accomplishing so much through you so soon.   700
ORESTES: When they bestow a glad deed on a man
So he averts misfortune from his people,
Extends his kingdom, makes his frontiers safe,
And ancient enemies flee or are slain,
Then he has cause for thanks, because a god
Has granted him life's prime and final joy.
Me they selected as a butcher, as
My mother's murderer, though I did revere her,
And then, avenging shamefully a deed
Of shame, destroyed me with a nod. Believe me,   710
They meant to ruin Tantalus's house,
And I, the last thereof, shall not die free
Of guilt nor honorably.
PYLADES: The gods do not
Avenge the fathers' misdeeds on the son;
And each man, good or evil, carries off
His own reward with his own action. We
Are heirs to parents' blessings, not their curses.
ORESTES: Their blessing did not bring us here, I fancy.
PYLADES: And yet it was at least the high gods' will.
ORESTES: Their will it is, then, that destroys us.   720
PYLADES: Do as they bid you do, and wait. Once you
Have brought Apollo's sister to him and
Once both of them, united, dwell at Delphi,
Reverenced by a nobly thinking people,
That high pair will be graciously disposed
Toward you for that deed's sake, and they will rescue
You from the Subterraneans. None of them
Has so far dared come to this sacred grove.

ORESTES: Thus I will have at least a quiet death.

PYLADES: I think quite differently, and not without   730
   Some cleverness I have linked up things past
   With things to come and have it all worked out.
   Perhaps the great work has been ripening
   This long while in the planning of the gods.
   Diana longs to quit this harsh shore of
   Barbarians and their blood-stained human victims.
   We were appointed for that noble purpose,
   It is enjoined on us, and we have strangely
   Been brought by fate already to this portal.

ORESTES: With rare skill you entwine the gods' devices   740
   And your own wishes neatly into one.

PYLADES: What good is human shrewdness if it does
   Not harken heedfully to that high will?
   A noble man who has done many wrongs
   Is summoned by a god to some hard action
   And charged to end what seemed impossible
   To us. The hero triumphs, by atonement
   Serving the gods and this world that reveres him.

ORESTES: If I am destined to live on and act,
   Then from my laden brow let some god take   750
   Away the giddiness which on this path,
   Wet with my mother's blood, keeps dragging me
   Down toward the dead. And let him mercifully
   Dry up the spring that keeps bedashing me
   As it spurts up out of my mother's wounds.

PYLADES: Wait with more calm! You make the evil worse
   And take the Furies' office on yourself.
   Just let me do the thinking, and be quiet.
   If our joint strength is needed for some action,
   Then I will call on you, and we will both   760
   Advance with well-planned daring to achieve it.

ORESTES: I hear Ulysses speaking.

PYLADES: Do not scoff.
   Each man must choose the hero after whom

He toils to scale the pathways up Olympus.
Allow me to acknowledge that, to me,
Cunning and shrewdness do not seem disgraceful
To any man who is bent on bold deeds.
ORESTES: I like one who is brave and yet straightforward.
PYLADES: Therefore I have not asked you for advice.
  One step already has been taken. From   770
  Our guards I have cajoled much information.
  I know there is a strange and godlike woman
  Who has been holding this blood-law in check;
  A pure heart, prayer, and incense are the things
  She offers to the gods. This kindly woman
  Is much extolled; they think she is descended
  From the race of the Amazons and that
  She has fled to escape some dire misfortune.
ORESTES: It seems that her enlightened sway lost force
  In the offender's presence, whom a curse   780
  Pursues and covers like a widespread night.
  The pious bloodlust sets the ancient custom
  Free of its check in order to destroy us.
  The savage notions of the king will kill us;
  A woman can not save us if he rages.
PYLADES: Lucky for us it is a woman! Men,
  Even the best of them, become enured
  To cruelty, and in the long run make
  A law out of the thing which they abhor,
  Grow harsh from habit and unrecognizable.   790
  A woman will stand fast by one decision
  That she has made. You may more surely count
  On her in good things as in evil.—Quiet!
  She comes. Leave me alone with her. I dare
  Not name our names to her at once or trust
  Our fate to her without reserve. Go now,
  I'll seek you out before she talks to you.

        [*Exit Orestes.*
        Enter Iphigenia.]

IPHIGENIA: Declare, O stranger, whence you have come here.
   It seems to me I should compare you rather
   To a Greek than to any Scythian.[4]   800
               (*She removes his chains.*)
   The freedom I give you is ominous,
   And may the gods avert what now impends!
PYLADES: O lovely voice! O welcome, welcome sound
   Of one's maternal tongue in a strange country!
   The blue hills of my fathers' harbor I,
   A captive, see before my eyes again,
   Welcome anew. And of this joy let me
   Assure you: I too am indeed a Greek.
   I had forgotten for a moment how
   Much I have need of you, and I allowed   810
   My mind to dwell on your august appearance.
   O tell me, if some destiny has not
   Sealed up your lips, from which one of our houses
   It is you trace your godlike ancestry.
IPHIGENIA: The priestess, chosen and ensanctified
   By her own goddess, now addresses you.
   Let that suffice you; tell me who you are
   And what disastrously prevailing fate
   Has brought you to this place with your companion.
PYLADES: I can tell you quite easily what evil   820
   Pursues us with its tedious company.
   O if you could grant us with equal ease
   The cheering glance of hope, exalted lady!
   We are from Crete, and sons of King Adrastus:
   I am the younger, Cephalus by name,
   And he Laodamas, the eldest of
   The house. Between us was a middle brother,
   Harsh and wild, who in the earliest play
   Of youth already spoiled our joy and concord.
   We quietly obeyed our mother's word   830
   As long as our sire's strength fought before Troy;
   But once he had come, booty-laden, home

And soon thereafter died, we brothers were
At odds for kingdom and inheritance.
The eldest had my preference. He slew
Our brother. For that blood-guilt he is driven
With vehemence by the Fury round about.
But to this savage shore we have been sent
By Delphian Apollo with high hope.
Within his sister's temple he bade us   840
Expect to find the blessed hand of help.
As you know, we were captured and brought here
And marked for you as sacrificial victims.

IPHIGENIA: Troy fell? Dear man, assure me that it did.

PYLADES: It fell. May *you* assure us of deliverance!
And hasten the assistance that a god
Has promised us. Have pity on my brother.
O speak some words of kindness to him soon.
But spare him when you speak to him, I beg
You earnestly, for he is easily   850
Disturbed and shaken to his inmost being
By joy and sorrow and by memories.
A feverish madness sometimes comes upon him
And his free, noble mind on those occasions
Becomes the prey of the tormenting Furies.

IPHIGENIA: As great as your misfortune is, I urge you:
Forget it until you have satisfied me.

PYLADES: The lofty city, which for ten long years
Resisted the whole army of the Greeks,
Lies now in ruins, not to rise again.   860
But many graves of our best men make us
Recall the shore of the barbarians.
Achilles lies there with his handsome friend.

IPHIGENIA: So you divine forms too have turned to dust!

PYLADES: And Palamedes, Telamonian Ajax,
They never saw their fatherland again.

IPHIGENIA: He does not speak about my father, does
Not name him with the slain. He is alive, then?

And I will see him. O take hope, dear heart!

PYLADES: But blessèd are the thousands who there died   870
　　The bittersweet death at their foemen's hands;
　　For dismal horrors and a dreary end
　　For those returning home a hostile and
　　An angry god bestowed instead of triumph.
　　But does the voice of humankind not reach you?
　　To utmost distances it bears the news
　　Of the unheard-of things that happened then.
　　Can it be possible the grief that fills
　　Mycenae's halls with sighs reiterated
　　Should be a secret from you?—Clytemnestra,   880
　　With Ægisthus' help, ensnared her spouse
　　The day of his return and murdered him!—
　　Yes, you hold that king's house in reverence!
　　I see your bosom vainly fights against
　　This unexpected, monstrous news I tell.
　　Are you the daughter of a friend of theirs?
　　Or were you born adjacent to that city?
　　Do not conceal it, and bear me no grudge
　　For having been the first to tell this horror.

IPHIGENIA: Speak on. How was the fearful deed committed?   890

PYLADES: The day of his arrival, when the king,
　　Refreshed and soothed, stepped from his bath and asked
　　To have his garment from his spouse's hand,
　　The wicked woman cast around his shoulders,
　　Around his head, a many-folded web
　　That artfully entangled its broad meshes;
　　And as he strove in vain to disengage
　　Himself as from a net, Ægisthus struck him,
　　The traitor, and enwrapped thus in a shroud
　　The mighty king descended to the dead.   900

IPHIGENIA: And what reward was the accomplice's?

PYLADES: A bed and kingdom he already had.

IPHIGENIA: So wicked lust inspired the shameful deed?

PYLADES: And the profound sense of an old revenge.

IPHIGENIA: And what offense had the king given *her*?

PYLADES: By such a grievous deed that, if there were
 Excuse for murder, she would be excused.
 To Aulis he enticed her, and since some
 Divinity denied the Greeks their sailing
 By violence of winds, he brought his daughter,   910
 His eldest-born, Iphigenia, up
 Before Diana's altar, and she died
 A victim for the welfare of the Greeks.
 They say that an aversion was thereby
 Stamped so deep in her heart that she acceded
 To love-suit from Ægisthus and herself
 Enmeshed her husband in the nets of ruin.

IPHIGENIA (*veiling her face*):
 It is enough. You will see me again.
     [*Exit.*]

PYLADES (*alone*): The fate of this king's house seems to have left her
 Profoundly moved. Whoever she may be,   920
 She probably herself once knew the king
 And was, to our good fortune, sold here from
 Some noble family. Be still, dear heart,
 And let us with good cheer and prudently
 Steer toward the star of hope that gleams for us. (925)

ACT III

Iphigenia. Orestes.

IPHIGENIA: Unhappy man, I loose your fetters now
In token of a still more painful fate.
The freedom that this sanctuary grants
Is, like the bright and final glimpse of life
For one far gone in illness, a sign of death.   930
I still can not and must not tell myself
That you are lost! How could I consecrate
The two of you with murderous hand to death?
And no one whosoever dares to touch
Your heads as long as I am priestess of
Diana. But if I refuse my duty
Which the incensed king now demands of me,
He will choose one of my attendant maidens
As my successor, after which I can
Assist you only with my ardent wish.   940
O worthy countryman, the lowliest
Of knaves that touched at our ancestral hearth
Is, in a foreign land, supremely welcome.
How can I show you joy enough and blessing,
Who bring to me the images of heroes
Whom I had learned to reverence from childhood
And who refresh my inmost heart, bestowing
Upon it the touch of a fair, new hope?
ORESTES: Do you withhold your name and lineage
With prudent purpose, or may I know who   950
It is who comes like an immortal to me?
IPHIGENIA: You shall know who I am. But now tell me

What I learned only half way from your brother,
The deaths of those who, coming home from Troy,
Met with a harsh and unexpected fate
In silence at the thresholds of their dwellings.
I was brought young to this shore, it is true;
But well do I remember the shy glance
Which I once cast with wonderment and with
Timidity upon those heroes. They   960
Rode forth as though Olympus opened up
And sent the figures of illustrious ages
Of yore down to strike fear in Ilium.
And Agamemnon was most glorious
Of all! O tell me: he died, coming home,
By the craft of his wife and of Ægisthus?

ORESTES: He did.

IPHIGENIA: Alas for you, ill-starred Mycenae!
So Tantalus's grandsons have sown curse
On curse with full and frenzied hands! Like weeds
That wave their wild heads, all around them strewing   970
Seed thousandfold, they have begotten close-
Kinned murderers unto their children's children
For endless fury of retaliation!—
Disclose what in your brother's speech the darkness
Of fear so suddenly concealed from me.
How did the last son of that mighty race,
That gracious boy destined to be his father's
Avenger in times to come, how did Orestes
Escape the day of blood? Did a like fate
Enmesh him with Avernus' nets as well?[1]   980
Is he alive yet? Does Electra live?

ORESTES: They are alive.

IPHIGENIA: O lend me, golden Sun,
Your fairest rays and lay them down with thanks
Before Jove's throne! For I am poor and mute.

ORESTES: If you are linked by friendship to that house,
If you are bound to it by closer ties,

As is betrayed to me by your fair joy,
Then grip your heart and hold it fast! For sudden
Lapse back into the depths of grief must be
Unbearable for one in joy. I see   990
You only know of Agamemnon's death.
IPHIGENIA: Do I not have enough with that grim news?
ORESTES: You have heard no more than the half of horror.
IPHIGENIA: What else? Orestes and Electra live.
ORESTES: You have no fears for Clytemnestra, then?
IPHIGENIA: She can be saved by neither hope nor fear.
ORESTES: No, but her own blood did give her her death.
IPHIGENIA: Speak clearer words, leave me to guess to longer. 1000
Uncertainty is beating her dark wings
A thousandfold around my fearful head.
ORESTES: The gods, then, have selected me to be
The tidings-bearer of a deed which I
Should so much like to bury in the soundless
And hollow cave of night? Against my will
Your gracious lips compel me; they may even
Inquire for something painful and receive it.
    The day their father died, Electra hid
Her brother in a place of safety. Strophius,   1010
Their father's brother-in-law, gladly took him
And brought him up along with his own son,
Who, Pylades by name, formed fairest ties
Of friendship with the boy who thus arrived.
As they grew up, there grew up in their souls
A burning wish to avenge the king's death.
Unnoticed, garbed as foreigners, they reached
Mycenae, as if they were bringing there
The sad news of Orestes' death together
With his ashes.[2] There the queen received   1020
Them well; they gained their access to the house.
Orestes made himself known to Electra;
She fanned the fire of revenge in him
Which in his mother's sacred presence had

Died down to embers. Silently she led
Him to the place at which his father died
And where an old, faint trace of wantonly
Spilled blood still stained the frequently washed floor
With ominous and palely faded streaks.
She there described for him with tongue of fire   1030
Each circumstance of that outrageous deed,
Her own life spent in servile misery,
The haughtiness of the secure betrayers,
And all the dangers now impending for
The children of a mother turned stepmother;
She forced upon him there that ancient dagger
Which had in Tantalus's house raged grimly,
And Clytemnestra died by her son's hand.

IPHIGENIA: Immortal gods who live in blessedness
    The pure day long on clouds forever new,   1040
    Have you kept me apart these many years
    From human beings, held me so close to
    Yourselves, committed to my care the child-like
    Employment of attending to the holy
    Fire, and drawn my soul up like a flame
    In everlasting, pious clarity
    Unto your dwelling places, only so
    That I might feel my house's horrors later
    And more profoundly?—Tell me now of that
    Unfortunate! Tell me about Orestes!—   1050

ORESTES: O if one only could tell of his death!
    How foaming from the slaughtered woman's blood
    His mother's ghost
    Rose and cried unto Night's primeval daughters:
        "Let not the matricide get away!
        After the criminal! To you he is consecrate!"
    They stopped and harkened, and their hollow gaze
    Looked round about them with the eagle's craving.
    They stirred amid the blackness of their caves
    And out of corners came gliding their companions,   1060

Doubt and Remorse, so softly up to join them.
Before them rose a smoke of Acheron,[3]
And in its billowing cloud there spins forever
The image of the perpetrated deed
Bewilderingly around the guilty head.
And they with authorized destruction tread
The lovely ground of earth which gods have sown
And whence an ancient curse drove them long since.[4]
And their swift foot pursues the fugitive,
Allowing rest but to scare up anew.   1070

IPHIGENIA: Unhappy man, you are in a like case
And feel what that poor fugitive endures!

ORESTES: What are you saying? Why is my case like?

IPHIGENIA: Like him, a brother's murder weighs you down;
Your younger brother has already told me.

ORESTES: I cannot bear, great soul, that you
Should be deceived by an untrue report.
A stranger, wily and accustomed to
Deceit, may for another stranger weave
A web of lies to trip him; between *us*   1080
Let there be truth.
I am Orestes! and this guilty head
Is bending toward the pit and seeking death;
It shall be welcome in whatever form!
Whoever you may be, I wish you rescue;
I wish my friend the same—but not for me.
You seem to tarry here against your will.
Contrive your plan of flight, but leave me here.
Let my dead body hurtle from the cliff
And let my blood stream smoking to the sea   1090
And pass its curse to this barbarian shore!
May both of you go back home to fair Greece
And there begin a kindly life anew.
                    (*He withdraws.*)

IPHIGENIA: So thou dost come, Fulfillment, fairest daughter
Of mightiest Father, down at last to me!

How your form looms immense before me here;
My glance can scarcely reach up to your hands,
Which, filled with fruit and wreathèd garland-blessings,
Bring down to me the treasures of Olympus.
As kings are known by superfluity   1100
Of gifts—for to them that must seem but little
Which thousands find to be great wealth—so you,
Ye gods, are to be recognized by gifts
Long hoarded up and wisely held till ready.
For you alone know what can do us good,
You see the far-flung reaches of the future
When every evening's misted veil of stars
Conceals the prospect from us. Calmly you
Lend ear unto our supplications begging
So childishly for haste; but your hands never   1110
Pluck unripe the golden fruit of heaven;
And woe to him who in his obstinate
Impatience takes them and eats to his death
Of that sour food. O do not let this long
Awaited, scarcely dreamed-of happiness
Pass like the shade of a departed friend
Away from me in vain with tripled sorrow!
ORESTES (*who comes back to her*) :
　　If you are praying for yourself and Pylades,
　　Do not name my name with your other two.
　　You will not save the criminal whom you   1120
　　Have joined, and you will share his curse and pain.
IPHIGENIA: My destiny is closely linked with yours.
ORESTES: By no means! Let me go to death alone
　　And unaccompanied. If you hid me in
　　Your very veil, guilt-laden as I am,
　　You could not hide me from those sleepless ones;
　　Your presence, O immortal one, can only
　　Force them aside, not frighten them away.
　　They dare not tread this sacred forest's floor
　　With their audacious feet of crushing bronze;   1130

Yet from the distance here and there I hear
Their ghastly laughter. Wolves will wait that way
Around a tree in which a traveler
Has taken refuge. They lie in wait out there
Beyond; and if I were to leave this grove,
They would arise and shake their serpent-hair,
And stir the dust on every side, and drive
Their quarry on before them in his flight.

IPHIGENIA: Can you, Orestes, hear a friendly word?
ORESTES: No, save it up for some friend of the gods.   1140
IPHIGENIA: But they are giving you new light of hope.
ORESTES: Through smoke and vapor I see the dull shine
Of death's own river lighting me to hell.
IPHIGENIA: Have you Electra, just one sister only?
ORESTES: I knew that one; the eldest was, however,
Saved from our house's wretchedness in time
By kindly fate, though it seemed horrible
To us. O cease your questions and do not
Yourself join the Erinyes; they blow
The ashes from my soul maliciously   1150
And will not let the final embers of
My house's conflagration burn away
And die with me in silence. Must that fire,
Thus fanned deliberately and fed with sulphur
Of hell, burn my tormented soul forever?
IPHIGENIA: I bring sweet-scented incense to that flame.
O let love's pure breath, gently wafted, cool
The burning deep within your breast. Orestes,
My dear one, can you not hear what I say?
Has the attendance of the gods of terror   1160
So caused the blood to dry up in your veins?
Does some spell, turning you to stone, steal through
Your limbs as from the grisly Gorgon's head?⁵
O, if the voice of shed maternal blood
Can summon you with dull sound down to hell,
May not a stainless sister's word of blessing

Call down gods of assistance from Olympus?
ORESTES: It calls! It calls! Are you bent on my ruin?
Is there some vengeance-goddess hidden in you?
Who are you, you whose voice so hideously   1170
Turns back my inmost being on its depths?
IPHIGENIA: Your inmost being tells you who I am.
Orestes, it is I! Iphigenia!
I am alive!
ORESTES: What? You?
IPHIGENIA: My brother!
ORESTES: Leave me!
I warn you, do not touch these locks of mine!
As from Creusa's bridal raiment, fire[6]
Is struck and spread unquenchably from me.
Leave me! Like Hercules, I want to die
A death of shame, and closed within myself.
IPHIGENIA: You will not perish! O, if I could only   1180
Hear one calm word from you! Resolve my doubts
And let me also have some reassurance
Of happiness I have so long besought.
Both joy and sorrow sweep alternately
Across my soul. An awesome horror drives
Me back from the strange man, and yet my heart
Impels me mightily on toward my brother.
ORESTES: Is this Lyaeus' temple?[7] Is the priestess
Seized uncontrollably by holy frenzy?
IPHIGENIA: O hear me! Look at me! See how my heart   1190
After a long, long time is opening to
The bliss of kissing the head of the dearest
Person whom the world can hold for me,
Of clasping you within my arms, which were
Outstretched before to empty winds alone!
O let me! Let me! The eternal fountain
Does not more brightly pour down from Parnassus
From cliff to cliff into the golden valley
Than joy now flows up surging from my heart,

Surrounding me as with a blissful sea.   1200
Orestes! O my brother!
ORESTES: Lovely nymph,
  I do not trust you or your flattery.
  Diana asks that priestesses be stern
  And will avenge the profanation of
  Her holy place. Take your arm from my breast.
  And if you wish to love and save some youth
  And seek to offer him sweet happiness,
  Then turn your kind heart to my friend, a man
  More worthy. He is wandering along
  That path there on the cliff; go seek him out,   1210
  Direct him and spare me.
IPHIGENIA: Compose yourself,
  My brother, realize whom you have found!
  Rebuke your sister for pure joy of heaven,
  And not for reckless, guilty passion.
  O take illusion from his staring eyes,
  So that this moment of our utter joy
  Does not make us thrice wretched! She is here,
  Your long lost sister. For the goddess swept me
  Up from that altar and bore me to safety
  To her own sanctuary here. You are   1220
  A captive, marked for sacrificial slaughter,
  And find the priestess to be your own sister.
ORESTES: Unhappy, wretched woman! May the sun
  Then see the final horrors of our house!
  Electra is not here? so she could be
  Destroyed along with us and not prolong
  Her life for still more grievous fate and pain.
  Good, priestess: I will follow to the altar;
  Fratricide has been a common habit
  Among our ancient clan; and I thank you,   1230
  Gods, for deciding my extermination
  Without children. And let me warn you: do not
  Be too fond of the sun or of the stars;

Come, follow me to the dark realm below!
As dragons spawned amid the sulphur-pit
Attack their fellow-spawn and eat them up,
Our frenzied family destroy each other.
Come down with me still innocent and childless!
You gaze at me with pity? Do not do so!
It was with such looks Clytemnestra tried   1240
To gain some access into her son's heart;
But his arm, upraised, struck her to the heart.
My mother fell!—Appear, indignant ghost!
Close up your circle and advance, you Furies,
Be present at this welcome spectacle,
The last and ghastliest you have prepared!
Not hatred, not revenge now whets her dagger,
My loving sister is compelled to do
This deed. Do not weep. You are not to blame.
I have loved no one since my earliest years   1250
The way that I could love you, O my sister.
Yes, wield your knife, do not hold back at all,
Slash wide this breast and open up a path
For all the rivers that seethe here within.

           (*He collapses in exhaustion.*)

IPHIGENIA: This happiness and misery I cannot
   Endure alone.—Where are you, Pylades?
   Where can I come to find your help, dear man?

           (*She goes out searching.*)

ORESTES (*rousing from his stupor and getting up*):
   Another draught! Out of the waves of Lethe
   Hand me the last cool goblet of refreshment.
   Life's spasm will be quickly washed away   1260
   And my heart cleansed; my spirit soon will flow
   In quiet, yielding to oblivion's spring,
   To you, ye shades, into eternal mists.
   In your peace let the son of earth, much driven
   About, come graciously to quench his thirst!
   What whispering do I hear among the branches?

What sound comes rustling out of yonder twilight?
Already here to see the newest comer!
What is this host that splendidly rejoices
Together like a princely house assembled?   1270
They walk in peace, the old and young, and husbands
With wives; how godlike and how like each other
They seem to move, these forms. Yes, it is they,
The forebears of my house!—There with Thyestes
Walks Atreus in familiar conversation,
With the lads darting playfully around them.
Is there no enmity among you here?
Has vengeance been extinguished with the sunlight?
Then I too must be welcome, and I may
Join in the solemn pomp of your procession.   1280

Welcome, fathers! Orestes greets you,
The last man of all your race and line;
He has reaped that which you had sown:
With curses oppressed, he has descended.
But here every burden is lighter to bear:
Accept him, accept him into your midst!—
You, Atreus, I honor, and you, Thyestes;
Here we are all rid of enmity.—
Show me my father, whom I saw only
Once in my life!—Is it you, my father?   1290
And leading my mother so tenderly?
If Clytemnestra may give you her hand,
Orestes too may go up to her
And say to her: See your son!—
Both of you: see your son! Bid him welcome!
In our house during the earthly life
Greeting was murder's surest of watchwords,
Yet the olden race of Tantalus
Has its joys on the further side of the night.
"Welcome!" you cry, and receive me well.   1300
O take me to the old man, my ancestor.[8]
Where is the old one? Let me see him,

That beloved man and much revered
Who used to sit in the councils of gods.
You seem to shudder? You turn away?
What is it? The peer of gods is in pain?
Alas! The all-too-powerful ones
Have riveted horrible torments
To that hero's breast with iron chains.

(*Enter Iphigenia and Pylades.*)

Have you two also so soon come down?   1310
Hail, my sister! We still lack Electra:
May some kindly god quickly send us down
That *one* as well with gentle arrows.[9]
As for you, poor friend, I must pity you.
Come along, come along, to Pluto's throne
To greet our host as befits new guests!

IPHIGENIA: You brother-sister pair who for mankind
   Bring up the fair light over the broad heavens
   By day and night and who may not shine on
   The dead departed, save us, brother and sister!   1320
   Thou dost, Diana, love thy gracious brother
   Above all else that earth and sky can offer,
   And thou dost turn thy virgin countenance
   Toward his eternal light with silent yearning.
   O let not my sole, late-discovered brother
   Rave in the darkness of insanity.
   And if thy will, since thou hast hid me here,
   Be now accomplished, and if thou wilt give
   Thy blessèd help to me through him and also
   To him through me, release him from this curse   1330
   Before the precious time of rescue fades.
PYLADES: Now do you know us, and this sacred grove,
   And this light which does not shine on the dead?
   Do you feel your friend's and your sister's arms
   As they still firmly hold you up alive?
   Take stout grasp of us; we are not empty shades.

Mark now my word and listen closely! Pull
Yourself together! Every moment counts,
And our return depends on slender threads
Spun now, it seems, by a well-wishing Parca.   1340
ORESTES (to Iphigenia):
O let me for the first time with free heart
Experience pure delight clasped in your arms!
Ye gods, who walk abroad with flaming might
And as you walk consume the heavy clouds,
Who, graciously-severe, upon the earth
Pour down the long-sought rain in raging streams
Amid the thunder's voice and roar of winds,
Yet presently resolve the shuddering dread
Of men to blessings, changing anxious awe
To joyous glances and loud gratitude   1350
When, in the raindrops on fresh-quickened leaves,
The new sun is reflected thousandfold
And Iris of the lovely hues with light
Hand parts the grey veil of the final clouds,—
O let me too, clasped in my sister's arms
And at my dear friend's heart, enjoy and keep
With total gratitude what you grant me!
   The curse is lifting; my heart tells me so.
To Tartarus pass the Eumenides,[10]
I hear their going, and they close behind them   1360
The doors of bronze with far-receding thunder.
The earth exhales refreshing fragrance and
Invites me to its plains for full pursuit
Of life's delights and high accomplishment.
PYLADES: Do not let slip the precious time we have!
And may the wind that swells our sails be first
To bring our utter joy up to Olympus.
Come! We need swift decision and resolve.   (1368)

ACT IV

IPHIGENIA: Once the immortals destine
          Manifold confusions
          For one of the dwellers of earth,
          Once they ready for him
          Utterly shattering changes
          Over from joy to sorrow
          And from sorrow to joy,
          Then, be it close by his city
          Or on a distant shore,
          They undertake to provide
          Him with a tranquil friend,
          So that in hours of need   1380
          There may be help at hand.
Shed blessings, gods, upon our Pylades
And on whatever he may undertake.
He is the arm of the young man in battle,
The old man's shining eye in the assembly,
For his soul is at peace, and it contains
The sacred, inexhaustible endowment
Of calm; for one much buffeted about
He fetches help and counsel from its depths.
He tore me from my brother, at whom I   1390
Had gazed and gazed in wonderment, unable
To realize my happiness; I would not
Release him from my arms and did not sense
The nearness of the danger that surrounds us.
They now have gone to carry out their plan
Down by the sea, where, hidden in a cove,
The ship with their companions is awaiting

455

Their signal. They gave me a shrewd reply
With which to make the king an answer if
He sends more urgent orders to perform   1400
The sacrifice. Oh, I can see quite well
That I must let myself be guided like
A child. I never learned to use deceit
Or how to trick things out of people. Woe!
O woe to lies! They do not liberate
The heart as other words true-spoken do.
They do not comfort us, they strike alarm
In one who secretly invents them, and,
Like arrows sped and by some god averted
And made to miss their mark, they backward fly   1410
To strike the archer. Worry after worry
Wavers across my heart. Perhaps the Fury
Will fiercely seize my brother once again
Upon the ground of the unhallowed shore.
Will they discover them? I think I hear
Armed men approaching!—Here!—The messenger
With rapid step is coming from the king.
My heart pounds and my soul is clouded over
As I catch sight of that man's countenance
Whom I must now address with falsity.   1420

[Enter Arkas.]

ARKAS: Make haste now, priestess, with the sacrifice.
   The king is waiting and the people with him.
IPHIGENIA: I would obey your sign and do my duty,
   But that an unexpected obstacle
   Intrudes itself between me and compliance.
ARKAS: What is it that impedes the king's command?
IPHIGENIA: A chance event of which we are not master.
ARKAS: Declare it so I may report it to him,
   Because he has resolved on both men's deaths.
IPHIGENIA: Such is not yet the gods' determination.   1430
   The elder of these men is burdened with
   The crime of bloodshed of one close of kin.

The Furies hound him on his trail; indeed
The evil came upon him in the inner
Temple itself, and that pure place has now
Been desecrated by his presence. I
Am hurrying with my maidens to perform
A mystic consecration at the seashore
And dip the goddess' statue in fresh waves.
Let none disturb our silent journey there.   1440

ARKAS: I shall with speed inform the king of this
  New obstacle; do not begin the holy
  Task until he has sent his permission.

IPHIGENIA: But that is left up wholly to the priestess.

ARKAS: So odd a circumstance the king must know of.

IPHIGENIA: His counsel, like his command, will alter nothing.

ARKAS: The powerful are often asked for form's sake.

IPHIGENIA: Do not insist on what I should refuse.

ARKAS: Do not refuse a good and proper thing.

IPHIGENIA: I will comply if you make no delay.   1450

ARKAS: With speed I shall bring this report to camp,
  With speed I shall be back here with his answer.
  Would that I could take him a further message
  Resolving all the things that now distress us,
  For you have left a true man's word unheeded.

IPHIGENIA: I have done gladly all that I could do.

ARKAS: It still is not too late to change your mind.

IPHIGENIA: That simply does not lie within my power.

ARKAS: You term impossible what costs you effort.

IPHIGENIA: Your wish misleads you to think it possible.   1460

ARKAS: Will you so calmly risk all that you have?

IPHIGENIA: I have laid it in the hands of the gods.

ARKAS: They tend toward human means to rescue humans.

IPHIGENIA: All things depend upon their slightest hint.

ARKAS: And I tell you it lies within your hands.
  It is the king's own irritated feelings
  Alone that bring these strangers bitter death.
  The army long since weaned their minds away

From cruel sacrifice and bloodstained office.
Yes, many a man whom an adverse fate   1470
Has borne to alien shores, has learned indeed
How godlike is a friendly human face
Encountered by a hapless wanderer
Thus buffeted about on a strange border.
O do not fail us when you can so help us!
You easily can finish what was started,
For Gentleness, which comes in human form
Down from the skies, can nowhere build a kingdom
More readily than where, all dark and wild,
A new folk full of life and strength and courage,   1480
Abandoned to itself and dread misgivings,
Endures the heavy weight of human life.

IPHIGENIA: O do not agitate my soul, which you
    Can not prevail upon to do your will.

ARKAS: As long as time is left, one does not stint
    Exertion or a good word's repetition.

IPHIGENIA: You but distress yourself and cause me sorrow,
    And both in vain; therefore please leave me now.

ARKAS: It is to sorrow that I make appeal;
    Your sorrow is a friend and counsels well.   1490

IPHIGENIA: It seizes on my soul with vehemence,
    But yet without effacing my repugnance.

ARKAS: Can lofty souls feel such repugnance for
    A kindness that a noble man extends?

IPHIGENIA: Yes, when the noble man improperly
    Seeks, not my gratitude, but to possess me.

ARKAS: A person who feels no affection never
    Is at a loss for words of self-excuse.
    I shall inform the prince of what has happened.
    O if you only would rehearse within   1500
    Your soul how nobly he has treated you
    From your arrival to this present day!

                    [Exit.]

IPHIGENIA (alone): At this man's words I feel my heart reversed

At an unfitting moment suddenly
Within my bosom. I am terrified!—
For, as the tide in swift streams swelling breaks
Over the rocks that lie amid the sand
Along the shore, so was my inmost being
Submerged beneath a stream of joy. I held
What was impossible clasped in my arms.   1510
It seemed as if a cloud were softly closing
Again about me, lifting me above
The earth, and lulling me once more into
That slumber which the kindly goddess once
Disposed around my brow when her arm grasped
And rescued me.—My heart seized on
My brother with unprecedented force;
I harkened only to his friend's advice,
My soul urged forward only to save them.
And as a sailor gladly turns his back   1520
Upon the crags of a deserted island,
So Tauris lay behind me. Now the voice
Of this true man has reawakened me,
Reminding me that here too I abandon
Human beings. Doubly hateful to
Me is deception. O my soul, be still!
Do you begin to waver now and doubt?
The firm ground of your solitude you must
Abandon now! And once again embarked,
The waves will take you in their rocking, sad   1530
And fearful you will not know world or self.

[Enter Pylades.]

PYLADES: Where is she? so that in swift words I may
    Bring her the cheerful tidings of our rescue!
IPHIGENIA: You see me full of care and expectation
    Of the sure comfort that you promised me.
PYLADES: Your brother has been cured! We trod upon
    The rocky ground of the unhallowed shore
    And on the sand in cheerful conversation.

The grove remained behind us; we forgot it.
More splendidly and still more splendidly   1540
There blazed around his head with all its curls
The glorious flame of youth; his full eye shone
With hope and courage, and his free heart gave
Itself completely to the joy and pleasure
Of saving you, his rescuer, and me.

IPHIGENIA: All blessings be upon you! From your lips
Which have pronounced such good things may there never
Be heard the sound of sorrow or lament!

PYLADES: I bring still more, for splendidly attended
Like princes is Good Fortune's way of coming.   1550
We did find our companions there as well.
Within a rocky cove they had concealed
The ship and sat in sad expectancy.
They caught sight of your brother and they all
Leaped up exultant, urgently requesting
The hour of departure to be hastened.
Each hand is eager to lay hold of oars,
And from the land a light breeze even spread
Its lovely pinions, as we all observed.
So let us hurry! Lead me to the temple   1560
And let me get into the sanctuary
And reverently seize on our objective!
I will be able by myself to carry
The goddess' statue on my well-trained shoulders;
O how I yearn to bear that welcome burden!

>   (*As he is speaking these last words he goes
>   toward the temple without noticing that Iphi-
>   genia is not following him; finally he turns
>   around.*)

You stand and hesitate—you do not speak!
You seem confused! Some new calamity
Opposes our good fortune, then? Declare it!
Did you send to the king that shrewd reply

That we had previously agreed upon?   1570
IPHIGENIA: I did, dear man; and yet you will rebuke me.
  The sight of you already is reproof.
  The king sent me his messenger, and as
  You prompted me to speak, I spoke to him.
  He seemed to be amazed and urgently
  Desired first to report this strange rite to
  The king and to hear what his orders were;
  And I am now awaiting his return.
PYLADES: Alas for us! The peril hovers now
  About our heads anew! Why did you not   1580
  Hedge yourself prudently with priestess' rights?
IPHIGENIA: I never have used them as a concealment.
PYLADES: You will, pure soul, destroy yourself and us
  Together. O, why did I not foresee
  Such a predicament and teach you also
  How to elude such a demand!
IPHIGENIA: Blame me
  Alone, the fault is mine, I realize.
  And yet I could in no way else confront
  That man who reasonably and seriously
  Asked what my heart acknowledged was his right.   1590
PYLADES: The outlook grows more menacing; but all the same
  Let us not falter or betray ourselves
  By thoughtlessness and over-haste to action.
  Wait calmly for the messenger's return,
  And then stand firm, no matter what he brings:
  For ordering such rites of consecration
  Lies with the priestess and not with the king.
  If he demands to see the foreign man
  Who is so heavy burdened down with madness,
  Decline to do so, as if you had both   1600
  Of us well guarded in the temple. Give
  Us time to flee in haste and steal the holy
  Treasure from this harsh, unworthy people.
  Apollo sends the best of omens, and

Before we have fulfilled his stipulation,
He has fulfilled his promise like a god.
Orestes has been cured, he is set free!—
O take us, favoring winds, with him set free,
Unto the rocky isle the god inhabits,[1]
Thence to Mycenae, so it may revive,   1610
So from the ashes of the burned-out hearth
The household gods may joyously arise
And lovely fire may shine about their dwellings.[2]
Your hand shall be the first to strew the incense
Before them out of golden vessels. You
Shall bring well-being and new life across that threshold,
Atone the curse, and deck anew your people
In splendor with the blossoms of fresh life.

IPHIGENIA: When listening to you, beloved man,
My soul, touched by the sunlight of your words,   1620
Turns up and faces toward sweet consolation
The way a flower turns up toward the sun.
How precious are a friend's words of assurance;
A solitary person pines away,
For lack of that celestial strength, in silence.
For thoughts and resolutions ripen slowly
Within the bosom, and a loving person's
Presence would develop them with ease.

PYLADES: Farewell. I go in haste to reassure
Our friends who wait in longing expectation,   1630
Then I will come back quickly and, concealed
Within that thicket, listen for your sign—
What are you pondering? A silent sadness
Wafts over your free brow all of a sudden.

IPHIGENIA: Forgive me! Like light mists across the sun,
Light care comes drifting on across my soul
With trepidation.

PYLADES: Do not be afraid!
Fear has allied itself deceitfully
With Peril, for those two are close companions.

IPHIGENIA: I term that care a noble one that warns me   1640
　Not to betray maliciously and rob
　The king who has become my second father.
PYLADES: You flee from someone who would kill your brother.
IPHIGENIA: It is the same man who has shown me kindness.
PYLADES: What Need compels is not ingratitude.
IPHIGENIA: Ingratitude it is,—by Need excused.
PYLADES: Before both gods and men, in your case, surely.
IPHIGENIA: My own heart is not satisfied, however.
PYLADES: Excess of scruple is a mask for pride.
IPHIGENIA: I do not analyse, I merely feel.   1650
PYLADES: If you feel rightly, you revere your action.
IPHIGENIA: Unstained alone the heart approves itself.
PYLADES: You have so kept yourself here in the temple;
　Life teaches us to be less strict both with
　Ourselves and others; you will learn that too.
　So wondrously is mankind constituted,
　So various are his knots and interweavings,
　That no one can stay pure and unconfused
　Within himself or with his fellow men.
　Nor are we called upon to judge ourselves.   1660
　To walk our way and keep our eyes fixed on it
　Is mankind's first and foremost obligation:
　They seldom judge aright what they have done
　And almost never prize what they are doing.
IPHIGENIA: You almost sway me to share your opinion.
PYLADES: Is swaying needed when choice is ruled out?
　To save yourself, your brother, and a friend
　There is but one way; can we help but take it?
IPHIGENIA: O let me hesitate! for you would not
　Do such wrong calmly to a man to whom   1670
　You felt yourself indebted for kind treatment.
PYLADES: If we are lost, a still more harsh reproach
　Awaits you, and it will include despair.
　You are not used to losing, obviously,
　Since, to escape a major evil, you

Won't sacrifice so much as one false word.

IPHIGENIA: If I but had a man's heart in my bosom,
Which, when it entertains a daring notion,
Will shut itself to every other voice!

PYLADES: It is in vain that you refuse; the iron   1680
Hand of Necessity commands, and its
Stern beckoning is supreme law, to which
The gods themselves must bow. In silence rules
Eternal Destiny's unhearing sister.
What she enjoins upon you, bear, and do
As she commands. The rest you know. I shall
Be back here quickly to receive the fair
Seal of deliverance from your sacred hand.

[*Exit.*]

IPHIGENIA (*alone*): I must comply, for I see my own people
In urgent danger. But alas for me!   1690
My own fate makes me ever more distressed.
O, may I not still salvage that soft hope
That I had cherished in my solitude?
Is this curse to endure forever? Is
This house then never to arise again
With a fresh blessing?—All things else decline!
The best of happiness, life's fairest strength
Will slacken finally: why not this curse?
Have I then hoped in vain, preserved out here
And cut off from my house's destiny,   1700
To expiate with pure hand and pure heart
Some future day that dwelling so defiled!
Within my arms my brother scarcely has
Been cured from dire ill by a sudden marvel,
A ship long prayed for scarcely comes in sight
To take me to a harbor of my forebears,
When deaf Necessity with hand of brass
Imposes sin twofold upon me: stealing
The sacred statue much revered and trusted
Into my keeping, and deceiving someone   1710

To whom I owe my life and destiny.
O let not an aversion spring up in
My bosom finally! And may the hatred
That those primeval gods, the Titans, feel
Toward you, Olympians, not rend my tender
Bosom also with its vulture claws![3]
Save me and save your image in my soul!
   My ears are humming with an ancient song—
I had forgotten it, and gladly so—
The song the Parcae once sang shuddering   1720
When Tantalus fell from his golden chair;
They suffered for their noble friend; grim were
Their hearts, and full of dread the song they sang.
Our nurse, when we were young, would sing it to
Us children, and I noted it with care.

> In fear of the gods let
> The race of man stand!
> Dominion they hold
> In hands everlasting,
> With power to use it   1730
> As they may see fit.

> One whom they exalt
> Should fear them twice over.
> On cliffs and on clouds
> Are chairs set out ready
> At tables of gold.

> If discord arises,
> The guests may be cast,
> Abused and dishonored,
> To the depths of the dark   1740
> And there wait in vain,
> Amid gloom and in fetters,
> For judgment with justice.

> Those others, however,

Sit endlessly feasting
At tables of gold.
And striding from mountain
Across unto mountain,
They scent from the chasms
The smoking breath 1750
Of the stifling Titans
Like a thin cloud of odor
Up-wafting from sacrifice.

These rulers avert
The eyes of their blessing
From whole generations,
Declining to see
In the grandson the grandsire's
Once well-beloved features
Now mute but eloquent. 1760

So sang the Parcae.
The old one, the exile,
He harkens in hollows
Of night to these songs,
Thinks children and grandchildren,
And shakes his head. (1766)

ACT V

Thoas. Arkas.

ARKAS: Confused, I must admit I do not know
Which way I should turn my suspicion now.
Is it the captives who are secretly
Devising flight? Or can it be the priestess   1770
Who is assisting them? A growing rumor
Claims that the ship that brought those two men here
Is still concealed within some bay or other.
And that man's madness, and this consecration,
And all this holy pretext for delay
Call loudly for suspicion and precaution.
THOAS: Summon the priestess here immediately.
Then go and swiftly, sharply, search the coast
Down from the headland to the goddess' grove.
Forbear to probe its sacred depths, but lay   1780
A prudent ambush, fall upon them, seize
Them where you find them, as your custom is.
                    [*Exit Arkas.*]
Rage wildly alternates within my bosom,
First toward her whom I had held so holy,
Then toward myself, who by indulgence and
By kindness made her apt for treachery.
A human being soon adjusts to slavery
And soon learns to obey, if freedom is
Completely taken from him. Had she fallen
Into the hands of my rough ancestors,   1790
And if the holy savagery had spared her,
She would have been content to save herself

467

Alone, she would have gratefully accepted
Her fate, and would have termed it duty to
Shed alien blood before the altar
As need required. But as it is,
My kindness rouses rash desires in her.
In vain I hoped to join her fate to mine;
She now schemes for a private destiny.
By flattery she won my heart, and now   1800
That I resist that, she is seeking her
Own way by cunning and deceit, and all
My kindness seems to her a right of old.
                    [*Enter Iphigenia.*]
IPHIGENIA: You sent for me? What brings you to us here?
THOAS: You have delayed the sacrifice; why so?
IPHIGENIA: I have explained all that to Arkas, clearly.
THOAS: I wish to hear from you in more detail.
IPHIGENIA: The goddess grants you respite for reflection.
THOAS: This respite seems most opportune for *you.*
IPHIGENIA: If your heart has been steeled for this barbaric   1810
    Decision, you should not have come! A king
    Who asks inhuman actions will find henchmen
    Enough who for reward and favor will
    With greed accept half of the action's curse;
    But his own presence still remains unblemished.
    He sits within his stormcloud plotting death
    And lets his messengers descend with flaming
    Destruction on the luckless mortal's head,
    While he serenely moves off in his storm,   1820
    An unscathed god across the heights of sky.
THOAS: The holy lips intone a savage song.
IPHIGENIA: No priestess I, just Agamemnon's daughter.
    The unknown woman's word you reverenced,
    Now you abruptly give the princess orders?
    No! From my youth I learned how to obey,
    My parents first, then a divinity,
    And in obedience I always felt

My soul most gloriously free; submission,
However, to a man's uncouth commands
I never did learn, either there or here. 1830
THOAS: An ancient law, not I, gives you this order.
IPHIGENIA: We seize with eagerness upon a law
That serves our passion as an instrument.
It is another and more ancient law
That bids me to resist you now, the law
By which all aliens are sacred.
THOAS: These captives seem to be dear to your heart,
For in your sympathy and agitation
You have forgotten the first rule of prudence:
Not to irritate the man in power. 1840
IPHIGENIA: Whether I speak or not, you still can know
What is and always will be in my heart.
Will memory of a kindred destiny
Not open any closed-up heart to pity?
How much more mine! In them I see myself.
Before the altar I myself once trembled
And early death once awesomely surrounded
Me as I knelt; the knife was lifted up
That was to pierce my living bosom through.
My inmost being cringed in reeling horror, 1850
My eyes grew dim, and—then I woke up safe.
Are we not bound to pay in turn to other
Unfortunates what the gods granted us?
And knowing this, and me, you still would force me?
THOAS: Obey your office, not your human master.
IPHIGENIA: Do not seek to extenuate the harshness
That takes advantage of a woman's weakness.
I am as free-born as a man. And if
The son of Agamemnon stood before you,
And if you asked improper things of him, 1860
He has a sword and has an arm to wield it
In his defense of the rights of his heart.
But I have only words, and it beseems

A noble man to value women's words.

THOAS: I value them above a brother's sword.

IPHIGENIA: The fate of weapons wavers back and forth,
And no wise warrior underrates his foe.
But Nature has not left the weak defenseless
Either, against insolence and harshness.
She gives them joy in stratagem and cunning   1870
So they may dodge, delay, and circumvent.
Indeed, the man of power deserves the use of these.

THOAS: Precaution shrewdly parries cunning wiles.

IPHIGENIA: And no pure soul will have recourse to them.

THOAS: Do not imprudently pass your own sentence.

IPHIGENIA: O if you could but see how my soul struggles
To drive courageously away at first
Attack an evil seeking to possess it!
Do I stand here defenseless, then, against you?
My fair request, that gracious suppliant's branch   1880
More mighty in a woman's hand than sword
Or weapon, you reject and thrust aside:
What else is left me to defend myself?
Shall I beseech the goddess for a marvel?
Is there no strength in my soul's inner depths?

THOAS: The fate of those two foreigners disturbs you
Excessively, it seems. Who are they, pray,
For whom your spirit is so greatly roused?

IPHIGENIA: They are—they seem—I think that they are Greeks.

THOAS: They are compatriots of yours? and doubtless   1890
Awakened in you fair hopes of return?

IPHIGENIA (after a silence):
Do men alone, then, have the right to do
Unheard-of feats? Can only men clasp things
Impossible to their heroic bosoms?[1]
What is termed great? What lifts to awe the souls
Of minstrels as they tell their oft-told tales,
Except what bravest men began with chances
Unlikely of success? He who by night

Stole up alone upon the enemy,
Then as an unexpected flame seized on   1900
The sleepers and raged in among the wakers
And finally, as hard-pressed by the wakened
He fled on foemen's horses, but with booty,—[2]
Shall he alone be praised? Or he alone
Who, spurning roads of safety, boldly went
A-roaming through the mountains and the forests
To clear the highwaymen out of a district?[3]
Is nothing left for us? Must gentle woman
Renounce her innate right, turn wild and fight
Against wild men, and wrest from you the right   1910
Of swords like Amazons who take revenge
In blood for their oppression? Back and forth
In my heart ebbs a daring enterprise;
I cannot help but meet with great reproach,
And even with dire harm, if I should fail;
Yet on your knees, ye gods, I lay it, and
If you are true, as you are said to be,
Then show it by your help and glorify
Truth through me!—Yes, I confess, O king,
A secret fraud is being perpetrated.   1920
You will in vain ask for those prisoners;
For they have gone—gone searching for their friends
Who with their ship are waiting by the shore.
The elder one, who was afflicted here
But who has now been cured—he is Orestes,
My brother, and the other one is his
Devoted friend since childhood, Pylades
By name. Apollo sends them here from Delphi
With his divine command to carry off
Diana's statue and to bring his sister   1930
Back to him there, in recompense for which
He promises deliverance to the man
Stained with his mother's blood and hounded by
The Furies. To your hands I thus entrust

Both remnants of the house of Tantalus.
Destroy us—if you *can*.

THOAS: You think the rough
And barbarous Scythian will hear the voice
Of truth and human decency that Atreus
The Greek would not hear?

IPHIGENIA: All men hear it, born
Beneath whatever sky they may, and through
Whose bosoms flows the fountainhead of life[4]   1940
Pure and unhindered.—What are you devising,
O king, in silence deep within your soul?
If it is our destruction, kill me first!
For now that there is no deliverance left
For us, I realize the ghastly peril
Into which I over-hastily
And wilfully have plunged my loved ones. Ah!
They will stand bound before me. With what looks
Can I take farewell of my brother then,   1950
Whose murderess I am? O, I can never
Again look into his beloved eyes!

THOAS: How the deceivers with their artful falsehoods
Have cast their nets about the head of one
Long cloistered and who readily lent ear
To their desires!

IPHIGENIA: No, no, O king! I could
Have been deceived, but these are loyal men
And true. And if you find them otherwise,
Then leave them to their fate and send me off
To exile as a punishment for folly   1960
Upon the bleak shore of some craggy island.
But if this man is my so long-besought
And much-loved brother, then release us; be
Kind to the brother as well as the sister.
My father died because of his wife's guilt,
And she died from her son. The final hope
Of Atreus' line now rests with him alone.

Let me with pure heart and pure hand go over
The sea and purify our family.
You will stand by your word!—If to my people   1970
Return were ever possible, you swore
To let me go. It now is possible.
A king will not, like vulgar men, consent
Out of embarrassment just to be rid
One moment of the suppliant; nor will
He promise for contingencies he hopes
Will not arise. He feels his full worth only
When he can gladden those who wait in hope.

THOAS: Impatiently, as fire contends with water
And, hissing, seeks extermination of   1980
Its enemy, so does the anger in
My bosom show resistance to your words.

IPHIGENIA: O let your mercy, circled round about
With joy and praises and thanksgiving shine
Upon me like the steady altar-flame.

THOAS: How often has this strain brought me to calm!

IPHIGENIA: O, offer me your hand in sign of peace.

THOAS: You ask a great deal in so short a time.

IPHIGENIA: To do good things does not require reflection.

THOAS: It does! for sometimes out of good comes evil.   1990

IPHIGENIA: O, it is doubt that turns good into evil.
Do not reflect; grant as your feelings prompt you.

(Enter Orestes under arms.)

ORESTES *(speaking into the wings)*:
Redouble your best efforts! Hold them back!
For these few moments only! Do not give
Way to the mob, protect my and my sister's
Way to the ship.

(to Iphigenia, without seeing the king)
            Come! We have been betrayed.
We have but small space left for flight. O hurry!

(He catches sight of the king.)

THOAS (*putting his hand to his sword*):
  Before me no man with impunity
  Shall wield a naked sword.
IPHIGENIA: Do not profane
  The goddess' dwelling place with rage and murder!   2000
  Command your people to lay down their weapons,
  And hear your priestess, hear your sister.
ORESTES: Tell me,
  Who is this man who threatens us?
IPHIGENIA: Revere
  In him the king who is my second father.
  Forgive me, brother, but my childlike heart
  Has placed our entire fate within his hand.
  I have confessed the plan of you two men
  And thereby saved my soul from treachery.
ORESTES: Then will he peaceably grant our return?
IPHIGENIA: Your flashing sword forbids my answering that.   2010
ORESTES (*putting up his sword*):
  Speak, then. You see that I obey your word.

            (*Enter Pylades, and soon after him
            Arkas, both with drawn swords.*)

PYLADES: Do not delay! Our men are summoning
  Their final strength. By giving ground they will
  Be driven slowly back down to the sea.
  But what discourse of princes do I find here!
  This is the monarch's reverend head I see!
ARKAS: With calmness, as befits you well, O king,
  You stand here and confront your enemies,
  This insolence shall instantly be punished.
  Their men retreat and die, their ship is ours;   2020
  One word from you and it will be in flames.
THOAS: Go and proclaim a truce. No man of mine
  Shall harm the foe so long as we are speaking.

            (*Exit Arkas.*)

ORESTES: I will accept this truce. Dear friend, assemble

What men of ours are left and wait in patience
To see what end the gods assign our doings.
(*Exit Pylades.*)

IPHIGENIA: Deliver me from care before I start
　To speak. I fear harsh quarrel if, O king,
　You do not lend ear to the gentle voice
　Of reasonableness, or you, my brother,　　　　　　　2030
　Do not control the rashness of your youth.

THOAS: I shall restrain my anger, as beseems
　The elder. Answer me. By what do you
　Attest that you are Agamemnon's son,
　This woman's brother here?

ORESTES:　　　　　　　　　　Here is the sword
　With which he slew the doughty men of Troy.
　I took it from his murderer and begged
　The heaven-dwellers to bestow on me
　The great king's arm and courage and good fortune
　And to grant me a better death than his.　　　　　2040
　Select one of the nobles from your army,
　Confront me with the best one of them all.
　As far as earth sustains the sons of heroes,
　No alien is refused such a request.

THOAS: By ancient custom here such privilege
　Was never granted strangers.

ORESTES:　　　　　　　　　　Then begin
　A different custom with yourself and me!
　In following it whole nations will translate
　Their rulers' action into sacred law.
　And let me not fight solely for our freedom,　　　　2050
　But let me, as an alien, fight for aliens.
　If *I* die, then their sentence will have been
　Pronounced along with mine; but if good fortune
　Allows me to prevail, let no man ever
　Set foot upon this shore without his being
　Met by the swift glance of a helpful love,
　And let all men depart therefrom consoled!

THOAS: You seem to be, youth, not unworthy of
   The line of ancestors in whom you glory.
   The count is large of brave and noble men   2060
   Who here attend me, but I still can face
   The foe myself at my age, and I am
   Prepared to try the chance of arms with you.
IPHIGENIA: By no means! For such bloody testimony
   There is, O king, no call! Withdraw hands from
   Your swords, and think of me and of my fate.
   A quick fight may immortalize a man,
   And even if he falls, the songs will praise him.
   But the unending tears thereafter shed
   By the surviving and deserted woman   2070
   No future age will count, and poets speak
   No word about the thousand days and nights
   Of weeping when a silent soul consumes
   Itself in vain with yearning to bring back
   The lost and suddenly departed friend.[5]
   An apprehension warned me at the outset
   Lest deception of some pirate might
   Abduct me from a place of safety and
   Traduce me into bondage. Diligently
   I questioned them, I probed each circumstance,   2080
   I asked for signs, and now my heart is certain.
   See here on his right hand the birthmark which
   Resembles, as it were, three stars, and which
   Appeared the very day that he was born.
   The priest said that it meant a grievous deed
   To be done by that hand. Then I am further
   Convinced twice over by this scar that furrows
   His eyebrow here. Once, when he was a child,
   Electra, quick and heedless as her manner
   Always was, dropped him out of her arms.   2090
   He struck against a tripod—[6] It is he—
   Must I speak too of his resemblance to
   His father, and the exultation of

My heart, as further proofs of my conviction?
THOAS: Even if your words resolved all doubts
　　And I restrained the anger in my heart,
　　Recourse to arms would still be needed to
　　Decide between us. I can see no peace.
　　They came here, as you have yourself acknowledged,
　　To steal my sacred statue of the goddess.   2100
　　Do you think I will calmly let them do so?
　　The Greeks have often turned their greedy eyes
　　On far-off treasures of barbarians—
　　The golden fleece, fine horses, lovely daughters;[7]
　　Not always did their force and guile, however,
　　Get them home safely with their stock of plunder.
ORESTES: The statue shall, O king, not cause us discord.
　　We now perceive the error which a god
　　Cast like a veil about our heads when he
　　Bade us set out upon our journey here.   2110
　　I had begged him for counsel and deliverance
　　From the Furies' company; he answered:
　　"If you will bring to Greece the sister who
　　On Tauris' shore now tarries in the temple
　　Against her will, the curse will be removed."
　　This we construed to mean Apollo's sister,
　　While he had *you* in mind! Your harsh bonds are
　　Now stricken off, and you, O holy one,
　　Are now restored to your own people. I
　　Have been healed at your touch; in your embrace   2120
　　The evil seized upon me with its claws
　　For the last time, and horribly it shook
　　Me to the very marrow; then it fled
　　Off like a serpent to its lair. Through you
　　I now enjoy the day's broad light once more.
　　Magnificent and fair now seems to me
　　The goddess' counsel. Like a sacred statue
　　Into which a city's fate is charmed
　　Unalterably by mystic words of gods,[8]

She took you, the protectress of the house,   2130
Away and kept you in a holy stillness
Unto your brother's and your people's blessing.
Then when all rescue on the wide earth seemed
To have been lost, you give us back all things
Again. Allow your soul to turn to peace,
O king! Do not prevent her from completing
The consecration of her father's house,
From giving me back to my now pure hall
And placing on my head my ancient crown.
Requite the blessing that she brought to you   2140
By letting me enjoy my closer right.
Men's highest glory, violence and cunning,
Are by the truth of this exalted soul
Now put to shame, and pure and childlike trust
In a high-minded man meets with reward.

IPHIGENIA: Remember your sworn word and let yourself
Be swayed by this speech from an upright man's
True lips. O look at us! It is not often
You have occasion for such noble action.
You cannot well refuse it; grant it soon!   2150

THOAS: Then go!

IPHIGENIA: Not thus, my king! Without your blessing,
With your ill-will, I shall not part from you.
O do not banish us. A friendly guest-right
Must be the rule between us: that way we
Are not cut off forever. For you are
As dear to me as ever was my father,
And this impression is fixed in my soul.
And if the least among your people ever
Brings to my ear the cadence of the voice
I am so used to hear from you, or if   2160
I see the poorest man dressed in your manner,
I shall receive him like a god, I shall
Myself prepare a couch for him, myself
Invite him to a seat beside the fire,

Inquiring news of you and of your fate.
O may the gods give you well-merited
Reward for your good deeds and for your kindness!
Farewell. O turn your face toward us and give
Me back a gracious word of parting now!
For then the wind will swell the sails more gently   2170
And tears more soothingly flow from the eyes
Of those who part. Farewell, and as a pledge
Of ancient friendship give me your right hand.

THOAS: Farewell!   (2174)

NOTES

1. The crime of Tantalus the Titan was variously identified in antiquity:

> (a) he stole ambrosia and nectar (immortality-bestowing food and drink of the gods) and gave them to mankind;
>
> (b) he served his own son as food for the gods, to test their omniscience;
>
> (c) he betrayed the secrets of the gods;
>
> (d) he boasted in overweening pride (*hybris*) of his association with the gods.

Goethe disregards the first two of these, vaguely alludes to the third, and stresses the fourth.

For his crime Tantalus was condemned to Tartarus,—which Homer describes as a pit as far below Hades as earth is below heaven,—there to stand up to his chin in water beneath a loaded fruit-tree, both water and fruit forever receding as he sought to satisfy his thirst and hunger.

2. Pelops competed with Oenomaüs in a chariot race for the hand of Hippodamia. With the promise of half of his future kingdom, if he won, Pelops bribed Myrtilus, his opponent's charioteer, to loosen the linch-pins in his opponent's chariot-wheels, with the result that Oenomaüs was killed in the race. Instead of keeping his promise to Myrtilus once he had become king, Pelops had the charioteer thrown into the sea. The drowning man cursed his murderer and all of Pelops' descendants.

3. Chrysippus was Pelops' first son, by the nymph Axioche. See the genealogical chart at the end of the Introduction to this play.

4. The motif of Hippodamia's suicide, like other details of Iphigenia's narrative, derive from the *Fabulae* of C. Ilius Hyginus.

5. Euripides, Hyginus, and Ovid (*Metamorphoses* xii, 27) tell of Iphigenia's rescue from death at the sacrificial altar; Sophocles (in *Electra*) and Æschylus (in *Agamemnon*) say she died there at Aulis.

ACT II

1. The Furies, who haunt murderers. They come from the ghost realms of the underworld, and hence are "Subterraneans," (line 581).

2. Pylades was outlawed as an accomplice in Clytemnestra's murder.

3. Goethe here follows Euripides' *Electra,* where it is related that an old servant stole the lad Orestes away and took him to Strophius, King of Phocis, who had married Agamemnon's sister Anaxibia; Pylades, the son of Strophius, was therefore Orestes' cousin. See the genealogical chart at the end of the Introduction and also lines 1009-1014 of Act III.

4. To the Greeks almost any nomad north and east of the Black Sea was a "Scythian."

ACT III

1. The lake, nine miles west of Italian Naples, which was, according to Italian lore, the entrance to the underworld.

2. Again Goethe tells the story as Sophocles told it in *Electra.*

3. A river of the underworld.

4. The Furies were forced off the earth and into the underworld by the gods at the same time when the gods defeated and imprisoned the Titans.

5. The Gorgon Medusa's head turned beholders to stone.

6. The bridal raiment which jealous Medea sent to her rival Creusa burst into flames and consumed the bride.—Hercules died of a poisoned shirt.

7. Lyaeus—Bacchus.

8. Tantalus.

9. Both Apollo and his sister Artemis could shoot unseen arrows of death against mortals.

10. The Eumenides, literally "the gracious ones," is the euphemistic name for the Furies.

ACT IV

1. The island of Delos.

2. The (Roman) gods of the hearth, known as the Lares and Penates.

3. Old reliefs represent the Titans as having vulture claws.

ACT V

1. Perhaps as Hercules clasped and strangled the Nemean lion.

2. Like Ulysses or Diomedes who in Book X on the *Iliad* raided the camp of the Thracians to prevent the latter from helping the Trojans.

3. Like Theseus in dealing with Sciros, Procrustes, etc.

4. The "fountainhead of life" = *fons vitae*, a periphrasis for "God."

5. Laodamia's tears moved the gods to return her husband Protesilaus to her from beyond death for three hours' time. (See Wordsworth's poem, *Laodamia*.)

6. Euripides' *Electra* mentions such a scar, acquired while chasing a fawn.

7. The golden fleece was stolen from the land of Colchis by Jason.—Hercules took the magical horses of Laomedon when he captured Troy.—Beautiful daughters, e.g. Ariadne of Crete, Helen of Sparta, Medea of Colchis.

8. Such a statue was the palladium, or sacred image of Athene, which fell from the skies and which preserved Troy until it was stolen by Ulysses and Diomedes.

TORQUATO TASSO

From childhood Goethe had been familiar with the principal work of the Renaissance Italian poet Torquato Tasso, *Jerusalem Delivered* (*Gerusalemme Liberata*), the long narrative poem about the heroic feats of the First Crusade. When he came to read the biography of Tasso by Giovanni Battista Manso, his attention was caught by an episode depicting the poet's hopeless love for the Princess Leonore d'Este. Amid rather different circumstances Goethe was himself in the grip of a hopeless love for Charlotte von Stein. Here, then, was a congenial "historical situation" for a drama, such a drama as would serve as a channel of confession for his own frustrated passion. Ironically, Tasso's love for the Princess d'Este was a figment of biographer Manso's imagination, as Goethe was ultimately to discover, but without the false *datum* the play would not have been started. Before the play was completed, however, it would come to include much more than a story of unrequited love.

The "inventive day" was March 30, 1780, according to Goethe's diary. The first draft of *Iphigenia,* itself a sort of memorial to Frau von Stein, had had its première in the ducal garden a year before and was now in the second stage of its ten-year evolution to final form. *Tasso* was to endure a similar limbo of delay. Composition was not started until the following October 14th. By March of 1781 the prose text had advanced, apparently, into the second Act. On April 20th his customary morning note to Frau von Stein said: "My entire soul is with you. . . . Today I shall be diligent." Slow progress went on into the summer and then petered out.

Two Acts in poetic prose were among the various unfinished projects that Goethe took with him to Italy in 1786. During the stormy voyage to Sicily in March of 1787 he stayed below decks to mull over his plans for the play. A year after that, nothing further had been written. In 1788 he came upon the new biography of Tasso by the Abbate Pierantonio Serassi, which contained no love story but which did show the poet as opposed by Antonio Montecatino. Under that name Goethe could collect and focus all the opposition to Tasso and thereby give his drama a different orientation altogether. But that required rethinking the entire matter. Most of the actual composition was therefore postponed until after his return to Weimar, so that the blank-verse text, as we have it, was realized between June 1788 and June 1789. Publication followed in 1790. Moreover, reports of Goethe's "pagan" life in Italy had displeased Frau von Stein, so that her reception of the returning traveler was cool. Coolness was answered with coolness, and thus the final *Tasso* was accomplished in freedom from the spell that first inspired it.

At first glance *Tasso* seems like a second *Iphigenia*: limpidly pure blank verse, five good characters caught in a painful dilemma, dramaturgy close to the Racinian formula, Charlotte von Stein once again cast as a princess of exquisite moral sensitivities, and the author himself, not crime-haunted like Orestes, to be sure, but headed all the same for madness of a different sort. We may also point out that *Tasso*, like *The Lover's Whim*, begins with two ladies twining garlands in a lovely garden, and, like *The Lover's Whim*, it reaches its dramatic climax in a certain kiss. Yet the substance of *Tasso* is almost as distantly removed from *Iphigenia* as from that one-Act pastoral.

The principal distinction from *Iphigenia* lies in the fact that the five good characters in *Tasso* are not wholly good. Indeed, the play's conflict arises out of their relatively slight flaws. All five of them are intelligent persons of good will, long acquainted, and associating almost as a family; they are at leisure in a gracious country house, and no external disaster impends. Yet they quarrel atrociously, and at the final curtain the hero is a broken man.

Duke Alfonso has been like a generous father to Tasso, his poet in residence, and he has been immensely patient at the endless delays over completing *Jerusalem Delivered*. Poet and poem are necessary to his fame as a patron of the arts. In the very hour of the poem's completion, Tasso vows to take the work to a different patron, and Alfonso is understandably exasperated.

The visiting Countess Leonore Sanvitale, the least good of the five characters, feels neither any adulterous passion for the youthful Tasso nor any ill-will toward her hosts, but, if the poem *is* to be taken elsewhere, why should she and her husband not be the ones to reap the glory from it? With a malice that is almost subconscious she tends to side with Tasso in the quarrel and thereby makes things worse.

The Princess Leonore d'Este, Alfonso's sister and the Charlotte von Stein equivalent, is a fragile creature who has recovered from a deadly illness to live guardedly and intensely. It would be unfair to call her a professional convalescent, but as one who has come face to face with death she is hypersensitive and to some degree unwholesomely ethereal. Her genuine fondness for Tasso is sisterly and benign, but as a princess she rather "descends unto" this commoner, never once considering that *his* feelings might be less than ethereal, never once considering that her ready talk of love in Renaissance-Platonic terms might have an ambiguous ring for him. Unwittingly she condescends to him; unawares she wounds his pride. When, at the height of his frenzy, he kisses her by force, she is scandalized and shocked.

In 1577, the approximate date of the play's action, the historical Tasso was age thirty-three, but Goethe makes him an immature youth whose ardors are within imperfect control. Not only does he live in a world all his own, but in his adoration of Art and in his awareness of his poetic gifts, he had made the perilous assumption that, as an aristocrat by merit, he is the equal of these aristocrats by birth. He even tends to forget their wealth and power and his own economic dependence upon them. Recklessly he defies them all.

Fifth and last-introduced of the characters is Antonio Montecatino, a mature and accomplished man of the world, vigorous, self-assured, and with impeccable courtly manners. He has just returned from a difficult and successful mission of diplomacy in Duke Alfonso's interest, a mission that has averted war and even gained territory for his master. Let the historical Antonio have been what he may, in the Antonio of the drama we see yet another aspect of the multifaceted author; we see Goethe the polished courtier, prime minister of Weimar, and man of practical affairs who could and did effectively organize a fire department and manage a theater budget.

As the play opens, the two Leonores are twining wreaths, one of flowers, one of laurel leaves. The Duke amicably joins them. Along comes Tasso with his completed poem, which he presents to his lord.

At Alfonso's bidding, his sister places the laurel crown upon Tasso's head. The youth is ecstatic at receiving this honor in the midst of "his family" and from a beloved hand. Just then Antonio arrives. Instantly all attention is shifted to him and to his successful mission. To him the little coronation is a pretty game, though he speaks at length in praise of Ariosto, the poet upon whose sculptured bust the other wreath has been set. Tasso stands silent, mortified and outraged.

In Act II the Princess soothes his hurt feelings and expresses the wish that he cultivate Antonio's friendship. Her wish is his command, and directly he approaches Antonio with an impetuous "Let us be friends!" and, like a foolish child, adding: "We must be friends because the Princess wishes it." Antonio finds him preposterous. They quarrel. Tasso draws his sword and challenges Antonio to let weapons decide their argument. The Duke comes upon them so and sternly sends Tasso to his room like a misbehaving boy.

Act III presents the two Leonores and Antonio in discussions of the situation. Act IV brings each of them individually to consult with the "prisoner" and ends with a soliloquy by Tasso in which all persons are seen in nightmarish distortion as malignant and bent on his harm. Even the Princess is evil, and the wild harangue ends on the words "She too! She too!" From Antonio, however, he has cunningly extracted a promise of intercession with the Duke in a plan to "escape."

Reluctantly Alfonso authorizes this escape at the beginning of Act V. But now Tasso wants his poem back, allegedly to amend it further, and again the Duke reluctantly agrees. Then comes the Princess, sisterly and loving, to persuade Tasso not to leave. He mistakes her meaning and in frantic passion seizes her and kisses her. In horror she struggles free and rushes away. The stunned Tasso sees Antonio confronting him.

Abjectly he declares himself Antonio's prisoner. Flaring wildly up, he reviles everyone, the conniving, whorish Princess most of all, and then recoils from his own blasphemies. In total spiritual collapse he throws himself upon the mercy of this self-possessed man, but not without first remembering that the power of poetry is still his:

> And if men in their torment must be mute,
> A god gave me the power to tell my pain.

On the psychological level *Tasso* is an acute and profound analysis of the author's spiritual malaise in the earlier 1780s, the malaise that drove him to precipitate flight to Italy and an absence of two years. It is also a superbly fine dramatic poem, analogous to chamber music of a subtle and complex kind. Its musical counterpart may be found in the latter trios and quartets of Beethoven.

TORQUATO TASSO

A Play in Five Acts

1780–1790

CHARACTERS

ALFONSO THE SECOND, Duke of Ferrara
LEONORE D'ESTE, Sister of the Duke
LEONORE SANVITALE, Countess of Scandiano
TORQUATO TASSO
ANTONIO MONTECATINO, Secretary of State

The scene is at Belriguardo, a pleasure palace.
Time: around 1577.

ACT I

A garden spot adorned with herms of the epic poets, downstage right of Vergil, downstage left of Aristo.
The Princess. Leonore.

PRINCESS: You look at me and smile, Eleonore,
    And look back at yourself and smile again.
    What is the matter? Tell me as your friend.
    You seem bemused, and yet you seem quite pleased.
LEONORE: Oh yes, my Princess, I behold us both
    With pleasure here so rustically adorned.
    We look like truly happy shepherdesses,
    And we are busy, too, like happy ones.
    We're twining wreaths. Here, this one, bright with flowers,
    Keeps growing more and more beneath my hand.   10
    You, with your loftier mind and nobler heart,
    Chose for yourself the slender, fragile laurel.
PRINCESS: The branches I have woven in my thoughts,
    They have already found a worthy head.
    With gratitude I place them here on Vergil.
                (She crowns the bust of Vergil.)
LEONORE: Then I will set my own full, joyous wreath
    On Master Lodovico's lofty brow—
           (She crowns the bust of Ariosto.)
    Let him whose jests will never fade away
    Receive at once his share of this new springtime.
PRINCESS: It is obliging of my brother to   20
    Bring us so early out into the country.
    We can be by ourselves and dream our way
    For hours back to the poets' golden age.
    I love this Belriguardo, for I spent

Many a day of happy childhood here,
And this new greenness and this sunlight brings
Me back the feeling of that bygone time.

LEONORE: Oh yes, we find ourselves in a new world!
    The shade of these eternally green trees
    Already gladdens, and the murmur of   30
    These fountains quickens us anew to life.
    Young branches sway upon the morning wind.
    The flowers in the beds gaze up at us
    In friendly fashion with their childlike eyes.
    With confidence the gardener unroofs
    The hothouse for the oranges and lemons,
    The blue sky over us is in repose,
    And on the far horizon there the snow
    Of distant mountains melts to fragrant mist.

PRINCESS: The springtime would be very welcome to me   40
    If it did not deprive me of my friend.

LEONORE: Do not remind me in these gracious hours,
    O Princess, of how soon I must depart.

PRINCESS: Whatever you are leaving, you will find
    Again, and doubly, in that mighty city.

LEONORE: My duty summons me, love summons me
    Back to my husband, who has been so long
    Without me. I bring him his son, who has
    So swiftly grown this year, so swiftly formed,
    And I will share in his paternal joy.   50
    Florence is vast and splendid, but the worth
    Of all of its accumulated treasures
    Can never match Ferrara's precious jewels.
    The people made a city of that city,
    Ferrara gained its greatness through its princes.

PRINCESS: Through the good human beings rather, who
    By chance met here and for good fortune formed
    Alliances.

LEONORE: Chance scatters what chance gathers.
    A noble person will attract the noble

And can retain them firmly, as you do.   60
Around your brother and around yourself
Assemble minds that are quite worthy of you.
And you are worthy of your great forefathers.
Here was enkindled the fair light of learning,
With joy, and of emancipated thought,
When barbarism still enclosed the world
With heavy gloom. While I was yet a child
My ear rang with the names of Ércole
Of Este and Ippólito of Este.
Ferrara was, with Rome and Florence, much   70
Praised by my father! Many was the time
I yearned to go there; and now here I am.
Here Petrarch was received, here he was fostered,   .
And Ariosto found his models here.
No great name can be named by Italy
Which this house has not harbored as its guest.
And it is advantageous entertaining
A genius: if you give a gift to him,
He leaves a finer one behind for you.
The place where once a good man has set foot   80
Is consecrate; a hundred years thereafter
His word and deed resound unto the grandchild.
PRINCESS: Yes, if the grandchild warmly feels, as you do;
    I often envy you that happy fortune.
LEONORE: Which you enjoy serenely, purely, as
    Few others do. My full heart forces me
    To say straight off what I acutely feel;
    You feel it better, feel it deeply, and —
    Say nothing. Momentary seeming does
    Not dazzle you, sharp wit does not beguile you,   90
    And flattery glides vainly to your ear.
    Firm stands your mind and faultless your good taste,
    Your judgment true, your sympathy is great
    With greatness, which you know as your own self.
PRINCESS: You should not lend this supreme flattery

The raiment of the intimacy of friendship.
LEONORE: The friendship is quite just, and it alone
    Can know the total compass of your worth.
    Let me give opportunity and fortune
    Their share as well in your accomplishment;   100
    You have it, all the same, and such you are.
    And the whole world reveres you and your sister
    Before all the great women of your time.
PRINCESS: That, Leonore, can move me but little
    When I consider just how small one is,
    And what one is, one owes to other people.
    For my skill in the ancient languages
    And best things from times past, I thank my mother;
    Yet neither daughter ever was her equal
    In learning or in excellence of mind,   110
    And if one of us is to be compared
    With her, Lucretia surely has that right.
    I can assure you also that I never
    Regarded as a rank or a possession
    What Nature or what luck bestowed on me.
    When clever men discourse I am delighted
    That I can understand just what they mean.
    Let it be an opinion of a man
    Of ancient times and of his actions' worth,
    Or let some branch of learning be the topic   120
    Which by extension through experience
    Will profit human beings and uplift them:
    Wherever noble men's discourse may lead,
    I gladly follow, for I do so with ease.
    I like to hear disputes of clever men
    When speakers' lips with light grace play upon
    The forces which so cheerfully and yet
    So fearsomely bestir the human breast;
    Or when the princely eagerness for fame
    And aggrandizing of possession forms   130
    The thinker's theme, and when the fine astuteness

Of an astute man deftly set in motion,
Instead of cheating us, gives us instruction.
LEONORE: Then following that serious entertainment
Our ear and inner sense repose with pleasure
Upon the rhymes provided by the poet
Who with his gracious tones instills emotions
Of utmost loveliness into our souls.
Your lofty mind encompasses vast realms,
While I like best to dwell upon the island   140
Of poetry amid the laurel groves.
PRINCESS: In this fair land the myrtle tends to grow,
They have sought to assure me, more than all
The other trees. And though the Muses are
Full many, one more rarely seeks to gain
A friend and playmate from among their number
Than one is glad to meet the poet who
Seems to avoid and even flee from us
And seeks for something which we do not know
And which perhaps he does not know himself.   150
How nice, then, it would be if he should meet us
Some lucky hour and with sudden rapture
Discovered in us the treasure which he long
Had searched for and in vain through the wide world.
LEONORE: I must admit the justice of your jest,
It hits its mark in me, but not profoundly.
I honor every man and his true worth
And I am being only just to Tasso.
His vision scarcely tarries on this earth,
His ear perceives the harmony of Nature;   160
What history provides, what this life gives,
His heart at once and willingly takes up:
Things scattered far and wide his mind assembles
And his emotions give life to things lifeless.
He can ennoble what seemed base to us,
And things esteemed turn in his sight to naught.
Within this private magic circle walks

That admirable man and draws us on
To walk with him and share experiences.
He seems to come close to us, yet remains   170
Afar; he seems to look at us, and spirits
May strangely stand before him in our stead.
PRINCESS: You have described the poet well and fondly
Who hovers in the realm of his sweet dreams.
I feel, however, that reality
Attracts him strongly too, and holds him fast.
Those lovely songs which we from time to time
Discover fastened to our trees and which,
Like golden apples, make a fragrant, new
Hesperia, do you not recognize   180
Them all for gracious fruits of a true love?
LEONORE: I too take pleasure in those lovely pages.
And with his diverse mind he glorifies
A single picture throughout all his rhymes.
At times he lifts it up in shining glory
Unto the starry sky, himself adoring
Like angels over clouds before the picture;
Then he pursues it through the quiet meadows,
Entwining every flower in his garland.
If the adored one leaves, he consecrates   190
The path that her fair foot has lightly trodden.
Concealed in thickets like the nightingale,
He fills the grove and air with harmonies
Of his laments poured from his lovesick heart.
His charming grief, the blessed melancholy
Entices every ear, all hearts must follow —
PRINCESS: And if he were to name his subject, he
Would call it by the name of Leonore.
LEONORE: That is your name as much as it is mine.
I would resent it if it were another.   200
I am delighted that he can conceal
His feeling for you in that double meaning.
And I am pleased that he remembers me

Amid the gracious sounding of that name.
There is no question here of any love
That seeks to be the master of its object,
Or would exclusively possess it and
In jealousy forbid its view to others.
When in his blissful contemplation he
Concerns himself with your worth he may also   210
Take his delight in my own slighter person.
He does not love us, — pardon my so speaking!
From all the spheres he conjures what he loves
Down into the one name which we both bear
And he communicates his feelings to us;
We seem to love the man, and we love only
In him the highest things that we can love.

PRINCESS: You have gone very deeply, Leonore,
Into this science, and you tell me things
Which almost touch upon my ear alone   220
And scarcely penetrate into my soul.

LEONORE: What? You, a Plato scholar, and not grasp
What a mere novice dares to prattle of?
It must be that I have too gravely erred.
And yet I am not wholly wrong, I know.
Amid this gracious school Love does not show
Himself, as formerly, as a spoiled child;
He is the youth who wed with Psyche and
Who in the privy-council of the gods
Has seat and voice. He does not rage so wanton   230
From one heart to another, back and forth.
He does not seize straight off on form and beauty
With sweet misjudgment, and he does not pay
For sudden rapture with disgust and loathing.

PRINCESS: Here comes my brother. Let us not betray
The turn our conversation took again.
We would have to endure his joking, as
Our costume met his mockery before.

                    (Enter Alfonso.)

ALFONSO: I have been looking everywhere for Tasso
    And do not find him — even here with you.   240
    Can you not give me any news of him?
PRINCESS: I saw him little yesterday, and not
    At all today.
ALFONSO: It is his long-time failing
    To seek seclusion more than company.
    If I forgive him for avoiding motley
    Throngs of people and preferring to
    Commune in quiet freely with his mind,
    I still can not approve that he avoids
    The very circle which his friends comprise.
LEONORE: If I am not in error, you will soon,   250
    O Prince, transmute your blame to gladsome praise.
    I saw him from afar today; he had
    A book and tablet, wrote, and paced, and wrote.
    A hurried word that he spoke yesterday
    Seemed to announce to me his work's completion.
    He troubles only with correcting small points
    To lay a worthy offering at last
    Before your grace, which has done so much for him.
ALFONSO: He shall be welcome *when* he brings it, and
    Acquitted for a long, long time to come.   260
    Much as I sympathize with his long efforts,
    Much as the great work pleases me and must
    Please me in many ways, nevertheless
    My own impatience is increasing too.
    He can not finish it, can not get through;
    He keeps on changing, slowly moves ahead.
    Stops once again, and keeps on cheating hopes.
    One is indignant seeing pleasure that
    One thought so near postponed to times remote.
PRINCESS: But I praise the discretion and the care   270
    With which he moves step by step to his goal.
    By favor of the Muses only will
    So many rhymes shape firmly to a whole!

And his soul cherishes this impulse only:
His poem must be rounded to a whole.
He will not heap up tale on pretty tale
That entertain delightfully and then
Like empty words delude and fade away.
Leave him alone, my brother. Time is not
The measure of a work of quality.   280
And if posterity is to enjoy it,
The artist's own times must forget themselves.

ALFONSO: Let us, dear sister, work together here,
As we have often done to our advantage.
If I am over-zealous, mitigate;
And if you are too mild, I will press harder.
Thus we perhaps will see him all at once
At the goal where we have so long desired him.
And then the fatherland and all the world
Will be astounded at the work achieved.   290
I shall have my own share in the renown,
And he will be inducted into life.
A noble man cannot owe his formation
To any narrow circle. Fatherland
And world at large must have effect on him.
He must learn to endure both praise and blame.
He must be forced to know himself and others
Aright. Seclusion will no longer lull him
With praise. Foes *will* not and friends *may* not spare him.
The youth will then exert his strength in struggle,   300
Feel what he is, and soon perceive his manhood.

LEONORE: Then you will still do everything for him,
My Lord, as you already have done much.
A talent forms itself in solitude,
A character amid the stream of life.
O may he form his spirit like his art
On your instruction, and may he no longer
Shun human beings, and may his suspicion
Be not transformed at last to fear and hatred!

ALFONSO: Only one who does not know human beings 310
  Will fear them, and a man who shuns them will
  Misjudge them. Such is his case, and by stages
  A free mind comes to be perplexed and chained.
  Thus he is often vastly more concerned
  About my favor than beseems him, and
  He has mistrust of many who, I know,
  Are not his enemies. If it bechances
  A letter goes astray, or a domestic
  Transfers from his own service to some other,
  Or if a paper gets out of his hands, 320
  Immediately he sees design, betrayal,
  And malice undermining his own fate.
PRINCESS: Let us, beloved brother, not forget
  A man can not get outside of himself.
  And if a friend upon a walk with us
  Should hurt his foot, we would prefer to walk
  More slowly and extend our hand to him
  Gladly and willingly.
ALFONSO: It would be better
  If we could heal him and were rather to
  Try out at once a cure upon a surgeon's 330
  Reliable advice, and then proceed
  On the new path of fresh life with the cured man.
  And yet, my dear ones, I hope never to
  Take on myself the guilt of the harsh surgeon.
  I'm doing what I can to inculcate
  His heart with confidence and with assurance.
  I frequently give him decisive signs
  Of favor before many people. If
  He makes complaint to me, I have it seen to,
  As I did do when recently he thought 340
  His room was burglarized. If nothing is
  Then found, I show him calmly how I see it.
  And since one must use every means, I practice
  Patience, as he does deserve, with Tasso.

And you, I know, both willingly support me.
I have now brought you to the country and
Myself return this evening to the city.
You will just for a moment see Antonio;
He comes from Rome to fetch me. We have much
To settle and discuss. Decisions must   350
Be made, and many letters must be written.
All these things force me back into the city.

PRINCESS: Will you allow us to accompany you?

ALFONSO: Remain in Belriguardo, go together
  Over to Consandoli. Enjoy
  The lovely days entirely at your leisure.

PRINCESS: You cannot stay with us? Can the affairs
  Not be done here as well as in the city?

LEONORE: You take Antonio away at once
  Who would have had so much to tell of Rome?   360

ALFONSO: It won't do, children. But I will come back
  With him as soon as possible, and then
  He shall recount to you, and you shall help
  Me in rewarding him, who once again
  Has made such great exertions in my service.
  And once we have got our discussions over,
  Then let the swarm come in, so things will be
  Gay in our gardens, and a beauteous lady,
  If I should seek one, may be glad to meet
  Me also, as is fitting, in the coolness.   370

LEONORE: We'll look the other way quite cheerfully.

ALFONSO: And yet you know that I can be indulgent.

PRINCESS (looking off stage):
  I have been watching Tasso coming. Slowly
  He moves his steps, then stops at intervals
  All of a sudden as if undecided,
  Then comes on faster toward us, and then stops
  Again.

ALFONSO: If he is thinking and composing
  Do not disturb his dreams and let him walk.

LEONORE: No, he has seen us, he is coming here.
                    (Enter Tasso with a book bound
                         in parchment.)
TASSO: I come up slowly to present a work,   380
  And still am hesitant to give it to you.
  Too well I know it still remains unfinished
  However much it might seem to be ended.
  But though I was concerned about presenting
  It to you uncompleted, new concern
  Compels me now: I should not like to seem
  Too anxious, nor to seem ungrateful either.
  And as a man can only say: "Here am I!"
  So friends considerately will rejoice,
  So I can only say: "Accept it now!"   390
                    (He presents the volume.)
ALFONSO: You quite surprise me with your gift and make
  This lovely day a festival for me.
  And so at last I hold it in my hands
  And call it in a certain sense my own!
  I long have wished you might make up your mind
  And finally tell me: "Here! It is enough."
TASSO: If you are satisfied, then it is finished;
  For it belongs to you in every sense.
  If I considered all the effort spent,
  If I looked at the ink-strokes of my pen,   400
  Then I might well declare: "This work is mine."
  But if I look more closely at what gives
  This poem dignity and inner value,
  I see that I have it from you alone.
  If Nature kindly gave me the fair gift
  Of poetry from generous caprice,
  Capricious Fortune had thrust me away
  From her with fierce and wrathful violence;
  And if the fair world had resplendently
  With all its plenitude caught the boy's gaze,   410
  My youthful mind had early been beclouded

By my dear parents' undeserved privation.
If ever my lips opened up to sing,
It was a mournful song that poured from them
And I accompanied with my gentle tones
My father's sorrow and my mother's anguish.
And it was you alone who raised me up
Out of a narrow life to lovely freedom,
Who lifted every care off of my head
And gave me liberty so that my soul   420
Was able to expand in valiant song.
Whatever praise my work may now obtain
I owe to you, for it belongs to you.

ALFONSO: A second time you merit every praise
    And tactfully honor both yourself and us.

TASSO: Could I but say what I acutely feel,
    That what I bring I have from you alone!
    The youth of no achievements — could he have drawn
    This poem from himself? The shrewd direction
    Of lively warfare — did he think that up?   430
    The art of weapons mightily displayed
    By every hero on the day appointed,
    The captain's sense, the bravery of knights,
    How vigilance and cunning are subdued,
    O did you not inspire all that in me,
    My wise and valiant Prince, as if you were
    My Genius who could take delight in making
    His high, his unattainably high being
    Manifest through a mere mortal man?

PRINCESS: Enjoy the work now which gives us delight.   440

ALFONSO: Rejoice in every good man's approbation.

LEONORE: Rejoice now in your universal fame.

TASSO: For me there is sufficient in this moment.
    I thought of you alone as I reflected
    And wrote; to please you was my highest wish,
    To entertain you was my furthest goal.
    One who does not see the world in his friends

Does not deserve to have the world hear of him.
Here is my fatherland, here is the circle
In midst of which my soul is glad to dwell.   450
Here I give ear, here I note every hint.
Here speaks experience, erudition, taste,
I see world and posterity before me.
The masses make an artist shy and muddled;
Only those like you, who understand
And feel, they shall alone judge and reward!

ALFONSO: If we stand for world and posterity,
It is not seemly merely to receive.
The splendid token that rewards a poet,
Which even heroes, who have need of him,   460
Unenvying behold upon his head,
I see right here upon your forebear's brow.
           (pointing to the herm of Vergil.)
Was it a genius or coincidence
That wove and brought it? Not for nothing does
It chance to be here. I hear Vergil say:
"Why honor ye the dead? They had their joy
And their reward while they were still alive.
Now if you so admire and reverence us,
Then give unto the living ones their share.
My marble image has been crowned enough: 470
These verdant branches should belong to life."
         (Alfonso beckons to his sister; she takes the
           wreath from the bust of Vergil and approaches
           Tasso. He falls back.)

LEONORE: What? You refuse? But see whose hand presents you
The beautiful, imperishable wreath!

TASSO: O let me hesitate! I do not see
How I can ever live beyond this hour.

ALFONSO: In the enjoyment of the fine possession
Which frightens you for the initial moment.

PRINCESS *(as she holds the wreath aloft):*
You grant me the unwonted pleasure, Tasso,

Of saying to you wordless what I think.

TASSO: Kneeling I accept the lovely burden   480
    From your dear hands upon my feeble head.
                (He kneels; the Princess places
                  the wreath upon him.)

LEONORE *(applauding)*:
    Long live the poet for the first time crowned!
    O how the wreath befits the modest man!
                (Tasso stands up.)

ALFONSO: It is the symbol merely of the crown
    That shall adorn you on the Capitol.

PRINCESS: And up there louder voices will acclaim you;
    Here friendship gives reward with gentle lips.

TASSO: O take it off my head again, take it
    Away! It scorches every lock of hair,
    And like a ray of sunlight that might strike   490
    Too hot upon my head, it burns the power
    Of thought out of my brow. A heat of fever
    Excites my blood. Forgive! It is too much!

LEONORE: This branch affords protection rather to
    The man's head who must walk amid the fervent
    Regions of renown, and cools his brow.

TASSO: I am not worthy of the coolness which
    Should only blow upon the brows of heroes.
    O raise it up, ye gods, transfigure it
    Among the clouds so that it floats on high   500
    And higher out of reach! so that my life
    May be eternal progress toward that goal!

ALFONSO: Achieving early, one learns early to
    Esteem the fair possessions of this life.
    Enjoying early, one will not by choice
    In this life do without what he once had;
    And once possessing, one must be in armor.

TASSO: And donning armor one must feel within
    His heart a strength that never will desert him.
    Ah, it deserts me even now! In fortune   510

It fails me now, the innate strength that bade me
Steadfastly meet misfortune and with pride
Confront injustice. Has my joy dissolved,
And has the rapture of the present moment
Dissolved the very marrow in my limbs?
My knees collapse beneath me! Once again
You see me bowed, O Princess, down before you.
Hear, then, my plea and take the wreath away
So that, as though awakened from a dream
Of beauty I may feel a life new-quickened.   520
PRINCESS: If you can quietly and humbly bear
    The talent which the gods have given you,
    Then learn to bear these branches also, for
    They are the finest thing that we can give you.
    The head which they have once touched worthily,
    About that brow they will forever hover.
TASSO: Then let me go away in shame. Within
    The deep grove let me hide my happiness,
    As formerly I hid my sorrows there.
    There I will walk alone, no eye will there   530
    Remind me of my undeserved good fortune.
    And if by chance a lucid fountain shows
    Me there a man in its pure mirror, resting
    In thought and oddly crowned in the reflection
    Of sky between the trees, between the rocks,
    Then it will seem as if I were beholding
    Elysium upon that magic surface
    Created. I will ponder and inquire:
    Now who may this departed spirit be?
    The youth of ancient times? Engarlanded   540
    So fair? Who will tell me his name? His merits?
    A long time I will wait and think: If only
    Another one and still another would
    Come and join him in friendly conversation!
    O to behold the heroes and the poets
    Of ancient times assembled by this fountain,

O to behold them here inseparable
Forever as in life they were united!
Thus by its power does the magnet join
Things iron with things iron fast together   550
As equal striving joins heroes and poets.
Homer forgot himself, and his whole life
Was consecrated to thought of two men,
And Alexander in Elysium
Makes haste to seek out Homer and Achilles.
O if I only might be present to
Behold those souls supreme united then!

LEONORE: Awake! Awake! And do not make us feel
You fail to recognize the present time.

TASSO: It is the present time that so exalts me.   560
I only seem far off, I am enraptured!

PRINCESS: I am delighted, when you speak with spirits,
To hear you talk so humanly with them.

> (*A page steps up to the Prince and quietly
> delivers something.*)

ALFONSO: He has arrived, right at the best of times.
Antonio! — Bring him here. — Ah, here he comes.

> (*Enter Antonio.*)

Welcome! who bring good news and your own self
At one and the same time.

PRINCESS: Our greetings to you!

ANTONIO: I hardly dare to say what satisfaction
Gives me a new existence in your presence.
In your sight I again find everything   570
That I so long have missed. You seem to be
Pleased with what I have done and have accomplished,
Thus I have my reward for every care,
For many a day endured now with impatience
And wasted now deliberately. We have,
Then, what we want, and there is no more quarrel.

LEONORE: My greetings to you also, angry as
I am. You come just when I have to leave.

ANTONIO: So that my good luck may not be quite perfect
    You take a lovely part away at once!   580
TASSO: My greetings also! I too hope joy from
    The presence of the much experienced man.
ANTONIO: You'll find me genuine if ever you
    Choose to look over from your world to mine.
ALFONSO: Although you have informed me in your letters
    Of what you did and how things fared with you,
    I still have many things to ask about
    And by what means the business was accomplished.
    Upon that strange and wonderful terrain one's step
    Must be well gauged if it is finally   590
    To lead you to your proper purposes.
    A man who bears in mind his lord's advantage
    Will have no easy time of it in Rome;
    For Rome takes everything but gives you nothing,
    And if one goes there to get something, he
    Gets nothing, unless he in turn gives something,
    And he is lucky if he gets it then.
ANTONIO: It is not my demeanor or my skill
    Whereby I carried out your will, my Lord.
    What shrewd man would not find his master in   600
    The Vatican? No, many things concurred
    Which I could turn to our advantage. Gregory
    Respects and greets you and sends you his blessing.
    The aged man, the noblest on whose head
    A crown's weight ever lay, recalls with joy
    When he embraced you with his arm. The man
    Discriminant of men knows you and values
    You highly. And for your sake he did much.
ALFONSO: I am glad of his good opinion in
    So far as it is honest. But you know   610
    That one sees kingdoms lying small enough
    Before one's feet down from the Vatican,
    Not to speak of mortal men and princes.
    Just mention what it was that helped you most.

ANTONIO: Good! if you wish: the Pope's own lofty mind.
    For he sees small things small and great things great.
    In order that he may control a world
    He yields with friendly good will to his neighbors.
    The strip of land that he surrenders to you,
    He knows its worth, like the worth of your friendship.   620
    There must be calm in Italy, he wants
    To see friends close to home, keep peace along
    His borders, so the might of Christendom,
    Which he controls with power, may destroy
    Both Turks and heretics on either side.
PRINCESS: And are the men known whom he favors more
    Than others, who in confidence approach him?
ANTONIO: Experienced men alone possess his ear,
    And only energetic ones his favor
    And confidence. He, who from youth had served   630
    The state, controls it now and influences
    Those courts which years before he saw and knew
    As Nuncio and frequently directed.
    The whole world lies as clear before his gaze
    As the advantages of his own state.
    To see him operate is to admire him
    And be glad when the world discovers what
    He long has quietly prepared and managed.
    There is no finer sight in all the world
    Than to behold a Prince astutely ruling,   640
    Or see a realm where all obey with pride,
    Where each man thinks to serve himself alone
    Because he is asked only to do right.
LEONORE: How ardently I long to see that world
    Just once close by!
ALFONSO: But surely to work in it?
    For Leonore will not just look on.
    It would be very nice, my friend, however,
    If we could sometimes also get our hands
    Into the mighty game— Is that not so?

LEONORE *(to Alfonso):*
    You want to tease me, but you won't succeed.   650
ALFONSO: I owe you a great deal from other days.
LEONORE: Today I will remain, then, in your debt.
    Forgive me, and do not interrupt my questions.
                (to Antonio)
    Has he done much to help his relatives?
ANTONIO: He has done neither less nor more than proper.
    A man of power who does not look after
    His own will be condemned, and by the people
    Themselves. With quiet moderation Gregory
    Knows how to use his relatives who serve
    The state as honest men, and thus fulfills   660
    With one concern two allied obligations.
TASSO: Does learning and does art likewise enjoy
    Protection from him? Does he emulate
    The mighty princes of the ancient time?
ANTONIO: He honors learning as far as it is
    Of use to rule the state, make peoples known;
    Art he esteems as far as it adorns
    And glorifies his Rome, makes palaces
    And temples works of wonder on this earth.
    Nothing must be superfluous around him!   670
    To pass, a thing must serve and be effective.
ALFONSO: And do you think that we can finish up
    The business soon? no further obstacles
    Will be presented to us here and there?
ANTONIO: I would be much deceived if this dispute
    Were not directly settled and forever
    Just by your signature and a few letters.
ALFONSO: Then I will praise these days of my life now
    As a time of advantage and good fortune.
    I see my boundaries enlarged and know   680
    Them safe for times to come. This you have managed
    Without a clash of swords, for which you well
    Deserve a civic crown. And that our ladies

Shall weave you from the nearest oak-leaves and
Emplace it on your brow this lovely morning.
Meanwhile, Tasso has enriched me also:
He has now won Jerusalem for us
And thus put modern Christendom to shame,
By cheerful courage and severe exertion
Attaining a remote and lofty goal.   690
And for his efforts you behold him crowned.

ANTONIO: You solve a riddle for me. With amazement
   I noticed two men crowned as I arrived.

TASSO: If you see my good fortune with your eyes,
   I only wish that with the very same
   Glance you might look upon my spirit's shame.

ANTONIO: I long have known Alfonso is excessive
   In his rewards, and you discover now
   What all his people long ago discovered.

PRINCESS: When once you find out what he has achieved   700
   You will see we are just and moderate.
   We are the first and silent witnesses
   Of the applause the world will not deny him
   And future years will grant him ten times over.

ANTONIO: Through you he can be certain of his fame.
   Who would presume to doubt when you give praise?
   But tell me who has set this wreath upon
   The brow of Ariosto?

LEONORE: My hand did so.

ANTONIO: That was well done! It decks him beautifully;
   The laurel's self would not so well adorn him.   710
   As Nature decks her inwardly rich heart
   With garb of green and motley color, he
   Garbs everything that can make human creatures
   Worthy of respect and of affection
   In flowery raiment of his fable-fiction.
   Contentment, wisdom, and experience,
   And mental vigor, taste, and pure sense for
   The truly good, these in his poems seem,

In spirit and in person also, to
Repose as under flower-bearing trees, 720
Enfolded in the snow of the light blossoms,
Enwreathed with roses, whimsically ringed around
With wanton magic play of Amoretti.
The spring of plenty bubbles close at hand
With view of many-colored wondrous fishes.
The air is filled with rarities of fowl,
As copse and meadow are with unknown herds;
Roguishness half concealed in verdure listens,
From time to time out of a golden cloud
Wisdom intones exalted maxims, while 730
Upon a well-tuned lute wild madness seems
To rage about, now one way, now another,
And yet hold temperately to faultless rhythm.
Whoever ventures up beside this man
Deserves the wreath for sheer audacity.
Forgive me if I seem myself possessed
And, like a man in ecstasy, can not
Take heed of time or place or what I speak;
For all these poets, all these wreaths, the festive
And rare array of lovely ladies, they 740
Transport me from myself to a strange land.
PRINCESS: A man who can so well appreciate
One merit will not fail to see the other.
Some day you shall point out in Tasso's songs
What we have felt but only you perceived.
ALFONSO: Antonio, come along! I still have much
To ask about which I am curious.
And then till set of sun you shall be at
The ladies' disposition. Come! Farewell. (749)

(Antonio follows the Prince,
Tasso, the ladies.)

ACT II

A room.
The Princess. Tasso.

TASSO: My steps pursue you with uncertainty,   750
    O Princess, and within my soul thoughts rise
    Without proportion and coherent order.
    Seclusion seems to beckon me and whisper
    Complaisantly: "Come and I will resolve
    The newly risen doubts within your breast."
    But if I cast a glance at you, or my
    Attentive ear hears one word from your lips,
    Then I feel a new daylight all around me
    And all my fetters fall away from me.
    I will confess to you that the man who   760
    Came to us unexpectedly did not
    Wake me with gentleness from my fair dream.
    His manner and his words affected me
    In such a wondrous way that more than ever
    I feel myself divided and again
    Am in confusing conflict with myself.
PRINCESS: It is impossibie that an old friend
    Who has long led an alien life far off
    Should at the moment when he comes back to us
    Be found precisely as he was before.   770
    He has not altered in his inner self.
    Allow us a few days to live with him
    And then the strings will gradually be tuned
    Until felicitously a harmony
    Is realized again. If he then comes
    To know more closely what you have achieved

513

In all this time he certainly will place
You up beside the poet whom he now
Opposes to you as a towering giant.

Tasso: The praise of Ariosto from his lips,   780
My Princess, caused me more delight than it
Could have offended me. It is a comfort
For us to have praise lavished on a man
Who stands before us as a mighty model.
In quiet heart we can say to ourselves:
If you achieve a portion of his merit
A portion of his fame can not escape you.
No, what disturbs my heart within its depths,
What even now fills up my entire soul,
Were those forms of that other world which circles,   790
Alive, unresting, and tremendous, there
Around one great, uniquely subtle man
In orderly completion of the orbit
Which that demigod has dared assign it.
I harkened eagerly and heard with pleasure
The assured words of the experienced man.
Alas, the more I harkened, more and more
I foundered there before myself, I feared
That I would vanish on those rocks like Echo,
And like a mere non-entity be lost.   800

Princess: And yet so short a time before you felt
How heroes and poets live for one another,
How heroes and poets seek out one another,
And neither needs feel envy of the other?
The feat that merits song is admirable,
But it is also fine to bring abundance
Of feats to future times through worthy songs.
Content yourself with gazing on the world's
Wild course, as from a shore, out from the safety
Of one small state that grants you its protection.   810

Tasso: Did I not with amazement first see here
How splendidly the brave man is rewarded?

I came here as an inexperienced boy
At a time when one festival upon
Another seemed to make Ferrara mid-point
Of the earth. O what a sight it was!
The spacious square whereon skilled Valor was
To show itself in all its glory formed
A circle such that it is hardly likely
The sun will shine upon a second time.   820
Here sat the fairest ladies in a throng,
And in a throng the first men of our age.
One's gaze ran through the noble crowd with wonder,
Exclaiming: "All these the fatherland has sent here,
That single, narrow land surrounded by
The sea. And they together constitute
The most illustrious court that ever sat
In judgment over honor, worth, and virtue.
Go through them one by one, you will find none
Of whom his neighbor needs to be ashamed!" —   830
And then the barriers were all thrown open.
Then horses stamped and shields and helmets gleamed,
Then grooms thronged in, then trumpet fanfares rang,
And lances shattered with a splitting sound,
Helmets and shields with blows resounded, dust
Swirling enveloped for a moment both
The victor's glory and the vanquished's shame.
O let me draw a curtain over all
That far too brilliant spectacle so that
Before that splendid sight my own unmerit   840
May not be too intensely clear to me.
PRINCESS: Although that noble circle and those feats
      Enflamed you then for toil and emulation,
      I still could certify for you, young friend,
      At that same time the quiet creed of patience.
      Those festivals you praise, and which were praised
      To me at that time by a hundred tongues,
      And many years since then, I did not see.

Off in a quiet place to which the furthest
Echo of joy could fade away with scarcely   850
An interruption, I had to endure
Much pain and many grievous thoughts as well.
With wings outspread Death's image hovered there
Before my eyes and blocked the prospect outward
Into the world that is forever new.
Only by slow degrees did it withdraw
And let me glimpse, as through a veil, the many
Hues of life, all wan, but grateful still.
I saw its vivid figures gently stir again
And when I stepped forth, still supported by   860
My ladies, for the first time from my sick-room,
There came Lucretia full of joyous life
And with her hand presented you to me.
You were the first in that new life of mine
To meet me, new and quite unknown before.
I had great hopes for you and me; that hope
Has up to now not disappointed us.

Tasso: And I, bewildered by the tumult of
The surging throng, bedazzled with such splendor,
And agitated by hosts of emotions,   870
Walked silently along beside your sister
Through the tranquil hallways of the palace,
Then stepped into the room where you appeared
Before us presently supported by
Your ladies— What a moment! O forgive me!
As one bewitched by frenzy and delusion
Is lightly healed by presence of a godhead,
So I was cured of all my fantasies,
Of all my mania, of every false
Impulse, by one glance into your gaze.   880
If raw desires had formerly been lost
In the pursuing of a thousand objects,
I now stepped back within myself for shame
And came to know that which is worth desiring.

Thus one may search the wide sands of the sea
In vain to find a pearl that lies enclosed
And hidden in the quiet of a shell.

PRINCESS: It was a lovely time that then began,
And had my sister not wed the Duke of
Urbino and removed from us, years would   890
Have flown by in untroubled happiness.
Unfortunately we now too greatly miss
The cheerful mind, the heart replete with courage
And life, the rich wit of that gracious woman.

TASSO: I realize, and all too well, that since
The day of her departure no one could
Make up for you the pure delight you lost.
How often it has wrenched my heart! How often
I told the quiet grove my grief for you!
"Alas!" I cried, "Her sister has sole right,   900
Sole fortune to be precious to this dear one?
Is there no other heart in whom she might
Confide, no other soul of equal temper
With hers? Have mind and wit been quite extinguished?
Was this one woman, excellent as she was,
All things in all?" O pardon me, my Princess!
I often thought then of myself and wished
I might mean something to you. Very little,
Yet something, not with words, but with my actions
I wished to be so, show you by my life   910
Just how my heart was vowed to you in secret.
But I did not succeed, and far too often,
Through error, I did things that caused you pain,
Outraged the man to whom you gave protection,
Confused unwisely what you wished resolved,
And always at the moment when I wanted
To come more near, felt far and farther off.

PRINCESS: I have not, Tasso, ever failed to see
Your true intent, and I know you are zealous
In working your own harm. But where my sister   920

Could get along with anyone soever,
You scarcely seem to make out with a friend,
Not even after many years.
TASSO: Condemn me!
But tell me then where is the man or woman
Whom I may venture to address and talk to
With free heart as I dare to talk to you?
PRINCESS: You should do more confiding in my brother.
TASSO: He is my Prince! — But do not think that any
Wild impetus to freedom swells my bosom.
Man is not born so that he may be free.   930
And for a noble one no happiness
Is finer than to serve a Prince whom he
Reveres. He is my Lord, and I perceive
The total compass of that lofty word.
I must learn to be silent when he speaks,
And do as he commands, no matter how
Intensely heart and judgment contradict him.
PRINCESS: But with my brother that is not the case.
And now we have Antonio back again,
You are sure of a new and clever friend.   940
TASSO: I had so hoped; now I despair of it
Almost. How profitable association
With him would have been for me, and how useful
His counsel in a thousand instances!
He has, I dare say, all I lack. Yet — though
All gods conjoined to bring gifts to his cradle,
Unfortunately the Graces stayed away,
And one who lacks gifts from those gracious ones
May well own much, may well give much away,
But none can ever rest upon his bosom.   950
PRINCESS: Yet he may be confided in, and that
Is much! You must not ask for everything
From one man, and he does what he has promised.
Once he declares himself to be your friend,
He will provide whatever you may lack.

You two must be allied! I will be pleased
To bring this thing about before too long.
Only, do not resist, as is your habit.
Thus we have long had Leonore here,
Who is refined and lovely and with whom   960
It is not hard to get along, yet you
Have not been close to her as she desired.

TASSO: I have obeyed you, otherwise I would
Have held aloof instead of going nearer.
As amiable as she appears to be,
I don't know how it is, I rarely could
Be wholly frank with her, and even when
It is her purpose to please friends, one senses
The purpose and one is put off by it.

PRINCESS: On this path, Tasso, we shall never find   970
Companionship! This path leads us astray
To wander on through solitary thickets
And silent valleys; more and ever more
The personality is spoiled and seeks
To reestablish in its inner being
The golden age which it finds lacking outside,
However little this attempt succeeds.

TASSO: O what a term my Princess there expresses!
The golden age, O whither has it fled?
For which all hearts in vain are filled with yearning!   980
When on the free earth human beings roamed
Abroad in their enjoyment like the happy herds;
When a primaeval tree on bright-hued meadow
Afforded shade for shepherdess and shepherd,
And younger shrubs entwined their tender branches
Familiarly about a yearning love;
Where clear and still on sand forever pure
The supple stream embraced the nymphs so softly;
Where in the grass the startled serpent vanished
Quite harmlessly, where the audacious faun,   990
Soon chastised by the doughty youth, took flight;

     Where every bird in freedom of the air
     And every beast through hill and valley roving
     Told man: Whatever pleases is allowed.
PRINCESS: My friend, the golden age is doubtless past,
     But good men will establish it anew.
     And if I may state how I understand it:
     The golden age with which the poet often
     Beguiles us, that same golden age existed,
     It seems to me, as little then as now.   1000
     And if it did exist, it surely was
     What may recur repeatedly for us,
     For kindred hearts still chance on one another
     And share enjoyment of the lovely world.
     But in the motto one word must be changed,
     My friend: What is befitting is allowed.
TASSO: O if a general court consisting solely
     Of good and noble human beings would
     Decide what is befitting; and not have
     Each man deem proper what is useful to him.   1010
     We see how for the mighty and the clever
     All thrives, and he permits himself all things.
PRINCESS: If you would learn precisely what is fitting,
     Do no more than inquire of noble women.
     It is above all others their concern
     That everything that happens is befitting.
     Propriety erects a wall around
     The tender, easily offended sex.
     Where rules morality, there they rule also,
     Where impudence controls, they count for nothing.   1020
     And if you make inquiry of both sexes:
     Men strive for freedom, women for decorum.
TASSO: You term us coarse, unruly, feelingless?
PRINCESS: Not that. But you strive for far-off possessions,
     And all your striving must be violent.
     You make bold to act for eternity,
     Whereas we only want to own a close

And limited estate upon this earth,
And want it to endure for us steadfastly.
Of no man's heart can we be sure, no matter   1030
How warmly it surrendered once to us.
Beauty, which you seem to esteem alone,
Is transitory. What remains has no
More charm, and what has no more charm, is dead.
If there were men who prized a female heart
And who could realize just what a gracious
Treasure of fidelity and love
Can be contained within a woman's breast;
If memory of uniquely lovely hours
Would vividly remain within your souls,   1040
If your glance, otherwise so penetrating,
Could also penetrate the veil that age
Or illness casts upon us; if possession
Which is supposed to give tranquillity
Did not make you lust for another's goods;
A splendid day would have appeared for us,
Then we would celebrate our golden age.
TASSO: You speak words which rouse powerfully within
My bosom cares that were half lulled asleep.
PRINCESS: What do you mean? Speak frankly with me, Tasso.   1050
TASSO: I often heard it said, and recently
Have heard it said again, and had I not
Heard, I would still have thought it: noble princes
Are suing for your hand! And what we must
Expect, we fear and we could utterly
Despair. For you will leave us, it is natural.
How we will bear it, though, I do not know.
PRINCESS: Have no fears for the present moment. I
Might almost say: have no fears whatsoever.
Here I am glad to be and glad to stay;   1060
I still know no engagement that would tempt me.
And if you want so much to keep me, show
Me so by harmony and make yourself

A happy life, and through you, one for me.

TASSO: O teach me how to do the possible!
  To you are dedicated all my days.
  When my heart is unfolded to praise you,
  To give you thanks, then only do I feel
  The purest happiness that man can know;
  Divinest things I learned through you alone.   1070
  Thus earthly gods from other humans are
  Distinguished, just as high fate is distinguished
  From the advice and will of even those
  Men who are most astute. So much they let
  Pass by unnoticed as light wavelets rippling
  Before their feet, when we see mighty wave
  On mighty wave; they do not hear the storm
  That rages all around and overthrows us;
  They barely hear our plea for help and let
  The air be filled with sighs and lamentation,   1080
  As we do with poor children of small mind.
  You often have, O godlike one, had patience
  With me, and like the sun your glance has dried
  The dew that welled from underneath my eyelids.

PRINCESS: It is entirely proper women should
  Treat you in friendly fashion, for your poem
  Glorifies the sex in many ways.
  Gentle or brave, you have consistently
  Presented them as lovable and noble,
  And though Armida does appear as hateful,   1090
  Her charm and love conciliate us quickly.

TASSO: Whatever things reecho in my poem,
  I owe them all to one, to one alone.
  No unclear, immaterial image hovers
  Before my brow, now dazzlingly approaching
  My soul and now retreating. I have seen
  It with my very eyes, the archetype
  Of every virtue and of every beauty.
  What I have copied from it will endure:

Heroic love of Tancred for Chlorinda,   1100
Erminia's quiet faithfulness unnoticed,
Sophronia's greatness and Olinda's pain,
These are not shadows by illusion bred;
I know they are eternal, for they *are*.
And what has any better right to last
For centuries and have prolonged effect
More than the secret of a noble love
Confided modestly to lovely song?

PRINCESS: Shall I tell you another excellence
Which has been caught unnoticed by this poem?   1110
It lures us on and on; we listen and
We listen, and we think we understand;
And what we understand we cannot blame;
And thus this poem finally wins us over.

TASSO: O what a heaven you disclose for me,
My Princess! If this splendor does not blind me,
I see eternal happiness unhoped-for
Descending gloriously on golden rays.

PRINCESS: No further, Tasso! There are many things
Which we must seize upon with vehemence,   1120
But others can be ours through self-restraint
Alone and through renunciation. Such,
They say, is virtue, such, they say, is love,
Which is related to it. Mark this well.

                    [Exit.]

TASSO *(alone):*
Is it allowable to raise your eyes?
Do you dare look about? You are alone!
And did these columns hear what she pronounced?
And need you fear these silent witnesses
Of highest happiness? There now is rising
The sun of a new day of my existence,   1130
With which the former will not be compared.
Descending low the goddess swiftly lifts
The mortal up. What a new sphere reveals

Itself before my vision, what a realm!
How richly is the ardent wish rewarded!
I dreamed that I was near to highest bliss,
And *this* bliss is beyond all of my dreams.
Let one who was born blind conceive of light
And colors as he may; if the new day
Appears to him, it is as a new sense.   1140
Foresensing, heartened, staggering drunk with joy,
I enter on this path. You give me much,
You give as earth and heaven shower gifts
Upon us lavishly and with full hands,
And in return ask only what a gift
Like this entitles you to ask of me.
I must renounce, I must show self-restraint,
And thus deserve that you confide in me.
What have I ever done that she could choose me?
What must I do now to be worthy of her?   1150
She could confide in you, and hence you are.
Yes, Princess, to your words and to your gaze
Let my soul be forever consecrated!
Ask anything you will, for I am yours!
Let her send me to seek for toil and peril
And fame in foreign lands, or let her hand me
The golden lyre amid the tranquil grove,
Ordain me for repose and praise of her:
Hers am I; forming me she shall possess me.
For *her* my heart has hoarded every treasure.   1160
O had capacity a thousand-fold
Been given me by a god, I scarcely could
Express my word-transcending adoration.
The painter's brush, the poet's lips, the sweetest
That on the early honey ever fed,
These I could wish to have. No, Tasso shall
Henceforth not stray in solitude and moody
And weak among the trees and human beings!
He is no more alone, he is with *you*.

O if the noblest of all feats would here   1170
Present itself before me visibly
Ringed round with grisly peril! I would throw
Myself upon it, gladly risk the life
That I now have from her hands — I would challenge
The finest human beings as my friends
To come with noble forces and perform
Impossibilities upon her beck
And call. Rash man, why did your mouth not hold
Back what you felt till you could lay yourself
Yet far more worthily before her feet?   1180
That was your purpose and your wiser wish.
But be it so! It is far finer to
Receive a gift like this unmerited
Than half and half to fancy that one might
Have had a right to ask for it. Look cheerily!
It is so great, so vast, what lies before you,
And hopeful youth entices you again
Into a radiant and unknown future.
— Swell high, my heart! — Climate of happiness,
Accord your favor to this plant for once!   1190
It strives toward heaven, and a thousand branches
Grow forth from it, unfolding into blossoms.
May it bear fruit, and O may it bear joy!
And may a dear hand pluck the golden apples
Off from its fresh and richly laden boughs!
            [Enter Antonio.]
Welcome to you whom I behold now, as
It were, for the first time. No man was ever
More admirably announced to me. Hence, welcome!
I know you now and I know your full worth;
I offer heart and hand unhesitating   1200
And hope that you will not disdain me either.
ANTONIO: Fair gifts you offer me, and generously,
    I recognize their value as I should,
    Hence let me hesitate before I take them.

I do not know yet whether I in turn
Can offer you the same. I should not like
To seem in over-haste nor seem ungrateful;
Let me be prudent and concerned for both.

TASSO: Who will blame prudence? Every step in life
Reveals how indispensable it is.   1210
But it is finer when the soul informs us
Where we have no need of its circumspection.

ANTONIO: On that score let each man ask his own heart,
For he must pay for his mistake himself.

TASSO: So be it, then. I have performed my duty.
I have revered the Princess's command,
Who wants to see us friends, and have presented
Myself to you. Hold back, Antonio, I could not,
But I shall surely not impose myself.
Time and acquaintance will perhaps bring you   1220
To ask more warmly for the gift which you
Now coldly put aside and almost scorn.

ANTONIO: A self-restrained man often is termed cold
By those who think themselves more warm than others
Because a fleeting heat comes over them.

TASSO: You censure what I censure, what I shun.
I too am capable, young as I am,
Of putting permanency over fervor.

ANTONIO: Most wisely so! Be always of that mind.

TASSO: You are entitled to advise me and   1230
To warn me, for you have Experience at
Your side as proven and long-standing friend.
Still, credit that a quiet heart does harken
To every day's and every hour's warning
And practices in secret all the virtues
Your strictness thinks to teach as something new.

ANTONIO: It is agreeable to be concerned
With one's own self, if that but serve a purpose.
By introspection no man can discover
His inmost heart; by his own measure he   1240

Will judge himself too small, or else, alas,
Too great. Man knows himself through man alone
And only life can teach him what he is.

Tasso: I hear you with approval and respect.

Antonio: And yet at these words you are doubtless thinking
Something quite different from what I intend.

Tasso: In this way we will not come any nearer.
It is not sensible, it profits nothing
To misjudge any man deliberately,
Let him be who he may. I hardly needed   1250
The Princess's command, I quickly knew you:
I realize you wish and do the good.
Your own fate leaves you wholly unconcerned,
You think of others, give support to others,
And on the lightly changeful wave of life
Retain a steadfast heart. So I perceive you.
What would I be if I did not approach you
And did not eagerly seek to acquire
A portion of the treasure you are hoarding?
I know you won't regret it if you open   1260
Your heart, I know that you will be my friend
When once you know me, and I long have needed
Just such a friend. I feel my inexperience
And youth no cause for shame. About my head
The future's golden cloud still gently hovers.
O take me, noble man, unto your bosom
And consecrate me, rash and inexperienced,
Unto the temperate usages of life.

Antonio: All in a single minute you ask for
What time alone can grant with careful thought.   1270

Tasso: Within a single minute love will grant
What effort barely gains in length of time.
I do not ask this of you, I demand it.
I call upon you in that virtue's name
That vies in the allying of good men.
And shall I name a further name to you?

The Princess hopes for it, *she* wishes it —
Eleonore — she wants to bring me
To you and you to me. O let us meet
Her wish! Let us both go before that goddess   1280
And offer her our service, our whole souls,
United, to perform the utmost for her.
Once again! — Here is my hand! Clasp it!
Do not step back, refuse yourself no longer,
O noble man, and grant me the delight,
The best good human beings know, of yielding,
Without reserve, in trust, up to a better.

ANTONIO: You go with all sails crowded. It would seem
You are accustomed to win out, to find
The roads smooth everywhere and gates wide open.   1290
I willingly allow you every worth
And every lucky chance; but I see only
Too clearly we still stand too far apart.

TASSO: In years, in tested merit, that may be;
In courage and in will I yield to none.

ANTONIO: It is not will that coaxes high feats up,
And courage will imagine shorter ways.
A man who has achieved his goal is crowned;
A worthy one will often lack a crown.
There are, however, facile crowns, and there   1300
Are crowns of very different sorts. Sometimes
They can be comfortably achieved on strolls.

TASSO: What godhead freely grants to one and sternly
Refuses to another, such a prize
Will not be every man's to wish and will.

ANTONIO: Give Luck the credit over other gods
And I will listen, for his choice is blind.

TASSO: But Justice also wears a blindfold and
Has closed eyes in the face of all delusion.

ANTONIO: A lucky man may well extol Good Luck,   1310
And for the service may impute to him
A hundred eyes, shrewd choice, and strict discernment,

Call it Minerva, call it what he will,
Accept a gracious gift as a reward,
And take chance trimmings for well won adornment.

Tasso: You need not speak more plainly. This is quite enough!
I now see deep into your heart and know
You for a lifetime. O would that my Princess
Also knew you this way! Do not waste
The arrows of your eyes and of your tongue!   1320
You aim them futilely against the wreath,
The never-fading wreath upon my head.
First be so great as not begrudge me it
And then perhaps you may contest me for it.
I deem it sacred, a supreme possession.
Show me the man who has achieved the thing
That I am striving for, show me the hero
Of whom the stories merely told the tale,
Show me the poet who may be compared
With Homer and with Vergil, yes, and what   1330
Goes further still, show me the man who ever
Deserved with triple merit that reward
And yet was three times more than I ashamed
Of that fair crown, — then you will see me on
My knees before the god who so endowed me,
Nor would I rise until that god transferred
That mark of honor from my head to his.

Antonio: Till then, admittedly, you merit it.

Tasso: Appraise my worth: I will not shrink from that.
But I have not deserved contempt. The crown   1340
That my Prince deemed me worthy of and which
My Princess' hand entwined for me shall not
Be cast in doubt by sneers from anyone!

Antonio: Your high tone and swift heat do not beseem you
With me, and are not seemly in this place.

Tasso: What you presumed here may beseem me also.
Has truth perhaps been banished from this place?
Is the free mind imprisoned in the palace?

Must noble men endure oppression here?
Highness is here, I fancy, in its proper place,   1350
The highness of the soul! May it not joy
In presence of the great ones of this earth?
It may and shall. We come close to a Prince
By noble blood alone, ours from our forefathers,
But why not by the mind that Nature granted
Not great to every man, as she could not
Give every man a line of noble ancestors.
Smallness alone should feel uneasy here,
And envy, that appears to its own shame,
Just as no spider's filthy web may be   1360
Allowed to cling upon these marble walls.

ANTONIO: You prove me right yourself in spurning you!
And so the over-hasty boy would get
By force the grown man's confidence and friendship?
Ill-bred as you are, do you think you're good?

TASSO: Far rather what you choose to term ill-bred
Than what I could not help but term ignoble.

ANTONIO: You still are young enough that proper training
Can teach you something of a better way.

TASSO: Not young enough to bow in front of idols;   1370
To brave defiance with defiance, old
Enough.

ANTONIO: Where lip and lyre decide the contest
You do come off the hero and the victor.

TASSO: It would be rash to boast about my fists;
They have done nothing, but I trust in them.

ANTONIO: You reckon on forbearance, which has only
Spoiled you too much in arrogant good fortune.

TASSO: That I am grown to manhood, I now feel.
You are the last with whom I should have liked
To try the hazard of a pass with weapons,   1380
But you rake fire on top of fire until
My inmost marrow scorches and the painful
Lust for revenge seethes foaming in my breast.

So if you are the man you boast of, face me.

ANTONIO: You know as little who, as where, you are.

TASSO: No sanctuary bids us bear abuse.
You blaspheme and you desecrate this place,
Not I, who offered you my confidence,
Respect, and love, the finest offerings.
Your spirit has defiled this paradise   1390
And your words now defile this stainless room,
Not my heart's surge of passion which now rages
At suffering the slightest spot of soilure.

ANTONIO: What lofty spirit in that pent-up bosom!

TASSO: Here is still room to give that bosom vent.

ANTONIO: The rabble also vent their hearts with words.

TASSO: If you're a nobleman as I am, show it.

ANTONIO: Such am I, but I know, too, where I am.

TASSO: Come down then where our weapons may avail.

ANTONIO: You should not challenge, and I will not come.   1400

TASSO: Such obstacles are welcome to a coward.

ANTONIO: The coward threatens only where he's safe.

TASSO: With joy I can dispense with that protection.

ANTONIO: You compromise yourself, this place you cannot.

TASSO: The place forgive me for enduring this!
                    (He draws his sword.)
Draw or come after, if I am not to
Despise you, as I hate you, evermore!
                    [Enter Alfonso.]

ALFONSO: In what contention do I chance upon you?

ANTONIO: You find me standing calmly, O my Prince,
Before a man whom rage has seized upon.   1410

TASSO: Ah, I adore you as a deity for
Restraining me with just one glance of warning.

ALFONSO: Recount, Antonio, Tasso, and inform me
How did dissension get into my house?
How did it seize upon you, carrying off
In frenzy sane men from the path of proper
Behavior and of laws? I am astonished.

TASSO: I do not think that you quite know us both.
   This man, renowned as sensible and upright,
   Has treated me maliciously and rudely   1420
   Like an ill-bred and an ignoble man.
   I had approached him trustfully, but he
   Thrust me away; I in persistent love
   Pressed on, and ever more, more bitterly
   He did not rest till he had turned the purest
   Drop of blood in me to gall. Forgive me!
   You found me like a madman here. This man
   Is all to blame if I incurred a guilt.
   He was the one who fiercely fanned the fire
   That seized me and offended me and him.   1430
ANTONIO: His high poetic flight swept him away!
   You did, O Prince, address me first and asked
   Of me. Then let me be permitted to
   Speak second after this rash talker now.
TASSO: O yes! Relate, relate it word for word!
   And if you can put every syllable
   And every look before this judge, just dare!
   Disgrace yourself now for a second time
   And testify against yourself! And I
   Will not deny one breath or pulse-beat of it.   1440
ANTONIO: If you have any more to say, then say it.
   If not, be still and do not interrupt me.
   Did I, my Prince, or did this hothead here
   Begin the quarrel? Which one was it who
   Was in the wrong? That is an ample question
   Which for the moment must wait in abeyance.
TASSO: What? I should think that that was the first question,
   Which one of us is right and which is wrong.
ANTONIO: Not just the way the unrestricted mind
   May fancy it.
ALFONSO: Antonio!
ANTONIO: Gracious Lord,   1450
   I honor your behest, but keep him quiet.

Once I have spoken, he can talk again.
You will decide. Thus I will merely say:
I cannot argue with him, I can neither
Accuse him, nor defend myself, nor offer
Myself to give him satisfaction now.
For as he stands, he is not a free man.
A heavy law holds sway above him, which
Your favor at the most can mitigate.
He made threats to me here, he challenged me,   1460
He hardly hid his naked sword from you,
And had you, Lord, not intervened between us,
I too would stand here now as one disloyal,
Accessory to guilt, and shamed before you.

ALFONSO *(to Tasso):*
    You have not acted well.

TASSO: My own heart, Lord,
Acquits me; yours will surely do the same.
Yes, it is true, I made threats, challenged him,
And drew. But how insidiously his tongue
Offended me with well selected words,
How sharp and swift his fang injected its   1470
Fine venom in my blood, how he enflamed
The fever more and more, — you can't imagine!
Calmly, coldly, he kept at me, drove
Me to the highest pitch. O you don't know
Him, you don't know him, you will never know him!
I warmly offered him the finest friendship
And he threw my gift down before my feet.
Had my soul not flamed up with passion, it
Would be eternally unworthy of
Your favor and your service. If I did   1480
Forget the law and this place here, forgive me.
On no spot can I ever be abject,
On no spot can I bear humiliation.
If this heart ever, be it where it may,
Fails you and fails itself, then cast me out

And neṽer let me see your face again.

ANTONIO: How easily this youth bears heavy burdens
And shakes off faults like dust out of a garment!
It would be quite amazing, were the magic power
Of poetry not so well known, that loves   1490
So well to sport with the impossible.
I have my doubts, my Prince, that you and all
Your followers will look upon this deed
As being quite so insignificant.
For majesty extends its high protection
To every man that comes to it as to
A goddess and to its inviolate
Abode. As at the altar steps, all passion
Will hold itself in check upon her threshold.
There no sword gleams, no threatening word is uttered,   1500
Offense itself demands no vengeance there.
Broad fields provide sufficient open space
For fury and implacability.
No coward threatens there, no man takes flight.
These walls your fathers founded here upon
Security, and for their dignity
Made strong a sanctuary, solemnly
Maintaining peace by heavy penalties.
There prison, death, and exile overtook
The guilty; neither did regard for persons   1510
Or clemency restrain the arm of justice.
The wicked man himself was terror-stricken.
Now after long and splendid peace we see
Raw fury staggering back again in frenzy
Into the jurisdiction of right conduct.
Judge, Lord, and punish! Who can walk within
Set limits of his duty if the law
And if his Prince's power does not shield him?

ALFONSO: More than you both have said or ever could say
My own impartial mind gives me to hear.   1520
You would have done your duty vastly better

If I did not have to pronounce this judgment.
For right and wrong are close-related here.
If from Antonio you sustained offense,
Then he must give you satisfaction in
Some way or other, as you will demand.
I would prefer it if you chose me for
The arbitration. Meanwhile, your crime, Tasso,
Makes you a prisoner. As I forgive you,
I will alleviate the law for your sake.   1530
Leave us, Tasso. Stay in your own room,
Your own sole guard and by yourself alone.
TASSO: Is this, O Prince, your sentence as a judge?
ANTONIO: Do you not recognize a father's mildness?
TASSO *(to Antonio):*
  To you I have no more to at say present.
                    (to Alfonso)
  O Prince, your solemn sentence gives me over,
  A free man, to imprisonment. So be it!
  You deem it just. Your sacred word obeying,
  I bid my heart be still to deepest depths.
  This is so new to me that I almost   1540
  Do not know you, myself, or this fair place.
  But this man I know well — I will obey,
  Although I still could say a lot of things,
  And ought to say them, too. My lips fall silent.
  Was there a crime? It seems at least that I
  Am being looked on as a criminal.
  Speak my heart as it may, I am a captive.
ALFONSO: You make it graver, Tasso, than I do.
TASSO: It is incomprehensible to me.
  O not incomprehensible exactly,   1550
  I am no child. I almost think I must
  Have grasped it. Sudden light does dawn on me
  But in an instant closes up again.
  I hear my sentence only, and I bow.
  There are too many useless words already!

Acquire henceforth the habit of obeying.
You, feeble man, forgot where you were standing,
The gods' hall seemed to stand on equal earth
With you, and now the steep fall overwhelms you.
Obey with a good will, for it befits   1560
A man to do with good will what is painful.
First take this sword that you had given me
When I went with the Cardinal to France.
I wore it with no fame, nor yet with shame,
Not even here today. This hopeful gift
I yield up with a heart profoundly moved.
ALFONSO: You do not feel how I am minded toward you.
TASSO: Obedience is my lot, and not to think!
    Unfortunately a splendid gift's refusal
    Is what my destiny requires of me.   1570
    Nor does a crown befit a captive: I
    Remove the mark of honor from my head
    Myself, that I thought given for all time.
    That finest fortune was vouchsafed too early
    And, as if I had overreached myself,
    Is taken from me all too soon.
    You take yourself what no one could take from you,
    And what no god will give a second time.
    We human beings have most wondrous trials;
    We could not bear it, were it not that Nature   1580
    Endowed us with a blessed levity.
    Distress invites us to play recklessly
    And coolly with possessions beyond price,
    And willingly we open up our hands
    For such a thing to slip past all recall.
    There is a tear united with this kiss,
    Devoting you to transitoriness.
    It is permissible, this mark of weakness.
    Who would not weep when an immortal thing
    Itself is not safe from annihilation?   1590
    Come, join this sword, which had no part, alas,

In winning you, and, twined about it, rest,
As on the coffin of the brave, upon
The tomb of my good fortune and my hope.
I willingly lay both before your feet,
For who is well armed if you are in anger,
And who adorned, Lord, if you fail to note him?
I go, a captive, to await my judgment.

> (*At the Prince's sign, a page picks up the sword and wreath and carries them away.*)

ANTONIO: Where is the boy's wild raving taking him?
In what hues does he paint his fate and merits?   1600
Restricted, inexperienced, youth considers
Itself as a unique and elect being
To whom all is allowed above all others.
Let him feel punished; punishment is good
For youth, and the adult will thank us for it.

ALFONSO: Punished he is; I only fear: too much.

ANTONIO: If you wish to deal leniently with him,
Then give him back, O Prince, his liberty
And let the sword then settle our dispute.

ALFONSO: If opinion so requires, that may be done.   1610
But tell me, how did you provoke his anger?

ANTONIO: I scarcely can say how it came about.
I may perhaps have hurt his human feelings,
But as a nobleman I gave him no
Offense, and at the height of anger no
Improper word escaped his lips.

ALFONSO: So seemed
Your quarrel to me, and what I thought at once
Is all the more confirmed by what you say.
When grown men quarrel, one may justly hold
The shrewder one responsible. You ought   1620
Not to be angry with him; guiding him
Would more become you. But there still is time.
This is no case that would require a duel.
As long as peace remains to me, I want

Just so long to enjoy it in my house.
Restore a calm, you can do so with ease.
Lenore Sanvitale will first seek
With gentle lips to sooth his agitation.
Then go to him, and in my name restore
His total liberty to him and gain   1630
His confidence with honest, noble words.
Perform this just as soon as possible.
You will talk to him like a friend and father.
I want peace made before we go away,
And nothing is impossible to you
When once you will. Best we delay an hour,
Then let the ladies gently finish up
What you began; when we ourselves get back,
They will have wiped out every trace of this
Abrupt impression. It appears, Antonio,   1640
That you will not get out of practice. You
Have barely finished with one task, when back
You come and straightway get yourself another.
I trust you will succeed in this one also.
ANTONIO: I am abashed, and in your words I see
    My guilt as in the clearest mirror. With
    Alacrity a man obeys a master
    Who can persuade us as he gives commands.   (1648)

ACT III

THE PRINCESS *(alone):* Where does Eleonore stay? Concern
  More painfully with every moment stirs   1650
  My deepest heart. I scarcely know what happened,
  I scarcely know which one if them is guilty.
  If she would only come! I should not like
  To speak yet with my brother or Antonio
  Until I am more calm, till I have heard
  How things now stand and what may come to be.
           [Enter Leonore.]
  What news do you bring, Leonore? Tell me,
  How do things stand now with our friend? What happened?
LEONORE: I could not learn more than we know already.
  They harshly clashed, and Tasso drew his sword,   1660
  Your brother parted them. It seems, however,
  That it was Tasso who began the quarrel.
  Antonio walks about conversing with
  His Prince, while Tasso on the other hand
  Remains alone and banished in his room.
PRINCESS: Antonio provoked him certainly
  And coldly gave the high-strung youth offense.
LEONORE: I have the same opinion, for there was
  A cloud upon his brow when he arrived.
PRINCESS: Alas, that we fail so completely to   1670
  Observe the pure, mute signal of the heart!
  A god speaks very softly in our bosoms,
  Softly and audibly, and shows us what
  We should accept and what we should avoid.
  Antonio seemed to me this morning much
  More gruff, withdrawn into himself, than ever.

When Tasso went up to him then, my mind
Gave me a warning. Just observe the outer
Appearance of the two, in face, in voice,
In look, in gait. All points in opposition;   1680
They cannot ever give each other love.
But that dissembler, Hope, persuaded me
And whispered: Both of them are rational men,
Both noble, erudite, and both your friends.
What bond is surer than that of good men?
I urged the youth and he agreed completely;
How warm and fine his acquiescence was!
O had I only spoken with Antonio!
I hesitated; there was little time,
I shrank from recommending urgently   1690
The youth to him in the first words I spoke;
I trusted to good manners and politeness,
In social usage which is interposed
So smoothly even between enemies,
And from the tested man had no fear of
A rash youth's over-haste. But it is done.
The evil was far off, now it is here.
O give me counsel! What is to be done?
LEONORE: You feel yourself how difficult it is
To counsel after what you tell me. Here   1700
Is no like-minded men's misunderstanding;
Words could set that aright, or weapons could,
If needs be, easily and happily.
But these are two men, as I long have felt,
Who must be enemies because great Nature
Did not form one man from the two of them.
And if they were shrewd for their own advantage,
They would ally themselves as friends together.
Then they would stand as one man and would walk
Along through life with joy and might and fortune.   1710
I had so hoped, but now I see, in vain.
Today's dissension, be it as it may,

Can be composed, but that gives no assurance
For future times, not even for tomorrow.
It would be best for Tasso, I should think,
To travel for a time away from here.
Why, he could go to Rome, and Florence too;
There in a few weeks I could meet him and
Could work upon his spirits as a friend.
Meanwhile, Antonio, who has become   1720
So alien to us, you would be bringing
Closer to you and to your friends once more.
In that way time, that does so much, perhaps
Might grant what now seems quite impossible.
PRINCESS: You want the pleasure for yourself, my friend,
    While I must do without. Is that quite nice?
LEONORE: You will not do without, except for what
    You could not now enjoy in any case.
PRINCESS: Am I to send a friend away so calmly?
LEONORE: Retain him, whom you only seem to banish.   1730
PRINCESS: My brother will not willingly release him.
LEONORE: When he sees it as we do, he will yield.
PRINCESS: Condemning oneself in a friend is hard.
LEONORE: Yet you will save your friend thus in yourself.
PRINCESS: I do not cast my vote for it to happen.
LEONORE: Then look for greater evil yet to come.
PRINCESS: You pain me, while unsure if you are helping.
LEONORE: We soon shall learn which one of us is wrong.
PRINCESS: And if it is to be, ask me no longer.
LEONORE: One who can make decisions, conquers sorrow.   1740
PRINCESS: I cannot quite decide, but be it so
    If he is not to be away for long —
    Let us be watchful for him, Leonore,
    That he not suffer want in times to come
    And that the Duke may willingly advance
    His stipend to him even while abroad.
    Talk with Antonio, for with my brother
    He has much influence and will not hold

This quarrel against us or against our friend.

LEONORE: One word from you would, Princess, have more   1750
                             weight.

PRINCESS: I am not able, as you know, my friend,
  To ask things for myself and for my own
  The way my sister of Urbino can.
  I live my life so quietly, and from
  My brother gratefully accept whatever
  He can and wishes to provide me with.
  I used once to reproach myself for this,
  But I have overcome that feeling now.
  A friend of mine would often scold me for it.
  "You are unselfish," she would say to me,   1760
  "And that is splendid; but you are so much so
  That you can have no just perception of
  Your friends' requirements either." I admit it
  And must therefore put up with that reproach.
  Hence I am all the better pleased that I
  Now really can be of use to our friend.
  I do receive my mother's legacy,
  And I will gladly help toward his support.

LEONORE: And I too find myself in a position,
  O Princess, where I can help as a friend.   1770
  He does not manage well, and where he lacks,
  I will be able to assist him nicely.

PRINCESS: Take him away, then, and if I must do
  Without him, you shall have first claim on him.
  I realize it will be best that way.
  But must I praise this sorrow once again
  As good and wholesome? That was my fate ever
  From childhood, I am used to it by now.
  But happiness is no more than half lost
  If we did not count its possession certain.   1780

LEONORE: Deserving as you are, I hope to see
  You happy.

PRINCESS: Happy? O Eleonore!

Who ever is quite happy? — I might term
My brother so, for his great heart endures
His destiny with ever equal courage.
But what he merits, never has been his.
And is my sister of Urbino happy?
That lovely woman, great and noble heart!
She bears no children to her younger husband
And he esteems her and does not hold it   1790
Against her, but no joy dwells in their house.
What was the good of all our mother's wisdom,
Her learning of all kinds, and her great mind?
Could it protect her from mistakes of others?
They parted us from her; now she is dead.
She did not leave us children with the comfort
That she died reconciled unto her God.

LEONORE: O do not look at what all persons lack,
Consider what remains for each! What, Princess,
Does not remain for you?

PRINCESS: Remain for me?   1800
Patience, Eleonore! I could practice that
From childhood up. While sister, brother, friends
Gregariously had joy in games and parties,
My illness kept me shut within my room,
And in the company of many ailments
I early had to learn to do without.
One thing there was that charmed my solitude,
The joy of song; I used to entertain
Myself myself, I lulled my pain, my yearning,
My every wish, to sleep with gentle tones.   1810
Grief often turned to pleasure then, and even
The sense of sadness turned to harmony.
That happiness was not allowed me long,
The doctor took that too away; his strict
Command bade me be still. I was to live,
To suffer, and to renounce the least small comfort.

LEONORE: So many friends came in to see you, and

You now are well and take delight in life.
PRINCESS: Yes, I am well, which means I am not ill;
    And I have many friends whose faithfulness   1820
    Does make me glad. I also had a friend —
LEONORE: You have him still.
PRINCESS: But I shall lose him soon.
    The moment when I first caught sight of him
    Meant much to me. I hardly had recovered
    From many sufferings, and pain and illness
    Had only just departed; timidly
    I looked at life again, joyed in the daylight
    Again, and in my brother and my sister,
    And with new strength inhaled sweet hope's pure fragrance.
    I ventured to look further forward into   1830
    Life's vistas, and out of the further distance
    Came forms of friends approaching me. And then,
    Eleonore, came my sister and presented
    This youth to me; he came led by her hand,
    And, to confess quite frankly, my soul seized
    Upon him and will hold him fast forever.
LEONORE: Have no regrets on that score, O my Princess!
    To recognize nobility is gain,
    A gain that never can be wrested from us.
PRINCESS: Things beautiful and excellent are to be feared,   1840
    As flame is, that is of such splendid use
    So long as it burns only on your hearth,
    So long as it shines for you from a torch,
    How lovely! Who can or who wants to do
    Without it? Once it eats abroad unguarded,
    How wretched it can make us! Leave me now.
    I have been garrulous and should conceal
    Even from you how weak I am, and ill.
LEONORE: The illness of the spirit is relieved
    Most easily by grieving and confiding.   1850
PRINCESS: I shall be healed soon if confiding heals:
    To you I give full confidence and pure.

Alas, my friend, I have made up my mind:
Let him depart. But I already feel
The long protracted suffering of those days when
I am deprived of what gave me delight.
The sun no longer will lift from my eyelids
His beautiful, transfigured dream-impression;
The hope of seeing him no more will fill
My scarce awakened mind with joyous yearning;   1860
My first glance down into our gardens will
Seek him in vain amid the dewy shadows.
How pleasingly the wish was gratified
To be with him on every cheerful evening!
How our companionship increased the wish
To know and understand each other better.
Each day our spirits tuned themselves more truly
In pure and ever purer harmonies.
But what a twilight now descends before me!
The sun's resplendency, the happy feeling   1870
Of lofty day, the thousandfold world's bright
And radiant presence are all empty and
Veiled deep within the mist that is around me.
Before, each day was a whole life to me;
Foreboding's self was still, and care was silent,
And under joyous sail, the river bore us
Along on lightest waves without a rudder.
Now terrors of the future overwhelm
My heart in stealth amid the dismal present.
LEONORE: The future will return your friends to you   1880
    And bring new joy and happiness as well.
PRINCESS: Whatever I possess I like to keep.
    Change brings diversion but does little good.
    In youthful yearning I have never reached
    With greed into strange persons' urns of fate
    To seize perchance upon some object for
    My own requiring, inexperienced heart.
    I had to honor him, therefore I loved him;

I had to love him, for with him my life
Became a life such as I never knew.   1890
I told myself at first: Withdraw from him!
I yielded, yielded, and came ever closer,
So sweetly lured and yet so harshly punished.
A pure and true possession now escapes me;
For joy and happiness an evil spirit
Now gives my longing corresponding sorrows.

LEONORE: If a friend's words can give no consolation,
The quiet power of the lovely world
And better times will unperceived restore you.

PRINCESS: The world indeed is beautiful! Across   1900
Its breadth so much of good moves back and forth.
Alas, that it forever seems to move
By just one step away from us
And lure our fearful yearning on through life,
Step after step, up to our very graves!
It is so rarely human beings find
What seemed to have been theirs by destiny,
So rarely that they ever can retain
What once their hands successfully have seized on!
What first submitted to us, wrenches free   1910
And we relinquish what so avidly
We clutched. There is a happiness; we know
It not, or knowing, know not how to prize it.
[Exit.]

LEONORE *(alone):* How sad I feel for that fine, noble heart!
How sad the lot that now falls to Her Highness!
She loses — and do you think you will gain?
Is it so needful that he go away?
Or do you make it needful, to obtain
The heart and talents for yourself which up
To now you have shared with another — shared   1920
Unequally? Is acting thus quite honest?
Are you not rich enough? What do you lack for?
Husband and son, possessions, rank and beauty,

You have what one would like to give you. He
Engages us in our own special field.
He lacks a thousand little things, which to
Procure a woman gladly bends her efforts.   2070
He likes to wear the finest linen, or
A silken garment with embroidery.
He likes to see himself in fine array;
Ignoble stuff that suits a lackey only
He cannot bear, and everything of his
Must be becoming, fine, and good, and noble.
And yet he has no skill in getting all
These things himself, or when he does possess them,
In keeping them; he always lacks for money,
For prudent care. He will leave one thing here,   2080
And leave another there, — he never comes
Back from a journey but that one third of
His things are missing, — then again his servant
Will steal from him. And so, Antonio,
One needs to take care of him all year long.

ANTONIO: And that care makes him dear and dearer still.
  O happy youth, to have shortcomings reckoned
  As virtues, be so handsomely allowed
  To play the boy still while a man, be able
  To boast about his lovely weaknesses!   2090
  You would have to forgive me, my fair friend,
  If I were to become a trifle bitter.
  You don't tell all, — what he presumes, for instance,
  And that he is more shrewd than people think.
  He boasts two flames of love! ties and unties
  The knots now one way, now another, and
  By *such* arts wins *such* hearts! Would anyone
  Believe it?

LEONORE: Good! That very fact will prove
  That it is only friendship that impels us.
  And even if we traded love for love,   2100
  Would we not cheaply pay that splendid heart

That quite forgets itself and in devotion
Lives for its friends amid a lovely dream?
ANTONIO: Go on and spoil him, more and ever more,
    Allow his selfishness to pass for love,
    Offend all friends who dedicate themselves
    To you with loyal souls, pay that proud man
    Your voluntary tribute, and destroy
    The worthy circle of a common trust!
LEONORE: We are not quite so partial as you think,   2110
    We do admonish our young friend in many
    Cases; we want to educate him so
    He can enjoy himself more and give others
    More to enjoy. What is blameworthy in him
    Is not by any means obscured from us.
ANTONIO: Yet you praise many things that should be blamed.
    I long have known him, for he is so easy
    To know, and too proud to conceal himself.
    He sinks into himself as if the world
    Were all inside his heart and he were wholly   2120
    Sufficient to himself within his world,
    And all around him disappears for him.
    He drops it, lets it go, thrusts it away,
    And rests upon himself. — Then suddenly
    As an unnoticed spark ignites the mine,
    In joy, grief, whim, or anger, he explodes;
    Then he wants to grasp everything and hold it,
    Then must be done whatever he may fancy,
    Within a moment's space must come about
    What ought to be prepared through length of years,   2130
    Within a moment's space must be removed
    What effort scarcely could resolve in years.
    He asks from himself the impossible
    So that he may in turn ask it of others.
    His mind wants to assemble ultimates
    Of things together; scarcely one from millions
    Of human beings can succeed in that,

And he is not the man. He falls at last,
No wise improved, right back into himself.

LEONORE: He harms himself, he does no harm to others. 2140

ANTONIO: He does hurt other people all too much.
Can you deny that in the moment of
The passion that so swiftly seizes him
He will presume to blaspheme and abuse
The Prince, the Princess' self, or whomsoever?
Just for the moment, to be sure. However,
That moment will recur, for he controls
His mouth as little as he does his heart.

LEONORE: I should imagine, if he went away
From here for a brief time, it would be good 2150
For him and also profit others too.

ANTONIO: Perhaps; perhaps not. Right now it is not
To be considered; for I do not want
The burden of the error on my shoulders.
It might appear that I drove him away,
And I do not drive him away. For all
I care, he can stay at our court in peace.
And if he wishes to be reconciled
With me, if he can follow my advice,
Then we can get along quite tolerably. 2160

LEONORE: Then you hope to have influence upon
A spirit that you recently thought hopeless.

ANTONIO: We always hope, and it is better in
All things to hope than to despair. For who
Can calculate what all is possible?
He is dear to our Prince. He must stay with us.
And if we try in vain to educate him,
He will not be the only one we bear with.

LEONORE: I did not think you so impartial, so
Devoid of passion. Your mind swiftly changed. 2170

ANTONIO: Age must have one advantage, after all;
If; namely, it cannot escape from error,
It can control itself immediately.

You were at first concerned with reconciling
Me with your friend. Now I ask that of you.
Do what you can so this man finds himself
And everything is back again to normal.
I shall myself go to him just as soon
As I find out from you that he is calm,
And just as soon as you think that my presence   2180
Will not make matters worse. And yet, whatever
You do, do it within the hour. Alfonso
Is going back this evening yet, and I
Shall be accompanying him. Meanwhile, farewell.

[Exit.]

LEONORE *(alone):* This time, my friend, we are not in agreement.
My own advantage does not go along
Today with yours. Hence I shall use the time
In trying to win Tasso over. Quickly!   (2188)

ACT IV

A room.

Tasso *(alone):* Have you awakened from a dream, and has
    The fair illusion left you suddenly?   2190
    Did sleep subdue you on a day of highest
    Pleasure, and does it now hold and torment
    Your soul with heavy fetters? Yes, you wake
    And yet you dream. Where have the hours gone
    That played about your head with wreaths of flowers?
    Or those days when your spirit with free yearning
    Pierced through the blue that heaven spread afar?
    Yet you are still alive, you touch yourself,
    You touch yourself and are not sure you live.
    Is it my fault, is it another's fault   2200
    That I now find myself here as one guilty?
    Have I infringed a law, that I must suffer?
    Is not my entire fault a merit rather?
    I looked at him, and I was swept away
    By good will and the heart's deceitful hope
    That, bearing human features, he was human.
    Thus I went up to him with open arms
    And I encountered locks and bolts, no heart.
    O I had thought it out so cleverly
    How I was going to receive the man   2210
    Who this long time had seemed suspicious to me!
    But whatsoever has befallen you,
    Yet hold fast to one thing of certainty:
    I did see *her!* She stood right there before me!
    She spoke to me, and I did hear her speak!
    Her glance, her tone, and her words' lovely meaning,

555

Those are forever mine, time cannot rob me
Of them, nor destiny, nor yet wild fortune!
And if my spirit soared aloft too fast,
And if I all too swiftly gave vent to   2220
The flame within my bosom which devours
Me now, I still do not regret it, and
Though my life's fate were thereby lost forever,
I would devote myself to her and gladly
Go at her bidding though it called to ruin.
So be it! I still showed that I was worthy
Of that exquisite trust that gives me life,
That gives me life now at this very hour
That forcibly throws open the black portal
Of a long time of grief. — Yes, it is done!   2230
The sun of fairest favor sets for me
All of a sudden. Now the Prince averts
His gracious glance from me and leaves me here
To stand lost on a dismal, narrow path.
Those ugly winged things of double omen,
The loathly retinue of ancient Night,
They swarm forth now and whir about my head.
O where, O where shall I direct my step
To flee these noisome things that whiz about me,
And to escape from the abyss before me?   2240

[Enter Leonore.]

LEONORE: What has bechanced? Dear Tasso, did your zeal
And your suspicious thought so goad you on?
What happened? We are all in consternation.
Your gentle temper, your complaisant way,
Your rapid glance, and your just understanding
Whereby you give to each man what belongs
To him, your equanimity that bears
What noble men soon learn to bear but vain
Men seldom, wise control of tongue and lip —
Dear friend, I almost fail to recognize you!   2250

TASSO: And what if all those things had now been lost?

What if you came upon a friend whom you
Thought rich and found him suddenly a beggar?
You are quite right, I am myself no longer,
And yet I am such just as much as ever.
It seems to be a riddle, but is not.
The quiet moon that gives you joy by night
And with its shining lures your eye and spirit
Irresistably, it floats by day
An insignificant, pale, little cloudlet.   2260
I am outshone by splendor of the day.
You do not know me, I know myself no longer.

LEONORE: I do not understand what you are saying,
  The way you put it, Friend. Explain yourself.
  Did the gruff man's offense hurt you so deeply
  That you completely fail to recognize
  Yourself and us as well? Confide in me.

TASSO: I am not the offended one; you see
  Me punished here because I gave offense.
  The sword would cut the knot of many words   2270
  Quite easily and fast, but I am captive.
  You hardly know — do not, dear friend, be frightened —
  But you now find your friend inside a jail.
  The Prince is punishing me like a schoolboy.
  I will not argue with him, cannot do so.

LEONORE: You seem to be upset more than is proper.

TASSO: Do you think me so weak, so much a child,
  That such a fall could shatter me at once?
  The thing that happened does not hurt me deeply;
  What hurts me is the thing it signifies   2280
  For me. Just let my enviers and foes
  Alone to act. The field is free and open.

LEONORE: You entertain a false suspicion of
  Many of them, I have convinced myself.
  Nor does Antonio bear you such ill-will
  As you imagine. And today's vexation —

TASSO: I set that quite aside, and only take

Antonio as he was and still remains.
His stiff-necked shrewdness always did annoy me,
His everlasting playing of the master.   2290
Instead of seeing if his hearer's mind
Is not already on the proper track,
He lectures you on things that you felt better
And more profoundly, does not hear a word
You say to him, and will misjudge you always.
To be misjudged, misjudged by a proud man
Who smilingly thinks he is so superior!
I am not old enough or wise enough
That I should merely smile back and endure it.
Sooner or later, it could not go on,   2300
We had to break; and later it would only
Have been just that much worse. I recognize
One master only, just the one who feeds me;
Him I will gladly follow, but no other.
I must be free in thinking and creating;
In action the world hems us in enough.
LEONORE: He often speaks of you with high esteem.
TASSO: Forbearingly, you mean, subtly and shrewdly.
And that is what annoys me, for he can
So smoothly speak, with such condition, that   2310
His praise becomes disparagement and nothing
Hurts you worse or more deeply than praise from
His mouth.
LEONORE: O if you only could have heard,
My friend, the way he used to speak of you
And of the talent gracious Nature gave you
Above so many. He unquestionably
Feels what you are and have, and he esteems it.
TASSO: A selfish spirit, O believe me, cannot
Escape the torments of its narrow envy.
A man like that may well forgive another   2320
His fortune, rank, and honor, for he thinks:
That you yourself will have if you so wish,

And persevere, and Fortune favors you.
But what has been alone conferred by Nature,
What lies beyond the reach of all exertion,
Forever unattainable by effort,
What neither gold, nor sword, nor shrewdness, nor
Persistence can achieve, that he will not
Forgive. He grant me that? He, who with stiff
Mind fancies he will force the Muses' favor?   2330
Who, when he strings the thoughts of many poets
Together, seems to see himself a poet?
He will far sooner grant my Prince's favor,
Which he would like to limit to himself,
Than that high talent which those Heavenly Ones
Have given to the poor and orphaned youth.
LEONORE: O if you saw as clearly as I see it!
    You are mistaken, he is not that way.
TASSO: If I mistake him, I mistake him gladly!
    I see him as my most insidious foe   2340
    And would be desolated if I had
    To see him as more lenient. It is foolish
    To be fair-minded all the time; that is
    Destruction of oneself. Are human beings
    So fair of mind toward us? O no! O no!
    The human being in his narrow nature
    Requires the double feeling, love and hate.
    Does he not need the night as well as day
    And sleep as well as waking? No, I must
    From now on look upon this man as object   2350
    Of my profoundest hatred; nothing can
    Deprive me of the pleasure of imagining
    Him worse and worse.
LEONORE: If you, dear friend, will not
    Desist from this opinion, I can hardly
    See how you can remain here at this court.
    You know what weight he carries, and must carry.
TASSO: How totally superfluous I have

Been here this long time, I well know, fair friend.

LEONORE: That you are not, that you can never be!
You know how glad the Prince is, and how glad   2360
The Princess is to live with you; and when
The sister from Urbino comes, she comes
Almost as much for your sake as her brother's
And sister's sake. They all alike think well
Of you, and each has total trust in you.

TASSO: O Leonore, what kind of trust is that?
When has he ever said a word to me,
A serious word, about his state? If ever
There was a special case where, even in
My presence he consulted with his sister   2370
Or others, he did not ask my opinion.
Always it was: "Antonio will be coming!
We must write to Antonio! Ask Antonio!"

LEONORE: Instead of thanking him, you are complaining.
If he is pleased to give you total freedom,
He pays you honor, as he can pay honor.

TASSO: He lets me be, because he thinks me useless.

LEONORE: You are not useless just because inactive.
Care and vexation you have held so long,
Like a beloved infant, at your bosom.   2380
I have considered often, and consider
It as I will, — upon this splendid ground
Where Fortune seemed to have transplanted you,
You do not thrive. O Tasso! — Shall I say it?
Shall I advise you? — You should go away.

TASSO: O do not spare the patient, dear physician!
Give him the remedy, do not consider
If it is bitter. — If he can recover,
That is the thing to ponder, wise, good friend!
I see it all myself, it is all over!   2390
Him I can well forgive, me he can not.
They need him, and, alas, do not need me.
And he is shrewd, and I, alas, am not.

And he works to my harm, and I can not,
I do not like to harm him back. My friends,
They let it pass, they see it otherwise,
They barely make resistance, and should fight.
You think that I should leave. I think so too —
So then, farewell. I will endure that also.
You parted with me — may the strength and courage   2400
Be granted me to part with you as well.
LEONORE: O, from a distance everything looks purer
Which from near-by we find bewildering merely.
Then you will realize perhaps what love
Surrounded you on every side, what value
The loyalty of true friends has, and how
The wide world does not take the place of close ones.
TASSO: That we shall see. From childhood I have known
The world, the way it leaves one destitute
And lonely quite without concern, and goes   2410
Its way like sun and moon and other gods.
LEONORE: If you heed me, my friend, you never shall
Go through this sad experience again.
If you take my advice, you will go first
To Florence, and a friend will there most kindly
Look after you. Be of good cheer. That friend
Is I myself. I go to meet my husband
There in the next few days, and I can give
No greater joy to him or to myself
Than if I bring you with me to our midst.   2420
I shall not say a word, you know yourself
To what kind of a Prince you will be coming,
What kind of men that lovely city holds
Within its bosom, and what kind of women.
You do not speak? Consider well! Decide.
TASSO: It is delightful, what you say, so wholly
In keeping with the wish I entertain.
Only, it is too new. I beg you, let
Me think it over. I will soon decide.

LEONORE: I go away now with the fairest hopes 2430
    For you and us and also for this house.
    Consider, and if you consider rightly,
    You hardly can conceive a better plan.
TASSO: Just one more thing, beloved friend! Tell me,
    How is the Princess now disposed toward me?
    Was she annoyed with me? What did she say? —
    She did blame me severely? Speak quite freely.
LEONORE: Since she knows you, she easily excused you.
TASSO: Have I lost in her eyes? Don't flatter me.
LEONORE: Women's favor is not so lightly lost. 2440
TASSO: Will she release me gladly if I go?
LEONORE: If it is for your welfare, certainly.
TASSO: Will I not lose the Prince's favor too?
LEONORE: In his magnanimity you can rest safely.
TASSO: And will we leave the Princess all alone?
    You go away; though I meant little to her,
    I still know that I did mean something to her.
LEONORE: A distant friend provides us very friendly
    Association, if we know him happy.
    This will succeed, and I see you made happy, 2450
    For you will not leave here unsatisfied.
    The Prince so ordered, and Antonio
    Will come to see you. He himself now blames
    The bitterness within him which so hurt you.
    Receive him calmly when he comes, I beg you.
TASSO: In every sense I can stand up to him.
LEONORE: And Heaven grant me still before you go,
    Dear friend, to open up your eyes and show you
    That no one in the entire fatherland
    Hates, persecutes, or works you secret harm. 2460
    You surely err, and as you formerly
    Wove verse for others' joy, so now, alas,
    In this case you have woven an odd web
    To harm yourself. I shall do everything
    To rip it all asunder, so that you

May walk the fair pathway of life in freedom.
Farewell. I shall hope for a good word soon.
                        [Exit.]
TASSO *(alone):* I am to recognize that no one hates me,
   That no one persecutes me, that all cunning
   And all the secret webs were solely spun   2470
   And woven of themselves inside my head!
   I'm to confess that I am in the wrong,
   That I to many do injustice, who
   Have not deserved it of me! And this in
   An hour when my full right lies clear before
   The countenance of the sun, as does their craft.
   I am to feel profoundly how the Prince
   Grants me his favor with an open heart,
   Apportions gifts to me in bounteous measure.
   Just at the moment when he, weak enough,   2480
   Lets his eye by my enemies be darkened
   And surely lets his hands be fettered too!
   That he is being deceived, he cannot see,
   And that they are deceivers, I can't show him;
   So that he may be quietly deceived,
   So that they may deceive him comfortably,
   I am to bide in silence, even yield!
   And who gives me this counsel? Who so shrewdly
   Urges me with true and fond opinion?
   Lenore herself, Lenore Sanvitale,   2490
   My tender friend! Aha! I know you now!
   O why did I put trust in her lips ever?
   She was not honest, though she showed me ever
   So much her favor or her tenderness
   With her beguiling words! O no, she was
   And still remains a crafty heart; she turns
   Toward favor with a soft and clever tread.
   How often I have willingly deceived
   Myself about her too! Yet basically
   My vanity alone deceived me. Good!   2500

I knew her, yet kept flattering myself;
She is this way with others, I would say,
But with you it is frank and true opinion.
And now I see it, see it all too late.
I then was favored, and she clung so softly
To one who had been favored. Now I fall,
She turns her back on me, as Fortune does.
She comes now as a cat's-paw of my foe,
She glides up to me here and with smooth tongue
The little serpent hisses magic tones.   2510
She seemed so lovely! Lovelier than ever!
What healing was in her lips' every word!
Yet flattery could not conceal for long
Her false intention from me. The opposite
Appeared too clearly written on her brow
Of everything she said. I quickly feel it
When someone seeks the pathway to my heart
And does not mean it from the heart. I am
To leave? For Florence, as soon as I can?
And why for Florence? I see that quite well.   2520
There rules the new house of the Medici,
Not, to be sure, in open enmity with
Ferrara, but still silent envy with
A cold hand holds the noblest souls apart.
If I receive distinguished tokens of
Their favor from those noble princes there,
As certainly I might expect to do,
The hangers-on would soon make my devotion
And gratitude suspicious; they would succeed.
Yes, I will leave, but not the way you wish.   2530
Yes, I will go, and further than you think.
What is there for me here? Who holds me back?
O every word I understood too well
That I enticed from Leonore's lips!
From word to word I barely caught it, now
I know the whole of what the Princess thinks —

Yes, yes, that too is true, do not despair!
"She will release me gladly if I go,
If it is for my welfare." O! I wish
She had a passion in her heart that would   2540
Destroy me and my welfare! Far more welcome
Would be the death that seized me, than this hand
That coldly, stiffly, lets me go — I go! —
Be on your guard now and let no appearance
Of friendship or goodwill deceive you. No one
Deceives you unless you deceive yourself.

[Enter Antonio.]

ANTONIO: I come to have a word with you here, Tasso,
    If you can and desire to hear me calmly.
TASSO: Action, you know, is still forbidden me.
    It well befits me to wait and to listen.   2550
ANTONIO: I find you tranquil, as I wish to do,
    And gladly speak to you from my free heart.
    First I dissolve, and in the Prince's name,
    The tenuous bond that seemed to hold you captive.
TASSO: Caprice now sets me free, as once it bound me.
    This I accept and do not ask for trial.
ANTONIO: Then let me say to you: It seems that I,
    By words, have hurt you deeply and still worse
    Than I myself, stirred up with many passions,
    Had realized. No word of insult dropped,   2560
    However, indiscreetly from my lips.
    As nobleman you've nothing to avenge,
    And as a man you won't refuse forgiveness.
TASSO: Which thing would hit the harder, hurt or insult,
    I will not now inquire. The former pierces
    The inner marrow, the latter cuts the skin.
    The dart of insult turns back on the man
    Who meant to wound; a sword well wielded will
    Soon satisfy opinions of all others —
    But an offended heart recovers slowly.   2570
ANTONIO: Now it is my turn to say urgently

To you: Do not draw back, fulfill my wish,
And the wish of the Prince who sends me to you.
TASSO: I know my duty, and I will give in.
As far as possible, all is forgiven.
The poets tell a story of a spear
That could by friendly application cure
A wound which it had once itself inflicted.
The tongues of human beings have that power;
I shall not hatefully resist it now.　　　　　　　2580
ANTONIO: I thank you, and I wish that you would put
Me, and my will to serve you, to the test
Immediately with confidence. Tell me,
How can I help you? I will gladly do so.
TASSO: You offer just what I myself was wishing.
You brought me back my liberty again;
Now get for me, I beg, the use of it.
ANTONIO: What can you mean? Explain that in plain terms.
TASSO: You know that I have finished up my poem.
It still lacks much of being truly finished.　　　　　　　2590
Today I did present it to the Prince,
But hoped to ask a favor as I did so.
To make request of him at the same time.
A number of my friends I find assembled
Just now in Rome; some have expressed already
In letters to me their opinions of
Some passages; I have been able to
Use much, but many things seem to require
Yet further study; several passages
I should not like to change unless they can
Convince me more than has been done so far.　　　　　　　2600
All that can not be done through written letters,
Their presence would resolve the problems quickly.
I meant to ask the Prince myself today,
But found no chance. Now I dare not attempt it
And can hope for this leave through you alone.
ANTONIO: It does seem ill-advised for you to leave

Just at the moment when your finished work
Commends you to the Prince and to the Princess.
A day of favor is a day of harvest,
One must be busy as soon as it ripens.   2610
And if you go away you will gain nothing
And maybe lose what you have gained already.
A mighty goddess is the present moment.
Learn to perceive her influence: stay here.
TASSO: There's nothing that I need to *fear*. Alfonso
Is noble, he has always shown himself
Magnanimous to me. And what I *hope* for,
I want to thank his heart for, not obtain
A grace by stealth; nor will I take from him
What he could then regret once having given.   2620
ANTONIO: Then do not ask him to release you now.
He will do so reluctantly, and I
Fear almost he will not do it at all.
TASSO: He will be glad to, if correctly asked,
And you can do that as soon as you wish.
ANTONIO: But tell me, what grounds am I to allege?
TASSO: Just let my poem speak from every stanza!
What I intended merits praise, far though
My goal may have outdistanced my achievement.
There was no lack of industry and effort.   2630
The cheerful course of many lovely days,
The quiet spaces of so many nights,
Were all devoted to that holy poem.
I modestly had hopes of coming close
To those great masters of the ancient time,
Of boldly calling our contemporaries
Out of long sleep to noble feats, and then
Perhaps of sharing fame and peril of
A holy war with noble Christian armies.
And if my poem is to wake the best   2640
Of men, it must be worthy of the best.
What I have finished I owe to Alfonso;

Now I should like to owe him full completion.

ANTONIO: That very Prince is here, as well as others,
Who can guide you as well as Romans can.
Complete your poem *here,* here is the place,
Then go to Rome to put it into action.

TASSO: Alfonso first inspired me, and will be
The last one surely to give me instruction;
Advice from you and from the clever men   2650
Whom our court has assembled, I prize highly.
You shall decide in case my friends in Rome
Fall short of totally persuading me.
But I must see them all the same. Gonzaga
Has formed a court for me, to which I must
Present myself, and I can hardly wait.
Flaminio de' Nobili, Angelio
Da Barga, Antoniano, and Speron Speroni!
You surely know these men. — What names those are!
With confidence and with concern alike   2660
They fill my mind, which gladly bows before them.

ANTONIO: You think of yourself only, not the Prince.
I tell you he will not release you now;
And if he does, it will be with reluctance,
You surely will not ask what he will not
Grant willingly. Must I be intercessor
For something I myself can not approve?

TASSO: Will you refuse me the first service when
I put your proffered friendship to the test?

ANTONIO: True friendship is shown by refusal at   2670
The proper time, and often love confers
A harmful gift by thinking more about
The asker's wishes than about his welfare.
You seem to me at just this present moment
To think good what you eagerly desire,
And to demand right now what you most want.
An erring man makes up by vehemence
For what he lacks in truth and strength of forces.

My duty bids me moderate as far
As possible the haste that sends you wrong.   2680
TASSO: I long have been familiar with this tyranny
Of friendship, which of all the tyrannies
Seems most intolerable to me. You think
A different way, and fancy therefore
You have the right opinion. I concede
That you desire my welfare; only do not
Ask me to look for it along your path.
ANTONIO: Am I to do you harm right at the start,
Cold-bloodedly, with full clear consciousness?
TASSO: I will deliver you from that concern!   2690
You will not hold me from it by these words.
You did pronounce me free, and this door which
Leads to the Prince stands open for me now.
I leave the choice to you. You, or else I!
The Prince is leaving. This is not the moment
For tarrying. Choose quickly. If you do
Not go, I'll go myself, come what come may.
ANTONIO: Let me obtain a brief postponement only
From you, and wait until the Prince returns.
Just not today!
TASSO: No, no! This very hour   2700
If possible! My feet are burning on
This marble pavement here; my mind can not
Find rest until the open roadway dust
Is swirling all around me in my haste.
I beg you! You can see how awkward I
Would stand in speaking with my master at
This moment; you see — How can I conceal it? —
That at this moment I can not command
Myself; no power in this world can do
So either. Chains alone could hold me back!   2710
Alfonso is no tyrant, he pronounces
Me free. How gladly I obeyed him once!
Today I cannot so obey. Just for today

Leave me in freedom so my mind can find
Itself. I will return to duty quickly.

ANTONIO: You make me dubious. What shall I do?
I clearly see that error is contagious.

TASSO: If I am to believe you wish me well,
Get what I want as far as you are able.
The Prince will then release me, and I will   2720
Not lose his favor, will not lose his help.
That I will owe to you, and I will thank you.
But if you hold an old grudge in your heart,
If you prefer me banished from this court,
If you want to destroy my fate forever
And drive me helpless into the wide world,
Then stick to your opinion and oppose me!

ANTONIO: Because I am to harm you anyway,
I will, O Tasso, choose the way you choose.
The outcome will decide who was in error!   2730
You want to go away! Then I predict:
You scarcely will have turned your back upon
This house when your heart will long to be back,
And stubbornness will drive you on. Dejection,
Perplexity, and grief in Rome await you.
And you will fail your purpose there as here.
I say this now no longer to advise you.
I am foretelling only what will happen,
And I invite you now beforehand to
Confide in me when worst has come to worst.   2740
I shall speak to the Prince now, as you ask.

[Exit.]

TASSO *(alone):* Go on, and go with the conviction that
You have persuaded me to what you will.
I'm learning to dissimulate, for you
Are a past master, and I catch on quickly.
Life forces us to seem, in fact to be,
Like those whom we had boldly, proudly, once
Despised. I now perceive quite plainly all

The artfulness of this fine court intrigue!
Antonio wants to drive me out of here   2750
Without its seeming that he drives me out.
He plays the wise one, the considerate one,
Just so I may be found inept and sick,
Appoints himself my guardian to debase
Me to the level of a child, whom he
Could not force as a lackey. Thus he clouds
The Prince's brow, the vision of the Princess.
He thinks that they should keep me: Nature did
Endow me after all with some fine talent,
But then again unfortunately accompanied   2760
The lofty gift with many weaknesses,
With pride unbounded, with exaggerated
Sensitivity and gloomy mind.
There's nothing for it; destiny so formed
This one particular man this way, so people
Must take him just the way he is, endure him,
Put up with him, and some fine day, maybe,
Enjoy from him, as unexpected gain,
Some things or other which can give them pleasure.
But as for other matters, he must be   2770
Allowed to live and die as he was born.
Do I still see Alfonso's steadfast mind?
Defying foes and stoutly shielding friends,
Do I see him as he confronts me now?
Oh yes, I now see fully my disaster!
It is my fate that everyone will change
Toward me alone, but toward all others will
Stand firm and true and sure, will lightly change
At just a breath, and in a moment's time.
Did not this man's arrival of itself   2780
Destroy my fate completely in one hour?
Did it not overthrow the structure of
My happiness from its most firm foundation?
O must I live to see this yet today?

Yes, just as everyone once thronged to me,
So everyone deserts me now; as each
One sought to draw me to himself and hold me,
So they all cast me off now and avoid me.
And why is that? Does he alone outweigh
The weight of my worth in the scales and all   2790
The love that I once had in such abundance?
Yes, everyone flees from me now. You too,
Beloved Princess, you withdraw from me!
She has not in these dismal hours sent
A single token of her favor to me.
Have I deserved that of her? — You poor heart,
For whom it was so natural to adore her! —
When I but heard her voice, how my breast was
Shot through with inexpressible emotion!
When I beheld her, day's bright light was dimmed   2800
For me; past all resistance her eye would,
Her lips would, draw me on, my knees would hardly
Support me, and I needed all
My strength of mind in order to stand upright
And not fall down before her feet; I hardly
Was able to dispel that ecstasy.
Hold fast, my heart! And you, clear mind of mine,
Be not here overclouded! Yes, she too!
Do I dare say it? I scarcely believe it;
I do believe it and want to suppress it.   2810
She too! She too! Excuse her fully, but
Do not conceal it from yourself: she too!
O these words, which I ought to doubt as long
As any breath of faith still lives within me,
Yes, these words, they engrave themselves like one
Of Fate's decrees on the bronze tablet-margin
Of the full-written tables of my torment.
Now only are my enemies made strong,
Now I am robbed forever of my strength.
How can I fight if *she* is in the army   2820

Opposed? How can I bide in patience if
She does not from afar lend me her hand?
If *her* glance does not meet the suppliant?
You did make bold to think it, did express it,
And it is true, before you could be frightened.
And now before despair with claws of bronze
Rips up your senses, tears them all asunder,
Accuse the bitter destiny, repeat
And then repeat again: She too! She too!   (2829)

ACT V

A garden.
Alfonso. Antonio.

ANTONIO: At your behest I went a second time   2830
  To Tasso, and I have just come from him.
  I spoke to him, I pressed him urgently,
  But he will not give up his point of view
  And ardently pleads with you to release him
  So he may go to Rome for a brief time.

ALFONSO: I am annoyed, I will admit to you,
  And I would rather tell you that I am
  Than hide it and make the annoyance greater.
  He wants to leave, then. Good! I will not keep him.
  He wants to go away, to Rome. So be it!   2840
  Just so as Scipio Gonzaga does
  Not get him from me, that shrewd Medici!
  That is what has made Italy so great,
  Each neighbor vying with all others to
  Possess the better men and make use of them.
  A Prince who does not gather talents round him
  In my eyes is a General without
  An army, and whoever does not hear
  The voice of poetry is a barbarian,
  Whoever he may be. I found this one   2850
  And chose him; I am proud to have him serve me,
  And since I have done so much for him thus far,
  I should not like to lose him without cause.

ANTONIO: I am embarrassed, for I bear the blame
  Before you for what happened here today.
  I too am willing to admit my error;

574

It now is for your favor to forgive.
But if you could imagine that I have
Not done the utmost to conciliate him,
I would be inconsolable. O speak   2860
To me with gracious mien so that I once
Again may get control and trust myself.
ALFONSO: Antonio, no, on that score be assured.
By no means do I put the blame on you.
With this man's mind I am too well acquainted,
I only too well know what I have done,
How often I indulged him, how much I
Forgot that it was actually for me
To give him orders. Man can make himself
Master of many things; necessity   2870
And length of time will hardly bend his mind.
ANTONIO: When others do a great deal for one man,
It is but fitting that the one in turn
Should diligently ask himself what helps
The others. One who has so trained his mind,
Who has ransacked all sciences and all
The knowledge that it is vouchsafed to us
To know, should he not be obliged twice-over
To rule himself? And does he think of that?
ALFONSO: It seems we're not supposed to be at rest!   2880
As soon as we plan to enjoy ourselves,
A foe is given us to test our valor,
A friend is given us to test our patience.
ANTONIO: Man's first and foremost duty, choosing food
And drink, since Nature has not bounded him
So straitly as the beasts, does he fulfill it?
Does he not rather let himself be lured
Like children by what gratifies his palate?
When does he mingle water with his wine?
Sweet things and spices and strong drink, one after   2890
The other he consumes with eager speed
And then complains about his turbid mind,

His fiery blood, his all too vehement being,
And puts the blame on Nature and on Fate.
How bitterly and foolishly I often
Have seen him argue with his doctor, comic
Almost, if anything is comic that
 Torments a man and plagues his fellow creatures.
"I have this trouble," he says plaintively
And much chagrined: "Why do you vaunt your skill?   2900
Make me get well!" — "All right!" replies the doctor,
"Then don't eat this and this." — "I can't do that." —
"Then take this medicine." — "Oh no; It tastes
So vile, my nature just revolts at it." —
"Well, then, drink water." — "Water? That I won't!
I am as water-shy as rabid people."
"Well, then, there is no help for you." — "Why not?"
"Your trouble will go on and gather trouble,
And if it doesn't kill you, it will bother
You more and more with every day." — "Fine! What   2910
Are you a doctor for? You know my trouble,
And you should know the remedies as well,
And make them palatable, so that I need
Not suffer to get rid of suffering."
You smile yourself, but is it not the truth
That you have heard him say this very thing?
ALFONSO: I've heard it often and excused it often.
ANTONIO: It is most sure that an intemperate life
    Just as it gives us wild, oppressive dreams,
    Will in the end make us dream in broad daylight.   2920
    What else is his suspicion but a dream?
    Step where he may, he thinks he is surrounded
    By enemies. No one can see his talent
    But that he envies him, and none can envy
    But that he hates and fiercely persecutes him.
    Thus he has often burdened you with his
    Complaints: forced locks and intercepted letters,
    Poison and daggers! What all won't he fancy?

You had these things investigated, did so yourself;
Did you find anything? Hardly the semblance.   2930
No Prince's patronage will make him safe,
No friend's devotion can assuage his feelings,
And will you promise peace and happiness
To such a man, and look for joy from *him?*
ALFONSO: You would be right, Antonio, if I looked
    To find in him my own direct advantage.
    But it is my advantage that I do
    Not look for direct and immediate profit.
    Not all things serve us in the selfsame way.
    He who needs much must use each thing in its   2940
    Own fashion; thereby he will be well served.
    That is the lesson that the Medici
    Have taught us, that the Popes themselves have shown.
    With what consideration, with what princely
    Patience and forebearance those men have
    Borne many a great talent which seemed not
    To need their wealthy favor, yet did need it!
ANTONIO: Who is not well aware of it, my Prince?
    Life's pains alone teach us to prize life's goods.
    While still so young he has attained too much   2950
    For him to savor it contentedly.
    O if he were obliged to work and earn
    What now is offered him with open hands,
    He would exert his powers manfully
    And would from step to step be satisfied.
    But a poor nobleman already has
    Attained the goal of his best wishes when
    A noble Prince selects him for his court
    Associate and with a generous hand
    Removes him from all want. If he gives him   2960
    His confidence and favor too, and seeks
    To raise him over others, to his side,
    Be it in war, in business, or in talk,
    Then I should think the modest man might honor

His happiness by silent gratitude.
And Tasso has, on top of all of this,
A young man's finest happiness: his country
Has recognized him and has hopes for him.
Believe me, his capricious discontent
Rests on broad cushions of his lucky fortunes.   2970
He comes; release him graciously, and give
Him time in Rome, in Naples, or wherever
He will, to look for what he has missed here,
And what he can find only here again.

ALFONSO: Does he want to go back first to Ferrara?

ANTONIO: He wants to stay on here in Belriguardo.
    The most important things that he needs for
    His trip he will have sent him by a friend.

ALFONSO: I am content. My sister will go back
    Directly with her friend, and I on horseback   2980
    Will still reach home before them. You will follow
    As soon as you have tended to his needs.
    Give orders to the castellan for what
    He needs so he can stay here at the castle
    As long as he may wish and till his friends
    Have sent his luggage to him, and till we
    Send him the letters which I am quite willing
    To write to Rome. But here he comes. Farewell.
                    [Exit Antonio. Enter Tasso.]

TASSO *(with reserve):* The favor which you have so often shown me
    Appears to me today in its full light.   2990
    You have forgiven what I thoughtlessly
    And insolently committed in your presence.
    My adversary you have reconciled,
    You will permit me to absent myself
    From your side for a time, and you are willing
    Magnanimously to keep your favor toward me.
    I now depart in total confidence,
    And hope that this brief respite will cure me
    Of everything that now oppresses me.

My spirit shall uplift itself anew,   3000
And on the path that I first trod with joy
And vigor, cheered and heartened by your glance,
Shall once again be worthy of your favor.

ALFONSO: I wish you happiness upon your journey
And hope you will come back to us entirely
Cured and in cheerful mind. Well satisfied,
You then will bring us back twofold reward
For every hour you have deprived us of.
I shall write letters for you to my people
And friends of mine in Rome, and I much wish   3010
That you will everywhere keep in close touch
And have full confidence in them, as I
Consider you, though absent, as my own.

TASSO: You overwhelm, O Prince, with favor one
Who feels himself unworthy and can not
So much as thank you at the present moment.
Instead of thanks I make a plea to you!
My poem lies most closely at my heart.
I have done much, and have spared neither effort
Nor diligence upon it, but too much   3020
Of it is wanting still. So I should like
To put myself to school once more down where
The spirit of great men still hovers round,
And hovers with effect. My song would then
More worthily rejoice in your approval.
O give those pages back to me which I
Now know with shame to be in your possession.

ALFONSO: You will not take away from me today
What you have hardly brought to me today.
Between you and between your poem let   3030
Me step as intercessor. Take care not
To injure by strict diligence the lovely
Naturalness that now lives in your rhymes,
And do not hear advice from every side!
The thousandfold ideas of as many

Different men, who contradict each other
In life and in opinions, these the poet
Will wisely take as one and not shrink from
Displeasing many so that he may that
Much better please so many others. Yet   3040
I do not say that here and there you should
Not modestly make some use of the file.
I herewith promise you that in short time
You will receive a copy of your poem.
From your hand it will stay in my hands, so
That I, together with my sisters, may
First really have some pleasure in it. If
You bring it back more perfect, we shall then
Enjoy it with a higher pleasure and
In some points warn you only as a friend.   3050

TASSO: Embarrassed only, I repeat my plea:
   Please let me quickly have the copy. My
   Whole mind now dwells upon this work, and now
   It must become the thing it can become.

ALFONSO: I quite approve the impulse that so moves you!
   And yet, if it were possible, good Tasso,
   You should enjoy the free world for a brief
   Time and amuse yourself, improve your blood
   By taking of a cure. Then you would find
   The excellent harmony of senses thus   3060
   Restored would give you what you now are seeking
   In vain in all your gloomy zealousness.

TASSO: My Prince, it seems that way; yet I am healthy
   When I can yield to my own industry,
   And hence my industry will make me well.
   You long have seen how I do not thrive in
   Free luxury. Tranquillity gives me
   The least tranquillity. This temperament
   Of mine, I feel, alas, is not disposed
   By Nature to drift down upon the days'   3070
   Soft element to the broad seas of time.

ALFONSO: All that you think and do, leads you deep down
    Into yourself. On every side of us
    There lie abysses dug by destiny,
    The deepest being here within our hearts,
    And it gives us delight to plunge therein.
    I beg you, tear yourself away from *you*.
    The man will gain all that the poet loses.

TASSO: It is in vain that I repress that impulse
    Which surges day and night within my bosom.   3080
    When I can neither write nor meditate,
    Life is no longer life for me. Try to
    Forbid the silkworm to continue spinning
    Though it is spinning on to its own death.
    It will evolve its precious weft from deep
    Within its inner self and will not cease
    Till it has cased itself in its own coffin.
    O would that a good god would give us also
    The destiny of that same enviable worm,
    To spread our wings abroad with speed and joy   3090
    In a new valley of the sun!

ALFONSO: Hear me!
    You give a double pleasure of life to
    So many people; learn, I beg you,
    To know the value of the life that you
    Still have with ten-fold riches now. Farewell.
    The sooner you return to us, the more
    Superbly welcome to us you will be.

                [Exit.]

TASSO *(alone):* So hold still firm, my heart, that was quite right!
    It is hard for you, it is the first time
    You can and choose thus to dissimulate.   3100
    You heard, that was not his true person speaking,
    Those were not his own words; it seemed to me
    An echo of Antonio's voice was sounding.
    O have a care! You will be hearing it
    From all sides from now on. Be firm, be firm!

It is a question of a moment yet.
One who learns late in life how to dissemble
Has the advantage of an honest look.
It will work if you only practice on them.
          (after a pause)
You gloat too soon in triumph. There she comes.   3110
The gracious Princess comes! O what emotion!
She enters; in my bosom my vexation
And my suspicion are dissolved in sorrow.
          [Enter the Princess.]

PRINCESS: You think of leaving us, or rather you
     Will stay behind in Belriguardo for
     A time yet, Tasso, then depart from us?
     I hope it will be for a short time only.
     You go to Rome?

TASSO: I will direct my way
     There first, and if my friends receive me kindly,
     The way I hope they will, then I perhaps   3120
     Will give the final touches to my poem
     With patience and great care while I am there.
     I will find many men assembled there
     Who well may be termed masters of all sorts.
     In that first city of the world does not
     Each spot, each stone, speak audibly to us?
     How many thousands of mute teachers beckon
     In solemn majesty and friendly-wise.
     If I do not complete my poem *there,*
     I never will complete it. But, alas,   3130
     I feel no luck attends on any project.
     Change it I will, but never finish it.
     I feel, I feel indeed that mighty art
     That nourishes us all, that strengthens and
     That quickens wholesome minds, will ruin me,
     It will drive me away. I hurry forth.
     I want to get to Naples.

PRINCESS: Do you dare?

The strict proscription has not yet been lifted
Which fell upon you and your father both.
TASSO: Well may you warn me, I have thought of that.   3140
I will go in disguise. I will assume
The poor coat of a pilgrim or a shepherd.
I will slip through the city where the movement
Of thousands easily conceals the one.
And I will hurry to the shore and find
A boat at once with willing, kindly people,
With peasants, who have come from market and
Are going home, with people of Sorrento.
For I must hurry over to Sorrento.
There lives my sister, who once used to be,   3150
With me, my parents' joy amid their sorrow.
I will be quiet in the boat and then
Will step in silence on the land and softly
Go up the path, and at the door will ask:
"Where does Cornelia live? Would you please show me?
Cornelia Sersale." Friendly-wise
Some spinstress will point out the street for me
And indicate the house. I will climb higher.
The children will run after me and stare
At my wild hair and at the gloomy stranger.   3160
I will come to the threshold. Open stands
The door, and I will step into the house —
PRINCESS: Look up, if that is possible, O Tasso,
And recognize the danger you are in!
I spare your feelings, or I would say to you:
Is it quite noble to speak as you speak,
Is it quite noble to think only of
Yourself, as if you did not hurt friends' hearts?
Is what my brother thinks concealed from you?
Or how both of us sisters value you?   3170
Have you not felt it and not recognized it?
Has everything been changed in a few minutes?
O Tasso, if you want to go away,

Do not leave grief and care behind for us.
              (*Tasso turns away.*)
How comforting it is, when some friend is
About to go away for a brief time,
To give him some small gift, if it is only
A new cloak or a weapon. But to you
One can give nothing more, because you throw
Away in anger everything you own.   3180
You choose the black smock and the pilgrim's wallet
And the long staff, and voluntarily
Go off in poverty and take from us
What you with us alone might well enjoy.
Tasso: Then you would not drive me away entirely?
O sweetest words, O fair and precious comfort!
O plead my cause! Take me in your protection! —
Leave me in Belriguardo here, transfer
Me to Consandoli, or where you will!
The Prince is owner of so many castles,   3190
So many gardens that are tended all
Year long, in which you hardly walk *one* day,
Perhaps no more than for a single hour.
Yes, choose the most remote of them which you
Will not be visiting for years on end
And which perhaps is lying now untended,
And send me there! And there let me be yours!
How I will take care of your trees, and cover over
The lemon trees with boards and bricks in autumn
And see them well protected with bound rushes.   3200
The lovely flowers in the flowerbeds
Will strike broad root, and every spot and pathway
Shall be kept clean in perfect tidiness.
And let me take care of the palace too!
I'll open windows at the proper times
So dampness will not damage the fine paintings;
The walls so beautifully adorned with stuccoing,
I'll clean them with a gentle feather-duster,

The pavement floor will shine with spotlessness,
Not one stone, not one brick shall be displaced,   3210
No grass shall grow out of a single crack.
PRINCESS: I find no remedy within my heart
And find no solace for you or — for us.
My eye looks round to see if some god might
Not send us help, might not reveal to me
A healing herb, a potion of some kind,
That would bring your mind peace, and peace to us!
The truest word that flows forth from my lips,
The best of curatives no longer works.
I have to leave you, and yet my heart can   3220
Not give you up.
TASSO: Is she the one, ye gods,
Who speaks now with you and takes pity on you!
And could you fail to know this noble heart?
And in her presence was it possible
Faint-heartedness once seized and overwhelmed you?
No, it is *you,* and I too now am I!
O go on speaking and from your lips let
Me hear all comfort! O do not withdraw
Your counsel from me! Speak: What shall I do?
So that your brother can forgive me, so   3230
That you yourself might be glad to forgive me,
So that you all might count me once again
With joy among your own? O tell me that!
PRINCESS: It is but little that we ask of you.
And yet it seems to be too much by far.
You should entrust yourself to us as friend.
We shall ask nothing from you which you are
Not when you are contented with yourself.
When you yourself are pleased, you give us pleasure,
You only sadden us when you avoid it.   3240
And though you do sometimes make us impatient,
It is that we would like to help you and
Unfortunately we see there is no help

If you yourself will not seize the friend's hand
Which, yearningly extended, does not reach you.
TASSO: It is your very self, the way you met
Me like a holy angel that first time.
Forgive the mortal man's dull vision if he
At certain moments failed to recognize you.
He knows you now again! His soul is opened   3250
Fully, adoring none but you forever.
My heart is wholly filled with tenderness —
She, she stands before me. What emotion!
Can it be aberration draws me to you?
Or madness? Is it heightened sense, which can
Alone seize on the highest, purest truth?
Yes, it is the emotion which alone
Upon this earth can give me happiness,
And which alone made me so miserable
When I resisted it and tried to banish   3260
It from my heart. I meant to fight against
This passion, and I fought and fought with my
Profoundest being, impiously destroyed
My very self, which you belonged to wholly —
PRINCESS: If I, O Tasso, am to hear you further,
Then moderate this heat, which frightens me.
TASSO: But will a goblet's brim retain the wine
That foams and runs and boils and overflows?
With every word you lift my happiness,
With every word your eye more brightly shines.   3270
I feel myself in inmost soul transformed,
I feel myself disburdened of all pain,
Free as a god, and owe it all to you!
The power ineffable that masters me
Streams from your lips. Yes, you make me entirely
Your own, and nothing of my total self
Henceforward will belong to me again.
My eye grows dim with light and happiness,
My senses fail, my foot no longer bears me.

You draw me to you irresistibly   3280
And my heart surges toward you without check.
You have completely won me, and forever,
So take my entire being unto you!
                    (*He falls into her arms and presses
                    her to him.*)
PRINCESS (*thrusting him aside and hurrying away*):
    Away from me!
LEONORE (*who has been visible for a time in the   ackground,
    hurrying up*): What happened? Tasso! Tasso!
                    (*She follows the Princess.*)
TASSO (*on the point of going after them*):
    My God!
ALFONSO (*who for a time has been seen approaching with
    Antonio*): He's lost his senses! Hold him fast!
                    (*Exit.*)
ANTONIO: O if, as you are always thinking that
    You are surrounded by your foes, some foe
    Were standing by you now, how he would gloat!
    Unhappy man, I hardly find my breath!
    When something wholly unexpected happens,   3290
    When our gaze chances on some monstrous thing,
    Our mind stands stock still for a time, for we
    Have nothing which we can compare to it.
TASSO (*after a long pause*):
    Fulfill your office, I see it is you!
    Yes, you deserve the princely confidence.
    Fulfill your office and proceed to torture
    Me slowly, now the staff is broken for me,
    To death. Go on and draw, draw out the arrow
    So I may fiercely feel the barbed hook
    That tears my flesh!   3300
    You are the tyrant's precious instrument;
    Be prison keeper, be the torturer,
    How well, how fittingly both things become you!
                    (*toward offstage*)

Yes, go, then, tyrant! You could not dissemble
Until the very last, gloat in your triumph!
You have the slave now well in chains, you have
Him saved aside for torments well thought out.
Go on, I hate you! And I fully feel
The loathing that the upper hand occasions
That pounces impiously and with injustice.   3310
        (after a pause)
At last I see myself now banished here,
Driven away and banished like a beggar.
They crowned me to be led up to the altar
Adorned like any sacrificial victim!
And they enticed from me on this last day
My sole possession in this world, my poem,
With smooth words got it for themselves and kept it!
In your hands is my sole possession which
Could have commended me in any place
And which alone could save me from starvation!   3320
I clearly see why I should take vacation.
It is a plot, and you are leader of it.
So that my poem does not get perfected,
So my name may not spread abroad still further,
So enviers may find a thousand flaws,
So I at last may be forgotten wholly,
That's why I should get used to idleness,
That's why I should indulge myself, my senses.
O worthy friendship, precious thoughtfulness!
I thought that the conspiracy was loathsome   3330
Which was spun round me restless and unseen,
But it has now become more loathsome still.
And you, you Siren, who so tenderly,
Celestially enticed me, now I see
You suddenly! But why, O God, so late!
But we so willingly deceive ourselves
And honor reprobates who honor us.
No, human beings do not know each other;

Only galley slaves know one another
Who pant for breath chained to a single bench;   3340
Where none has anything to ask and none
Has anything to lose, they know each other;
Where each man frankly says he is a scoundrel
And takes his fellow-men for scoundrels too.
But we politely mistake other people
So that they will mistake us in their turn.
How long your sacred image hid from me
The courtesan who plays her little tricks.
The mask now falls, and I behold Armida
With all charms stripped away. — Yes, that is you!   3350
Foreknowingly my poem sang of you!
And then the wily little mediatrix!
How deep degraded I see her before me!
I hear her rustle of light footsteps now,
I know the circle now round which she stole.
I know you all! Let that suffice for me!
If misery has robbed me of everything,
I praise it still; it teaches me the truth.

ANTONIO: I hear you, Tasso, with astonishment,
Much as I know how lightly your rash mind   3360
Pitches from one extreme point to the other.
Reflect a bit, and overcome this rage.
You blaspheme, you permit yourself word after
Word which can be forgiven in your grief
But which you never can forgive yourself.

TASSO: O do not talk to me with gentle lips,
From you I want to hear no words of wisdom!
Let me have this dull happiness, so as
Not to reflect, and then to lose my mind.
I feel my very inmost bones all mangled   3370
And I am still alive to feel the pain.
Despair in all its fury seizes me
And in the hellish torment that consumes me
Blaspheming is a tiny sound of pain.

    I want to go away! If you are honest,
    Then show it, and let me get out of here!
ANTONIO: I will not leave you in this great distress.
    And if your self-control fails you entirely,
    My patience certainly shall not fail me.
TASSO: Then I must give up to you as a captive?   3380
    I do give myself up, and so it's over.
    I offer no resistance, that is best —
    Then let me painfully repeat once more
    How beautiful it was, what I have squandered.
    They're going away — O God, I see the dust
    Already rising from their carriage wheels —
    Foreriders out ahead — There they go, there
    They disappear! Did I not come from there?
    Now they are gone, and they are angry with me.
    O if I could but kiss his hand once more!   3390
    O if I could but say farewell again!
    Could only once again say: "O forgive me!"
    And hear him saying: "Go, you are forgiven!"
    But that I do not hear, will never hear —
    O I will go! Let me just say farewell,
    Just say farewell! But give, O give me back
    The present time for just a moment yet!
    Perhaps I will get well again. No, no,
    I am cast out, am banished, I have banished
    Myself, and I will never hear that voice   3400
    Again, and I will never meet that glance
    Again, No, never —
ANTONIO: Let a man's voice remind you who is standing
    Beside you here, not without being touched:
    You are not quite so wretched as you think.
    Be strong! You give in too much to yourself.
TASSO: And am I then as wretched as I seem?
    Am I as weak as I appear before you?
    Has everything been lost? Has sorrow not,
    As if the earth had quaked, transformed the building   3410

Into a gruesome heap of shattered rubble?
Is there no talent left now to divert
Me thousandfold and to support me?
Is all the strength extinguished which once stirred
Within my heart? Have I become a nothing,
An utter nothing?
No, everything is here, and I am nothing!
I have been stolen from myself, and she
From me!

ANTONIO: Though you seem utterly distraught,
Compose yourself. See yourself as you are!   3420

TASSO: Yes, you remind me at the proper time! —
Will no example out of history
Avail? No noble man come to my sight
Who suffered more than I have ever suffered,
So by comparison I may be steadied?
No, all is lost! — One thing alone remains:
The gift of tears is given us by Nature,
The cry of anguish, when at last a man
Can bear no more — To me above all else —
She left me melody and speech in grief   3430
To cry out all my plenitude of anguish,
And if men in their torment must be mute,
A god gave me the power to tell my pain.

*(Antonio steps up to him and takes
him by the hand.)*

O noble man! You stand secure and silent,
I only seem to be a storm-tossed wave.
Reflect, however; do not gloat in triumph
For all your power! Mighty Nature, who
Gave this rock firm foundation, also has
Conferred mobility upon the wave.
She sends her storm, and then the wave is driven   3440
And rolls and swells and, foaming, overturns.
Upon that wave the sun was mirrored once
So beautifully, and constellations rested

Upon that bosom, which then gently swayed.
The splendor now has vanished, peace has fled. —
I know myself no longer in my peril
And am ashamed no longer to confess it.
The helm is shattered and the ship is cracking
On every side. With an exploding noise
The ground is riven underneath my feet!   3450
I now throw both my arms around you. Thus
The helmsman at the very last clings to
The rock on which he was about to founder.   (3453)

OTHER DRAMAS AND DRAMATIC PROJECTS OF THE WEIMAR PERIOD

After the month and more of embarrassing uncertainties about his invitation to Weimar, Goethe arrived there on November 7, 1775 with all plans tentative. As matters worked out, he was to make his home there for the remaining fifty-six years of his life.

The state was of modest size by the standards of the time, miniscule by modern standards, with a history unknown before 975 and obscure before 1200. For some centuries it was ruled by Counts, becoming a duchy as late as 1547. Its hereditary dukes, with rare exceptions, had played conventional and minor roles in central European history, and of late their line had been hovering close to extinction. In 1758 Duke Constantine had died short of his twenty-first birthday, leaving his nineteen-year-old widow to manage the government, to rear his heir Charles Augustus, then aged nine months, and to bear a second son four months after her consort's death. Thus when Goethe arrived in latter 1775, he was himself twenty-six years old, Dowager Duchess Anna Amalia was thirty-six, the now reigning Charles Augustus was eighteen, with a bride, Duchess Luise, even younger. It had been on the way home from their wedding that the newlyweds had passed through Frankfurt and pressed the author of *Götz* and *Werther* to come and join their court.

The Dowager Duchess had managed her regency well. Her choice of a tutor for her son had been Wieland (of *Gods, Heroes, and Wieland*), and it was Wieland who had proposed making Weimar the intellectual and artistic capital of the German-speaking world, or at least of its Protestant half. The importation of Goethe was the second step toward that goal, and by far the most important one. At Goethe's recommendation Herder was brought in the following year as court chaplain, but with all possible free time to pursue his scholarly work. By 1789 Schiller had come to live in Jena, the "other town" of the duchy, but not until the middle 1790s did he move to Weimar itself. By 1798 the extraordinary first group of the *Romantiker* were making Jena their center. In short, Wieland's vision was being fulfilled beyond all expectations. The capital city, we need to understand, had a population of about 5,000 persons, who inevitably basked in the sun of the ducal court. Charles Augustus himself was an enlightened, if absolute, ruler, responsible only in unusual circumstances to the Catholic Emperor in Vienna, who had some three hundred such vassal princes under his nominal control.

Within two months of arrival Goethe was writing friends that he felt quite at home in Weimar and might "stay on for a while." On June 11, 1776 he was appointed a member of the Duke's privy council, with a good stipend, and this was only the first of his official and unofficial duties which, over the years, came to comprise an awesomely long list. His association with drama began early and assumed many forms.

In 1774 the local theater had burned down, but two amateur groups, of the court and of the town, were continuing to present theatricals. For the use of the court group a local builder was constructing a combination ballroom-and-theater, which was opened in the last days of 1775, and there, in February of 1776, Goethe organized his first entertainment. It was a kind of pageant, occupying an interlude during a court ball, and it portrayed the temptations of Saint Anthony. The Seven Deadly Sins were mimed, Pride being enacted by Goethe himself decked out in elaborate array in quite realistic imitation of a peacock. (See frontispiece)

Drawing on the membership of both amateur groups, he went on to more complex presentations. Roles were eagerly accepted by courtiers, functionaries, and townsfolk, and occasionally by the Duke or his younger brother Constantine. The court choir lent singers when needed, and these were supported by the tiny court orchestra of seven or eight players. Gradually "extra help" was hired, but even in the heyday of the Weimar theater there had to be double and triple casting and actors had to sing and dance as occasion demanded. The *corps de ballet* was strictly home talent. For public performances there were both ticket sales and ducal support, but for the court entertainments the Duke naturally bore all costs. The first professional actress to be hired, in November 1776, was the beautiful and gifted Corona Schröter, who created an epoch both in the theater and in our author's life.

For the public theater that came eventually into existence, Goethe was impresario, director, and business manager, approximating the office that Englishmen of Shakespeare's time termed the Master of the Revels, and for the court entertainments the title was exact. Frequently he also served as actor. When *Fellow Culprits* was staged on January 9, 1777, he played Alcest. The following October he took three roles in his own *Annual Fair at Plundersville*. After that performance there was a banquet and dancing until dawn. In 1778 he played the title role in Cumberland's *The West Indian*, recently translated from the English, the role of the father being taken by the noted professional, Ekhof, as guest performer. On April 6, 1779 the famous garden performance of *Iphigenia in Tauris,* in the original prose version, saw Goethe playing Orestes opposite Corona Schröter in the title role, with the Duke as Pylades and with guest professionals as King Thoas and Arkas. According to an often-quoted poem of 1782, "the poet himself, to his secret chagrin, had, in case of need, to trim the candlewicks" (presumably of the footlight candles).

Above all, as resident dramatist, he created numerous works, serving, we remind ourselves, both court and public. A large block of those works may best be reviewed by abandoning chronology for the time being and considering them under the three headings of operetta texts, court pageants, and certain personal dramas.

I. OPERETTA TEXTS

By "operetta" we mean, in Goethe's case, the native German variety of the genre known as the *Singspiel,* which was much in vogue in the 1770s and 1780s but which had not yet received its ultimate transfiguration in Mozart's *The Magic Flute* of 1791. The libretto of a *Singspiel* might be comic or sentimental but not tragic. It was normally in prose, but could be in verse. What audiences favored was a play with a simple story line which would accommodate relatively simple music in the form of solos, duets, trios, and choruses. *Erwin and Elmire,* hitherto unperformed, was such a work, and now in the summer of 1776 it was brought to the Weimar stage, set to music by the Duchess mother in collaboration with the professional musician Schweizer. Its success paved the way for four more *Singspiel* texts by Goethe.

1. *Lila,* with music by the resident composer Baron von Seckendorf, was written for the birthday of the young Duchess Luise on January 30, 1777, and, to a significant degree, the story was about her. Even in its première this delicate little work was fully meaningful only to the inner circle of persons who were aware of Luise's hypersensitivity and her unhappiness in marriage to Charles Augustus. The source work was a French play in which the hero lapses into hallucinatory melancholia upon hearing the false report of his fiancée's death; his friends enter into his illusions and act out his fancies until they bring him back to health. Goethe reverses this situation: it is now the young wife Lila who has sustained the nervous shock. As the *Singspiel* begins, she has retreated to a garden house in the palace park and refuses to see anyone except a faithful maidservant. By night she roams the gardens in terror of fancied monsters.

As in *Erwin and Elmire,* a somewhat overlong Act I, entirely in prose, spells out the dramatic situation in detail, closing with the proposal of a physician, Dr. Verazio, that all concerned parties impersonate the monsters and by demonstràting their harmlessness effect Lila's recovery. Acts II, III, and IV, comprising eighteen pages of the total twenty-eight, are garden scenes. The prose dialogue is courtly, the lyrics are gracious but a trifle bland, partly because they continue the dialogue in most cases and do not stand apart as independent songs. In the joyous finale the troubled lady is restored to her dear ones and to her husband's embrace, while the concluding lines banish all unwholesome phantoms. With great tact the author has reassured Luise that Charles Augustus sincerely loves her. The impression conveyed by the total work is that of an older brother's tender admonitions to a troubled sister. Forty years later Goethe was to characterize this libretto as "a psychic cure."

2. *Jery and Bätely,* written in December 1779 and revised as late as 1828, was a particular favorite of Goethe's. The continuous

action is contained within twenty-two pages of print. The setting is before an Alpine cottage in Canton Uri, "William Tell country," which the author had recently visited, but the Swiss local color that Goethe felt sure he had captured eludes the modern reader.

Heart-whole young Bätely is happy with life on this upland farm and with keeping her father's cottage, caring not a whit for the swains who have been pining for her and seemingly indifferent to Jery, who is still pressing his suit. Along comes young Thomas, formerly of this region but more recently a soldier, and to him Jery confides his despair. Thomas makes him a bet that he can win Bätely for his luckless friend. Upon meeting Bätely, Thomas finds her cheerful and hospitable, until the girl sees that his interest is sentimental. She informs him in no uncertain terms that this cottage is not an inn and bids him be off. Thomas tries various means of coaxing her back out of the house, and when these all fail, he has his men drive his herd of cattle into the meadow of this hostile person. He also rips up part of a bridge and breaks cottage windows. Bätely's father is outraged but helpless. The neighbors refuse to help because Bätely has broken the hearts of their sons. Jery comes back, engages Thomas in a fist fight—and loses. Then, at the sight of Jery disheveled and bloody, Bätely is suddenly filled with loving concern. All comes right in the end, and a chorus of neighbors, after assembling by horn calls on the cliffs, calls down a general approval.

The prose dialogue is exceptionally vivid and realistic, some of the best Goethe ever wrote, and its length is in proper proportion to the total work. The lyrics, as in *Lila,* form part of the dialogue and are not particularly poetical.

3. *The Fisherman's Daughter (Die Fischerin)* owed its very conception to the open-air setting where an entertainment was called for. From 1781 the Duchess mother took up summer residence each year on her estate at Tiefurt on the River Ilm, and there a party of house guests, seated out-of-doors after nightfall of July 22, 1782, were presented with this *Singspiel.* In such a setting a continuous one-Acter was inevitable. Three roles and a chorus account for the entire work, as was the case with *Jery and Bätely,* and eighteen printed pages suffice to contain the full text.

Despite a happy ending, the emphasis is on mildly eerie effects, beginning with the famous *Erlking* ballad, sung by Corona Schröter as the fisherman's daughter. To the hero is assigned a second "spooky" ballad, *Der Wassermann,* about a supernatural merman who woos an earthly bride, only to have her drown when he takes her to his watery home. The final chorus is also in "folkish" vein, being roughly parallel to the nursery rhyme of "Who Killed Cock Robin?"

The heroine, named Dortchen ("Little Dorothy"), is impatiently waiting for her father and her prospective husband Niklas outside the fisherman's cottage where the three of them live. Her menfolk, she complains, allow her to drudge for them without paying her much heed or affection. Tonight once again they are late and supper is spoiled from waiting. To punish them she will hide somewhere and leave evidence to suggest she has drowned. The two men come home, approaching in a real boat up the River Ilm, and gradually become alarmed at Dortchen's absence. They send to the neighbors for help. Across the darkness the audience then glimpsed lanterns moving along the banks of the Ilm as the gathering chorus of neighbors search for the missing girl. At the height of the suspense Dortchen reappears. Her lesson has succeeded, Niklas sets their wedding for tomorrow, and all ends happily.

This time the principal lyrics are memorable, though there are also dialoguized verses, and the prose dialogue is excellent in the difficult suspense-building scene with the two men. The somewhat oafish father has particularly good lines in a genre role any good actor would be grateful for.

4. *Scherz, List und Rache* (*Jest, Guile, and Revenge*), of latter 1784, is a four-Act libretto that prints up to thirty-eight pages. The entire text is in verse, much of it in free verse, and three characters—Scapin, Scapine, and the Doctor—account for all the action; there is no chorus. By the names we perceive that we are in the realm of the old Italian *commedia dell'arte,* though echoes of Molière may also be distinctly heard.

Scapin and Scapine are husband and wife; the Doctor is a rascal who has cheated them out of an inheritance. To recover their money and get their revenge, the pair gain access to the Doctor's house, Scapin as a servant (who claims to exist without food), Scapine as a patient. Just as the Doctor is about to administer some medical concoction or other to the "lady," Scapin throws old rags on the kitchen hearth, fills the house with smoke, and cries "Fire!" When the distracted Doctor gets back to his patient, he finds her in a death-agony from poison. Before his eyes, she "dies" and enters "hell," describing the infernal sights so wildly that the Doctor is happy to pay Scapin handsomely to remove this woman from his premises. In Act IV he comes upon her "corpse," still not wholly dead, in his cellar and for a second time pays handsomely to be rid of her. Suddenly the two schemers resume their normal personalities and taunt the old fellow with the total repossession of their lost inheritance.

The invention is faithfully in the tradition of the old Italian clowning, horseplay and all, and without a touch of sentiment. Not a trace of "psychology," not a trace of "philosophy." In fact, the action is so continuously rapid that we wonder how the performers could have breath enough to sing or how, indeed, any music could have been accommodated. Yet E. T. A. Hoffmann did set it to music in 1801. Twenty years later Goethe ruefully admitted that lyric elements were lost in the shuffle and that German audiences had no taste for Mediterranean farce, where unrepentant villainy gloats in triumph over equally unrepentant villainy.

As stories, these four *Singspiel* texts are remarkably varied. If *Lila* put much emphasis on costumes, sets, and dancing, the other three use a bare minimum of resources, though the open-air setting of *The Fisherman's Daughter* was a stroke of genius and hardly to be repeated. Not one of the four ever received adequate musical treatment, nor would any generation since 1800 have thought of them as particularly suitable for musical treatment. They stand, then, as literary pieces.

II. THE *MASKENZÜGE* AND OTHER OCCASIONAL WORKS

For certain occasions Goethe composed quasi-dramatic pieces which were not self-contained works like the above libretti, but wholly dependent on the immediate circumstances. In these cases, masked and costumed persons entered, singly or in procession, silently mimed certain actions, held certain tableaux, and withdrew. Meanwhile a master of ceremonies read or recited verses that identified the maskers and amplified the thoughts and compliments being mimed. For Duchess Luise's birthday on January 30, 1781, for example, a group of Lapplanders, possibly three in number like the Magi, came up to the guest of honor, offering we know not what, while the master of ceremonies stated, in verse, that these persons were Lapplanders and that they would gladly have brought the Northern Lights as a birthday gift, save that Luise's glory would outshine that phenomenon. Only the six quatrains conveying this much are preserved from an unknown total.

For such a procedure English has no word, "pantomime" and "masquerade" being equally misleading, hence we keep the German term *Maskenzüge,* "costumed processions," and list six preserved or partially preserved examples from Goethe's pen. Most of them embody a dramatic idea.

1.   For January 30, 1781, the "Lapplanders," as mentioned.

2.   For January 30, 1798, four stanzas in *ottava rima* explain the laying of palms of peace at Luise's feet. The allusion is to the Treaty of Campo Formio of October 17, 1797, which was to have made a final adjustment between revolutionary France and the rest of Europe.

3.   For January 30, 1802, five stanzas in *ottava rima* introduce allegories of the various genres of poetry.

4.   For January 30, 1806, four stanzas of a hymn to Luise, set to the tune of "God Save the King," or, for Americans, "My Country, 'tis of Thee."

5.   For January 30, 1810, twenty-seven stanzas in *ottava rima* present the components of "Romantic (i.e., medieval) Poetry." "Minnesinger" and "Heroic Poet" open and close the series, which includes the four seasons, "the North," various virtues, and Brunehild [*sic*] and Siegfried (from the *Nibelungenlied*), along with other representative personages from the medieval German narrative poems.

6.   For December 18, 1818, the thirty-page text, not counting Goethe's own six-page synopsis in prose, of a *Maskenzug* performed for the visiting Dowager Empress of Russia. More than thirty masked

figures represent the arts and sciences of Weimar, the River Ilm, the season, and the works of the three most illustrious authors of the duchy: Wieland, Goethe, and Schiller. *Faust,* interestingly enough, is represented in the person of Mephistopheles, who himself speaks his seventy lines. As for Schiller, then thirteen years dead, the allegories mime and the master of ceremonies speaks *about: The Bride of Messina, William Tell, Wallenstein,* the *Demetrius* fragment, and the *Turandot* translation; not a word about the "politically dubious" early plays, or even about *Mary Stuart* and *The Maid of Orleans.*

This summary has swept us chronologically far ahead: Goethe was thirty-two when he wrote the quatrains about the Lapplanders, going on seventy when he wrote the elaborate "Glories of Weimar." In 1818 the Duke was sixty-one. The Duke Apparent, Charles Frederick (1783–1853) was thirty-five, married to a Russian princess since 1804, and father of a six-months-old son, Charles Alexander (1818–1901). Luise was now Duchess mother, and it was the *new* young Duchess who requested the "Glories of Weimar" in honor of the visit of her mother, the Dowager Empress of Russia.

For almost forty adult years Goethe had furnished specimens of this very specialized sort of drama, but a decade later, when he was approaching age eighty, he gave the genre its ultimate form in Act I of *Faust, Part II.* Under the caption of *Spacious Hall (Weitläufiger Saal),* lines 5065–5986 present a *Maskenzug* with *speaking* characters. The scene is the medieval court of an anonymous emperor, by which was meant any court, any center of power, wealth, and culture. Faust, the conjuror, offers the untold spiritual riches of the arts, but the greedy emperor and his fickle courtiers can see nothing but material coins and jewels. The result is pandemonium and failure, but in good Faustian fashion the failure is a spur to yet vaster achievements by the never-sated hero.

Two other occasional dramas may be grouped with the foregoing. The first, in verse to a total of eleven pages, is dedicated to the Duchess mother, Anna Amalia, and is dated to approximately 1800. Its nature is proclaimed in the erudite Greek title of *Palaeophron and Neoterpe,* which may be freely paraphrased as "Traditional and Innovative." These two personifications conduct the entire dialogue, save for the Spirit (*Genius*) who blesses their union. The thought is that artistic innovators must consult the masterpieces of old, but that no person must deny the current time by trying to live exclusively with the art works of the past. (To this notion Horace had devoted much of the long Epistle, II, 1, around 14 B.C.)

On the other hand, the thirty-one-page *What We Offer* (*Was wir bringen*) is a vivid little piece, in prose and verse, for six characters plus extras. For several years the Weimar troupe gave summer performances at Lauchstädt, some two hundred kilometers northeast of Weimar, to which Halle University students often came. The theater building was in such sorry condition that the students declared it was no better than a sheep shed, and certainly there was no denying that on rainy days the spectators got wet under the leaky roof. A new building was constructed, and for the opening on June 26, 1802 Goethe composed this pleasing work. The old building is itself allegorized as a ramshackle peasant cottage tenanted by old Father Märten and his aged spouse, Mutter Marthe. The latter is protesting her husband's plans for a new house when unexpected stangers come to call on them. The three charming young ladies prove ultimately to be allegorized forms of opera and drama, the enterprising young man who transforms the wretched old cottage into a palace proves to be the god Mercury, and the finale represents what the new theater building may become. Colorful costumes and amusing stage business make the work lively and altogether delightful. In the end, Märten and Marthe themselves become allegories of genre comedy, and Mercury offers the two of them, along with the more brilliant figures, to the future audiences of the Lauchstädt Theater.

III. THE PERSONAL DRAMAS

Besides dramatizing such public occasions, Goethe also had the habit of turning personal experiences into dramas. Not that he dialoguized his private diary entries under fictional names. Rather, he invented scenarios in which he could externalize and think through the problems weighing on his heart at any given point.

1. *Brother and Sister* (*Die Geschwister*), a one-Acter, in prose, for three characters, is the most poignant of these personal

dramas. The author's diary records it as "invented" on October 26, 1776, in progress on the 28th, and completed on the 29th. It was not published until 1787, and not until 1798 was it performed.

Wilhelm, a young merchant, has brought up Marianne from infancy by way of fulfilling a promise made to her dying mother, Charlotte, once his beloved. He has always claimed the girl as his sister, but now, to his distress, he admits to himself that he is in love with her. Marianne, on her part, is utterly devoted to him and, without realizing it, in love with him. Now comes Fabrice, Wilhelm's best friend, who announces *he* is in love with Marianne and who asks permission to propose marriage to her. In anguish, Wilhelm grants that permission. The girl, however, firmly declines the offer. As the three stand in confrontation the truth is told, "brother" and "sister" fall rapturously into each other's arms, and Fabrice must bitterly behold their happiness, with his own happiness destroyed.

Effective little work that it is, *Brother and Sister* becomes even more poignant when viewed as a statement from Goethe to the real-life Charlotte von Stein, his Iphigenia and his Princess of Este, that very-much-married lady, seven years his senior, and with a brood of children still increasing, who could be only a "sister" to him. By no coincidence did Wilhelm's deceased beloved bear the name of Charlotte, and the letter from which Wilhelm reads to Fabrice is surely part of an actual letter from Charlotte von Stein to Goethe. For readers aware of all this, there is a high emotional charge on the play; only experiment by performance could determine the precise effect on persons unaware of these circumstances.

2. The *Elpenor* fragment belongs to August–September of 1781. Its stately prose is so markedly iambic in cadence that a final version in blank verse must have been intended. Five characters are listed, one of whom does not appear in the extant two Acts.

Elpenor is a radiant youth on the threshold of manhood. From early years he has been raised by Queen Antiope, who believes him to be the son of her late husband's brother, King Lykus (whose name means "wolf"). On a journey long ago her husband and her own little boy had perished and she herself had sustained serious injury when nameless highwaymen attacked their party. From King Lykus she had begged to bring up *his* son until manhood, surrendering land and treasure in the bargain. The day is now at hand when the youth must rejoin his father, but, before he departs, his foster mother vows him to the identification and destruction of the murderers. Polymetis, the envoy from King Lykus, arrives. His monologue reveals that he was the captain of those murderers, acting at the behest of King Lykus, and that, as we guessed, Elpenor is Antiope's own lost son. With this monologue the fragment breaks off at the end of Act II.

The youthful hero has the name, but only the name, of the Elpenor whose ghost speaks to Odysseus in Book XI of the *Odyssey,* and the root of Greek *elpis,* "hope," probably dictated the choice. The scenario is largely of Goethe's invention, though Antiope and Lykus belong to the Theban cycle of classical story; the few ancient data used were doubtless gleaned from a handbook of mythology that drew on Pausanias, II, 6. The dramatic method, with its piecemeal disclosure of identities, is in the manner of *Oedipus the King.*

Under the date of August 8, 1781, Goethe's diary mentions a long walk and conversation with Duchess Luise, who was then in advanced pregnancy. *Elpenor* was begun on the 11th and continued on the 19th, but work ceased after September 10th, when Luise was delivered of a stillborn daughter. The "hope" of August had been for "an Elpenor" whose birth would mend the unhappy marriage of Luise and Charles Augustus. In short, *Elpenor* is a second *Lila,* but without a happy ending, indeed without any ending at all.

When, two years later, Luise bore the son and heir Charles Frederick on February 2, 1783, Goethe attempted to take up the play anew but found the subject repugnant to him. Fifteen years after that, in 1798, he chanced upon the manuscript once more and submitted it to Schiller's judgment without identifying the author. Schiller's reply was that the author was either a woman or else a man with extraordinary empathy for a woman's viewpoint. A more trenchant comment could hardly be made, since, charming as the youthful hero may be, interest lies primarily with the high-strung Antiope torn between tenderness and a festering passion for revenge. In 1806 Goethe included the fragment in a set of his collected works.

3.   *Proserpine. A Monodrama* was written for the composer Gluck, who had requested a work of consolation upon the death of a

young niece. To Goethe's mind the name of Gluck apparently suggested *Orfeo ed Euridice,* and the name of Euridice suggested the figure of Proserpine, who "also" descended young to the afterlife. The resulting product was this seven-page *scena* in varying meters, which presents Proserpine distraught with horror at being kidnapped away to the very entrance into the world of death. At a certain point she takes hope at seeing a pomegranate tree with the ripened fruit hanging from its branches. With delight she eats a few thirst-quenching kernels, and immediately the offstage voices of the Fates hail her as their queen amid the deathly realm. Curiously, there is no hint of any rebirth of the maiden with the coming of spring, as the classical myth had it: this Proserpine faces only the endless shadows and the embrace of an abhorred consort.

The uncertain date is likely to have been late in 1776, just after the arrival in Weimar of the beautiful Corona Schröter. At any rate, Corona declaimed the piece at the entertainments for Duchess Luise's birthday on January 30, 1778, where it constituted an episode in the comedy-medley entitled *The Triumph of Sensibility.* Ten years later Goethe admitted that its inclusion in such a medley was "blasphemous."

The works just reviewed occupy about two hundred fifty printed pages. The majority of them belong to Goethe's first decade in Weimar, 1776–86, and the rest—five *Maskenzüge, Palaeophron and Neoterpe,* and *What We Offer*—are in the spirit of that decade. Interesting, ingeniously invented and ingeniously varied, but minor. By a judgment more severe, they are the work of a gifted amateur, intended for performance by amateurs, for the entertainment of a court and a citizenry that were prolonging the fad for amateur theatricals which had started in France in the 1760s.

"Wilhelm Meister's Theatrical Mission"

At some point in 1777 Goethe began to collect his exalted ideas about drama into a prose narrative entitled "Wilhelm Meister's Theatrical Mission." The author's idealized self was the hero, under the name of "William (the) Master," in honor of the greatest dramatic artist of them all, the model of models, William Shakespeare. The theme of the novel was the hero's evolution—through experiences with all sorts of theater, toward mastery at acting. Concurrently, the exploration of all practical types of drama was to lead to a formula for the establishment of a valid dramatic art in German-speaking Europe.

Action and vivid adventures there were, and memorable characters, and fine lyric insets. For seven years Goethe worked intermittently at this novel, especially in the early 1780s, but around 1784 he stopped writing. Through the first half of the 1790s he revised it, adding and subtracting passages, reordering its six Books into five, and, more significantly, adding three wholly new Books (VI, VII, VIII) that had nothing to do with theater, and publishing it in 1795 as *Wilhelm Meister's Apprenticeship*. Most of the memorable characters were retained in their former roles, and the famous lyric insets were left in place, but the novel as a whole had surrendered liveliness for sober reflection and philosophical purpose. It enjoyed international fame.

Meanwhile the "Theatrical Mission" remained unpublished and unknown, until the manuscript was unexpectedly discovered in 1910 in Switzerland and published by scholars. Since 1910 more than one voice has been heard to remark that it is a more engaging work than the familiar *Apprenticeship*, and the present writer shares that minority opinion. What is important here is the fact that this splendid novel *about* drama was abandoned and left unfinished around 1784. A second point of significance is that the published *Apprenticeship* had the hero abandon the theater as a false life-course for *him*. The newly added Books VI, VII, and VIII direct Wilhelm, as we said, into wholly different regions; a belated sequel published in 1821 as *Wilhelm Meister's Journeyman Years* carries the hero still further away from the realm of the theater.

By 1784, however, it was not only the "Theatrical Mission" that was put aside. Major dramatic projects were already in limbo. *Iphigenia in Tauris* had been composed in prose in the latter 1770s and performed in 1779; since then it had been twice rewritten, still in prose and still unsatisfactory to the poet. *Tasso,* conceived in 1780 and partly written, also remained unfinished. *Egmont,* begun in 1775, was unfinished. The still earlier scenes of the *Urfaust* had never been finished, or even properly coordinated.

A kind of artistic paralysis had seized upon the author, the reasons for which were surely multiple and complex. We conjecture possible ones: time-consuming duties; that bizarre dedication in spiritual vassalage to Charlotte von Stein; too great involvement in the private lives of the ducal family; commonplace distractions; diversion of interest toward the natural sciences; a predictable slowing of life's river after the torrents and plunging cataracts of youth; necessarily slow accretions toward artistic maturity; dulling effects of routine and stability; compensatory dimming of excessive early brilliance. In any event, by 1786 and age thirty-seven Goethe seemed to be dying as an artist. No one realized that better than the man himself. At the beginning of September 1786, he abruptly pulled up stakes and departed for Italy. For twenty-two months he stayed in the southlands, and, to use his own expression, the time brought about his rebirth.

The Nausikaa Fragment; Italy and Return

On the way down he started a verse tragedy, *Ulysses on Phaea,* and in Sicily in the spring of 1787 he extended it to five pages, which go under the title of *Nausikaa.* On the basis of *Odyssey* VI, the island princess Nausikaa was to die of unrequited love for Odysseus. A wisp or two of the Sicilian springtime color the unpromising text.

Travel, studies, new acquaintances, and new experiences filled Goethe's southern months to the full. He studied plants, for instance, and elaborated a theory of botanical evolution. He studied painting and painted more than a thousand landscape pictures, mostly watercolors, enough to enable him to decide that painting, important as it was to him, was secondary in his life to literature. But he also resumed his literary work amid all his other pursuits. Early in 1787 *Iphigenia* emerged in its final blank-verse form. Succeeding months advanced composition of *Tasso. Egmont* was completed. The "Witch's Kitchen" scene was added to *Faust.* New poems were written. Even *Erwin and Elmire* and *Claudine of Villa Bella* were revised.

The "new life" was still upon him as he returned to Weimar in latter June of 1788. *Tasso* was completed in 1789. The poem sequences of the *Roman Elegies* and the *Venetian Epigrams* were produced in 1789–90. And in 1790 certain *Faust* scenes were published as *Faust.*

A Fragment, with the notion that the forty-year-old could do no more than this amount with the project of the twenty-four-year-old. He was laying the work to rest in order to devote time to his Wilhelm Meister novel, and he did indeed set to work on that revision. He also claimed his sexual birthright. When Charlotte von Stein received her knight-turned-pagan with coldness upon his homecoming, that spiritual bondage was cast off, and within three weeks' time Goethe took into his house twenty-three-year-old actress Christiane Vulpius, with whom he lived quite contentedly until her death in 1816. Moreover, he requested the Duke to be relieved of all official duties save those having to do with cultural matters. Charles Augustus consented, and without reduction in salary. We may add that the salary had been paid through Goethe's absence of nearly two years.

Meanwhile matters theatrical in Weimar had undergone small changes and small improvements. The combination ballroom-and-theater of 1776 had given way in 1780 to a better, though less than satisfactory, building. There had been increases in the number of actors and musicians, a stock of scenery and costumes had been accumulated, and a ducal subsidy had lent some stability to the enterprise. In 1783 a Dresden company, headed by a man named Bellomo, had been hired to give regular performances of plays, operettas, and even ballets, so that there was less dependence on amateurs, both onstage and backstage. Bellomo's performers, however, were mostly second-raters, and what depressed Goethe even more was the limited range of the German repertory, not only in Weimar, but everywhere else as well. Circumstances strongly implied that any "theatrical mission" was a lost cause.

IV. THE STAGE WORKS OF 1790–96

Upon his return from Italy, Goethe found matters pretty much as he had left them, with one important exception: dissatisfaction was being widely expressed both by the court and by the public. By 1790 the Duke and the Dowager Duchess had decided to make changes. Accordingly, Bellomo's company was dismissed in April of 1791 and a new acting company was organized. A dozen or so of new performers were engaged, and five or six of Bellomo's best people were kept on. A new theater building was inaugurated on May 7, 1791, and on the opening night Goethe delivered an address in which he emphasized that teamwork was to be the watchword for the new troupe: a play was more than the sum of its parts, it was a unity in which each performer had a part. Such an ideal may seem self-evident, but the fact was that it obtained in no German theater as of 1791.

Reluctantly Goethe assumed overall responsibility for the new enterprise. Such was the Duke's wish, and in duty he could not fail to comply. He, in consultation with the Duke, would control policies, but he did insist that a court official be appointed to supervise routine financial details. He also stipulated that his responsibilities should be limited to the six-month winter season; a deputy would have to look after the summer schedules in Lauchstädt. He further volunteered to create some new plays to vary the repertorial fare. Three such plays were, in fact, composed; a fourth remained a fragment.

1. *The Great-Cophta* (*Der Gross-Cophta*) of 1791 was the first of these. Originally a lighthearted *Singspiel* libretto and a product of the Italian journey, it was now rearranged as a five-Act comedy in prose. The complex plot is woven of three strands, which we briefly indentify as: the Diamond Necklace affair, the "operations" of Count Cagliostro, and a bittersweet love story of Goethe's invention.

The facts underlying the first of these were as follows. For some years a firm of Paris jewelers had been unable to sell a certain diamond necklace. Both Louis XV and Louis XVI had found it priced beyond their means. In 1785 a certain Countess de la Motte contrived to abscond with it. Her cat's-paw was the disgraced Cardinal de Rohan, who had gravely offended Queen Marie Antoinette. The Countess claimed sufficient influence with the Queen to effect a reconciliation, provided the Cardinal would purchase the necklace for Marie Antoinette by making a large downpayment and guaranteeing the balance with his own financial credit. In token of progress with her scheme she first gave the Cardinal forged letters of encouragement from the Queen, then she arranged for him a nocturnal interview in the Versailles gardens with a prostitute hired to impersonate the Queen. In this way the Countess obtained the necklace herself; accomplices disassembled it, smuggled the parts to London, and sold them.

The Cardinal de Rohan undertook this adventure only after consulting with the famous "Count Cagliostro." This adventurer had begun life in 1743 in Palermo as Giuseppe Balsamo. His title and the name Cagliostro were of his own invention. As a fugitive from Sicilian law, he had traveled to Italy, had picked up a wife-accomplice in Rome, had been inducted into Freemasonry in London, had traveled through eastern Europe as a practicing hypnotist, and, around 1780, had come to Paris as the protégé of the Cardinal de Rohan. He too had promised to regain the good will of Marie Antoinette for his sponsor, and on one occasion he did conjure a benevolent apparition of the Queen in a container of water for the Cardinal's encouragement. The apparition, however, was actually beheld only by a child-medium, "pure as an angel," who "interpreted" the vision. Apart from this "operation," the "Count" had no connection with the theft of the necklace.

When the firm of Boehmer & Bassenge found the downpayment on the necklace less than had been stipulated, they took the matter directly to the Queen, who, of course, knew nothing of the transaction. In the court trial of 1786 the Cardinal was acquitted of fraudulence but banished to the provinces; Cagliostro was acquitted but expelled from France; the Countess was sentenced to be flogged, branded, and imprisoned for life, but she contrived escape to London, where she occupied herself with writing defamatory "mémoires" about Marie Antoinette. Agitators chose to see the Queen as guilty despite the evidence, the trial verdicts were cited as an example of Louis XVI's despotic revenge, and the monarchy was popularly discredited.

All this was known to Goethe before he left for Italy, and he found it sinister and disquieting. Under the dates of April 13 and 14, the *Italian Journey* records a fascinating pair of vists made by Goethe to the Balsamo family in the poor quarter of Palermo, together with an account of the police dossiers compiled on "Cagliostro." Yet in composing his lighthearted libretto, *Die Mystifizierten,* a title which we paraphrase as "The Hoodwinked Initiates," the "Count" was depicted humorously and as the central figure.

When Goethe came to revise the libretto as the full-length play, *The Great-Cophta,* he was in a very different mood. With the Revolution in its second year and becoming more violent all the time, the

Cagliostro figure had to yield first place to the more sinister conspirators. Under the name of "Count Rostro" in the play, he poses as the envoy of "the Great-Cophta" and dominates simple initiates with such easy tricks as interrupting conversations to discourse with invisible spirits, entering a room before the servant has had time to announce his name, and conducting solemn interrogations that echo Masonic ritual. He is a preposterous quack, neither very funny nor very spooky. The Cardinal de Rohan, under the name of "the Canon" (*Domherr*), is a blundering fool with an amour, not a reconciliation, on his mind. The plot of the Countess de la Motte is conducted point by point by "the Marquise," whose accomplice is her husband, "the Marquis"; she sees through the Count's hocus-pocus but turns it to her own advantage, and the other characters are, to her, silly sheep to be herded as she wills. Thus the intrigues of the two scoundrels are running parallel and smoothly until they strike the obstacle of a pair of young lovers.

These young lovers are entirely of Goethe's invention. The first of them is "the Niece" of the Marquise—the persons in this play have titles but only two have names. This young girl with the look of dewy innocence upon her is already the mistress of the Marquis. She finds the hypnotist-charlatan frightening enough in himself, but panic seizes her when he announces that she is precisely the creature of total innocence that he needs to act as the Great-Cophta's medium. Hardly has he left the room when she throws herself at her aunt's feet, confesses her adultery, and begs to be excused from acting as the Great-Cophta's medium lest her guilt be instantly revealed in public. Cynically her aunt threatens to ruin her if she does *not* act as medium and if she does not also consent to impersonate "the Princess"—i.e., the Marie Antoinette figure—in the garden interview with the infatuated Canon. The second invented character is "Knight Greville," an initiate who comes to realize that the envoy of the Great-Cophta is a shameless impostor. By a final twist of the plot he overhears just enough of a conversation of the Niece to conclude that she is a willing accomplice in these dishonest transactions. In this overcrowded play we are asked to believe that these two young people loved at first sight and that the Knight's love turned sour at a word.

Act V presents the nocturnal garden scene but with reversed outcome. Before the principals have taken their places, the author contrives to clear the stage for a moment, and along comes a detachment of Swiss Guards with their commanding officer. Knight Greville has alerted the authorities, and what nowadays would be called a "stakeout" has been organized. As soon as the Switzers have retired to concealed positions in the shrubbery, the Marquise brings the Niece to the arbor, the Canon comes to implore the love of the imagined Princess, and the wretched girl plays out her coy role. Signal horns are heard in the distance. The Canon slips away. The Marquis comes to hurry the Niece off to a waiting carriage in which they will elope, but his wife arrives, demanding that the girl remain with her. At the height of the altercation the Switzers step out of the shadows to arrest all three of them. Other Switzers bring up the arrested charlatan, who vainly threatens supernatural reprisals. The jewels are recovered. Knight Greville denounces the guilty parties. Then, in a passionate outburst, the Niece admits her guilt but claims she was forced into the plot; she loves and respects the Knight but begs to be taken to a cloister for the rest of her life. The play ends with Knight Greville's remorse and his vow to save the girl from wasting her life away as a nun.

At the première of December 17, 1791 the Weimar audience was politely unenthusiastic. They knew perfectly well that they had just seen a dramatization of a scandal of six years ago, but they also knew that it did not end this way. The play was skillfully plotted, it provided the titillation of mystery and suspense, it had melodrama that was effective, the opening scene was striking, and so was the séance scene, but the work as a whole belied the word "comedy" (*Lustspiel*) in the subtitle without clearly establishing itself in some alternate genre. The author felt such contempt for Cagliostro that he could not make Count Rostro anything more than a small-time buffoon. In their fictionalized forms the conspirators also seemed petty. The Knight comes off as pompous and vindictive. Only the Niece could be interesting, but, depending on the interpreting actress, she will appear either pathetic or merely stupid. In real life these events were not concluded, joyously or otherwise, in a garden scene; rather, they were little puffs of wind before the onset of a cyclone. But of such a convulsion of nature the author gave no hint.

2. *The Civilian General* (*Der Bürgergeneral*) is a lively one-Act comedy in prose, performed in May of 1793 as a follow-up to Anton Wall's *Die beiden Billets,* which had delighted Weimar audiences and which was, in turn, an adaptation of *Les Deux Billets* (1779) by Voltaire's grand-nephew, the celebrated Florian (Jean-Pierre Claris, chevalier de Florian). Wall's hero, Schnaps the barber, is here put through "another adventure."

Röse and Görge—Rosie and Georgie—are twelve weeks married and still so much in love that they can hardly bear to be apart even when Görge is doing the farm work. Röse also takes good care of her father, though the old fellow complains that she neglects him. While Röse is off taking Görge his lunch, Schnaps the barber pays a call on old Märten, though the young people have forbidden him the cottage as a troublemaker.

Schnaps is a convert to the Revolution, and in his barber's satchel he has a Liberty Cap, a uniform, and other appurtenances of a secretly appointed "civilian General." His visit is for the secret parading of these for Märten's benefit. His objective is to rouse the German peasantry to rebel. The scene is interrupted by the arrival of Görge with a stick, but Schnaps hides overhead in the hay loft until he is gone. Then, by breaking open a wardrobe, Schnaps demonstrates how revolutionaries search for concealed persons. Social structure is explained by his dipping the aristocratic sour cream off the top of the milk in Röse's best milk crock. Considerable havoc has been wrought in the cottage before Görge arrives a second time, by way of the back door, and drives him away. Röse's cries now bring the village judge and a posse of peasants to the scene. The evidence—Liberty Cap, uniform, saber, and so on—is about to cause them all to be arrested when the local Nobleman chances by and sets everything to rights.

The Schnaps-Märten dialogue, which occupies half of the text, is a tour de force of crackling wit so rapidly traded as to leave any audience dazzled and any pair of actors breathless. This is glorious clown-banter, and at the same time excellent character portrayal. Goethe had a sharp ear for the peasant idiom, as well as a ready understanding for cranky oldsters. (The middle portion of *The Fisherman's Daughter* is another example.)

The difficulty with the play lies with the benevolent Nobleman—

who has no name. At the beginning he had stopped to chat amiably
with Röse and Görge in passing; at the end he serves as *deus ex
machina*. It was Schiller's excellent suggestion simply to omit this role
altogether, but Goethe was intent on the Nobleman's concluding
remarks: "we" are happy just the way we are; "we" are lucky to be
in a position where we can joke about Liberty Caps and other such
trash. Schiller was concerned only with dramatic effectiveness; Goethe
was solemnly concerned with delivering a warning against revolutionary propaganda among the German peasantry. Schiller also contemplated a good–natured "Sequel to Goethe's *Civilian General*," leaving an outline that occupies three printed pages, but the project was not
carried through.

3. *The Insurgents* (*Die Aufgeregten*, literally "Those who
have been stirred up") is subtitled "A Political Drama in Five Acts"
and dates from 1793. Paradoxically, the work must be described both
as complete and as incomplete.. Acts I, II, and IV are as we would
expect, but for most of Act III and the whole of Act V the author has
supplied a summary, as though he had not time or inclination to write
further.

The setting is an unidentified region of Germany. In the antecedent
action certain legal claims had been high-handedly settled in favor of a
noble family and to the detriment of the common people. "The
Countess" has just returned from Paris, where she formed the opinion
that revolutions result from injustices of a ruling class. Unbeknown to
her, local dissidents are plotting to force her to relinquish those old,
unfair claims. They will use firearms, they will attack her castle, and,
as we learn belatedly, they will kidnap her little son and hold him
hostage. The ringleader of the plot is the pompous and vindictive
Breme von Bremenfeld, Surgeon, who is a Schnaps-the-barber turned
nasty. Besides the other conspirators, the cast includes three young
ladies and certain suitors, for this play shall not be devoid of love
interest.

A page or so into Act III the author coolly writes: "Here there is a
lacuna which we shall bridge with narrative." A major scene is to
follow, over what is to begin as an afternoon drinking of tea in the
Countess's salon. Somehow, the entire cast will assemble, even to the

peasant extras. Arguments will arise, tempers will flare, but in between the hostile exchanges there will be urging of love suits and assignations for trysts, until the Act ends "rather tumultuously." Here, certainly, are the makings of a "scandalous scene" in the manner of Dostoevski, yet the implication is that the great issues of the French Revolution are being represented in miniature—around a tea table. The narrative concludes with the remark that "perhaps it will be regretted" that the author had not met the challenge of composing this scene.

Two pages of summary account for the unwritten Act V in its entirety. The scene is a moonlit corner of the castle garden where an ancient structure, in ruins and overgrown with brambles, conceals the entrance to a secret passageway of escape. The Countess, her little son, her daughter Friederike—who can handle firearms as well as any man—and others of her party are about to flee to safety. Actually, the document containing the concession of rights is all ready to hand over to the insurgents. The lady herself was all for appearing on a balcony and reading it aloud to the mob, but the spirited Friederike had declined to yield under duress. The Countess's intentions are already known to some of the rebels, who now arrive in support of the noble family, but Breme's hotheads also arrive in force, and they do *not* know of the concessions. Breme himself has known for years about the secret escape route and he means to corner the fugitives on their own property. Nevertheless there is still time to hear all the facts and in this final confrontation matters are settled to everyone's satisfaction.

4.   "The Girl from Oberkirch" makes too flippant a translation, and "The Maid of Oberkirch" may give a false impression, of the title **Das Mädchen von Oberkirch,** a play which announces itself as a "tragedy in five Acts." Six roles, plus numerous extras, are listed in the cast of characters, but eight pages of the opening Act are all that we have of the text. The subject, however, can be clearly discerned from the author's notes in conjunction with a 1795 magazine article that suggested the work.

Revolutionary leaders, in November of 1793, had asked a particularly beautiful German peasant girl to impersonate the Goddess of Reason on the desecrated altar of the Strassburg cathedral. The girl, whose name is Marie, consented in the hope that she would then be able to rescue her aristocratic family of employers. The play-text makes her the personal maid of a Countess. But the young Baron, nephew to the Countess, has so far broken caste restrictions as to ask her for her hand in marriage, and fearing to debase herself in his eyes by so infamous and irreligious an action, she refuses to carry out her promise. As a result, Marie and all of the noble family are sent to the guillotine.

All four of these plays, we note, have to do with the French Revolution, and in sequence they attest a progression on the author's part from cordial dislike into unqualified horror. Fifteen years later, in 1809, when Goethe was reminiscing about *Die Aufgeregten* with his secretary, Dr. Riemer, he delivered himself of certain remarks, which Riemer recorded. Daily, even hourly, reports of atrocities had so appalled him in the early 1790s that he loathed the Revolution, and only later and gradually had he come to realize its beneficent effects. People had wrongly called him a stand-patter, a regular defender of the *status quo*. Yet he had feared lest "the inevitable" in France be "artificially" imposed upon Germany. Repressive government was evil. There had to be change, even if change was not always for the better.

These observations, if we have properly grasped them, seem less than profound, at least for a mind of Goethe's scope. Significantly, however, he continued to ponder the stupendous phenomenon as long as he lived. A month before his death he was discussing the mémoires of Mirabeau with Eckermann, and on the night of March 21, 1832, the very last night of his life, he wished to read the mémoires of Narcisse Achille de Salvandy, recently published, on the same subject.

Characteristically, his mind sought some formula of compromise whereby old and new values could be reconciled. Characteristically too, he dreamed of expressing such a concept in dramatic form. In 1799, while reading a recently published book he had borrowed from Schiller, he discovered his dramatic subject, or more precisely, a human figure and a set of surrounding circumstances that would lend themselves to his purpose. Not one drama but a trilogy of dramas would be required to encompass the total plan. He thought about the project with much care, and with a secrecy that was most unusual with him, eventually starting work on Part I, which he entitled *The Natural Daughter* (*Die natürliche Tochter*). The play was finished and put into production. The première was given in the Weimar theater on Arpil 2, 1803, and though almost thirty years of life were yet left to him, this was to be—apart from *Faust, Part II,* of course— his last attempt at a poetic drama of high seriousness.

V. *THE NATURAL DAUGHTER*

The recently published (1797) book that Goethe borrowed from Schiller and read in 1799 was entitled *Mémoires historiques.* The writer called herself Amélie Gabrielle Stéfanie Louise de Bourbon-Conti. Indeed, it was to establish that identity for herself that she wrote the book. It was her claim that she was the much-wronged illegitimate daughter of the Prince de Conti and the Duchess de Mazarin: born in Paris in 1756, kidnapped and attested dead by her brother after he had sent her to Lons-le-Saunier in eastern France, where, under the name of Anne Louise Françoise Delorme, she married an attorney named Billet. This much served to make Goethe's Part I of a trilogy, i.e., to make *Die natürliche Tochter*; what followed in real life could not, except in the most general way, serve his further purpose. In real life, after her brother's death, the lady obtained from Louis XVI a pension derived from the Conti estate. In 1795 the Convention heard her plea anew, assigning her the confiscated property of an émigré and subsequently establishing her as the proprietress of a tobacco shop in Orléans. Long before her death in 1825, evidence had been published to show that she was, in fact, a chambermaid named Delorme and a cunning adventuress.

No adventuress would serve Goethe's purpose. He began by allowing her noble status, renaming her Eugenia, the Greek word for "noble-born," and reporting her kidnapping, the collusion of various persons in "proving" her death, and her acceptance of a stranger's offer of marriage at the last moment before a ship was to transport her to "the islands."

As Eugenia, she is of no identifiable country, though the era seems to be the recent past, or at least her father's antechamber is termed "sumptuous, modern" in the stage directions for Act III. Hers is the only specific name in the list of eleven characters. Her father is "the Duke" and uncle to "the King." He has brought her up in the provinces, growing ever fonder of her as the years passed, and now that her hostile mother has died, he introduces her anonymously into a royal hunting party. As he stands talking in the forest with his nephew the King, "the Count" hurries up with the news that she has been seriously hurt: with his own eyes he had seen her recklessly ride her horse down a cliffside; almost to the bottom, horse and rider had fallen headlong. She is brought, unconscious, on an improvised litter, to her father. She revives. Her identity is divulged. The King, impressed with her amazonian beauty, promises to bring her soon to his court. Thus far Act I.

In Act II we hear the sinister Secretary persuade the Governess to assist in the kidnap plot. In Act III we behold her father distraught with grief at the news of Eugenia's death in a second equestrian accident. With total aplomb the Secretary confronts that grief, which he had calculated in advance, and when the father inquires as to the circumstances, the Secretary summons "the Secular Priest" (*Weltgeistlicher*), who supervised the actual kidnapping. With total aplomb the Secular Priest relates his untrue story, assures the father that the corpse was so badly mangled that it cannot be shown, and adds that the coffin is so placed that he has it in view whenever he is at the altar. He recommends submission in meekness to the Higher Will.

Act IV brings Eugenia and her faithless Governess to the port city whence a ship will convey the girl to "the islands." At either side of the stage are the entranceways into a palace and into a church, while at the rear, through trees, the masts of ships are visible. These symbolize the three forces that control Eugenia's destiny. While she sits veiled and gazing off toward the sea, the Governess presents "a document" to the local Magistrate (*Gerichtsrat*). He shows dismay. In those steamy, unwholesome islands such a person as Eugenia will soon die. He engages her in conversation, learns that she most dreads leaving her native soil, learns that she is free to marry, and generously offers her security as his wife. The Governess urges acceptance of the offer. But Eugenia can be no man's wife.

In Act V the Governess reproves Eugenia for her stubbornness. In anguish Eugenia hails the passing Governor, who courteously offers assistance until he is shown the document. An Abbess accompanied by two nuns happens along. She offers Eugenia asylum until she is shown the document. A passing Monk listens to Eugenia's desperate plea but ends by recommending that she make the best of life in the islands. At last Eugenia demands to see that document for herself. It is the formal order of her banishment—signed by the King. The ship is now ready to sail. Just then a boy comes bringing a farewell gift of fruit from the Magistrate, and behind him is the Magistrate himself. Eugenia now asks to become his wife, or rather, his sisterly companion. When he has agreed to let her live in a remote cottage by herself, forgotten by the world, she proposes they go this very minute to the nuptial altar. As the final curtain falls, the future is all unknown.

The twentieth-century reader is likely to exclaim: "This is Kafka a century and more before the fact!" The parallels are indeed striking, but so are the nonparallels. The author of *The Trial* wrote from within the grisly political and social mystery he was depicting, the author of *The Natural Daughter* was diagnosing, from a distance, the causes of the French Revolution. Both writers aimed at creating a timeless myth in which an individual is annihilated by society, but where Kafka told his story in prose about a hapless male and a commoner, Goethe made his heroine a dispossessed princess and posed her statuesquely in a drama where all characters speak in exalted blank verse. More important, where *The Trial* ends in unequivocal doom, Parts II and III of Goethe's trilogy would surely have achieved a spiritual equilibrium.

All-pervasive corruption had suffocated the humanity out of state, church, monarch, aristocracy, and individuals in the mythical kingdom of this drama, as was the case, so Goethe believed, in pre-1789 France. Eugenia was "in somebody's way"—her ruthless brother's, as it happens—and once he has determined to "exterminate" her, no uncorrupted power dares rescue her. Advantage is all, truth is naught, and a human being has neither rights nor value. People feel actual pity, they even express their pity, but they politely decline to intervene. Even the Governess feels pity, but from greed for reward and from lust for the Secretary, she relentlessly, step by step, conducts Eugenia to her doom.

In her obscurity and "dead," Eugenia will wait, "by endurance accomplishing," to borrow Friedrich Hebbel's later phrase. In time the corrupt kingdom will collapse, her Magistrate husband, whose humanity has not been suffocated, will doubtless become a leader in the New Order, and Eugenia will "come back to life." Then, in some way, she will serve in the reconciliation of the old and the new values. Goethe's own Iphigenia had so mediated between Greeks and barbarians, and we suspect that the overall plan of Aeschylus's *Oresteia* underlay the over-all plan of Goethe's projected trilogy.

The cool reception of *The Natural Daughter* on April 2, 1803 must have disappointed Goethe, but not, as some have claimed, to the point of abandoning his project altogether. Reminders pricked his artistic conscience. In 1823, at age seventy-four, he planned to work on the sequel, and not until age eighty-two did he admit that time had run out. His fragmentary notes suggest a tragic end for Eugenia—the fate, perhaps of the "Maid of Oberkirch"?—and all his artistic life Goethe shrank from depicting tragic outcomes.

VI. THE YEARS 1800–25

The 1803 première of *The Natural Daughter* was presented, not in that new theater opened May 7, 1791, but in the even newer Weimar Theater inaugurated October 12, 1798 with Part I of Schiller's grand tragic trilogy *Wallenstein*. Lighting was now by oil lamps, not candles. Courtiers and functionaries sat in the balcony on either side of the ducal party, the working class in the gallery, citizens and students in the pit, at the rear of which Goethe had his own box. On occasion he might hand out cream tarts from there to small children. In a very real sense this was the Duke's theater, and audience decorum was enforced. The stage was a modest forty-foot square, yet in the seven years 1798–1805 it won immortality in the annals of drama.

There, under the personal direction of Goethe and Schiller,

audiences first saw Schiller's master plays: *Wallenstein,* Parts II and III (1799), *Mary Stuart* (1800), *The Bride of Messina* (1803), *The Maid of Orleans* (1804, belatedly), and *William Tell* (1804), as well as his special stage versions of: *Macbeth* (1800), Voltaire's *Mahomet* (1800, in Goethe's translation), Gozzi's *Turandot* (for Duchess Luise's birthday, January 30, 1802), Goethe's *Iphigenia* (1802), and Racine's *Phèdre* (for Luise's 1805 birthday). Operas of Gluck and Mozart had long been standard fare. In fact, when money was short *The Magic Flute* was given once again and the five hundred seats somehow accommodated eight hundred people. Goethe's own plays were performed. To the usual works by Lessing, *Nathan the Wise* was added. The classically oriented public was only lukewarm to Shakespeare in the old prose translations, but they were still lukewarm in 1803 to *Julius Caesar* in the new poetic version of August Wilhelm Schlegel. Experiments were made with Terence's *Andria* and *Eunuchus* in 1804, and in 1802 with August Wilhelm Schlegel's new "Greek drama" of *Ion;* that was the occasion when Goethe, from his box, shushed the snickering crowd. Also given were sorry plays by the popular Kotzebue and the equally sorry plays of the great actor Iffland, and many another forgotten piece. All in all, Goethe might well have conceded that Wilhelm Meister's theatrical mission had at last been accomplished, and if the success was in large part vicariously achieved by Schiller, Goethe did not for a minute begrudge his friend's fame. Moreover, without Goethe's long preparation, Schiller's achievement would not have been possible.

On May 9, 1805 Schiller died and an era closed. Before year's end Napoleon was in central Europe. On October 14, 1806 Goethe's own house was being looted by French soldiers while the Battle of Jena was being fought within cannon-sound of Weimar. The following day, October 15, 1806, Duchess Luise, in the Duke's absence, confronted Napoleon. The theater was closed and the ducal family was scattered.

As the tides of war swept eastward, the ducal family was reunited, and for the reopening of the theater on September 19, 1807 Goethe composed a nine-page *Prologue* in verse: the goddess of war rages, a fugitive woman seeks safety; at the moment of her despair star clusters are seen to spell out the name "Luise." In the second scene allegorized

Majesty and Peace speak a dialogue, near the close of which a memorial banner is unfurled for Dowager Duchess Anna Amalia, who had died the previous April.

Also in 1807, Goethe obliged a Vienna publisher with a thirty-page verse play entitled *Pandora,* in which the title character never appears because the work was left unfinished. The scenario presents the brothers Prometheus and Epimetheus—"Forethought" and "Afterthought"—the former a harshly practical demigod, the latter a gently contemplative one, and action centers around the rash brutality of the son of Prometheus. To stay the strife, Eos, goddess of the dawn, appears, but Epimetheus yearns for his lost wife Pandora, who may yet return as a mighty goddess to fulfill his lofty dreams.

In 1808 Napoleon was again in Weimar, and this time he held extended interviews with Goethe on October 8th and 10th. Each greatly admired the other. When next Napoleon passed through Weimar, on December 15, 1812, he was in full retreat from Russia and had time only to send Goethe his greetings. With Napoleon banished to Elba, Goethe complied in 1814 with a request from the actor Iffland for a celebration piece to be performed in Berlin. *The Awakening of Epimenides (Des Epimenides Erwachen)* is another of Goethe's allegories in near-operatic form; Faith, Hope, and Charity, among other figures, conjoin for the founding of European peace. Significantly, it avoids any recriminations against Napoleon just as it avoids any nationalistic pronouncements. The death of Iffland delayed performance until March 30, 1815 in Berlin, by which date, ironically, Napoleon had escaped from Elba and was once again marching on Paris. However, the Napoleonic aftermath ended at Waterloo on June 18, 1815, and in Goethe's long life the entire twenty-year career of Napoleon had been but an episode.

Meanwhile the Weimar Theater had continued under Goethe's direction, sometimes happily, sometimes not so happily, but never as it had been in those seven years from 1798 to 1805. Gradually the repertory changed. Experimental works had come and gone. On February 24, 1810 Zacharias Werner's new Gothic thriller, *The 24th of February,* was performed, but without follow-up, and Werner's career ended in early insanity. In 1812 Calderón's beautiful play of 1635,

Life Is a Dream, was presented. Back in 1808, however, Heinrich von Kleist's *The Broken Jug* had failed miserably, partly because Goethe, from aversion for both play and author, divided the one-Act comedy into three Acts and staged it with his usual statuesquely classical methods. Perversely he had sought to repaint a Breughel to resemble a Raphael. The frantic Kleist felt sure Goethe had ruined the play on purpose and talked wildly about challenging him to a duel. The matter was dropped, but Goethe's antipathy may well have been one factor among many in Kleist's suicide in 1811.

In latter 1808 there had been an unpleasantness with the excellent leading actress, Karoline Jagemann, who was the Duke's mistress; Goethe offered to resign from the theater, but the quarrel was patched up. Still, after thirty-two years, there was a cooling in the friendship between Charles Augustus and his resident genius. The break came nine years later. Over Goethe's objections, a new play called *Aubry's Dog* (*Der Hund des Aubry*) was given. As the star of the show a trained dog did stunts on the stage where Wilhelm Meister's lofty mission had once been realized. On the following day, April 13, 1817, Goethe was relieved of his theater duties. He had been in charge of the Weimar Theater officially for twenty-six years, since 1791, and for fifteen years before that, since 1776, he had been managing court theatricals: forty-one years in all.

VII.   *FAUST*

Through the first quarter of the nineteenth century Goethe realized projects of scope and distinction. Besides extensive writings on natural science (notably physics and biology), besides numerous poems, and not counting translations and shorter works, we may cite: the rounded-out *Faust, Part I* (1808); two novels: *The Elective Affinities* (1809) and *Wilhelm Meister's Journeyman Years* (1821); the larger portions of his autobiography (to age twenty-six), *Poetry and Truth* (1811–12–14), and the autobiographical *Italian Journey* (1816–17) and *Campaign in France* (1822). Since 1803, however, his dramas had been minor allegorizing pieces relying on support from music, dance, mime, and the skills of the costumer and the scene painter. It looked as though his theater career might end with the "Glories of Weimar" *Maskenzug* of 1818.

As of 1825 and age seventy-six, two unfinished projects still challenged him: the sequels to *The Natural Daughter* and the continuation of *Faust*. He hoped to do both, but the latter took precedence, partly because small starts had been made in 1800 and 1816, partly because public preference favored it. He set to work, and as the mighty plan of Part II was unfolding in the privacy of his study, evidence accumulated to show how interest was growing in Part I. Artists illustrated it, notably Delacroix in 1828; two French translations appeared, notably that by Gérard de Nerval in 1830; the one operatic version, Berlioz's *Scènes·de Faust,* so distressed Goethe in 1829 that he did not acknowledge receipt of the score. In 1819 Part I had been privately performed in Prince Radziwill's Berlin mansion, and now, in 1828, a public theater in Paris gave the work in French. At last Goethe reluctantly consented to a Weimar performance on August 29, 1829, the day after his eightieth birthday. Meanwhile composition of Part II continued, from 1825 to mid-August of 1831, at which point the five-Act work was placed under seals not to be broken while the author still lived. It was published after his death in 1832.

Almost sixty years earlier the scenes of the *Urfaust* had most certainly been intended as part of a play. Dismissal of the work in 1790 as "a fragment" probably indicated that Goethe *already* saw it was outgrowing the limits of the stage. In the completed Part I, published in 1808, some of the new additions were wholly stageworthy, some only partially so, and some would be necessarily deleted by any competent director. As the 4,612-line text stands, the high theme announced in the Faust-Mephisto compact (lines 1656–1706) dwindles away into a mere love adventure, which is itself inconclusive as far as the hero is concerned. People saw, as many still see, Part I as primarily a love story "about Faust, Margaret, and the Devil," though Margaret is not so much as mentioned until line 2605, more than half way through.

No one knew better than Goethe himself that Part I itself was *still* "a fragment," and he rightly objected to performances of it. Yet it continues to be staged. Three operatic versions do even greater violence to the author's intentions. Berlioz's *La Damnation de Faust* (1846) and Gounod's *Faust* (1859) limit themselves to Part I and within that limit distort the meaning, Gounod's libretto being offensively mawkish. Boito's *Mefistofele* (1868, revised 1875) makes its Act IV out of a few threads drawn from Goethe's Part II, but then, in its Epilogue, brings Faust back to his original laboratory for a Christian repentance and to his death before an open Bible. Thus Goethe's purpose has been continuously misrepresented by the spoken drama and on the lyric stage.

The five long Acts of Part II bring the total work to 12,111 lines, plus one scene in prose, more than four times the length of the uncut *Hamlet.* With the Margaret story of Part I now left to stand as a first experience made possible by the help of Mephistopheles, this Part II carries Faust on to other experiences: with government and economics, with science, with the philosophy of history, with generalship in war, and with empire building, while the closing scene shows Faust's spirit advancing after death toward still vaster and as yet unknown experiences. Any repentance for such onward questing is out of the question, any death-hour conversion is preposterous.

In its technique, Part II is a transfiguration of the procedures described for the *Maskenzüge* and for the small allegorizing dramas, and as such, it demands the widest exploitation of music, dance, mime, and spectacle. The five Acts may be defined as a series of cosmic myths, each broader in scope than its predecessor. In these myths there are both wit and wisdom, as well as visual action. The episodes "play," leaving the spectator to infer the "meaning." And the poetic conceptions are staggeringly grand.

There can be no question of cutting and combining to make "Goethe's *Faust*" a one-evening entertainment. It is *not* "the German counterpart of Marlowe's *Doctor Faustus.*" Any attempt to round out Part I by adding a death-scene from Part II would be like performing Act I of *Hamlet* and passing directly to the scene where Hamlet dies of the poisoned sword.

The total *Faust* is entirely stageworthy, and the world is the poorer for its not yet having been given in cyclical form under festival conditions. Four evenings would be required: 1. Part I (with appropriate cuts); 2. Part II, Acts I and II; 3. Act III; 4. Acts IV and V. In short, a parallel to the four evenings of Wagner's *Ring* cycle. Properly mounted, such a four-part *Faust* cycle would reveal Goethe as a dramatist unique in kind and enduringly great. Each of his plays translated in the present volume, and *The Natural Daughter* as well, has its own particular merit; each deserves performance before the public from time to time in what we term a permanent repertory of valid dramas; yet each in its particular manner may be described as contained within past eras, as are the memorable works of any other great author. The dramaturgy of each is a known quantity. The same statement applies even to the stage adaptations of *Faust. Part I.* But the total *Faust*, in the four-part cycle proposed, represents a new dramaturgy, a new kind of theater experience, a new synthesis of all the arts, as distinctly different from the performance of a single play as Wagner's *Ring* cycle in four-evening sequence is different from a performance of, say, *Die Meistersinger.* (The comparison is of dimensions only, not of subject matter.) Or perhaps the resources of filmmaking could be exploited to realize the immense possibilities of the work. In any case, the total *Faust* is of the future and has yet to be discovered.